R
2000
V.2

STUDIES IN ANTIQUITY AND CHRISTIANITY

The Roots of Egyptian Christianity
Birger A. Pearson and James E. Goehring, editors

Gnosticism, Judaism, and Egyptian Christianity
Birger A. Pearson

Ascetic Behavior in Greco-Roman Antiquity: A Sourcebook
Vincent L. Wimbush, editor

*Elijah in Upper Egypt: "The Apocalypse of Elijah"
and Early Egyptian Christianity*
David Frankfurter

The Letters of St. Antony: Monasticism and the Making of a Saint
Samuel Rubenson

Women and Goddess Traditions: In Antiquity and Today
Karen L. King, editor

*Ascetics, Society, and the Desert:
Studies in Early Egyptian Monasticism*
James E. Goehring

The Formation of Q: Trajectories in Ancient Wisdom Collections
John S. Kloppenborg

*Reading the Hebrew Bible for a New Millennium:
Form, Concept, and Theological Perspective*
Volume 1: *Theological and Hermeneutical Studies*
Wonil Kim, Deborah Ellens, Michael Floyd,
and Marvin A. Sweeney, editors

*Reading the Hebrew Bible for a New Millennium:
Form, Concept, and Theological Perspective*
Volume 2: *Exegetical and Theological Studies*
Wonil Kim, Deborah Ellens, Michael Floyd,
and Marvin A. Sweeney, editors

STUDIES IN ANTIQUITY AND CHRISTIANITY

The Institute for Antiquity and Christianity
Claremont Graduate University
Claremont, California

STUDIES IN ANTIQUITY & CHRISTIANITY

Reading the Hebrew Bible for a New Millennium

Form, Concept, and Theological Perspective

Volume 2: Exegetical and Theological Studies

Edited by
**Wonil Kim, Deborah Ellens,
Michael Floyd, and Marvin A. Sweeney**

TRINITY PRESS
INTERNATIONAL
HARRISBURG, PA

Trinity Press International, P.O. Box 1321, Harrisburg, PA 17105
Trinity Press International is a division of the Morehouse Group.

Cover art: *Isaiah*, James Jacques Joseph Tissot. 9⅞ x 4⅞ in. Photographer: Joseph Parnell. The Jewish Museum, New York / Art Resource, New York.

Cover design: James Booth

Library of Congress Cataloging-in-Publication Data
Reading the Hebrew Bible for a new millennium : form, concept, and theological perspective / edited by Deborah Ellens ... [et al.].
    p. cm. – (Studies in antiquity & Christianity)
    Includes bibliographical references and index.
    ISBN 1-56338-314-4 (pa : alk. paper)
    1. Bible. O.T. – Theology. I. Ellens, Deborah H. II. Studies in antiquity and Christianity.
    BS1192.5.A1 R43 2000
    230'.0411 – dc21
                                                            00-021124

Volume 2: Exegetical and Theological Studies
ISBN 1-56338-326-8

Printed in the United States of America

00   01   02   03   04   05   06   10   9   8   7   6   5   4   3   2   1

Contents

Preface

For over four decades, Rolf Knierim has stood at the forefront of methodological discussion concerning the development of exegetical theory and its application in the interpretation of biblical texts. To a large extent, his publications have played an extraordinary role in charting the course for future exegetical work as biblical scholarship has begun critically to reexamine some of its fundamental historical-critical postulates. Whereas early twentieth-century critical biblical scholarship aimed at the diachronic reconstruction of earlier or "original" text forms from which the present biblical text emerged, the late twentieth century has witnessed a decided shift to synchronically oriented exegetical methods or reading strategies that focus primary attention on the interpretation of the present form of the biblical text. This of course does not entail the elimination of diachronic concerns or historical reconstruction of the compositional process by which the biblical texts were formed, but it does point to the need first to come to terms with the biblical text as it stands without allowing preconceived views concerning the Bible's literary- or religio-historical development to dictate or unduly influence its interpretation. Rather than treat the present form of the biblical text as an obstacle to its interpretation or to the recovery of earlier text forms in which the "true" meaning of the Bible resides, Knierim's work takes seriously the literary character of biblical texts and emphasizes their communicative functions as the basis for biblical interpretation. Such work entails full consideration of the text's structure, generic characteristics, societal and literary settings, and conceptual underpinnings as the bases for articulating its messages, both to its ancient and to its modern audiences. It is only after the text has been assessed at this synchronic level that work may begin on attempting to reconstruct earlier text forms that might have existed prior to the present form of the text, and such work may begin only if the text shows evidence that such reconstruction is possible.

The seeds for such perspectives are already evident in Knierim's early work. Knierim, having been trained at Heidelberg in form- and traditio-historical exegesis by Gerhard von Rad and Claus Westermann, demonstrates in his 1957 *Inauguraldissertation* and his 1962 *Habilitationsschrift* (subsequently published as *Die Hauptbegriffe für Sünde im Alten*

Testament[1]) a careful concern for the precise definition of biblical terminology concerning sin and guilt in relation to its social, traditio-
historical, and literary contexts. Although the methods employed in this
study are largely oriented to the diachronic concerns of tradition criticism, Knierim's concerns are ultimately synchronic in that the goal of
this work is to understand the notions or concepts conveyed by the Hebrew terms *hata'*, *pasha'/pesha'*, and *'awah/'awon* as a basis for defining
the Bible's hamartiology, or systematic conceptualization of guilt and
sin. The term *ht'* refers to error of some sort, whether deliberate or unintentional; *psh'* refers to deliberate rebellion or crime; and *'wh* refers
to some deviation from a norm. All three terms form the basis for the
Bible's concept of sin and guilt, although the last term is preferred. The
terms may originate in nonsacral areas of life, but all entail human responsibility before G-d; they thereby presume the need for authoritative
action to punish the transgressor in order to rectify the problem that
the transgression has created.

Knierim's own preoccupation with the systematic conceptualization
of texts and their communicative functions underlies his seminal essay
"Old Testament Form Criticism Reconsidered."[2] This essay represents
more or less of a coming of age of form-critical theory in that it moved
well beyond past conceptualizations of the method, that is, the identification and reconstruction of the original short, self-contained units
that were embedded in the present form of the biblical texts and the
oral speech patterns or genres that formed the basis by which the original short units were formed and identified. Knierim recognizes biblical
texts as literary entities that are formed in the context of a societal or
life setting in which typical sociolinguistic forms of expression function and convey meaning. He questions the typical association between
genre and setting by noting that, beginning with Gunkel, the definition of genre has been ambiguous in that it is determined variously by
formal characteristics, settings, or content. Although typical forms of
language may function within specific social settings, it is possible for
such genres to function in settings in which they did not originate and
to be combined with other generic forms. Following the work of structural linguists such as de Saussure or Lévi-Strauss, he observes that
genres are generated by the preoccupations of the human mind rather
than by the sociohistorical settings in which they function and fulfill
needs. In short, genres are far more adaptable, both in terms of their
constitution and of their settings, than previous form-critical scholarship recognized. Furthermore, the literary and rhetorical character of

---

1. Gütersloh: Gerd Mohn, 1965.
2. *Int* 27 (1973) 435–68.

texts must be recognized; texts are generated to serve specific goals, and genres function within different texts and within different settings — institutional, stylistic, and literary — to serve those goals. Consequently, the structure of the text does not coincide with the structure of a genre; rather, textual structure serves the literary function and rhetorical goals of the text. Typical patterns of language do indeed appear within text, but Knierim correctly recognizes that texts are uniquely formulated and structured to serve their own rhetorical ends. The form critic must be prepared to assess this interrelationship between the typical and the unique in the interpretation of biblical texts.

The systematic conceptualization of exegesis is the topic of a second methodological essay, "Criticism of Literary Features, Form, Tradition, and Redaction."[3] Recognizing the challenges of subjectivity that had been made against traditional historical-critical methods, Knierim argues that such subjectivity "does not dissolve the task of historical exegesis,"[4] but calls upon the interpreter to be self-aware of his or her own assumptions and to account for them in interpretation. He also calls for an integration of the historical-critical methods — literary, form, tradition, and redaction criticism — in the overall exegetical task. Such integration is necessary to the integrity of exegesis, particularly as scholars were becoming increasingly aware of the importance of assessing larger literary units rather than the so-called short, originally self-contained literary units that had become the primary focus of historical-critical study. Certain changes in exegetical conceptualization and procedure were necessary. Literary criticism could no longer be identified simply with source criticism; plot development, characterization, style, and the rhetorical character of the text would have to be considered, among other factors. Form criticism would have to come to a new understanding of unique textual structures and the identification and function of genres within texts. Tradition criticism would have to account for the transmission of the traditions that appear within a text as well as for the text itself. Redaction criticism could no longer be considered as an exegetical afterthought; the exegesis of texts would have to start with the question of redaction criticism insofar as the present form of the text is the product of its redactors who shaped the text and defined its presentation. Finally, exegetes must be aware of the anthropological factor, that is, biblical texts were composed by human beings to address real situations and concerns. Insofar as they were concerned

---

3. In Douglas A. Knight and Gene M. Tucker, eds., *The Hebrew Bible and its Modern Interpreters* (Philadelphia: Fortress; Chico, Calif.: Scholars Press, 1985) 123–65.
4. Knierim, "Criticism," 124.

with theological — among other — matters, theological critique must also be a part of the process.

Finally, Knierim's monograph *Text and Concept in Leviticus 1:1–9*[5] constitutes his tour de force in exegetical methodology. Although it treats only nine verses at the beginning of the book of Leviticus, it constitutes a sophisticated primer on how to read a biblical text. It begins by assessing the role of these nine verses in relation to the larger unit of Lev. 1:1–3:17 in order to define the function of this text in relation to its larger literary context. It then embarks upon a detailed formal analysis of the present form of the text, including its syntactical, semantic, anthropological, and generic characteristics in order to define its communicative functions and its conceptual outlook and presuppositions. He emphasizes the means by which the text conceptualizes and presents the sacrificial ritual of the whole burnt offering, so that the structure of the text is determined by "the goal of the completed ritual itself."[6] The text cannot be classified generically as "ritual"; rather, it is an example of case law that prescribes a ritual procedure. Such a conceptualization points not only to ritual procedure itself, but to the overall conceptualization of the sacrificial cult of the temple and its role in addressing or resolving issues of guilt and sin. In short, such an analysis points ultimately to the theological conceptualization of the Bible at large.

Limitations of space of course prevent us from republishing all four of Knierim's works on exegetical methodology discussed above. Instead, we have republished the two articles as fundamental discussions of Knierim's thinking on the theory of exegesis and left readers to consult the two monographs on their own. Following these two essays, we have included a series of essays by scholars who have studied with Knierim, in order to illustrate the various facets of his methodological work in the interpretation of biblical texts. In doing so, it is our hope that such exegetical work and theoretical reflection will continue to guide the course of Hebrew Bible studies well into the twenty-first century.

MARVIN A. SWEENEY

---

5. FAT 2; Tübingen: J. C. B. Mohr (Paul Siebeck), 1992.
6. Knierim, *Text and Concept*, 89.

Abbreviations

CCAR	Central Conference of American Rabbis
CCSL	Corpus Christianorum: Series latina. Turnhout, 1953–
COut	Commentaar op het Oude Testament
CRINT	Compendia rerum iudaicarum ad Novum Testamentum
EdF	Erträge der Forschung
EKL	*Evangelisches Kirchenlexikon*
EncJud	*Encyclopaedia Judaica.* 16 vols. Jerusalem, 1972
FAT	Forschungen zum Alten Testament
FOTL	Forms of the Old Testament Literature
FRLANT	Forschungen zur Religion und Literatur des Alten und Neuen Testaments
HAL	Hebräisches und aramäisches Lexikon zum Alten Testament
HAT	Handbuch zum Alten Testament
HBT	*Horizons in Biblical Theology*
HDR	Harvard Dissertations in Religion
HKAT	Handkommentar zum Alten Testament
HSM	Harvard Semitic Monographs
HTR	*Harvard Theological Review*
IB	*Interpreter's Bible.* Ed. G. A. Buttrick et al. 12 vols. New York, 1951–1957
IBC	Interpretation: A Bible Commentary for Teaching and Preaching
ICC	International Critical Commentary
IDB	*Interpreter's Dictionary of the Bible,* Ed. G. A. Buttrick. 4 vols. Nashville, 1962
IDBSup	*Interpreter's Dictionary of the Bible, Supplementary Volume.* Ed. K. Crim. Nashville, 1976
Int	*Interpretation*
ITC	International Theological Commentary
JASO	*Journal of the Anthropological Society of Oxford*
JBL	*Journal of Biblical Literature*
JQR	*Jewish Quarterly Review*
JR	*Journal of Religion*
JRH	*Journal of Religion and Health*
JSOT	*Journal for the Study of the Old Testament*
JSOTSup	Journal for the Study of the Old Testament: Supplement Series
KAT	Kommentar zum Alten Testament

KHC	Kurzer Hand-Commentar zum Alten Testament
LCBI	Literary Currents in Biblical Interpretation
NCB	New Century Bible
NCBC	New Century Bible Commentary
NICOT	New International Commentary on the Old Testament
OBO	Orbis biblicus et orientalis
OBT	Overtures to Biblical Theology
OTL	Old Testament Library
OTS	Old Testament Studies
PTMS	Pittsburgh Theological Monograph Series
RB	*Revue biblique*
RGG	*Religion in Geschichte und Gegenwart*
SBAB	Stuttgarter biblische Aufsatzbände
SBLDS	Society of Biblical Literature Dissertation Series
SBLMS	Society of Biblical Literature Monograph Series
SBLSP	Society of Biblical Literature Seminar Papers
SBS	Stuttgarter Bibelstudien
SBSO	Shield Bible Study Outlines
SBT	Studies in Biblical Theology
SBTS	Sources for Biblical and Theological Study
ScEs	*Science et spirit*
ScrHier	Scripta hierosolymitana
SJOT	*Scandinavian Journal of the Old Testament*
SOTI	Studies in Old Testament Interpretation
TA	Theologische Arbeiten
TB	Theologische Bücherei: Neudrucke und Berichte aus dem 20. Jahrhundert
TBC	Torch Bible Commentaries
TDNT	*Theological Dictionary of the New Testament.* Ed. G. Kittel and G. Friedrich. Trans. G. W. Bromiley. 10 vols. Grand Rapids, 1964–1976
TDOT	*Theological Dictionary of the Old Testament.* Ed. G. J. Botterweck and H. Ringgren. Trans. J. T. Willis, G. W. Bromiley, and D. E. Green. 10 vols. Grand Rapids, 1974–
TEH	Theologische Existenz heute
THAT	*Theologisches Handwörterbuch zum Alten Testament.* Ed. E. Jenni, with assistance from C. Westermann. 2 vols. Stuttgart, 1971–1976

TLOT	*Theological Lexicon of the Old Testament*. Ed. E. Jenni, with assistance from C. Westermann. Trans. M. E. Biddle. 3 vols. Peabody, Mass., 1997
TLZ	*Theologische Literaturzeitung*
TOTC	Tyndale Old Testament Commentaries
TP	*Theologie und Philosophie*
TUMSR	Trinity University Monograph Series in Religion
VD	*Verbum Domini*
VT	*Vetus Testamentum*
VTSup	Supplements to Vetus Testamentum
WBC	Word Biblical Commentary
WMANT	Wissenschaftliche Monographien zum Alten und Neuen Testament
ZAW	*Zeitschrift für die alttestamentliche Wissenschaft*
ZBK	Zürcher Bibelkommentare
ZTK	*Zeitschrift für Theologie und Kirche*

OTHER ABBREVIATIONS

AV	Authorized Version
Dtr	Deuteronomistic
ET	English translation
FS	Festschrift
JB	Jerusalem Bible
LXX	Septuagint
LXX^A	Septuagint: Codex Alexandrinus
LXX^B	Septuagint: Codex Vaticanus
LXX^L	Septuagint: Greek cursive manuscripts boc2e2
LXX^M	Septuagint: Codex Coislinianus
LXX^N	Septuagint: Codex Basiliano-Vaticanus
MSS	manuscripts
MT	Masoretic Text
NEB	New English Bible
NJPS	*Tanakh: The Holy Scriptures: The New JPS Translation according to the Traditional Hebrew Text*
NRSV	New Revised Standard Version
OG	Old Greek
RSV	Revised Standard Version
RV	Revised Version

1

Criticism of Literary Features, Form, Tradition, and Redaction

Rolf Knierim

I. INTRODUCTION: ON HISTORICAL EXEGESIS

This review focuses on the development of the historical-critical method in the exegesis of the Hebrew Bible during the period following the Second World War. Although reference to actual exegetical results in the various areas of OT study will occasionally be unavoidable, the review will not concentrate on them. Nor will textual criticism and translation, normally considered parts of the historical-critical method, be the focus here.

It is the task of exegesis to interpret the Hebrew Bible as ancient literature, i.e., as written texts that came into existence in a distinct historical milieu and certainly do not exist without it. The methodology required for this task is to be distinguished from methods in archaeological, topographical, or historical research,[1] despite the fact that these fields contribute a wealth of background information on the historical nature of the texts and a critical correlative to their historical assessment. Yet the time has come, especially with the upsurge of additional methods of interpretation in recent years, to affirm that the method of historical interpretation must also be distinguished from hermeneutical methods that concentrate on the principles of relevance, validity, or accessibility of the ancient texts for us. This distinction must be upheld regardless of whether those methods are based on theological or philosophical preconceptions such as those offered by existentialism, universal history, process philosophy, aestheticism, psychology, Marxist philosophy, or any sort of metahistorical understanding of language. The distinction says nothing about or against the value of these hermeneutical systems, nor does it imply anything about the proper interrelationship of exegesis and hermeneutic in a system of interpretation encompassing both, a system on which there is as yet no general

Rolf Knierim, "Criticism of Literary Features, Form, Tradition, and Redaction," *The Hebrew Bible and Its Modern Interpreters*, ed. D. A. Knight and G. M. Tucker (Chicago: Scholars Press, 1985) 123–65. Reproduced by permission of the Society of Biblical Literature.

1. For a good example of this point, see C. C. Smith (71–106).

agreement. It merely emphasizes the need for a methodology that accounts in principle for the historical nature of the OT texts. Unless one can show that this nature is irrelevant, an appropriate methodology must begin with it, and hermeneutics itself must also account for it.[2]

The so-called historical-critical method has been both attacked and defended. This essay will point out some of the arguments that are no longer intrinsic to the method or are not adequately formulated and should therefore be abandoned or modified.

Biblical criticism, and with it historical exegesis, has been regarded as indispensable since the breakthrough of scientific studies in the field during the eighteenth century (Kraus, 1956:455). This does not mean, however, that the philosophical assumptions of the eighteenth century provide the reason for our historical study of the Bible. The dependence of the Old (and New) Testament on human and historical conditions is real and universal (Kraus, 1956:455, quoting Noth). In other words, historical exegesis is necessary because of the "historicality" of the Old Testament and not because of our dependence on the eighteenth century. Therefore, a statement such as Baumgärtel's (1957:185), saying that the autonomy of human thinking remains normative for biblical criticism, calls for qualification precisely because "autonomy" does not necessarily mean for us what it meant two hundred years ago. Suffice it to say that historical exegesis presupposes that autonomy of human judgment by which the interpreter is aware of the circle in historical interpretation and becomes subject to the heteronomy of the materials to be interpreted just as much as he or she is subject to our current assumptions. Yet one may add that the discovery of the circle itself, linking both the interpreter and the interpreted, does not dissolve the task of historical exegesis.

It should also be understood that historical exegesis is no longer based on or identified by the source theory of the Eichhorn-Graf-Wellhausen school and its philosophical assumptions and historical reconstructions, or by the method of classical literary criticism as a

---

2. This position is affirmed by Kaiser and Kümmel (1967:10), Koch (1969:102ff., 106ff.; and 3d German edition, 1974:336), Barth and Steck (xii, 2, 106), Fohrer et al. (12), Baumgärtel (1184–86); in principle also by Cazelles (101: "Not all biblical texts are historical...but all have a historical 'coefficient,' even if it is only the date of composition [or adaptation]. Failure to grasp this could well falsify their interpretation"), Fichtner (1221: "Die E.[xegese] at-licher Texte hat nach der wissenschaftlichen Methode der Auslegung antiker Texte zu geschehen"), Keck and Tucker (296, although their formulation could be interpreted differently: "The same methods of exegesis are applicable to the Bible as to any other document"; cf., however, 297, section b., second paragraph and especially the third paragraph), Hesse (1915), Kraus (1956:455: '...unerlässliche Aufgabe wissenschaftlicher Erforschung der Heiligen Schrift," following Noth's programmatic statement that the human and historical qualification of the OT word is real and limitless), and also by Krentz (61–63) and Habel.

whole (Kuhl, 1957:1231). While much is still owed to that school, historical exegesis must be identified by the historicality of the text itself and not by a certain view of that historicality. The historicality of the text is fundamental. Our understanding of the nature of the text is changing but not our understanding of its basic *historicality*. It is therefore essential that we distinguish between the recognition of the historicality of the texts, which is the essence of historical exegesis, and the more or less successful attempts to locate the texts historically (Fichtner: 1222; Horst: 1124), to define authorship (Grobel: 412). A statement such as Grobel's (412) that, "as with all literature, the answer to such questions is necessarily largely subjective," can at best be taken with reference to the unavoidable difficulties confronting each interpreter, in which case it becomes a truism. However, it must not be understood as discrediting historical exegesis on the grounds of "subjectivism."

Furthermore, it has been said that OT exegesis must, on the one hand, elucidate the historical facts as much as possible because God acts in history and that it must, on the other hand, also investigate how this history is presented in the Hebrew Bible (Fichtner: 1222). This statement amalgamates two separate methods: its latter part belongs indeed to historical exegesis, but its former part belongs to the task of history writing and not to exegesis. Inasmuch as exegesis is affected by this task, it must elucidate the historical circumstances of the texts, which again cannot be done without the support of historical research. The volume edited by Hayes and Miller is a telling example of this point. The statement that God acts in history may be itself a result of historical exegesis, but it is not the reason for or the basis of it. A similarly false reason is given by Kraus (1956:456), who defends historical criticism with reference to the historical intentions of the OT literature and says, "denn das AT ist im wesentlichen ein Geschichtsbuch und nimmt also allerorts auf die Historie Bezug" (1956:456: "For the Old Testament is essentially a book of history and, consequently, refers everywhere to history"). While it is true that much, but not all, of the Old Testament is preoccupied with history, it is not true that this preoccupation is the reason for historical exegesis. Again, the reason for historical exegesis is the historicality of the texts themselves and not their preoccupation with history.

A word must be added about the role of theology in exegesis. There was a time, also in the Society of Biblical Literature, when the inclusion of the theology of a text into its exegesis was considered unscientific speculation. Only "philological" and "historical" data were admissible, as if the theology is not at least as much a part of its historicality as its philological phenomena and its historical context. In the meantime it has been acknowledged that the Bible is a "book of faith" (Grobel: 413;

De Vries: 416), and it must be insisted that this "faith," wherever and however it is present in the texts, receives its proper place in historical exegesis. Otherwise, OT exegesis will fail to be what historical exegesis must be — a comprehensive effort to recover all data and all levels of meaning present in the text.

The atomization of methods and results in historical exegesis has become a major concern for everybody. Some have called it a scandal. Krentz, reporting on this situation, has said, "The *miserere*, the wretched state, of the discipline shows that exegesis has reached a crisis situation" (85). The situation is indeed critical, but it is senseless to push the panic button. The facts are irreversible, and in all probability the same development would occur were we to undo history and start over. More important, we belong to a privileged generation that has experienced and contributed to an enormous explosion of knowledge. Despite the dilemma caused by this explosion, constructive things have been, and are, happening both in published and unpublished ways, and the Bible, including both Testaments, is seriously studied, taught, and read by people in our day as seldom before. It could be that in the future people will be able to create a synthesis out of the indispensable raw materials that our atomistic generation has handed them. In the meantime, we should interpret our situation and draw appropriate consequences.

One of these consequences is that historical exegesis cannot be abandoned or replaced. Neither the atomization of its insights nor the contradictory results nor the degree of difficulty imposed by the nature of the texts nor the pluralism and imperfection of the methods themselves can exempt interpreters from the need to explain the historicality of the texts. As long as this reality confronts us, our options are either to improve the methods we have or to develop others that are better suited to explain the same phenomena. Significant efforts have been undertaken in recent years to improve existing methods, whereas better substitutes are nowhere in sight. Also, methodological shortcuts attempting either to supply us with an uncomplicated historical picture or to offer a quick, direct hermeneutical access to the texts are unrealistic.

One such substitute could be a simplistic application of canon criticism. Canon criticism, understood properly, is necessary as a part of historical exegesis; as such it may be an alternative expression for what has generally been called "tradition history." However, should it propose concentrating on the finally "canonized" text at the expense of the historical growth of the total tradition, it would be condemned to failure.

The new literary criticism as "the disciplinary study of pure literature" (Robertson, 1977:3) is another case in point. Robertson says,

"These scholars...are united in considering the Bible primarily and fundamentally as a literary document (as opposed, e.g., to considering it as a historical or theological document)....Their enterprise, viewed in the context of Western culture as a whole, is part of a turning away from a preoccupation with history and a turning toward language" (1976:547). It should be pointed out that, apart from the questions of the promise of this approach — its methodological appropriateness for the OT literature, its integrity, and also its own current atomization — the formulations through which Robertson sets this method apart from historical exegesis seem essentially guided by the goals set by this field of study and not the current understanding of historical exegesis. For historical exegesis studying the Old Testament as "historical" and "theological" is not "opposed" to studying it as a "literary document," and the concern with history secondary and subordinate to the primary interest in the language of the texts. After all, historical exegesis has had a long-standing interest in a need for an Israelite *Literaturgeschichte* inherited from Gunkel (Horst, 1958:1124ff.; Koch, 1969:102ff.). The difference, therefore, is between the inclusion and the exclusion of the historicality of the OT literature in our methods; the difference is not a historical and a theological assessment the OT literature "as opposed" to a purely literary assessment in the context of Western culture.

Another possible shortcut could be to replace the concern for "the conscious reflection of the author or the reader" by the concern for the "unconscious" in the texts as emphasized by psychology and structuralism (discussed by Cazelles: 99–100). This objection does not affect the possibility of the all-pervading presence of the unconscious. If the unconscious is understood as a metahistorical reality, it can complement historic exegesis. However, if concern for this reality is intended to replace the search for the historically determined realities, one would first have prove that human historicality is nonexistent and hence irrelevant for interpretation. Since "the text as it stands" is "the point of departure" (so Cazelles: 99), one would have to know that this text is merely the point of departure in the search for something else but not the focus of interpretation in its historic context and contingency.

Finally, Richter's postulate that the expression *"historisch-kritische Wissenschaft"* itself is no longer applicable (1971:17–18) must be mentioned. Richter is correct in saying that this expression grew out of the opposition to a type of systematic interpretation, that the cause for the opposition is no longer given, and that the "philological method" itself depends on systematic concepts. Thus, he wants to replace the traditional expression by the more encompassing term *(kritische) Literaturwissenschaft*. Ultimately, the search for the best expression is of secondary concern. What matters is that in such *Literaturwissenschaft* the one factor that cannot be ignored in the work of the OT literature is its historicality, which is different from the historicality of our own literatures. Hence, while the exegesis of the OT literature must be in tune with the method of *Literaturwissenschaft*, it must account for that specific kind of historicality. This is necessary because the term *Literaturwissenschaft* does not by definition express the differentiation between historically and societally different types of literature. It could be understood in the sense in which Robertson understands literary criticism, in which case Richter's term would be inappropriate for the exegesis of our historically determined texts. This must be stated apart from the question of what results a comparison of Richter's and Robertson's methods would yield. For these reasons, and not because of the origin of the term, we still prefer the expression "historical (-critical) exegesis." Moreover, Richter's own methodology, his exegetical publications, and those of his students are demonstrations of historical exegesis.

Another insight drawn from the critical situation is that the methods of historical exegesis, which were developed in the epistemological contexts of their time and emerged one by one in historical succession, need to be reconceptualized and integrated with one another. The order of presentation in our methodological textbooks and articles, as well as the different methodological systematizations, points out the problem. This problem has received increasing attention in recent years, and it will be addressed more specifically in the final section of this review. We begin with a discussion of each method and will conclude with a review of the problem of an integrated exegetical methodology.

II. THE INDIVIDUAL METHODS

Literary Features

The Heritage: Traditional Literary Criticism

The study of literary features originated in traditional literary criticism of the Hebrew Bible. Around 1900, literary criticism had developed into the literary-critical school. Its representatives, above all Wellhausen, had placed the literary-critical analysis of the scriptures at the center of their work (Eissfeldt, 1960:388–89). During the following decades this priority was supplanted by the plurality of methodological approaches generated by the rise of the religio-historical school, form criticism, and tradition history. At first this resulted in a diversification of the roles literary criticism continued to play in OT exegesis. While many scholars started early in varying ways, and with varying success, to combine literary criticism with other methods, particularly with form criticism and tradition history, other scholars continued to isolate literary criticism from these new methods, never integrating them all together in their publications. Probably the most striking and certainly the last example of this stance was Gustav Hölscher, whose *Geschichte der israelitischen und jüdischen Religion* (1922) was totally religio-historical in nature and had very little to do with literary criticism. Yet his *Geschichtsschreibung in Israel* (1952) is exclusively based on the method of the literary-critical school. A comparison of the first edition of Eissfeldt's *Einleitung in das Alte Testament* (1934) with the second edition (1956) shows literary criticism emerging from its isolation. While the first edition was strictly confined to the summary of literary-critical work, which along with a history of Israelite literature was one of the two main objectives of the literary-critical school, the second edition includes the results of form criticism, the discussion of the preliterary genres and their settings. Both progress and deficiency are clearly visible in this edition — progress in the adaptation of the results of a different method and deficiency in the juxtaposition of methods without their integration. This, then, was the place where literary criticism stood as a discipline in the mid-1950s, moving toward a broadening of its base but not yet free of an isolationist stance. Even though the alternatives had long been under way, literary critics were not yet capable of realizing that their discipline might have become part of an overarching exegetical method. An extreme reflex of this stance is a remark by Gustav Hölscher after Gerhard von Rad had become Hölscher's successor at Heidelberg in 1949 (also the year in which the first part of von Rad's commentary on Genesis appeared). Hölscher commented: "Das ist das Ende der Wissenschaft" (This is the end of science).[3] The impulses for change had to come from elsewhere.

In the early 1950s, von Rad tried to persuade Eissfeldt to write a compendium for students on the literary-critical method; Eissfeldt answered that it could all be found in his introduction.[4] It was only in subsequent years that summaries of the method began to appear in reference works such as *EKL*, *RGG*[3], *IDB*, and others, and more recently in *IDBSup* and in methodologically oriented monographs.[5]

---

3. The remark was made at that time to Dr. Erich Thier, lecturer in social ethics at the Theology Faculty, Heidelberg University, and was related to me orally by Thier in 1961, while we were neighbors in Heidelberg.

4. Related to me by von Rad around 1959.

5. See, among others, Barth and Steck (27–36), Baumgärtel (1186), Boecker (110–11), Cazelles (100), Fichtner (1221), Fohrer et al. (44–57), Freedman (72), Fretheim (838), Grobel (412), Habel (1–17), Horst (1124), Kaiser and Kümmel (15–18), Keck (547), Keck and Tucker (296–303), Koch (1969: 68–78), Kraus (1956:455–56), Kuhl (1957:1227–32), Rendtorff (1977), Richter (1971:50–69), and O. H. Steck (1975:27–36).

All these publications affirm literary criticism as a legitimate ex-egetical method. Yet none considers it the sole method to be used in isolation. While most of them reflect the understanding of traditional literary criticism, some see it in a refined way (Barth and Steck), some in an alternative way (Lohfink; Muilenburg; Schulte). Some redefine it in new way (Richter; Fohrer et al.), and others subordinate it to a differ-ent method altogether (Horst and Koch to form criticism, and Rendtorff to tradition history). The consensus on the need for literary criticism as such is based on the literary-historical character of the texts. An attempt to deny this factor and to replace literary criticism with other methods such as oral tradition history (Engnell) or form criticism (Reventlow) re-mains unpromising. On the other hand, the diverse positions presently expressed on the method itself indicate that its methodology has now become a central problem that is bound to stay with us for some time.

The Methodological Problem in Literary Criticism

Traditional literary criticism was guided by interest in the integrity or compositeness of texts; in the identification of such texts or layers of them as parts of larger literary works or layers, as fragments, or as redactional additions, such as introductions or conclusions, expansions, appendixes, brackets, glosses; in the reconstruction of the literary his-tory of a text in the context of the larger work, with major emphasis on the "original" or "authentic" layers; in the correlation of the literary history with the history of Israel; and in the assessment of the theology or religion especially of the sources. At present there is agreement on one goal of the literary-critical task: to establish the literary integrity or compositeness of a text unit. The terms "integrity" or "composite-ness" refer only to whether a text unit stems from the same hand, not to whether the text is "original" (*ursprünglich*, "Urtext"), authentic (*echt*), or uniform (stylistically homogeneous or heterogeneous). In the case of composite texts, the task is to separate the layers from one another and to establish their relative chronology. On every other question, however, there is a partial, if not a significant, diversity of opinion.

The relationship of small literary units to larger literary corpora (so-called "sources"), a problem only recently addressed in literary criticism, has become a point of major methodological diversity. The problem was programmed into the history of literary criticism, especially in the in-teraction between actual literary-critical work and its methodological design. As long as literary observations could be explained either by the source or fragment hypothesis, literary criticism did not have to be iden-tified as source criticism. However, as soon as the (new) documentary hypothesis about the Hexateuch had won out over the fragment hypothe-sis, literary criticism was defined as source criticism per se, even though many scholars continued to refute it as the sole solution to the problem.[6] Wellhausen himself is probably responsible more than anyone else for this development. His *Die Composition des Hexateuchs* is involved, from the first sentence to the last, with the assumption and discussion of the *Quellen*. This development probably explains why many have defined literary criticism as, or have related it simply to, source criticism (Baumgärtel: 1186; Horst: 1124; Kuhl, 1957:1231; Fichtner: 1221; Keck and Tucker: 300; Fretheim: 838; Tucker in Robertson 1977:viii; Koch, 1969:70), while others have understood it as also dealing with texts themselves (Kraus, 1956:455; Grobel: 412; Kaiser and Kümmel: 111; Keck: 547 ["Analyzes texts . . . possible use of sources . . . "]; Habel, although heavily involved with the discussion of sources; and Barth and Steck: 27 ["Einzeltexte . . . und grössere Textkomplexe . . . ": confined individual texts . . . and larger complexes of texts]). Most recently, however, coming from text linguistics on the one hand, Richter (1971:50–72), Fohrer et al. (44–57), and Hardmeier (28–51), and, on other hand, Rendtorff (1977), coming from tradition history, have insisted that literary criticism be dissociated from source criticism altogether and strictly confined to the smallest text units. The correlation of such units is considered to be a task of redaction criticism.[7]

To a certain extent, the differences in these positions are fundamental. Since they cannot be further analyzed in this paper, only four remarks will be made. (1) It is interesting to observe two reversed developments in literary criticism and in form criticism respectively. Form criticism, originally concerned with small units, has expanded its range to include larger literary corpora. By contrast, literary criticism, originally concerned with larger works, has turned its attention to small units. (2) It should be clear that, methodologically speaking, the identification of literary criticism with source criticism is wrong. The determination of sources is a possible result of literary-critical work but not its methodological principle. (3) A tension is emerging between two principles in methodology of literary criticism: the concern for the integrity or compositeness of a unit and the programmatic confinement to small units. These principles are neither congruous nor interchangeable. Large works as well as small units can have literary integrity. In either case the integrity of a text depends on whether or not it is the product of the same literary hand. It remains to be seen, therefore, whether large works, where they exist, can be excluded from the proper literary critical task. For as long as literary criticism is preoccupied with integrity of texts, its accounting for both small

---

6. See Eissfeldt (1956:132–43).

7. For demonstrations of this understanding see, among others, Richter (1963, 1970), Zenger, and Hardmeier.

units and large works through discernment of their constituent elements seems to be a genuine proposition. (4) The exclusion of larger works from literary-critical work is problematic also because it subordinates their determination to redaction criticism, suggesting that the distinctions held between authors, collectors, and strata, on the one hand, and editors or redactors of smaller or larger works, on the other, be abandoned. For example, the Deuteronomistic history, whether one sees it with Noth or with Cross (1973b), could only be understood as the work of a redactor; similar problems exist in the prophetic literature. In this respect, Weimar's approach, starting with the analysis of small units in order to arrive at a more refined picture of the larger works and then proceeding to the analysis of the redactional combination of these works, is not without reason.[8]

Methodological problems are involved in the relationship between the literary history, or the *Literaturgeschichte*, of the Old Testament, and the history of Israel. Initially, literary criticism combined the chronology of its assumed sources with the history of Israel. This combination proved to rest on, among other things, a simplistic understanding of the nature of the OT literature. Neither the layers of tradition in it nor its total range or generic character could be accounted for (see Koch, 1969:70–72). This deficit was theoretically discharged by Gunkel's proposal of a history of Israelite literature, initially outlined by Gunkel and Gressmann and carried out once by Hempel in 1934. This legacy has been upheld by Koch with his "Scheme for a Literary History of the Bible, "designed in the framework of the "History of Biblical Interpretation and the History of Language" (1969:106–8; 1974:333–42; see also Rendtorff 1977). But an updated implementation of the program is still to come. The reasons for the delay must be sought less in form criticism than in literary criticism itself. Both the attention directed to the OT as literature, with a host of revisions of and alternatives to the method, and the mushrooming new results indicate that literary criticism will have to play a conspicuous role in the foreseeable future before a new OT *Literaturgeschichte* can be written.

The problem of chronology is a major case in point. Among those who assume the existence of Pentateuchal sources, the opinions conflict sharply. While Kilian, Weimar, and Schulte have recently confirmed the existence of the old sources, Van Seters, Schmid, and Rendtorff have ascribed the sources (Van Seters, Schmid) or the unifying layers (Rendtorff) to the Deuteronomic time and thereafter. The situation is compounded further if one looks at the Sinai pericope. Perlitt, denying the Elohistic

---

8. This judgment is independent of Weimar's actual results, especially his contention that E is "vollständig überliefert" (i.e., preserved and transmitted in full) (165), which he has not substantiated.

origin of Exod 19:3–8, ascribes it to the time shortly before 587 B.C.E. (179).
Zenger, meanwhile, also assuming the existence of the older sources and
denying the Elohistic origin of Exod 19:3b, 8–9b, ascribes this passage
to the second Deuteronomistic redaction following the first postexilic
redaction (164–65). Mittmann's discussion, both agreeing and disagree-
ing with these two scholars on related passages, complicates the problem
even more. To be sure, all the scholars mentioned here operate on a
methodological level much more refined and even more rigid than traditional literary criticism has used, especially in terms of attention to
the text. And yet, while one may assume that the same methodological
criteria are at work for all of them, their results vary on both general and
specific points. One may explain these differences as the unavoidable
limit set by the texts beyond which there is room only for "subjective" conjecture. It seems, however, that the diversity still points back
to the methodological problem of what weight the specific criteria such
as tensions, breaks, brackets, doublets, style, and content have in any
given case and on what small or broad basis decisions can be justified.
Here the method itself is in need of further development. Of particular interest at this point is Barth and Steck's statement that doublets,
parallels, variations in vocabulary, differences in rhetoric and style, distinct thematic and phraseological features, and gaps or unevennesses
in texts can no longer be considered the sole criteria for literary-critical
analysis. They are relative and can become valid only when evaluated
together with the observations on form, content, and the traditions in a
text. This evaluation of the literary-critical criteria is certainly different
from that of Richter and Fohrer et al., who believe that these criteria
alone should be the basis for the determination of the literary layers
of a text. These different positions are in need of further critical comparison in conjunction with the testing of the methodological models
through actual exegetical work, most preferably on the same texts. The
new beginnings have been promising, but the future will have to show
which model, in its overall design as well as in its specifics, best serves
the goal, acknowledged by all, of establishing the relative chronology
within texts.

Another case in point is a new awareness of the relativity of words
such as author, collector, originality, or authenticity in literary criticism. Schmid, for example, wants to avoid the concept of "author"
and to do more justice to the literary phenomena by assuming a
Yahwistic "stratum," a *Schicht* (1976:17–18).[9] Rendtorff, too, speaks of

---

9. This proposal is not new, of course. Already Gunkel preferred to speak of *Schichten*
(layers, strata) rather than "sources."

Bearbeitungsschichten (1977:158–73). Related to this stance is Kilian's renewed inclusion of the activity of "collectors" and "revisers" (*Sammler
und Bearbeiter)* into the concept of "author" (304). A particularly interesting example is the difference in the interpretations of Gen 1:1–2:4a by
Steck and Schmidt. Schmidt has argued that this creation story is the result of the reinterpretation of an older text, a *Tatbericht.* In other words,
he had identified two "sources" in the present text. By contrast, Steck
has argued that the text has a genuine integrity dictated by the intention of its author. The fact that this author also uses older concepts by
no means points to different sources (1975: esp. 243–48). The difference
between these positions affects the criteria for establishing the integrity
or compositeness of a text as much as for identifying an author. Finally,
suffice it to say that words such as "originality" or "authenticity" are
commonly understood in the sense of an oldest discernible layer, but no
longer in the sense of *Urtext* or *Echtheit* versus less relevant secondary
accretions.

Last but not least, Hannelis Schulte proposes to solve the problem of
the Yahwist through investigation of *Epochenstil* and the isolation of the
specific theme "justice" and the genre *Führungsgeschichte* in the literary
corpora of an epoch. Hence, the work of the Yahwist probably extends
to 1 Kgs 2:46 (218), and its author can be identified as the grandson
of Abiathar (218). To be sure, operation with *Epochenstil* is another attempt to stay away from the concept of *Autorenstil* and converges with
the concept of strata, which attempts to account for the stylistic complexity in a work, or the work of an author. However, while others who
assume strata have opted for circles of authors, Schulte identifies the author personally, including the time of his work — between 910 and 900
B.C.E. plus or minus thirty years (216). Indeed, it is difficult to see how
the detection of the same theme and genre in various passages of several works of an epoch is enough to determine a specific author and the
procedure of his literary activities. This must be said, quite apart from
the question of whether J belonged to the tenth century, or indeed even
existed, and apart from the fact that Schulte's approach to literary criticism stands at the opposite end of the method suggested by structural
linguistics.

Alternative Approaches

Before the resurgence of traditional literary criticism in the 1960s (e.g.,
Fohrer, 1964; Elliger, 1966) and the emergence of structural linguistics
as a force in literary criticism, two major proposals were introduced that
called attention to the Hebrew Bible as literature. One came from James
Muilenburg, the other from Norbert Lohfink. Both of their approaches

rest on the methods of the classical science of literature.[10] Their different emphases seem to reflect more their individual reactions against specific aspects of the exegetical situation than different understandings of the science of literature. Generally speaking, their contributions were particularly important because they arose from the exegesis of texts, Deutero-Isaiah and Deuteronomy, respectively, that lay outside the narrative corpora, the domain of traditional literary criticism. Implied in this diversity of OT texts and methods is the overall question of whether the same method and the same process are commensurate with each of these literary types. This question has received insufficient attention in the literary-critical discussion.

Because form criticism had become increasingly preoccupied with the typical forces at work behind the texts, Lohfink called for a new recognition of the texts as texts. Influenced by Wellek and Warren and by Alonso Schökel, he proposed a "New Style Criticism" as the literary-critical task (10, 13). Its model was the analysis of the language in the context of the whole text and not on the lexical and syntactical level only (15).

Lohfink's method and his results have been criticized, and his actual results appear to have been surpassed (see Perlitt and Mittmann). It remains to be seen whether the method as such is to be discarded or if some of it will survive, and how. His particular kind of methodological correlation of literary criticism and form criticism certainly promised more than it could deliver. His attempt to identify an a priori accepted genre ("Covenant Formulary") in the stylistic structure of the text was just as indefensible as the literary-critical analysis of texts on the a priori assumption of sources.

Meanwhile, literary criticism had already received another impulse through Muilenburg's "rhetorical criticism." Muilenburg, too, was dissatisfied with form criticism's one-sided concentration on the originally short units and their generic typicality. In addition to that work, he called attention to the creative role of individual authors in smaller units as well as larger compositions. He proposed to analyze their style by identifying the rhetorical devices used in them. In turn, such analysis would allow him to recognize the individual oral style behind the written style and to establish the interdependence of written and oral literature (1953; 1956; 1969).

The viability of his criteria for identifying the style of compositions themselves, for demarcating rhetorical criticism from form criticism

---

10. The denunciation of this method as "aesthetic" is beside the point. The aestheticism of this method has itself been understood since Greco-Roman antiquity to be subject to norms intrinsic to higher literature. A different question is whether its norms and categories can be assumed to be partly or universally at work in the Israelite literature.

(compare the dependence of Lohfink's stylistic criteria on form criticism), and for correlating written and oral style may be questionable, but his call for the recognition of both the typicality and the individuality, the short units and the larger compositions, the oral and the written, and for the correlation of all in an integrated method remains a substantial legacy for exegesis. Thus, it is not coincidental that Muilenburg has generated a significant tradition of studies by his own students and others (see, e.g., Jackson and Kessler; Anderson: ix–xviii; Melugin: 1–10, 175–78).

Finally, impulses from the science of literature or from stylistic criticism have also come from others. For example, Meir Weiss proposes a method of "Total-Interpretation" of a biblical text as a holistic literary phenomenon. There are also new insights coming from the study of the ancient Near Eastern literature, particularly for poetry, but also for prose literature (Cross and Freedman, 1975; Robertson, 1972). In general, the new periodical *Semeia* now provides a specific outlet for new literary-critical studies, indeed for "experimental" work.

The new concentration on the Hebrew Bible as literature has generated an enormous resurgence of literary criticism in our generation. At the same time, the variety and diversity of models indicate that a consensus on the description of the literary-critical task is not yet in sight. Nevertheless, the situation in which we find ourselves is in no way comparable to the situation of literary criticism a generation ago.

Form

The Development of the Discussion

The exegetical interest in form had its beginnings in literary criticism, for which the determination of the structure or composition of larger literary works, the sources, was a major ingredient of methodology (Baumgärtel: 1186; Kraus, 1956:455; Grobel: 412; Keck: 547 ["Analyzes texts in order to determine their structure and composition"]; Hölscher, 1952:446–60, 196–209).[11] However, it was in the form-critical method that the determination of form as typical form gained a central place. Form criticism had started with the isolation of the small original units, the determination of their presumed oral origin, the so-called setting in life, and the generic classification of these units and of their function. This scope was broadened by von Rad, who investigated larger literary works form-critically (see Rendtorff, 1956:1304). Von Rad's impulse was

---

11. See Wellhausen's *Die Composition des Hexateuchs* (emphasis added). It would be interesting to study specifically Wellhausen's explicit and implicit arguments for "composition." Of course, literary criticism's understanding of "structure" or "composition" has to be distinguished from that in other fields.

carried in a specific direction by H. W. Wolff's works on the kerygmatic nature of J, E, D, and of "kerygmatic units" in the prophetic literature. The state of that development was the basis for the first German edition of Koch's *Was ist Formgeschichte?* (1964).

During the late 1960s and the early 1970s, the methodological discussion began to erupt as it had not done since the days of Gunkel. Major factors contributing to this development have been the impulses from ancient Near Eastern studies, especially on treaty and covenant, from the new stylistic and rhetorical criticism, from the study of oral literature, from structuralism, especially structural linguistics, and from careful scrutiny of the form-critical assumptions by some form critics themselves. The understandings of form or structure, genre, setting, function and/or intention, their interdependence, the relationship of genre and text, and of literature and orality, were affected. This state of the discussion is for the most part summarily, although often controversially, reflected in the latest German and English editions of Koch's work, in the exegetical methodologies of Richter, Steck, Fohrer et al., and in Tucker's article, which also lists most of the pertinent bibliography. Instead of recounting this development,[12] the following will attempt to highlight the points most central to the recent debate and to the future of form criticism.

The Focus of the Current Debate

The structure of the text itself has now received central attention in literary and form criticism (Richter, 1971:72–120; Fohrer et al.: 57–89; Koch, 1974:304–30, 1976:21–28; Campbell: 55–178; Hardmeier: 28–153). With some variations, a text is understood as an organic linguistic entity, as the elementary and self-contained unit of linguistic, oral or written, expression in a communication event. In principle, it supersedes the entities of the word and sentence levels. It is a "macrosyntactical unit" (Koch, 1976:11). Influenced by structural linguistics, one has accepted the assumption that a text involves both an element of expression and an element of signification and that, hence, as a whole it is a semantic phenomenon. The structure in which this phenomenon exists becomes the focus of analysis. This was also seen by Richter (1971:92–120) and Fohrer et al. (57–80), although "signification" and "content" are apparently not clearly distinguished by Richter. This compromises his assertion of the interdependence of expression and signification in the text structure and probably accounts for his belief that "content" plays no role in the investigation of the history of forms (1971:120). Of course, Barth and Steck (104–8) and Koch have questioned whether the

---

12. See my discussion (1973).

discussion of content can be dissociated from the analysis of the structure of a text, particularly with regard to the influence of content on the historicality of a text. Whatever the answer to that question may be, the analysis of structure in the correlation of expression (external) and signification (internal) structure is certainly within the domain of historical exegesis since it deals with the Hebrew text and its intrinsic components. On the critique of this issue, see Hardmeier (44–51).

Different from the task of the structural analysis of a text as such is the question of where or when in the exegetical process such analysis should be done. As is well known, Richter — followed by Fohrer et al. — has assigned it to a place within a seemingly logical, at any rate rigidly determined, sequential order. Their proposal has met with widespread opposition, but it nevertheless continues to be practiced in exegetical work. Three alternatives are conceivable. (1) The structural analysis of a text may be subsumed under literary criticism. This would not be new and would mean that the determination of the literary integrity of a text would be combined with, and supported by, the determination of its structure. In my own opinion, the integrity of a text cannot be ascertained at all without also, even primarily, the determination of its structural integrity. (2) The structural analysis may be subsumed under form criticism. This would mean that form criticism would finally incorporate the structural analysis of texts as texts into its methodology and, more important, that such analysis would become the starting point as well as the controlling basis for the subsequent identification of genre exemplars in the texts and the genres underneath them. (3) It may be done in isolation. This would highlight the distinctiveness of this methodological step and add a new method to those already known.

One may be tempted to evaluate these alternatives pragmatically rather than programmatically, but more is involved. It seems that neither the new emphasis on structural analysis of texts nor the demarcation of the distinctiveness of this step necessitates the introduction of a new exegetical method; methodological differentiation does not mean methodological separation. The methodological isolation of analyzing text structure deprives us of executing in actual exegesis what our assumptions about the nature of "text" suggest — its semantic and hierarchic unity, i.e., the interdependence not only of its elements of expression and signification but also of the individual (style, syntax, grammar) and the typical in its surface structure, and of the surface structure and depth structure as well.

More difficult is the question whether to subsume the analysis of text structure under literary criticism or form criticism. As the analysis of a text's integrity, the step belongs to literary criticism. As the analysis of a genre exemplar, it belongs to form criticism. Moreover, as the analysis of both the individuality and the typicality interdependent in a unit, it stands at the intersection of both methods. This result leads, ultimately, to the question of the methodological relationship between literary criticism and form criticism. Literary criticism is not concerned with the typical, except in the concept of an Israelite *Literaturgeschichte*. The interest of form criticism in the individual phenomenon has been ambiguous, but it has this potential. If the structural analysis of texts and of their individuality is considered an essential ingredient in determining their literary integrity, and if form criticism incorporates such structural analysis into its methodology, then the best place for it, possibly including the literary-critical task, seems to be as the initial step of the form-critical method. This possibility is part of Koch's long-standing position, which he and his team have now exemplified in the three volumes on Amos, *untersucht mit den Methoden einer strukturalen Formgeschichte*, 1976, including an extensive introduction on the method and design of the work. (For a discussion of the nomenclature of the various form-critical steps and for its critique, see now Hardmeier [283–93].)

Text and Genre

Scholars have become increasingly articulate and united in emphasizing that the detection of generic structures in a controlled way can occur only through comparison of the semantic structures of text entities. Even Koch and Richter agree on this point (Koch, 1973:811, 1976:22). The discussion about the so-called Covenant Formulary exemplifies the importance of this insight (Perlitt; McCarthy). Another case in point is provided by the different assessments of the rituals in Leviticus 1–7 by Rendtorff (1963) and Elliger. Indeed, approaching this problem through the text structures shows that the generic pattern of those rituals as claimed by Rendtorff cannot be verified.

The problem of understanding the defining genre has been discussed intensively. There is agreement that typical conventions of communication underneath the texts govern the typical structure of the texts, even though they are not identical with the structures of individual texts, and the generic text structures can be detected only through the synchronic and diachronic comparison of text structures.

Within this agreement, however, there are different emphases. Barth and Steck emphasize the correlation of form and content of a genre in the framework of its history, and they propose to use the word *Formgeschichte* for the exegetical process and the word *Gattungsgeschichte* for the history of a specific genre in a definitive setting (59–69). His caricature of traditional form criticism aside (1971:127–28; Koch, 1973:811), Richter sees genre on the basis of form alone, exclusive of content, as the structural pattern of a group of similar forms (1971:131). Similarly, Fohrer et al. speak of a *Strukturschema* (90) and differentiate between, among other things, the setting of genres and their history (93–97). Koch, on the other hand, understands genre as a texteme, as a structural or linguistic pattern (Sprachmuster, Strukturmuster; 1976:11) or as a "syntax of macrostructures" (1973:812) that is dependent on setting (custom and institutions, 1976:24; 1969) and provides the generative rules for the text performance so that individual texts can be regarded by definition as exemplars of genres (1976:11).

The latest and at the same time most comprehensive critical and constructive treatment of the subject was submitted by Hardmeier. It discusses all the relevant literature (except for Koch, 1976) and will have to be given central attention in future methodological discussion. Constitutive for Hardmeier's and Koch's point of departure is an advanced understanding of linguistic theory according to which texts are parts of linguistic acts of communication (52–105). The texts are products of the linguistic competence of societies and the generative factors in these societies. Inherent in these factors are semantically oriented "plans," abstract depth structures, or generic structures. These generic structures govern the structures of individual texts normatively. They are only detectable in the surface texts, although these surface texts also have components of text, individuality detectable particularly in their stylistic variability. Thus, the task is to distinguish the signals for the genre exemplar from those of individuality in the texts (258–301) and to develop the criteria for discovering the semantic components of genre exemplars.

There is no room here for a further report of Hardmeier's own development of this last point, but a methodology must distinguish between the conceptual model within which exegesis is done and the heuristic problem of verifying genre exemplars in texts and genres underneath them. The quest for verification is decisive. In our search for exemplars in the texts, we have only the texts and cannot presuppose what must be found out (i.e., the problem of circular conclusions). Naturally, this problem has been seen by Koch, Barth and Steck, Richter, Fohrer et al., Hardmeier, and others, and proposals have been made. However, one wonders what it means when Richter identifies a genre as an *Erzählung* (1971:142), a very general term, and speaks of a *prophetische Erzählung* (143) on the basis that such a narration has two parts — a speech prompting an action and an execution report. This pattern is certainly not typical only for prophetic narrations (see also Koch, 1973:810).

Occasionally, one refers to generic termini in the Hebrew literature itself (Fohrer et al.: 92–93; Hardmeier: 263, 284). Most recently, Kraus has proposed to reestablish our designations of the genres of the psalms based on the generic superscriptions of the psalms themselves (1978: 14–29) and has made a first effort in this direction.

The task referred to here is thorny. A discussion of Klaus Koch's generic identification of 2 Kgs. 1:6 (1974:309–14) demonstrates this difficulty. Koch is chosen, not because he might be wrong or because others have already solved the problem, but because he has submitted a detailed example of his approach. Koch detects in 2 Kgs. 1:6 a genre *Profezeiung* (P) with the following genre indicators: *Botenformel* v.6aα$_5$ (BF), *Lage-Hinweis* v.6aβ (LH), *Unheils-Wort* v.6bα (UW), and *Abschliessende Charakteristik* v.6bβ (AC). The rules generating the transformation from the genre (P) to the text are charted in a tree diagram on p. 314. The following sets of questions arise.[13]

First is a question concerning the generic structure. The whole prophecy (P) is subdivided into two parts, a *Rubrik* (BF) and a *Korpus* consisting of three parts itself: LH, UW, and AC. What is the relationship of the three parts of the *Korpus?* Koch juxtaposes them on the same level. Syntactically, this is difficult to verify, for AC (6bβ) is subordinate to UW (6bα) and not a second reference to LH (6aβ) in juxtaposition to UW. It seems that we have two sentences, not three, and that the indicators (לכן) and (כי), since they indicate generic components, must also be considered in view of their syntactical function and not in isolation from it. The syntactical order, however, can also be seen as a signal of two genre indicators that would affect the structure of the genre exemplar. What, then, are the criteria that verify the genre indicators?

Second, there are questions concerning the chosen generic terminology. (a) The messenger formula (BF) "thus Yahweh has spoken" is said to be a sort of legitimation (309), which is a definition according to its function. And while agreeing with this, because this definition may be important for the determination of a genre "prophecy," one must ask whether such a legitimizing BF did not also belong to the legitimation of nonprophetic messengers, apart from the fact that the BF is not unequivocally prophetic as such.

(b) What constitutes the determination of v.6aβ as LH? Koch, in his German translation, renders the passage in two separate sentences: "Kein Dasein eines Gottes in Israel? Du-sendend, zu ersuchen...!" (Does there not exist a God in Israel? You, sending to seek for ...) Leaving aside the question whether this translation is the only possible one, what constitutes its definition as LH? Is it the statement in question form in the first sentence or that in the second sentence, or both sentences together? Certainly, LH is not impossible, but what makes it unequivocal? Could it not be understood as an accusation in two parts,

---

13. In the following, Koch's abbreviations noted above are used.

in which the first part rationalizes or substantiates the accusation proper by pointing to the alternative, just as the LH has this function with regard to the following UW? Also, one may expect that the word LH can be expressed in a variety of verbal forms, one of which is the second person address, but this does not mean that every second person address form is to be generically classified as an LH. How do we determine the genre indicator in the second person address form in the second part of our passage? The same question can be asked with regard to the relationship of the question in the first part of the passage. And, finally, LH is not by definition a genre indicator for "prophecy," nor does it denote as such the semantic correlation to the following UW. This correlation was the reason Westermann rejected the words *Scheltwort* and *Drohwort,* which denoted unrelated entities, and replaced them with *Begründung* and *Ankündigung* (1960:46–49).

(c) Koch's choice of the term *Unheilsweissagung* (UW) is at least partly the result of his opposition to the judicial interpretation of these prophetic words as *Gericht.* Although the controversy about this issue is not unrelated to the generic definition of our passage, its a priori solution is not required for the evaluation of the problems concerning us here. We can, therefore, let UW stand. The term AC, however, is problematic. The word *"Abschliessend"* is at least ambiguous because it can mean the conclusion of the preceding part (UW) or of the whole. Syntactically, it belongs to the preceding. Structurally, Koch sets it on the same level as LH and UW and, hence, signalizes the conclusion of the whole as a self-contained entity. In what sense can this designation be understood as a genre indicator, and if it is so understood, why for "prophecy"? The same question affects the word *Charakteristik* in AC. This term is not confined to a certain tense. The word "you shall surely die," however, is future oriented, like the UW. Which establishes the genre indicator for "prophecy" in this sentence, *Charakteristik* or its future orientation? If it is the former, what is the basis for calling this sentence a *Charakteristik*? If it is the latter, is the word *Charakteristik* then a clear designation for what is characteristic in the sentence, i.e., for an indication of its generic nature? Finally, why is AC as such a genre indicator of "prophecy"?

Neither the LH nor the AC, taken independently, indicates unequivocally a genre "prophecy." And certainly this should not be expected, for it is their interdependence that determines which genre they indicate. In this case, however, the only indisputable genre indicator in the *Korpus* is the UW, which would then also determine the generic nature of the LH and AC. But this result raises new questions: Does every "prophecy" announcing evil, or every UW for that matter, have this threefold structure? And, if UW constitutes the whole structure, why call it "prophecy" and not "UW"? This definition would be supported just as much by the BF as that of prophecy. In this case, the BF would qualify the UW as a "prophetic UW," which appears in Koch's scheme as one of the two subdivisions of "prophecy." An implication of this is that the *supergenre* "prophecy" would then be constituted by the BF indicating the "prophetic," regardless of the nature of this corpus. Moreover, in its structural pattern the indicator UW would have to be replaced by a different indicator such as *Weissagung* (W), because UW indicates only prophecy of evil. Applied to the specific text laid out in Koch's tree diagram, this means that this text reflects the pattern of the subgenre UW regardless of whether or not it belongs to a supergenre P and should, therefore, be superscribed with "(prophetic) UW" and not with P.

Finally, the tree diagram identifying the two major parts as *Rubrik* (BF) and *Korpus* does not present the generic identity of this corpus. *Korpus* says nothing about "prophecy." Presumably what is meant is prophecy proper."

A third set of questions arises in regard to the context. Verses 5 and 6 are part of a larger context and its language; our unit should be understood in its horizon. At least three observations are pertinent. The messenger scenario is quite explicit in the total chapter, in the introduction to our unit as well as in the parallel of vv. 3–4. Furthermore, the officers sent to Elijah call him "man of God," not "prophet" (vv. 9, 10, 11, 12, 13). Finally, the king's own reaction (vv. 7–8) does not focus on the prophecy or whatever else it might be called. What was the generic horizon that guided or influenced the narrator? Does this context show unequivocal evidence of a genre "prophecy" in the speeches of the מלאך יהוה and the messengers?

In conclusion, in order to establish the structure and to determine the genre indicators of our unit within the immediate text unit and not outside it, we must encounter the immediate text unit in which it stands. The text unit is given in vv. 5–8 and its structure seems to signal that vv. 5–6 are a genre exemplar of dialogue and part of it, a substantiated, directly addressed, announcement of death, evil, in the framework of a messenger speech.[14]

---

14. The structure itself is as follows:

Report of the return of the messengers (5–8)	
I. Statement about the return	5a
II. Dialogue	5b–8
A. First round	5b–6
1. (King's) question (introduction + question)	5b
2. Answer (of messengers)	6
a. Narrative introduction	6aα_1
b. Answer	6aα_2–b

At any rate, the question at this point is methodological. How can we verify a genre exemplar and identify a genre when confronting a text, and not identify which of the propositions is finally correct? Once again we are indebted to Koch for his intensive effort to correlate form criticism as a whole with semantic linguistics, a first attempt of this kind which signaled a new era in the field. The further clarification of this issue is certainly one of the most important tasks immediately ahead, and progress on other important questions such as the relationship between oral and written language (see the essay by Robert C. Culley in this volume) and especially the determination of setting depends on it.

Additional Developments

In addition to the issues discussed thus far, developments in, or relative to, form criticism are emerging that deserve our attention.

We currently experience a distinct interest in the sociology of ancient Israel. The most recent works by Gerstenberger, Morton Smith, Gottwald, and Wilson are cases in point. While Gerstenberger has demonstrated in the "Complaints of the Individual" the remaining validity of a controlled reconstruction of a setting in the ancient Near East and the Old Testament through the classical approach of form criticism itself, Smith, Gottwald, and Wilson, each in his own way and on different subjects, have endeavored to describe societal realities in Israel through a sociologically controlled interpretation of the wider evidence.

For form criticism, the societal settings behind the texts are assumed to be the decisive generative forces for the emergence of generic texts. This assumption, however, has always meant that a comprehensive sociological picture of Israel's history is indispensable for form-critical

1) Statement about event	$6a\alpha_2$
2) Statement about speech	$6a\alpha_3$–b
a) Narrative introduction	$6a\alpha_3$
b) Speech	$6a\alpha_4$–b
(1) Messenger commission	$6a\alpha_{4+5}$
(2) Messenger speech	$6a\alpha_6$–b
(a) Messenger formula	$6a\alpha_6$
(b) Message	$6a\beta$–b
α. Accusation	$6a\beta$
aa. Rhetorical question	$6a\beta_1$
bb. Statement of fact	$6a\beta_2$
β. Announcement of death (evil)	6b
aa. Announcement proper	$6b\alpha$
bb. Reason	$6b\beta$
B. Second round	7–8a
C. Conclusion	8b

This format of the structure already contains the depth structure and could be directly transposed into the format of a tree diagram, just as Koch's tree diagram can be directly transposed into this format.

work. The only problem is that we have never had such a comprehensive picture, let alone the problem of the sometimes dubious reconstruction of settings via dubiously identified text patterns. In view of which, the above-mentioned works, besides some others, indicate not so much a new direction in form criticism itself, or in the sociology of religion for that matter, but certainly the execution of a long-standing program that is also decisive for the completion of the form-critical program. A new direction would evolve, however, if the sociological study of Israel's history and the study of the genres of the OT literature, each in its own right, would be programmatically correlated. Of such a programmatic correlation we have at best embryonic indications but neither a program nor an execution.

The attention to text structures has also opened the way, actually for the first time, for the correlation of the form critical method with the methods of rhetorical criticism and the criticism of literature. If one compares the text structures identifiable through the criteria of rhetoric, of literature, and of genre with one another, the discrepancies in one and the same text are obvious. The acrostic or any prosodic structure of a psalm, for example, is very different from, and in principle independent of, the generic structure of the psalm. Evidently, each of these structures is intrinsic to the textual phenomenon, and it makes no sense for us to carry out a methodological warfare among these different approaches. Instead, a methodology is necessary that enables us to correlate these approaches in such a way that the interrelationship of the rhetorical, literary, and generic structures in the same texts can be determined. Such a methodology has not yet been developed sufficiently. But actual studies in this direction are under way. Such studies should help us to advance our methodology just as much as they yield fresh exegetical insights. At any rate, this convergence of methods raises additional questions also for form criticism.

The relationship between orality and literality in many of our texts has long been of preeminent interest in form criticism. In fact, the assumption of the oral background of the OT literature stood at the cradle of the form-critical movement. What has always been a problem, however, is the lack of sufficient criteria by which to ascertain with certainty the degree and kind of oral language in our written texts. In spite of intensive work in this area during the last half-generation, definitive results and methodological concepts have remained elusive. Nevertheless, we are moving forward. In the area of Hebrew prosody, Michael H. Floyd has recently submitted the latest, and so far the most comprehensive, theory by which oral language can be discerned in Hebrew poetry. And in the area of royal judicial prose narratives, Charles Mabee has, through form-critical interpretation, established criteria that allow us to see the degree to which those written narratives reflect, or do not reflect, the language of actual oral judiciary processes. In both cases the results indicate that, while oral language does or may stand behind the written texts generally, the written texts are phenomena sui generis. They reflect a significant distance from the realm of oral language and cannot be considered as intending primary reproductions of oral texts. This development indicates that form-critical work as such must take seriously the problems of structure, genre, setting, and function/intention of written texts as literature in their own right in order to be better equipped for inquiring into the relationship between the written text and the oral background. The time is passing rapidly in which one could prematurely jump to conclusions about oral tradition before doing what must be done first: the form-critical assessment of the written text itself. The methodological consequences from this new direction as well as the substantive results promise to be far-reaching.

In conclusion, one more problem must be pointed out that needs to be taken up within form criticism. It concerns the methodological differentiation between form history and form sociology, between the diachronic and the synchronic aspects in form-critical work. It makes a difference whether we speak about, for example, an oral or a written tradition that stands diachronically behind a Genesis story and has led to it throughout a process lasting centuries, or whether we speak about a setting that lies synchronically underneath a complaint psalm. The forces at work that generate each of these two text types seem to be quite different and, hence, in need of a differentiating methodological description. However, the systematic, methodological clarification of this item and its application to the entirety of the OT literature is very much in the beginning stages.

Tradition

We are fortunate to have available a comprehensive account of the history of traditio-historical research by Douglas Knight (1973).[15] The results of this study are presupposed here, and we can attempt to systematize the current situation.

Current Methodological Positions

There seem to be some points of essential agreement. (1) We differentiate between the transmitted subject matters and the process of

---

15. See also the essays from several contributors in the volume edited by Knight (1977) on a variety of aspects of the field.

transmission; they are now called respectively traditions and transmission. (2) There is agreement that for the processes in both tradition and transmission we have to account for the possibilities of continuity as well as discontinuity. (3) There is agreement that oral and written influences are interdependent in the transmission of traditions. Oral transmission and written transmission are not by definition mutually exclusive, nor are they to be assigned to separate historical epochs. The determination of which of the two carried the process at a given time, or of the type of their interdependence, depends on the actual observations of specific materials. (4) There is agreement among those who have addressed the methodological issue that transmission history and tradition history deal with the transmission of the tradition of text units, whereas genre history is considered a separate question to be discussed together with genre (see Koch, 1969:38–39; Richter, 1971:142–64; Barth and Steck: 37–47, 70–78; Fohrer et al.: 99–136).

However, there are differences and disagreements. Whereas Barth and Steck (37) and Fohrer et al. (117) confine transmission history to the oral stage, Koch (1969:38–54) and Richter (1971:152) speak of both the oral and the, possibly, written stage.[16] On the question of whether form, content, or both are the subjects of inquiry, there are also variations. Barth and Steck, in the section on *Überlieferungsgeschichte* (37–45), allow for both form and content while in their separate section on *Traditionsgeschichte* (70–78) they allow for content only (conceptions, ideas, motifs). For Koch (8–54) and Richter (156), however, the emphasis on the forms is predominant while content is subordinate, whereas Fohrer et al. speak of "fixed semantic syndromes" of texts (108). Furthermore, Koch and Barth and Steck concentrate on the prehistory of text units in their entirety, especially Barth and Steck in *Traditionsgeschichte* (70), in contrast to the history of parts or elements of texts. Richter (1971:152–58) and Fohrer et al. (108), on the other hand, concentrate on generic elements in the units in form and content. The concentration on units in their entirety takes place for Richter (1971:72–125) in a separate exegetical step: the investigation of the history of a group of forms (or a form-group) and of the forms of a group. For Fohrer et al., the same concern is associated with genre criticism (81–99).

There is, finally, a remarkable terminological confusion that affects all the points just mentioned. Thus, the term *Traditionsgeschichte* is used by Kaiser (19–24) for that which grew out of *Formgeschichte*, the history of forms and genres. Koch did not use it in 1964/1969. For Barth

---

16. See, e.g., Noth, who used *Überlieferungsgeschichte* for the oral stages in his *Überlieferungsgeschichte des Pentateuch* and for the written stage in his *Überlieferungsgeschichtliche Studien*.

and Steck, it means only the history of conceptions and ideas to be researched analytically and synthetically. For Richter and Fohrer et al., it refers predominantly to the forms to be researched synthetically. The latter authors use *Traditions-Kritik* for the analytical process, *Überlieferungs-Kritik* for the analysis, and *Überlieferungsgeschichte* for the synthesis. Koch and Barth and Steck use *Überlieferungsgeschichte* for the designation of the historical process and not as a methodological term, but they, too, have their differences. For Koch, it describes the whole object of study, whereas it is confined for Barth and Steck to the process of transmission.

To be sure, all these terminological distinctions were generated by legitimate concerns, and we must not lay subjective blame on the scholars responsible for them. Nevertheless, the situation is a nuisance, and students as well as experts could spend their hours on more important things than on the analysis of the same words for different things or on different words for the same things in the various methodological and exegetical publications. While it is impossible to achieve rapid terminological uniformity because of the substantive differences, one could expect terminological consistency within a system. The book by Fohrer et al. is a case in point: they use the words *Kritik* and *Geschichte* as terms for methodological procedures, which is already problematical because *Geschichte* is not used only in this sense. The problem is aggravated by the fact that under *Kritik* they separate *Überlieferungs-Kritik* from *Kompositions-Kritik* and *Redaktions-Kritik* (118–19), whereas their *Überlieferungs-Geschichte*, the synthetic reconstruction, encompasses both the transmission of oral or written units and their composition and redaction (122). Hence, one should use sets of terminology that keep the designation of steps of research clearly separate from that of subjects researched. The traditional terms "analysis" and "synthesis" still make sense as names of the method. If they were adopted for all the exegetical steps, one could reserve the word "history" for both tradition and transmission and agree on the already used expression "History of the Transmission of Traditions" for the interdependence of tradition and transmission and for the entire field as well.

The substantive differences mentioned above are reflected not only in the methodologies but also in actual research. This item will be discussed in other sections of this volume, but two examples may be mentioned here.

In studies on the transmission of traditions, there are significant differences of both process and results between Magne Saebø and Paul D. Hanson in their studies on Zechariah 9–14. While both combine the two aspects of tradition and transmission, Saebø arrives at his results through exegesis of the history of the forms of his texts, while Hanson arrives at his results through exegesis of the traditional motif that determines the pattern of his texts (280–380).[17] Another example is the difference between Cross's approach to and results in his study of the Gilgal cult (1973a:90–142) and Eckart Otto's study, which is analogous to Koch's approach demonstrated in 1975 (38–57).

Finally, the problem of the relationship of the history of the transmission of traditions to history itself must be mentioned. It should be self-evident that the two areas involve separate methodologies just as they deal with distinguishable realities. It is also evident that in some corpora of tradition the insight into the history of the transmission of the traditions reveals how exceedingly difficult it is to ascertain anything specific about the historicity of the events themselves. The studies by Van Seters, Thompson, and Dever and Clark on the patriarchs are recent documentations of that difficulty. The methodological problem is whether to emphasize the distinctiveness of transmission history apart from the history of which it speaks,[18] or whether we have to accept Fohrer's "tradition comes from history" (1964:7, my translation). How can one affirm such a statement as a universal methodological principle in the context under debate? On the other hand, when disconnecting transmission history from history, are we not in danger of reestablishing a metahistory despite our reassurances of the hermeneutical circle in our understanding of transmission history? At least, do we not separate transmission history from a non-history before the tradition (see Kuhl, 1959b:1530; Coats: 913–14)?

Tradition and the Exegetical Task

The terminological and substantive differences mentioned above indicate that the methodology of the field is still influenced by the cumulative effect of its historical evolution (see Paulsen). This is true of the system of steps within the method and also of the relationship of the method itself to the other exegetical methods. When Gunkel, like Eichhorn, proposed in *Schöpfung und Chaos* to consider the entire transmission of the tradition in a text, i.e., to consider texts as traditions, he spoke of the history of their subject matter, of their *Stoff und Vorstellung*. In his *Die Sagen der Genesis*, the emphasis was on the genres and their history. And in his *Einleitung zu den Psalmen* there was more of an emphasis on the generic forms than anywhere else. Furthermore, for Gunkel, who introduced the word *Überlieferungsgeschichte* before *Formgeschichte*, there was no substantial difference between the two because

---

17. See also Steck (1967), who basically deals with the transmission of *Vorstellungen*.
18. See Koch's restrained position (1969:54–56).

both meant the attention to the prehistory of texts.[19] Some of the current
differences still reflect the shifts in Gunkel's own work, from which different methodological emphases have emerged. While Gunkel did not
understand these shifts as changes in method, neither did he balance
them in an explicit, integrated methodology.[20]

Furthermore, Gunkel did not intend to introduce a new method in
addition to the literary criticism prevailing at his time. He meant to replace literary criticism with a superior holistic method better suited to
explain the reality of the texts. This method is now one among others in
our methodology. Most important perhaps is the fact that he was not so
much interested in developing a method for the sake of methodology as
in developing it as an exegete who needed an approach to the texts that
was commensurate with their reality. This reality was the phenomenon
of the history of transmission of tradition in the texts. In this regard,
we still have nothing better to say. From this vantage point, however,
while we are greatly indebted to the scholars who have refined and correlated the methodology, we still have to press toward the formulation
of a methodology in which the integrity of the text history is demonstrated in the exposition of the unavoidable complexity of the exegetical
steps. In view of this goal, in which the methodological system is to be
oriented to the reality of the texts, it is most important that the system
be freed from the unintentional but actual influences of the historical
growth of the method.

Redaction

The work and understanding of redaction criticism were an outgrowth
of the nineteenth-century literary-critical school, especially its Pentateuchal criticism. Its understanding is best reflected by Eissfeldt:
"Pentateuchal criticism has become accustomed to use a unified terminology in so far as it denotes as redactors those who brought the
material together, in distinction to the compilers or authors of the individual 'documents,' 'books' or 'sources'" (1965:239) or: "There is a
distinction, for the most part clearly recognizable, between the author,

---

19. Kaiser's statement that "tradition criticism arises quite independently out of form
criticism or genre criticism" (22–23) reflects this view although historically, i.e., in the
progress of Gunkel's research, genre history grew out of tradition transmission history.
The English translation quoted here uses the terms "tradition criticism" and "form criticism," thus obscuring precisely the very reason for Kaiser's statement, which is the
assumption of history (*Geschichte* as the basis for the coherence of *Formgeschichte* and
Traditionsgeschichte; cf. Kaiser and Kümmel, 1963 [German original]: 22).

20. Those differences affect especially the relationship of the ideas and forms of
genre history and transmission/tradition history, the current methodological separation
of genre history from text history, and the relationship of transmission history to the
history of religions and culture.

organically shaping the material, and the redactor working mechanically" (1965:240). A redactor is understood in opposition to an author (see Koch, 1969:57).

This understanding has changed significantly through the influence of form criticism, and the most recent methodologies by Koch (1969: 57–59), Richter (1971:165–73), and Barth and Steck (48–53) reflect this change (see also Wharton). For all of them, redaction history concerns the entire history of the written texts from their first to their last literary layer, including the last gloss. Redaction is defined by the opposition "oral-written" (Koch; Barth and Steck) or "small and composed literary units" (Richter). Fohrer et al. are an exception (136–47). They distinguish between "composition" for layers before the final literary edition and "redaction" for their final composition. Here, "redaction" is defined by the opposition "earlier-later compositions" within the written tradition. Thus, we are currently confronted with three different methodological definitions of redaction.

The differences between the traditional understanding and the understanding expressed by Koch, Richter, and Barth and Steck are also reflected in exegetical publications in which redaction-critical/historical studies have been mushrooming during the last half-generation. A random sample shows that Thiel (e.g., 33–42), Rietzschel (e.g., 127–79), Wanke (e.g., 144–49), Mittmann (e.g., 168–69), Fuss (390–406), and Kilian (e.g., 284–313) operate essentially on the traditional assumptions of redaction criticism. They regard redactions as secondary compilations of primary sources, basic layers or blocks of literary traditions written by authors. Richter's position on the *Retterbuch* in Judges (1963) as expressed in his *Traditionsgeschichtliche Untersuchungen* is not clear. He does not emphasize redaction criticism, but he distinguishes between oral and written traditions, on the one hand, and between a *Verfasser* (1963:329–43, with elaborate emphasis) and successive *Erweiterungen* within the written traditions, on the other. If Richter understood the whole literary history as redaction history in 1963 (as suggested in 1971), then his "author" is also a redactor, and a subsequent distinction between an author-redactor and expansion-redactors becomes necessary. If he did not understand the whole literary history as redaction history, then he operated on the traditional distinction between author and redactors, a position different from the one taken in 1971.

On the other hand, Seitz (e.g., 303–5), Weimar (e.g., 91, 161–68), Zenger (e.g., 161–63), and Barth (e.g., 79–92, 208, 277) operate on the assumptions advanced by Koch, Richter, and Barth and Steck. They use the term "redactors" for the composers of original literary works or of blocks of original traditions (Barth, Seitz) as well as for the combiners of sources, such as the "Jehovist" (JE), even though they describe the activities of those combiners in the sense of the work of authors (Zenger, Weimar).[21]

These differences are by and large more than terminological. They result in part from a different understanding of the nature of the OT literature and in part from the different designs of the exegetical system. However, their existence indicates the need for a more critical clarification than has been offered so far of all the factors involving redaction criticism and its relationship to related exegetical steps. There is no room here for this task, nor for an analysis of the specific differences between the individual designs presented or practiced so far and their causes, but a few suggestions are in order.

First, the understanding of redaction and redactor should, speaking methodologically, be the same for all the literatures with which we are concerned and not be oriented to certain parts of the Hebrew Bible and the specific kinds of their literary transmission alone. It is precisely because of the different kinds of literary transmission of the various corpora of the OT literature, and within these corpora, that we need a consistent understanding of redactional activities that allows us to determine what is redactional in all of them and what is other than redactional.

Second, it can be observed in virtually all the publications past and present that verbs such as collect, compose, compile, combine, connect, assemble, and their respective nouns are used for the description of the activities of authors as well as of secondary redactors. This is not primarily the result of the fluctuating usage of words. Rather it indicates that both authors and redactors can use techniques of collecting, composing, compiling, combining, and connecting. In other words, these activities as such constitute neither a difference between authors and redactors nor the activities of redactors alone, if one understands under redaction the total process of the literary transmission of corpora. If this were so, one would have to add activities such as framing, expanding, adding, amending, inserting, interpolating, and glossing, and one would also have to reintroduce the figure "author" as one among several subcategories of those carrying on redactional activity. In sum, all the emphasis would have to rest on the distinctions within redactional activities, and the term redaction would become a superterm for almost all the literary activities concerning at least larger corpora.

Third, the antipathy of the traditional form-critical movement against the concept of author is known. There was good reason. To be sure, the understanding of redactors as opposed to authors must not be, and is no longer, depreciated as "mechanistic" or irrelevant, even as one may still

---

21. On the ambivalence on this issue in traditional redaction criticism, see Eissfeldt (1965:239).

prefer to admit to different degrees of literary creativity in our literature. However, the fact that we should not uncritically carry the notion of modern authorship into our concept of ancient Israelite texts does not mean that there are no authors to be found there. In some cases, it is indeed difficult to distinguish between what was newly created by an author and a corpus edited by a redactor. This difficulty comes partly from our insufficient insights and partly from the material itself, in which both factors interpenetrate. Such interpenetrations should be appreciated wherever they occur. Fohrer et al. could be on the right track in using "composers" for this phenomenon, but it is not typical for the totality of the OT literature. In many cases, one can clearly distinguish between the work characteristic of an ancient author and that of redactors. So long as we must not abandon the concept of author in principle, we will have to account for it methodologically. If we subsume it under "redactional activity," assuming that all redactors were authors or all authors were redactors, we lose the unavoidable distinction between characteristically different types of literary activities, and we also confuse the meanings of both words, which have exactly referred to those different types of literary activity in our modern languages. This distinction is even more important because both terms, author and redactor, refer to literary activities, which is why literary activity as such cannot be identified with redaction history alone, even as it was not identified with authors alone in the literary-critical school.

Finally, one should also avoid understanding redaction history as a term for a specific exegetical step rather than as a description of the phenomenon of the history of redaction itself. Barth and Steck (48) understand it as the process of synthesis, which is preceded by literary criticism as analysis (27–34). The assignment of literary criticism and redaction history to two separate exegetical processes, analysis and synthesis, evokes the question of the balance of their system, in which analysis and synthesis appear as correlative processes in the one method of *Überlieferungsgeschichte*.

III. THE UNITY OF HISTORICAL EXEGESIS

The work of OT scholarship during the last generation has been characterized by intensive methodological efforts, a process that has by no means come to an end. These efforts have focused not only on the individual methods but also on the method for the methods. Exegesis of texts is more than the application of individual methods, or even their cumulative application. At stake is the methodological unity in the plurality of the methods, a unity that should be commensurate with the unity and wholeness of the texts. This problem is generally recognized (see Grobel: 412–13; Fichtner: 1221–23; Cazelles: 100; Keck and Tucker: 296–300; Fretheim: 839; Kaiser: 24; Koch, 1976:100–110; Barth and Steck: 81–84; Richter, 1971:179–87; Fohrer et al.; 27–30, 148–71; Rendtorff, 1977:82, 143; among others). It is also recognized that the historical succession in which the methods emerged means neither that one method has replaced the others nor that the order in which we may apply them has to follow the sequence of their historical emergence (see Kuhl, 1957:1227). The historically developed methods must become parts of an exegetical system that has an integrity of its own.

However, there are differences among those who use and describe these methods systematically, quite apart from those who do exegesis in different ways. The partially controversial discussion surrounding the latest methodological designs already points to the need for further clarification of major problems intrinsic to the system's approach.

We can refer only in passing to the increasing number of publications in which selected methods are combined either explicitly or actually in exegetical work. The variability of such combinations seems to be as broad as the number of methods allows.[22] In many instances, these combinations are dictated by specific interests of the authors. In some, however, they seem to or do imply an author's understanding that he/she is doing comprehensive exegesis defined in principle by the dominant role of one method or a combination of methods.[23] The variety in these approaches also points to major differences in the systemic assumptions. This fact can be observed in the systemic differences in commentaries and commentary series.

In the published methodologies themselves, two issues are of particular importance: the sequence in which the exegetical steps should be employed and the supremacy of one method over all the others. Until the late 1960s, the sequence of the steps in exegesis does not seem to have been a methodological problem. It had been inherited from the exegetical tradition and consisted of the order of the methods' historical emergence, augmented where necessary by methods known from the classical philological tradition. Kaiser's arrangement of the steps (1963, trans. 1967) — text criticism, meter, literary criticism, form criticism,

---

22. For example, literary criticism is combined with form criticism, history, history of religion, rhetorical criticism, redaction criticism, linguistics, tradition history. In addition, form criticism is combined with tradition history, and tradition history with redaction criticism. See on this issue Horst (1124), Fichtner (1222), Kuhl (1959b:1530), and the titles in the bibliography of this essay.

23. See, e.g., Richter (1963), tradition history; Koch (1976), structural form criticism; Mittmann, literary criticism and tradition history; Weimar, redaction history; Rendtorff (1977), tradition history.

tradition history, concluding exegesis — is a clear example for both the cumulative character of the system and its self-evident logic.

The situation changed when Richter (1971) made a methodological issue out of the custom by demanding an unalterable sequence of steps consistent with an understanding of a science of OT literature: (1) exegesis of smaller units in the order literary criticism, form(s), genre, tradition (whereby the exegesis of forms, genre, and tradition has to branch out synchronically and diachronically); (2) exegesis of the large corpora, compositions, and redactions; (3) content. Fohrer et al. have adopted Richter's system with some refinements. These refinements consist of the addition of text criticism; an extra step for linguistic analysis after literary criticism; the division of tradition criticism into criticism of motif, tradition, and transmission; an explicit separation of composition criticism and redaction criticism; the application of all these steps to small units, except in part for redaction criticism; and the detailed and comprehensive exegesis of content, followed by the theological critique. However, they also leave no doubt that the sequence of steps is necessary because of the *Sache* (27).

Barth and Steck outline a different basic sequence. First, they undertake analytical steps moving backwards from text criticism to the Hebrew text. They then determine the text's oldest layer form-critically and from there move to the oral pre-stages through tradition history. They reverse the process to synthesis, by which tradition history is complemented by transmission history. Redaction history follows, and the comprehensive *Einzelexegese* concludes the process.

The similarities and differences in these models cannot be further analyzed at this point. Nonetheless, they are sufficient to indicate that the sequence of steps as such has become a methodological problem and that the clarification of this issue is now an urgent task for both substantive and didactic reasons.

Also at issue is the question of whether any particular method should govern all of exegesis. Koch's view on the matter is known. He has upgraded it (1976) by the concept of an all-encompassing *strukturale Formgeschichte*. Richter, Barth and Steck, and Fohrer have no such concept. For them, the all-encompassing step, if any, is the final comprehensive exegesis or the final synthesis that pulls together the results of all the previous steps. Rendtorff, on the other hand, proposes, on the basis of a forceful critique of the entire traditional model of exegesis, to reconstruct the exegetical method under the guidance of transmission history. Weimar is also moving toward redaction history as the encompassing model.

To be sure, in all of these cases the proposed dominant method is understood as pervading all the other methods without replacing them and not as one segment of the methodology alone. And in each case the reasons for a model are substantial and in no way mechanical. Yet just because this is the case, the different models suggest substantive and heuristic differences of larger proportions and once more indicate the transitional stage of the present methodological situation.

It is not the task of this review to outline the program of an exegetical methodology, but a few points should be mentioned which affect such a program. The very first task seems to be that we distinguish between our description of the specific exegetical steps and the traditional labels for our methods. Exegetical steps are means of access to the texts; these steps are developed in accordance with questions suggested by the texts. Some of these means of access are no longer necessarily to be associated with the traditional label of a specific method. The cluster of terms such as style, form, forms, form-group, groups of forms, structure, composition, rhetorical or generic pattern, and their diverse associations with literary criticism, form criticism, rhetorical criticism, redaction criticism, or their separate application, are a case in point. Another case of (mis)labeling is work being done under form *Geschichte* that is in fact either form sociology or tradition history, regardless of whether it is done analytically and/or synthetically. Form criticism has never seriously distinguished between the two steps. The fact that both aspects should not be separated does not mean that they must not be distinguished methodologically. In sum, the current situation no longer supports the assumption of a self-evident congruity of our descriptions of methodical steps and our traditional labels.

A second task should be to conceptualize the correlation of these steps in a system that responds to an integrated approach evoked by the texts and at the same time reflects the critical interdependence of method and actual exegetical work. With regard to the plurality of text traditions in the Hebrew Bible, it may still be asked whether we have to speak about systems in which the steps are applied selectively and in variable correlations. In other words, the question is whether or not we should allow for variability in the system of steps itself. The question of the sequence of steps is certainly important, but it can be addressed only in conjunction with their systemic conceptualization, and not before or without it. In this regard, none of the proposals submitted so far in the methodologies has remained uncontested. In fact, each raises serious questions at certain points, regardless of the contention of unalterable sequence.

The almost universal positioning of redaction criticism demonstrates this point. Richter said (1971) that no one has as yet demanded that it stand at the beginning; such a demand seemed to be absurd. Yet since then it has been advocated at least theoretically by Koch (1976:1,

31–32, 78ff.). Indeed, the rationale for this advocacy seems to be much stronger than is generally recognized. In fact, all the OT literature is without exception before us on the level of the final redaction. This final redaction implies not only mechanical work such as the framing and glossing of preserved texts but also the selecting, regrouping, and recomposing of texts, and even reformulating of traditional texts themselves. Theoretically, we cannot legitimately assume that we have any text before us in its preredactional form and content unless we can show evidence for that fact. It is much more problematic first to establish original texts from the present texts and then to identify the later layers than to identify the latest layers first and then to inquire into their prehistory. Even the famous delimitation of small units accorded to literary criticism ignores the fact that the texts of those units — their beginnings and ends, their position in the context, and their form and content — are at least also, even primarily, redactional phenomena. We cannot assume their present form to be older unless we have shown that they are not redactional. Such an assumption would require an *e silentio* redaction-critical judgment at the beginning, which is not exactly methodologically controlled exegesis. This factor alone raises questions about the methodological legitimacy of an exclusive focus on the small units at the beginning of the process with the redaction-critical step at its end. Certainly, it does not suggest a total reversal of the process, but it does raise the possibility, if not the necessity, of focusing from the outset on the interdependence of larger redactional works and their smaller units. If that were so, the conceptualization of the sequence of steps in the system would for this reason alone have to look quite different from anything that we have seen so far.

It is frequently asserted that the redactional layers are also deserving of interpretation, and not only the separate "sources." This assertion, legitimate as it is, is not a serious methodological issue. The methodological issue is the question of the place where redaction criticism comes into exegesis. Our exegetical tradition suggests that redaction criticism continues to be an appendix to literary criticism and that its proper role in the methodological system has not yet received the attention it deserves. This deficit affects our concept of the system in its entirety.

The question of the supremacy of one method over the others is too complex to be pursued in detail here. The differences of the proposals made are more than terminological in nature and affect the conceptualization of a holistic, integrated methodology. In this regard, it is important that we distinguish between a holistic conceptualization of the entire OT literature and a holistic conceptualization of the exegesis of texts. Nevertheless, the texts too are subject to such claims from form criticism, tradition history, science of literature, and perhaps redaction criticism. In this regard it is important that any claim distinguish between the usage of a label for a particular step as distinct from others and the usage of the same label for the process involving all the steps. If one considers that the unity of the system must be commensurate with the unity of the texts and recognizes that all of the aspects implied in the steps must play their role in setting forth that unity one could conclude that the more neutral term "historical exegesis" is sufficient for the time being.

Finally, historical exegesis should always be aware of the anthropological factor in the texts. This does not mean the human mind underneath the texts, nor does it mean that the focus of exegesis should move away from the texts to the humans behind them. The anthropological factor is the presence of the speakers and writers in their texts. These texts did not come into existence mechanically, even where redactors may have operated only mechanically. They owe their existence to human beings and to their concerns, attentions, efforts, decisions, learnedness, and intentions. These humans speak in the texts and are part of their historicality. To ignore this factor could mean another idealistic or mechanistic misunderstanding of the phenomenon "text": idealistic where the texts are treated as expendable shells of ideas or of meaning to be abstracted from the shells even where one stresses their semantic nature; and mechanistic where they are treated only as texts at our disposal despite our claims to the validity of the hermeneutical circle, while the humans who produced them are barred from their own texts by our methodologically sophisticated historical exegesis. These human beings were part of their historical texts. In fact, they are the real sources of the texts. The inclusion of this factor into the historicality of the texts is as important as the historical exegesis of the texts themselves. Taken seriously, it could add a set of questions to our methodology which so far has virtually totally eluded us. And surely, inasmuch as these human texts were concerned with theological matters, their theological concerns must also be an intrinsic part of historical exegesis, or it does not do its job. This means that the "theological critique" has to be part of all the exegetical steps and should not be relegated to a separate step at the very end of the exegetical process, as Fohrer et al. suggest (156–71). At the very least, the inclusion of the anthropological factor into historical exegesis can help us to encounter the spirit breathing in the texts and to avoid being killed by seeing only their letter.[24]

24. The manuscript of this essay was completed in September 1979. Once more I am greatly indebted to Ms. Eleanor Beach, my research associate in 1979 at the Institute for Antiquity and Christianity, for shepherding this article from my manuscript to the volume editors, and also to the editors themselves for their efforts. I dedicate this essay to Klaus Koch, eminent scholar, colleague, and friend, who in more than one way has set new horizons for OT studies and certainly for the methodological discussion itself.

Bibliography

Alonso Schökel, Luis. "Die stilistische Analyse bei den Propheten." In *Congress Volume: Oxford, 1959.* VTSup 7. Leiden: E. J. Brill, 1960.

———. "Genera Litteraria." *VD* 38 (1960).

Anderson, Bernhard. "The New Frontier of Rhetorical Criticism: A Tribute to James Muilenburg." In *Rhetorical Criticism: Essays in Honor of James Muilenburg.* Edited by J. J. Jackson and M. Kessler. PTMS 1. Pittsburgh: Pickwick, 1974.

Barth, Hermann. *Die Jesaja-Worte in der Josiazeit.* WMANT 48. Neukirchen-Vluyn: Neukirchener Verlag, 1977.

Barth, Hermann, and Odil Hannes Steck. *Exegese des Alten Testaments.* 4th edition. Neukirchen-Vluyn: Neukirchener Verlag, 1973.

Baumgärtel, Friedrich. "Bibelkritik, I. AT." In *RGG³*, Vol. 1. Tübingen: J. C. B Mohr (Paul Siebeck), 1957.

Boecker, Hans Jochen. "Pentateuch." In *EKL.* Vol. 3. Göttingen: Vandenhoeck & Ruprecht, 1959.

Campbell, Anthony F. *The Ark Narrative (1 Sam 4–6; 2 Sam 6): A Form-critical and Traditio-historical Study.* SBLDS 16. Missoula, MT: Scholar Press, 1975.

Cazelles, Henri. "Biblical Criticism, OT." *IDBSup* (1976).

Coats, George W. "Tradition Criticism, OT." *IDBSup* (1976).

Coote, Robert B. "Tradition, Oral, OT." *IDBSup* (1976).

Cross, Frank Moore, Jr. "The Cultus of the Israelite League." In *Canaanite Myth and Hebrew Epic.* Cambridge, MA: Harvard University Press, 1973a.

———. "The Themes of the Book of Kings and the Structure of the Deuteronomistic History." In *Canaanite Myth and Hebrew Epic.* Cambridge, Mass.: Harvard University Press, 1973b.

Cross, Frank Moore, Jr., and David Noel Freedman. *Studies in Ancient Yahwistic Poetry.* SBLDS 21. Missoula, Mont.: Scholars Press, 1975.

Dever, William G., and W. Malcolm Clark. "The Patriarchal Traditions." In *Israelite and Judaean History.* Edited by John H. Hayes and J. Maxwell Miller. Philadelphia: Westminster, 1977.

De Vries, Simon J. "Biblical Criticism, History of." In *IDB.* Vol. 1. Nashville: Abingdon, 1962.

Eissfeldt, Otto. *Einleitung in das Alte Testament.* 2d edition. Tübingen: J. C. B. Mohr (Paul Siebeck), 1956.

———. "Literarkritische Schule." In *RGG³.* Vol. 4. Tübingen: J. C. B. Mohr (Paul Siebeck), 1960.

———. *The Old Testament, An Introduction.* Translated by Peter R. Ackroyd from 3d German edition. New York and Evanston: Harper & Row, 1965.

Elliger, Karl. *Leviticus.* HAT 4. Tübingen: J. C. B. Mohr (Paul Siebeck), 1966.

Engnell, Ivan. *A Rigid Scrutiny: Critical Essays on the Old Testament.* Translated by John T. Willis. Nashville: Vanderbilt University, 1969.

Fichtner, Johannes. "Exegese I. Des AT." In *EKL.* Vol. 1. Göttingen: Vandenhoeck & Ruprecht, 1956.

Floyd, Michael H. "Oral Tradition as a Problematic Factor in the Historical Interpretation of Poems in the Law and the Prophets." Ph.D. dissertation, Claremont Graduate School, 1980.

Fohrer. Georg. *Überlieferung und Geschichte des Exodus.* BZAW 91. Berlin: A. Töpelmann, 1964.

Fohrer, Georg, et al. *Exegese des Alten Testaments.* Heidelberg: Quelle und Meyer, 1973.

Freedman, David Noel. "Pentateuch." In *IDB.* Vol. 3. (1962).

Fretheim, Terence E. "Source Criticism, OT." In *IDBSup* (1976).

Fuss, Werner. *Die deuteronomistische Pentateuchredaktion in Exodus 3–17.* BZAW 126. Berlin and New York: Walter de Gruyter, 1972.

Gerstenberger, Erhard. *Der bittende Mensch.* WMANT 51. Neukirchen-Vluyn: Neukirchener Verlag, 1980.

Gottwald, Norman K. *The Tribes of Yahweh.* Maryknoll, N.Y.: Orbis Books, 1979.

Grobel, Kendrick. "Biblical Criticism." In *IDB.* Vol. 1. (1962).

Habel, Norman. *Literary Criticism of the Old Testament.* Philadelphia: Fortress, 1971.

Hanson, Paul D. *The Dawn of Apocalyptic.* Philadelphia: Fortress, 1975.

Hardmeier, Christof. *Texttheorie und biblische Exegese.* BevT 79. Munich: Chr. Kaiser, 1978.

Hayes, John, and J. Maxwell Miller, eds. *Israelite and Judaean History.* Philadelphia: Westminster, 1977.

Hempel, Johannes. *Die althebräische Literatur.* Handbuch der Literaturwissenschaft. Wildpart-Potsdam: Akademische Verlagsgesellschaft Athenaion, 1934.

Hesse, Franz. "Schriftauslegung I. Im AT." In *RGG³.* Vol. 5. Tübingen: J. C. B. Mohr (Paul Siebeck), 1961.

Hölscher, Gustav. *Geschichte der israelitischen und jüdischen Religion.* Giessen: A. Töpelmann, 1922.

———. *Geschichtsschreibung in Israel.* Lund: CWK Gleerup, 1952.

Horst, Friedrich. "Literaturgeschichte, I. Des AT." In *EKL.* Vol. 2. Göttingen: Vandenhoeck & Ruprecht, 1958.

Jackson, Jared J., and Martin Kessler, eds. *Rhetorical Criticism: Essays in Honor of James Muilenburg.* PTMS 1. Pittsburgh: Pickwick, 1974.

Kaiser, Otto, and Werner Georg Kümmel. *Exegetical Method.* Translated by E. V. N. Goetchius. New York: Seabury, 1967.

Keck, Leander E. "Literary criticism." In *IDBSup* (1976).

Keck, Leander E., and Gene M. Tucker. "Exegesis." In *IDBSup* (1976).

Kilian, Rudolf. *Die vorpriesterlichen Abrahamsüberlieferungen.* BBB 24. Bonn: Peter Hanstein, 1966.

Knierim, Rolf. "Old Testament Form Criticism Reconsidered." *Int* 27 (1973).

Knight, Douglas A. *Rediscovering the Traditions of Israel.* SBLDS 9. Missoula, Mont.: Society of Biblical Literature, 1973.

Knight, Douglas A., ed. *Tradition and Theology in the Old Testament.* Philadelphia: Fortress, 1977.

Koch, Klaus. *Amos.* AOAT 20. Neukirchen-Vluyn: Neukirchener Verlag, 1976.

———. *The Growth of the Biblical Tradition: The Form-Critical Method.* Translated by S. M. Cupitt from 2d German edition. New York: Charles Scribner's Sons, 1969.

————. "Reichen die formgeschichtlichen Methoden für die Gegenwartsaufgaben der Bibelwissenschaft zu?" *TLZ* 98 (1973).

————. *Was ist Formgeschichte?* Neukirchen-Vluyn: Neukirchener Verlag, 1964.

————. *Was ist Formgeschichte?* 3d edition. Neukirchen-Vluyn: Neukirchener Verlag, 1974.

Köhler, Ludwig. *Deuterojesaja (Jesaja 40–55) stilkritisch untersucht.* BZAW 37. Giessen: A. Töpelmann, 1923.

Kraus, Hans-Joachim. "Bibelkritik, I. AT." In *EKL*. Vol. 1. Göttingen: Vandenhoeck & Ruprecht, 1956.

————. *Psalmen.* 5th ed. BKAT 15/1–2. Neukirchen-Vluyn: Neukirchener Verlag, 1978.

Krentz, Edgar. *The Historical Critical Method.* Philadelphia: Fortress, 1975.

Kuhl, Curt. "Bibelwissenschaft, geschichtlich: 1. Bibelwissenschaft des AT." In *RGG*[3]. Vol. 1. Tübingen: J. C. B. Mohr (Paul Siebeck), 1957.

————. "Traditionswesen in Israel." In *EKL*. Vol. 3. Göttingen: Vandenhoeck & Ruprecht, 1959a.

————. "Überlieferungsgeschichtliche Forschung." In *EKL*. Vol. 3. Göttingen: Vandenhoeck & Ruprecht, 1959b.

Lohfink, Norbert. *Das Hauptgebot.* AnBib 20. Rome: Pontifical Biblical Institute, 1963.

Mabee, Charles. "The Problem of Setting in Hebrew Royal Judicial Narrative." Ph.D. dissertation, Claremont Graduate School, 1977.

McCarthy, Dennis J. *Treaty and Covenant.* AnBib 21A. Rome: Pontifical Biblical Institute, 1978.

Melugin, Roy F. *The Formation of Isaiah 40–55.* BZAW 141. Berlin and New York: Walter de Gruyter, 1975.

Mittman, Siegfried. *Deuteronomium 1:1–6:3 literarkritisch und traditionsgeschichtlich untersucht.* BZAW 139. Berlin and New York: Walter de Gruyter, 1975.

Muilenburg, James. "The Book of Isaiah: Chapters 40–66, Introduction and Exegesis." *IB* 5. New York and Nashville: Abingdon, 1956.

————. "Form Criticism and Beyond." *JBL* 88 (1969).

————. "A Study in Hebrew Rhetoric: Repetition and Style." In *Congress Volume: Copenhagen, 1953.* VTSup 1. Leiden: E. J. Brill, 1953.

Noth, Martin. *Überlieferungsgeschichtliche Studien.* 2d edition. Darmstadt: Wissenschaftliche Buchgesellschaft, 1957.

Otto, Eckart. *Das Mazzotfest in Gilgal.* BWANT 107. Stuttgart: W. Kohlhammer, 1975.

Paulsen, Henning. "Traditionsgeschichtliche Methode und religionsgeschichtliche Schule." *ZTK* 75 (1978).

Perlitt, Lothar. *Bundestheologie im Alten Testament.* WMANT 36. Neukirchen-Vluyn: Neukirchener Verlag, 1969.

Rast, Walter E. *Tradition History and the Old Testament.* Philadelphia: Fortress, 1972.

Rendtorff, Rolf. "Beobachtungen zur altisraelitischen Geschichtsschreibung anhand der Geschichte vom Aufstieg Davids." In *Probleme biblischer Theologie: Gerhard von Rad zum 70. Geburtstag.* Edited by H. W. Wolff. Munich: Chr. Kaiser, 1971.

————. *Das überlieferungsgeschichtliche Problem des Pentateuch*. BZAW 147. Berlin and New York: Walter de Gruyter, 1977.

————. *Die Gesetze in der Priesterschrift*. 2d ed. FRLANT 62. Göttingen: Vandenhoeck & Ruprecht, 1963.

————. "Formen und Gattungen, I. AT." In *EKL*. Vol. 1. Göttingen: Vandenhoeck & Ruprecht, 1956.

Reventlow, Henning Graf. *Das Heiligkeitsgesetz formgeschichtlich untersucht*. WMANT 6. Neukirchen-Vluyn: Neukirchener Verlag, 1961.

Richter, Wolfgang. *Die sogenannten vorprophetischen Berufungsberichte*. FRLANT 101. Göttingen: Vandenhoeck & Ruprecht, 1970.

————. *Exegese als Literaturwissenschaft*. Göttingen: Vandenhoeck & Ruprecht, 1971.

————. *Traditionsgeschichtliche Untersuchungen zum Richterbuch*. BBB 18. Bonn: Peter Hanstein, 1963.

Rietzschel, Claus. *Das Problem der Urrolle*. Gütersloh: Mohn, 1966.

Robertson, David A. *Linguistic Evidence in Dating Early Hebrew Poetry*. SBLDS 3. Missoula, Mont.: Society of Biblical Literature, 1972.

————. "Literature, The Bible as." In *IDBSup* (1976).

————. *The Old Testament and the Literary Critic*. Philadelphia: Fortress, 1977.

Saebø, Magne. *Sacharja 9–14: Untersuchungen von Text und Form*. WMANT 34. Neukirchen-Vluyn: Neukirchener Verlag, 1969.

Schmid, Hans Heinrich. *Der sogenannte Jahwist*. Zurich: Theologischer Verlag, 1976.

Schmidt, Werner H. *Die Schöpfungsgeschichte der Priesterschrift*. WMANT 17. Neukirchen-Vluyn: Neukirchener Verlag, 1964.

Schulte, Hannelis. *Die Entstehung der Geschichtsschreibung im Alten Israel*. BZAW 128. Berlin and New York: Walter de Gruyter, 1972.

Seitz, Gottfried. *Redaktionsgeschichtliche Studien zum Deuteronomium*. BWANT 93. Stuttgart: W. Kohlhammer, 1971.

Smith, Clyde Curry. "Jehu and the Black Obelisk of Shalmaneser III." In *Scripture in History and Theology: Essays in Honor of J. Coert Rylaarsdam*. Edited by A. L. Merrill and T. W. Overholt. PTMS 17. Pittsburgh: Pickwick, 1977.

Smith, Morton. *Palestinian Parties and Politics That Shaped the Old Testament*. New York and London: Columbia University Press, 1971.

Steck, Karl Gerhard. "Tradition." In *EKL*. Vol. 3. Göttingen: Vandenhoeck & Ruprecht, 1959.

Steck, Odil Hannes. *Der Schöpfungsbericht der Priesterschrift*. FRLANT 115. Göttingen: Vandenhoeck & Ruprecht, 1975.

————. *Israel und das gewaltsame Geschick der Propheten*. WMANT 23. Neukirchen-Vluyn: Neukirchener Verlag, 1967.

Thiel, Winfried. *Die deuteronomistische Redaktion von Jeremia 1–25*. WMANT 41. Neukirchen-Vluyn: Neukirchener Verlag, 1973.

Thompson, Thomas L. *The Historicity of the Patriarchal Narratives*. BZAW 133. Berlin and New York: Walter de Gruyter, 1974.

Tucker, Gene M. "Form Criticism, OT." In *IDBSup* (1976).

Van Seters, John. *Abraham in History and Tradition*. New Haven, Conn.: Yale University Press, 1975.

Wanke, Günther. *Untersuchungen zur sogenannten Baruchschrift.* BZAW 122. Berlin: Walter de Gruyter, 1971.

Weimar, Peter. *Untersuchungen zur Redaktionsgeschichte des Pentateuch.* BZAW 146. Berlin and New York: Walter de Gruyter, 1977.

Weiss, Meir. "Die Methode der 'Total-Interpretation.'" In *Congress Volume: Uppsala, 1971.* VTSup 22. Leiden: E. J. Brill, 1972.

Wellek, Rene, and Austin Warren. *Theory of Literature.* 3d edition. New York and London: Harcourt Brace Jovanovich, 1975.

Wellhausen, Julius. *Die Composition des Hexateuchs und der historischen Bücher des Alten Testaments.* 4th edition. Berlin: Walter de Gruyter, 1963.

Westermann, Claus. *Basic Forms of Prophetic Speech.* Translated by H. C. White from *Grundformen Prophetischer Rede,* 1960. Philadelphia: Fortress, 1967.

Wharton, James A. "Redaction Criticism, OT." In *IDBSup* (1976).

Wilson, Robert R. *Prophecy and Society in Ancient Israel.* Philadelphia: Fortress, 1980.

Wolff, Hans Walter. *Gesammelte Studien zum Alten Testament.* TB 22. Munich: Chr. Kaiser, 1964.

Zenger, Erich. *Die Sinaitheophanie: Untersuchungen zu Jahwist und Elohist.* Forschung zur Bibel 3. Würzburg: Echter-Verlag, 1971.

2

Old Testament Form Criticism Reconsidered

Rolf Knierim

The historical manifestations of typical forms, especially the interrelationship of the various typicalities in linguistic entities, and their influence on individual texts are more flexible than form criticism has been prepared to assume.

Among the methods concerned with the exegesis of biblical texts, form criticism has had a prominent place since the beginning of our century.[1] Concentrating on the texts of the biblical literature as literary entities, form criticism has attempted to interpret these individual entities by discovering the matrices to which they owe their existence and which they reflect. And since a matrix is assumed to be typical in nature, individual texts emerging from it can be explained as specifications of a distinct typicality. The way form criticism has conceived of the typical is sociolinguistic and morphological; the linguistic types underlying the individual texts are genres that arise out of a typical societal or life setting. They are governed by patterns, appear in typical formulaic expression (*Formensprache*), convey a typical mood, and have a typical function.[2]

The explicit prerequisite in this conceptualization was, thereby, that the coherence of all these factors, at least that of the mood, the formulaic language, and the setting,[3] would have to be recognized in an attempt to identify a genre. Ascertaining that language was in ancient

Rolf Knierim, "Old Testament Form Criticism Reconsidered," *Interpretation* 27 (October 1973) 435–48. Reproduced by permission.

1. For a convenient discussion of the total method and its ramifications, cf. Klaus Koch, *The Growth of the Biblical Tradition, The Form Critical Method*, trans. S. M. Cupitt (New York: Charles Scribner's Sons, 1969). Gene M. Tucker, *Form Criticism of the Old Testament* (Philadelphia: Fortress Press, 1971).

2. Cf. the nucleus of the statement as quoted from Gunkel and discussed by Werner Klatt, *Hermann Gunkel* (Göttingen: Vandenhoeck & Ruprecht, 1969) 106–25, 128, 143ff.

3. This was Gunkel's program. In the actual history of the discipline, however, the emphasis shifted more to the triad structure (form), setting, and function, often to theme, plot, or occupation of mind (*Geistesbeschäftigung*). Cf. Volker Wagner, *Rechtssätze in gebundener Sprache und Rechtssatzreihen im israelitischen Recht* (BZAW 127; Berlin and New York: de Gruyter, 1972) 57, 59; Erhard Gerstenberger, *Wesen und Herkunft des apodiktischen Rechts* (WMANT 20; Neukirchen-Vluyn: Neukirchener, 1965) 66.

times much less individualized than it is in our days, that it was indeed patterned and governed by the structures of life itself, the form critics have operated on the basis of a hermeneutic of language according to which life and language correspond to one another: life creates language, and language reflects life and its meaning. The philosophical premises of this position have been discussed elsewhere so that we need not recount them here.[4] Neither can we afford to dwell even generally on the new avenues to biblical exegesis opened by the method and the wealth of results it has yielded. Instead, we are preoccupied at this juncture with a number of fundamental problems that are built into the very system of the form-critical method. In focusing on this concern, we are aware of the rapidly increasing number of voices that are also concerned with it.

I

One of the facts is that we are no longer so clear as to what exactly a genre is. More pointedly, it is doubtful whether this has ever been clear. A historical and comparative survey of the criteria for understanding genres, or of the factors assumed to constitute a genre, shows a perplexing methodological flexibility and inconsistency.[5]

1. Gunkel's own theoretical conceptualization of a genre as a coherent entity of mood, form, and setting was at best an ideal. In his exegetical work, their balance had to bend considerably. Identification of a genre was governed by formal symptoms,[6] by the setting,[7] or even by content.[8]

2. This ambiguity has pervaded many of the attempts at classifying genres, not only in the field of biblical scholarship. The attempts of the International Society for Folk Narrative Research to classify folk narrative (*Sagen*) have met so far with insurmountable obstacles and eluded any consensus.[9] One definition of *Sage* requires three constituents —

---

4. Cf. Klatt and Hans Joachim Kraus, *Die Geschichte der historisch-kritischen Erforschung des Alten Testaments* (Neukirchen: Neukirchener Verlag, 2d. ed., 1969).

5. Cf. Especially William G. Doty, "The Concept of Genre in Literary Analysis," *Proceedings*, ed. Lane C. McGaughy (SBL, 1972) 2, 413ff.; J. Arthur Baird, "Genre Analysis as a Method of Historical Criticism," 385ff.; Wolfgang Richter, *Exegese als Literaturwissenschaft* (Göttingen: Vandenhoeck & Ruprecht, 1971) 125ff.

6. Cf. Klatt, *Gunkel*, 143.

7. Ibid., 229.

8. Ibid., 217; Cf. Richter, *Exegese als Literaturwissenschaft*, 75ff. If I see correctly, the old differentiation of generic types between oral forms and written genres has been generally discarded and justly so.

9. Cf. Leander Petzoldt, ed., *Vergleichende Sagenforschung* (Darmstadt: Wissenschaftliche Buchgesellschaft, 1969).

one or more motifs, a fixed form, and, above all, a content of belief.[10] But others are content with less. For some interpreters, the narratives are constituted by the setting in which they are narrated.[11] This is especially true for the historical narratives, which are classed by the locality[12] or by the everyday life setting with which they are concerned.[13] For others, the aspect of the setting has to be complemented by other aspects, such as types of motifs characteristic of different regions.[14] For still others, setting becomes insignificant altogether. The puzzle of the so-called Migratory Legends is one of the reasons.[15] The use of the criterion of morphology has had more positive results. In this approach narratives are grouped according to genetic families that have relatively stable compositional skeletons.[16] But here, too, the basic criterion has had to be complemented with others, such as fixed thematic patterns[17] or the overall theme (e.g., the Sodom and Gomorrah theme).[18] Morphological classification has also been supplemented by the category of social function, as in the case of the *memorata* (*memorabilia*). These are grouped together because they serve to prove, explain, or illustrate, in addition to having a common form.[19] One attempt to classify the total spectrum of folk narrative used the three criteria of morphology, setting, and function intermittently.[20] And a projected, all-encompassing catalog differentiates between primordial — aetiological and eschatological — and historical narratives, on the one hand, and narratives dealing with supernatural forces and supernatural persons, on the other.[21]

3. What has been said about folk narratives is also true for the definition and classification of myths.[22] Myth itself is inseparably related to its ritual setting.[23] It creates reality through rituals. It is striking that the variations of mythical language are not created by the setting itself. Rather, they seem grounded in pre-rational structures of the mind.

The field of mythology helps to focus our problem. It shows that

---

10. Ibid., 309.
11. Ibid., 352.
12. Ibid., 310, 421.
13. Ibid., 328.
14. Ibid., 357, 359, 361, 364, 372.
15. Ibid., 310.
16. Ibid., 328.
17. Ibid., 326ff., 337.
18. Ibid., 315, 392, 395ff.
19. Ibid., 328, 342, 360.
20. Ibid., 328f.
21. Ibid., 368.
22. Cf. the interdisciplinary anthology, Karl Kerenyi, ed., *Die Eröffnung des Zugangs zum Mythus, Wege der Forschung XX* (Darmstadt: Wissenschaftliche Buchgesellschaft, 1967).
23. Ibid., 170, 186, 262ff., 271ff.

the order of interdependence between a setting and a genre can be reversible. Its linguistic form is by no means constituted by the setting. One would have to say that the genre constitutes and forms the setting. In other words, the genre "myth" creates the ritual "reality."

This also raises the questions of the nature of "genre" altogether. It can be conceived of as an external reproduction, in action and language, of the typical patterns in which the human mind perceives cosmic and social order. A genre such as myth can be understood as the expression of a "conceptual genre" of the mind.

This aspect cannot be taken lightly especially by those concerned with the form-critical interpretation of ancient texts. For it is well known that throughout most of the history of civilization, certainly at its early stages, the human institutions, and not only the cultic ones, were never thought of by their founders other than as earthly copies, images, and materializations of the primordial world. If, however, linguistic genres and institutional settings taken together can depend on preconceptualizations, we must revise one of the traditional form-critical assumptions. A genre is no longer to be constituted by its societal setting. A potential autonomy vis-à-vis setting can be attributed to generic language.

4. The centrality of this problem is indicated by its high visibility in different fields of research such as literature, folklore, myth and symbol, phenomenology of religion, linguistics, and, most vocally, structuralism. The range of publications is so vast that a few examples from different areas must suffice at this point.

There has been a tendency in literary criticism to relate genre and cultural convention to genetically transmitted structures that lie below or behind empirical reality. The Chicago or neo-Aristotelian school, represented by R. S. Crane, has developed the concept of "intrinsic genre." It means that individual texts, in this case poems, are immediately shaped by "the common symbolic operations of the human mind, and hence...the structures of meaning which, because they are basic and universal in man's experience, are in a sense given to poets rather than created by them."[24] This concept means that genres cannot be discovered except through individual texts intrinsically shaped by them. It also criticizes the traditional approach to poems on the basis of preconceived generic conceptualizations like epic, tragedy, and lyric. This has prevented interpreters from recognizing any of the actual structural principles in poems except for those already contained in their

---

24. R. S. Crane, *The Language of Criticism and the Structure of Poetry* (Toronto: University of Toronto Press, 1953) 116.

preferred definitions and models.[25] If I see correctly, the intrinsic genre of a text and the "structural principles" below it complement one another; the second expression refers to depth level, whereas the first one refers to the surface level on which it appears in individual texts.

5. This position is very close to that taken by the representatives of French structuralism. Claude Lévi-Strauss aims at discovering the fundamental patterns of the human mind that underlie its overwhelming diversity of expression.[26] He uncovers the unconscious structure underlying each institution and each custom, in order to obtain a principle of interpretation valid for other institutions and other customs.[27] When he does this, he appears in the company of those concerned with the discussion of genre. To be sure, the word "genre" scarcely occurs in structuralist language, and understandably so. Structuralism wants to identify those structures that underlie all forms of human expression and behavior and not primarily genres on the linguistic level. Nevertheless, the structuralist method becomes interesting for the discussion of genre precisely at the point where it assumes that the variable patterns of linguistic expression and human behavior are received in already structured forms from the patterns and schemata conceived by the collective consciousness on its prelinguistic level.[28] This assumption opens perspectives for the explanation of the possible origins and identity traits of generic language, which go, in principle, beyond the framework of interpretation provided by traditional form criticism. If the typical forms that pervade individual and diverse expression actually come from underlying matrices that the human mind generates, then the structuralists' particular notion of "structure" may be able to offer additional criteria for the identification of genres. This may be useful since we have reason to assume that typical linguistic entities may arise from and reflect origins other than social settings.[29]

6. It is generally known that the structuralists have depended on Ferdinand de Saussure for their differentiation between the prelinguistic activity of the human mind (*langue*) and the activity of language (*pa-*

---

25. Ibid., 146.

26. E. Nelson Hayes and Tanya Hayes, eds., *Claude Lévi-Strauss, The Anthropologist as Hero* (Cambridge and London: M.I.T. Press, 1970) 27.

27. Ibid., 27; cf. also p. 41 and e.g., Lévi-Strauss, *Structural Anthropology* (Garden City: Anchor Books, Doubleday & Co., 1967) 64, 81, 86; Gunther Schiwy, *Der französische Strukturalismus* (Rowohlts deutsche Enzyklopädie, 1971) 310.

28. Lévi-Strauss, *Structural Anthropology*, 55, 64; Hayes, *The Anthropologist*, 203; cf. Also Edmund Leach, ed., *The Structural Study of Myth and Totemism* (London: Tavistock Publications, 1967) 17–21, 49, 120ff.

29. The potential of structuralism for form criticism becomes especially evident in view of its goal to encompass both the patterns of human language and social behavior and to make them fruitful for cross-cultural comparisons.

role). Quite apart from the prominence that the methods of structural linguistics have recently received in biblical exegesis, there are two of its theories that may further exemplify the problem of genre concerning us here: one, the relationship between language and *langue,* the other the relationship between language and reality.

The first one builds on a fundamental distinction between the synchronic and the diachronic understanding of language. This theory holds that certain structures of language persist throughout the years whereas others change. As a result, both the persisting and the changing structures frequently affect and penetrate each other. In the language of form criticism this is the cause for the existence of "mixed genres."

The second and more important thesis holds that the synchronic structure of language is always related to a certain state of prelinguistic conceptualization *(état de langue).*[30] This raises a question: Are not the genres of the synchronic level predominantly constituted by the structuring preoccupation of the human mind *(langue)* rather than by sociohistorical settings? This second thesis suggests that such genres can coincide with the objective realities they refer to, but they do not have to.[31] The implication of this thesis coincides with the statements of an increasing number of biblical scholars, saying that language, including generically patterned language, has its independent mode of existence. It is, so to say, a setting of its own kind which is not necessarily representative of a social, or even any institutionalized, setting. This by no means implies, however, that a genre cannot be constituted by and reflect a certain setting. Nevertheless, the conclusion seems unavoidable that "setting," in the sense biblical form criticism has understood it, cannot be regarded indispensably as one of the factors that constitute genres, not if genre is understood as a linguistic phenomenon.

7. Before we consider the possible consequences of these observations for the understanding of genre and for the form-critical methodology as a whole, we should look at other aspects of the conceptualization of genre.

For André Jolles,[32] the one matrix that constitutes all the elementary genres *(einfache Formen)* and their artistic literary counterparts

---

30. Horst Geckeler, *Strukturelle Semantik und Wortfeldtheorie* (Munich: Wilhelm Fink Verlag, 1971) 185.

31. Cf. Geckeler, Ibid., 179ff.; cf. also Strauss, in Leach, *Structural Study of Myth,* 29. "The myth is certainly related to given empirical facts, but not as a re-presentation of them. The relationship is of a dialectic kind, and the institutions described in the myths can be the very opposite of real institutions."

32. *Einfache Formen* (2d rev. ed.; Darmstadt: Wissenschaftliche Buchgesellschaft, 1958).

is the occupation of mind *(Geistesbeschäftigung)*. This is different from
the structuralists' notion of the operation of the subconscious "human
mind." "Occupation of mind" means much more. It is that on which
man has, and sets, his mind. The different oral or literary genres receive
their distinct identities from the different modes of that occupation of
mind, its different concerns or orientations. If, for example, it is occupied with a distinctly confined reality of life such as work or family,
the form of the genre will be congruous with that reality; it will grow
out of it and reflect it. This is the *Sage*. And this genre grows out of
its setting because the setting is precisely the focus of its preoccupation. However, most of the other elementary genres such as fairy tale,
Memorabile, legend, novel, and joke, do not grow out of, or represent,
such a setting. These are not morphologically differentiated by their
settings, but rather by occupation with different concerns. It does not
matter here whether Jolles was right in some of his interpretations or
not. What matters is the fact that once more we are confronted with a
position according to which generic formations of language and literature have their correlatives in the typical operations of man's mind.
Genres are the forms of expression through which these mental operations function. For Jolles, generic identity is constituted by the typical
occupation of mind as it expresses itself in language. In view of Jolles's
impact, especially on Old Testament form criticism, it is worthwhile
to mention that his linguistically oriented understanding of genres
is significantly different methodologically from Gunkel's sociologically
oriented understanding.

8. Paul Bockmann adds yet another important nuance to the form-
critical discussion of literature. He emphasizes the interrelation of
language and the spirit of an age,[33] especially the interrelation of the
language of generic forms *(Formensprache)* and the changing human self-
understanding. He states that this interrelation subjects the genres to
their historicity. With the change of human self-understanding, the language of generic forms cannot escape transformation either. In view of
this fact, the question arises as to whether a normative concept of genre
based on fixed autonomous sets of structural elements can be meaning-
fully upheld at all.[34] A method oriented on such an understanding of
genre will find it very difficult to understand the formative forces. In
Bockmann's work, too, the category of setting plays a little role. And
instead of Jolles's "occupation of the mind," he emphasizes the context

---

33. *Formensprache, Studien zur Literarästhetik und Dichtungsinterpretation* (Darmstadt:
Wissenschaftliche Buchgesellschaft, 1969) 511.

34. Bockmann, *Formgeschichte der deutschen Dichtung* (Hamburg: Hoffman und Campe
Verlag, 3d. ed., 1967) 38f.

of the "spirit of the age," a position which is more sociohistorically oriented. Most important, however, he points out another tension in the form-critical method — the conflict between changing formal structures in language and literature on the one hand and morphologically defined genres on the other. As a result of this conflict, Bockmann switches away from the traditional Greco-Roman and medieval methodology of genre criticism, with its sophisticated system of generic classifications based upon morphology of language.[35] Instead, he turns to a methodology of form criticism in what is for him the proper sense of the word. The structural unity of literary works is the focus of attention, in the context of their contemporary literary conventions, so that a holistic interpretation may be achieved. This does not mean that genres fall out of sight. But they become subservient to the holistic form-critical interpretation and they figure in it only as much as they play a role in the historical transformation of forms.

9. Finally, new perspectives in the interrelation of composition, pattern, formulaic language, setting, and theme have come from the folklorists. Based on field studies about "The Singer of Tales,"[36] Lord has attempted to outline a morphology of oral and written poetry. The oral text of a poem is a composition essentially governed by three factors: a pattern of formulaic language (in lines or cola), a system of rhetorical devices (rhythm, line, boundary, alliteration, chiasm, inclusion, assonance) by which line is added to line, and the grouping of a set of ideas around a major theme which accounts for the unity of the whole. Generally, all these factors are traditional, that is, they represent both the tools acquired by the poet from the tradition of oral poetry and the raw materials that he has inherited. The formulas, the rhetorical framework, and the ideas of a theme are stable, but their organization in the actual composition of a poem is variable. Thus a poem itself exists as a thematic pattern outside of its actual performance, along with the devices of oral poetry. In its actual performance, and only there, it is composed into an oral text. This text never becomes normative. Only its pattern, the formulas, and the rhetorical devices are normative. An oral composition is, therefore, neither learned by memory nor recited. It is created ad hoc by the poet. But the poet has learned his pattern and is in command of his poetic techniques. He can play his instrument. At this point the setting comes into the picture in a twofold way. Setting appears, on the one hand, as the tradition which furnishes the poet with his poetic devices and his thematic pattern. On the other hand, it

---

35. Cf. the instructive book by Helmut Rahn, *Morphologie der Antiken Literatur* (Darmstadt: Wissenchaftliche Buchgesellschaft, 1969) 45–65.

36. Albert B. Lord, *The Singer of Tales* (New York: Atheneum, 1978).

appears as the situation of actual performance. Supported by his instrument, he creates the oral text in the market place, the inn, or a family
gathering in a house.[37]

The oral texts of a poem created by the singer in his performances
are not identical. Nevertheless, they are of the same kind because they
follow the same dictate under which oral poems are composed. As soon
as a poem is created for the purpose of writing, however, the resulting
text is different in kind from all the oral texts. Not only is there from
that point on a fixed text — an "original" — the writing itself stands
under a dictate of composition and orientation towards readers, which
changes the nature of the text, and it takes on the traits of the unique.[38]

The relevance of such a study for the form-critical methodology is
obvious. Most important, we possess evidence here for the indissoluble
coherence of an oral genre with its content, its form, and its setting. Its
conceptual pattern belongs to the setting of the guild which represents
the tradition. The textual materialization not only belongs to the setting, it literally owes its existence to the setting of its performance. As a
literary genre, however, it is removed from those settings and subjected
to the different conditions entailed in the situation of its writing. Beyond that, this case reveals something of the relationship between the
generic pattern and the individual contribution and something of the
relationship between oral and written tradition. But Lord is only concerned with the question of oral poetry and only with the genre and
setting of poetic tales at that. How much can it contribute to the problem of oral prose? Can it help to rediscover the particulars of its oral
style and composition, and, above all, its traditional conceptual pattern?
The only things we possess are the written texts and we are told that
the written text is different in kind both from an oral text and its pattern. To what degree are the criteria for the description of the poetic
tale and its setting applicable to the analysis of different genres and
their different settings — even other poetic ones? Does this method lend
itself to a kind of form criticism capable of identifying the thematic traditions, the formulaic language, and the linguistic composition of texts
much more than their genres? These questions may show that Lord's
method deals only with a segment of the materials with which biblical
form criticism is confronted. Therefore, while availing ourselves of it for
this segment, we must keep in mind the other approaches for dealing
with the generic variety of Old Testament literature.

---

37. Cf. the similar observations on the oral prose style of the Nordic sagas and the
setting of their performances by the saga-tellers before the Icelandic and Greenlandic assemblies, the royal courts, or on special festivals: Gustav Neckel, *Die altnordische Literatur*
(Darmstadt: Wissenschaftliche Buchgesellschaft, reprint of first edition, 1923) 104ff.

38. Lord, *The Singer of Tales,* 124ff.

10. The review of some fields concerned in one way or another with the problems of morphology, setting, genre, function, and typicality of language and its occupations shows a startling diversity indeed. It would be worthwhile to analyze the reasons for this diversity, but we will refrain from such analysis and, instead, cling only to one observation that brings us back to the point that gave rise to our review. Not only is the concept of genre developed quite differently in various approaches, even when approaches use the same combination of categories, but the categories may be weighted quite differently.

Rather than turning away from the confusion of these methodologies or demanding that they be coordinated under a uniting theory, we should ask whether or not similar observations can be made with regard to Old Testament form-critical scholarship. What could such an overall situation mean for a reconceptualization of the form-critical method itself? The vast amount of publications compels us to be selective and to concentrate on exemplary cases that exemplify the situation.

11. Use of the morphology of language and literature as a heuristic principle for the identification of genres has become one of the most visible trademarks of Old Testament form-critical scholarship. It has recently been advocated in a most programmatic way by Richter.[39] He relates form to the individual text and genre to a text-type. A genre is a structural model or scheme *(Strukturmuster)* of approximate value,[40] and the occurrence of at least two congruous or similar units is the foundation for its identification.[41] Richter demands that literary units be identified strictly on morphological grounds. However, he emphasizes that both the forms and the genres point to the settings where they originate or to the relations in life that constitute them.[42] The forms or genres and their setting are related to one another in such a way that genres can change their setting. The categories of content or concern must be separated from the criteria by which genres can be identified.

By correlating genre and setting, Richter is essentially in line with the traditional form-critical method, even though he refines it skillfully. The question concerning us here, however, is precisely this programmatic assumption that genres are constituted by their setting. In other words, the setting is assumed to provide or produce the matrix to which typical linguistic units owe their existence. To be sure, this assumption can be ascertained with regard to a great many forms, formulas,

---

39. *Exegese als Literaturwissenschaft*, 72–152.
40. Ibid., 132.
41. Ibid., 138f.
42. Ibid., 121, 133, 145ff.

and genres in the Old Testament. Thus the problem is not whether
generic language can depend on setting but whether this has to be assumed always. Can the assumption become an exclusive methodological
principle under which all Old Testament texts have to be understood
according to Richter's own statement?[43] Genre is an operational term,
that is, a term which implies something about the function of a genre,
namely, to point to its setting. If, however, setting means the matrix that
produces the structural models, we can ask whether this matrix could
not be something other than a setting in the traditional form-critical or
in Richter's sense. It could, for example, be the structure of an existential human situation, or Jolles's occupation of the human mind. At this
point, we are reminded of what has been said about the understanding
of the operation of mind in structuralism, structural linguistics, and by
Jolles. We are confronted with the possibility of language itself as an autonomous matrix of typical linguistic expressions. This is a possibility
for the Old Testament traditions as well.

Some form-critical research seems to follow this assumption. Claus
Westermann's studies in Genesis may be a case in point. By analyzing the models according to which the core of the original patriarchal
narratives is structured, he finds them reflecting the reality and the
typical situations of families with their problems. They are family narratives.[44] Their matrix is the setting of such family situations in such a
cultural milieu. The narratives in Genesis 1–11, however, are of a different kind. They are concerned with the world, the evolution of mankind,
and with the nature of man, his guilt and destiny. They are primordial
narratives.[45] Their matrix is the occupation of man's mind with these
realities, as is evident in the worldwide dissemination of their motifs.
For Westermann, both genres and their structural model apparently are
products of the occupation of the human mind. The only reason why
the matrix of the family narratives can be seen in their setting is the
narrator's preoccupation with that kind of reality.

Paul D. Hanson, in an important article on "Zechariah 9 and the Recapitulation of an Ancient Ritual Pattern,"[46] seems to follow a method
with similar implications. Taking this text as a whole, he discovers in
it all the structural components of an ancient Near Eastern genre that
he calls the "conflict myth" (p. 53). Its form and substance have had
an enormous influence on considerable portions of the Old Testament,

---

43. Ibid., 133.

44. "Arten der Erzählung in der Genesis," *Forschung am Alten Testament, Gesammelte
Studien* (Munich: Chr. Kaiser Verlag, 1964) 1–91.

45. Westermann, *Genesis 1–11*, Erträge der Forschung 7 (Darmstadt: Wissenschaftliche
Buchgesellschaft, 1972) 107f.

46. *JBL*, 92:37–59 (1973).

especially the "Divine warrior hymns" of the sixth- and fifth-century corpora. This genre is described by Hanson as a dominating "thought form," a motif "dominated by the mythopoeic view of divine action" but expressed in a vast diversity of form, style, and content. This diversity requires a basic stock of typical components necessary for the genre to be transformed into a text. It does not expect the genre to be cast once and for all into a fixed form.

Taken together, the work of Hanson, Westermann, and Richter raises some questions. There are well-known studies which establish genres on the basis of a fixed linguistic pattern, such as Beyerlin's and Baltzer's covenant formulary[47] and Jeremias's theophany.[48] Westermann and Hanson have provided studies that establish genres on the basis of a concern or motif that can take diverse forms in specific texts. Does not Richter's definition of genre as a structural model or scheme of approximate value fail to allow for both of these methods? If both fixed and variable text-types exist in our literature, methodological openness is demanded. We should not have to choose between two alternative methodological premises, namely between concepts of genre as a fixed or flexible structure. Insistence on one or the other becomes methodologically meaningless. Instead we should ask whether a certain text rests on the one or the other sort of generic pattern, whether this or that exegesis does more justice to it.[49]

Coming back to Hanson's description of the genre of conflict myth, we find another instance in which the assumption of a setting in life being the matrix of the genre plays virtually no role at all. Perhaps Hanson would like to affirm that it originated in an ancient Near Eastern cult festival. Even so, one could ask if the mythical conceptualization did not constitute the cult festival and its pattern rather than being constituted by it. Everything Hanson says indicates that the occurrence of this genre in Israel does not point to a setting from which it emerged, which it reflected, or to which it owed its existence. Does this not put Richter's assumption about the coherence between genre and setting in question? Hanson's example also points to the false dilemma in which a great number of form critical studies are caught. After a genre has been

---

47. Walter Beyerlin, *Origins and History of the Sinai Tradition,* trans. S. Rudman (Oxford: B. H. Blackwell, 1965). Klaus Baltzer, *The Covenant Formulary in Old Testament, Jewish, and Early Christian Writings,* trans. David E. Green (Philadelphia: Fortress Press, 1971. From 2d German edition, 1964).

48. Jörg Jeremias, *Theophanie,* WMANT 10 (Neukirchen: Neukirchener Verlag, 1965), criticized by Hanson for this position.

49. In view of this distinction, the frequent insistence either on fixed or on flexible patterns or formulaic language for the identification of a genre and their respective criticisms becomes methodologically meaningless.

identified with great effort on morphological grounds, those studies continue to look for a setting at any cost, postulating, creating, fabricating one even if there is no evidence for it — and all that simply because the methodology demands a setting without which a genre would be unthinkable. Our observations, however, indicate that the reason for the stubborn absence of settings may sometimes lie deeper than in the absence of internal or external evidence for them, or of the interpreter's genius to track them down. It may lie in the very nature of language itself.

If I understand correctly, Richter himself has taken a position different from the one referred to above in an article[50] in which he reviews Gerhard von Rad's thesis on the nature and origin of the Hexateuch.[51]

12. The need for a critical reevaluation of the form-critical dogma of the coherence of genre and setting has been advocated by New Testament scholars in recent years. Via has stated that the cardinal mistake of form criticism was its failure to grant in the interpretation of texts priority to their semantic character and unity.[52] Instead, it has preferred the extra-textual factor of the setting in life. And with explicit reference to the autonomy of the linguistic art-work, he moves away from the primary and almost exclusive function of the "setting in life" category saying that the language form is a category of its own. Güttgemanns also makes a fundamental criticism of the form-critical method[53] and asks for a new theory of literature of the biblical genres which is based on the discipline of linguistics.[54]

In summing up, the problem of the interrelation of genre and setting has not been critically examined enough in Old Testament form criticism to date. The coherence of the two can no longer be dogmatically upheld in the sense form criticism has done. Hence, the method must be designed in a way as to allow us to do justice to the nature of all texts. In such a design, the relationship between genre and setting must remain an open one, so that both can be related to, or kept independent of, one another as a text may require.

---

50. "Beobachtungen zur theologischen Systembildung in der alttestamentlichen Literatur anhand des kleinen geschichtlichen Credo," in *Wahrheit und Verkündigung, Festschrift Michael Schmaus* (Munich: Verlag Ferdinand Schoningh, 1967), I, 175–211.

51. *The Problems of the Hexateuch and Other Essays*, trans. E. W. T. Dicken (Edinburgh and London: Olive & Boyd, 1966).

52. Dan Otto Via, Jr., *The Parables: Their Literary and Existential Dimensions* (Philadelphia: Fortress Press, 1967).

53. Erhard Güttgemanns, *Offene Fragen zur Formgeschichte des Evangeliums*, Beiträge zur Ev. Theologie 54 (Munich: Chr. Kaiser Verlag, 1970) 44ff.

54. E. Güttgemanns, *Studia Linguistica Neotestamentica* (BevT 60; Munich: Chr. Kaiser Verlag, 1971) 79, 145, and passim.

II

There is another major problem in the form-critical method. It concerns the understanding of the relationship between a genre's structure, on the one hand, and its content, mood, function, intention, or concern, on the other.

The typical structure or pattern on which individual texts are based has been the key to the recognition of genres in virtually all the form critical studies. It rested on the insight that human beings express themselves through language by availing themselves of the typical patterns of expression conventional in their societies. The accuracy of this assumption could be demonstrated for a wide range of literatures — ancient Near Eastern and biblical, Greco-Roman, Medieval, and others as well. This has given the method a broad undergirding. As for the Old Testament, none of its parts has remained unaffected by this approach, be it the narratives, the laws, the prophetic or wisdom literature, or the Psalms.[55]

1. Gerhard von Rad has once more stressed the importance of poetic form for the communication of that which is on the human mind:

> [The peculiarity of poetry] cannot be separated from the intellectual process as if it were something added later; rather, perception takes place precisely in and with the poetic conception. One certainly cannot regard the phenomenon of the poetic expression as a transfiguration and a transformation, stemming from within a man, of experiences which, from the aesthetic point of view, are much less impressive, that is as a matter more of appearance than of reality. . . .[56] [In didactic poetry,] the possibility, indeed the necessity, of clothing one perception in one form and another in another, arose from the material itself as well as from the situation of the instructors. But one will not be able, in every case, to succeed in proving that specific perceptions could be expressed only in specific forms and not also in others. On the other hand, the chosen form was a neutral garb only in a very few cases, so it is necessary to say something about particularly characteristic forms.[57]

And, just as many genres of psalms, laws, or prophetic speeches have their characteristic patterns, so do the many genres of wisdom literature. They include "school question," the "teacher's opening sum-

---

55. Hermann Gunkel and Joachim Begrich, *Einleitung in die Psalmen* (HAT; Ergänzungsband; Göttingen: Vandenhoeck & Ruprecht, 1933) is certainly the most comprehensive treatment of a whole section of the Old Testament ever undertaken along this line.

56. Gerhard von Rad, *Wisdom in Israel* (Nashville: Abingdon Press, 1972); Ger., *Weisheit in Israel* (Neukirchen: Neukirchener Verlag, 1970) 24.

57. Ibid., 34f.

mons,"[58] the "proverb of comparison,"[59] the "maxim,"[60] the "numerical sayings,"[61] the "dialogue,"[62] the "plain statement" and "exhortatory sentence,"[63] and the "riddle."[64] These are all governed by certain structures without which they could not be what they are. Of course, this force of the form is especially predominant in those linguistic entities that are short.

As these examples show, there can be no doubt that in many cases the typical form either constitutes a genre, or else it is one of the constitutive factors. But a problem arises when genre is defined strictly on such morphological grounds, to the exclusion of "content" as one of its inherent elements.[65] This problem would be less complicated if one could show that in many cases definitions of genres on the basis of content were simply acts of methodological oversight and neglect.[66] However, there is a broad chorus of voices stating explicitly either that form, content, and setting,[67] or that form and content together are the factors that constitute a genre.[68] We are, therefore, not confronted with inadvertent mistakes, but with an explicit polarization. And it may well be that the reasons for the dissension lie deeper than has been shown.

As an approach to the problem we can ask whether the typical form, structural model, or scheme can be taken as the sole factor by which genres are constituted. A positive argument would have to show not only that the formal factors in language suffice for the recognition of genres in some cases. It would also have to show that formal factors are the only ones that constitute genres.

2. In view of such a proposition, we would, first of all, have to ask whether a structural model is by definition, that is, always, a genre.

The assumption that structure is all there is to genre is difficult to maintain.[69] For example, Richter's own definition of part of the J

---

58. Ibid., 18. Original German: *Schulfrage, Lehreröffnungsruf.*

59. Ibid., 29. Original German: *Vergleichsspruch.*

60. Ibid., 26. Original German: *Sinnspruch.*

61. Ibid., 35. Original German: *Zahlenspruch.* Cf. W. M. Roth, *Numerical Sayings in the Old Testament*, VTSup 18 (Leiden: E. J. Brill, 1964).

62. Von Rad, *Wisdom*, 40f. Original German: *Dialog.*

63. Ibid., 31 Original German: *Aussagesatz, Mahnsatz.* Cf. Hans-Jürgen Hermisson, *Studien zur israelitischen Spruchweisheit*, WMANT 28 (Neukirchen: Neukirchener Verlag, 1968).

64. Von Rad, *Wisdom*, 36f. Original German: *Rätselspiel.*

65. Richter, *Exegese als Literaturwissenschaft*, 125ff.

66. This is the main thrust of Richter's criticism, *Exegese als Literaturwissenschaft*, 125ff.

67. See above, footnote 3.

68. Cf., e.g., Doty, 'Genre in Literary Analysis," 434, who cites Tucker's review (Dialog, 5 [1966] 145) of Koch's *Was ist Formgeschichte?* (Neukirchen: Neukirchener Verlag, 1964); Hermisson, *Studien zur israelitischen Spruchweisheit*, 85; Von Rad, *Wisdom*, 30.

69. The understanding of "structural model" in the sense the word could have in

narrative in Exodus 3 as "religious 'statement-narrative'" (*religiöse 'Aussage-Erzählung'*)[70] points to the difficulty. The structural term "narrative" is deficient by itself. It allows for no distinction between narratives which are clearly of different types in spite of identical or similar stylistic patterns. The word "religious" refers to content; it has nothing to do with the "structural model."

Westermann's differentiations between "reporting" and "describing" praise[71] are based to a degree on grammatical distinctions, and the distinctions between "imperative" and "participial" hymns[72] are certainly based on grammatical models. But these models may not be the factors that constitute hymnic genres.[73]

As for the wisdom sayings, the meter and *parallelismus membrorum* are a constitutive structural model. But it is impossible to say that this structural model constitutes the genre. This would neither allow for a further differentiation among these sayings nor would it account for the fact that the same model was used in other forms of poetry, too.[74]

The same is true for the studies in legal and related genres. Certain grammatical forms such as imperative, jussive, prohibitive, vetitive, or certain syntactical constructions in casuistic laws, death-declarations, or curse formulations are undoubtedly part of the formulaic language of genres. But the problem remains whether these forms as such constitute the genres, and whether the genres avail themselves of only these forms.[75]

French structuralism can remain aside at this point. Richter's own proposal that at least two similarly structured units would have to be found within different parts of the Old Testament in order that we may see whether or not there is a genre (*Exegese*, 138) does not suffice. One would have to show that these two units, or even more, carry and govern a text unit in a typical way either as expression of a distinct setting, or of a typical occupation of mind, or as models of communication. In order to show this, one would not only need some similar units, but evidence that they convey something typical.

70. Richter, *Die sogenannten vorprophetischen Berufungsberichte*, FRLANT 101 (Göttingen: Vandenhoeck & Ruprecht, 1970) 80. Cf. the same generic definitions for the quite different scheme of Exodus 19 by Erich Zenger, *Die Sinaitheophanie*, Forschung zur Bibel 3 (Würzburg: Echter Verlag, 1971) 129.

71. *The Praise of God in the Psalms*, trans. Keith R. Crim (Richmond, Va.: John Knox Press, 1965).

72. Frank Crüsemann, *Studien zur Formgeschichte von Hymnus und Danklied in Israel*, WMANT 32 (Neukirchen: Neukirchener Verlag, 1969) 19ff., 81ff.

73. Gunkel-Begrich, *Einleitung in die Psalmen* (1933), already suffered from the tension between the identification of patterns and the definition of the genres of Psalms on different grounds.

74. Cf. Hermisson's critique of this problem (*Studien zur israelitischen Spruchweisheit*, 84ff., 137ff., 179ff., 187ff.) and his insistence on the variability of syntactical forms within the same genre (189).

75. Hermann Schutz identified a genuine genre, the "law of death" (*Todesrecht*) which is concerned with the violation of prohibitions involving capital offenses, on the grounds of a consistent pattern (*Das Todesrecht im Alten Testament*, BZAW 114 [1969] 5–84. Ger-

What has been said of the smaller units is all the more true for the larger ones. Structural models cannot be assumed to be constitutive of genres by definition. Westermann's scheme of judgment in the narratives of Genesis 3–11,[76] or Richter's call-report scheme, or Long's combination of the call scheme with a vision-report scheme,[77] or von Rad's scheme of the call followed by the public proof of the charisma,[78] or his "long didactic poem" (grosse Lehrdichtung),[79] or "didactic nar-

---

hard Liedke, however, has recognized, with good reason, the stylistic variability of both the casuistic and the apodictic laws and sought the criteria for that which constitutes the genres in the nature of different judicial authorities of which one proposes settlements (casuistic) whereas the other, the king, establishes death declarations (apodictic), (Gestalt und Bezeichnung alttestamentlicher Rechtssätze, WMANT 39 [Neukirchener Verlag, 1971] 11–153). The most radical criticism of a formalistic conceptualization was leveled by Volkmar Wagner who abolishes the category "apodictic law" altogether while saying that laws (Rechtssätze), regardless of their variable forms, are constituted by the logical coherence between a case and its legal consequences in statements concerned with legal issues. (Rechtssätze in gebundener Sprache und Rechtssatzungen im israelitischen Recht, BZAW 127 [Berlin and New York: de Gruyter, 1972]). As for the prohibitions, Gerstenberger has warned of undue formalism and emphasized the variability of forms of the genre (called by him "prohibitives"), (Wesen und Herkunft des "apodiktischen Rechts," WMANT 20 [Neukirchen: Neukirchener Verlag, 1965] 42ff., 50ff.). Wolfgang Richter, however, has identified a genre Mahnspruch (exhortation) strictly on the basis of the grammatical form of vetitive and a motivation which was used by teachers training youngsters of the upper classes for public service as a technique to intensify their teaching of the prohibitions (Recht und Ethos [Munich: Kösel Verlag, 1966] 41–68, 172ff.). In a recent article, Weinfeld has taken quite a different position. Asking for the origin of the apodictic style, he finds it in a dialogue pattern of legal instruction imposed by a king upon his subjects who in turn pledge the acceptance and fulfillment of the commandments. (M. Weinfeld, "The Origin of the Apodictic Law," VT 23 [1973] 63ff.). While I cannot believe that Weinfeld is correct in assuming this pattern to be the only origin of the apodictic style, I do believe that he has reintroduced an essential truth into the discussion, namely, that the forms under discussion can also belong to genres other than those for which Gerstenberger, Richter, and others have reserved them. They can, in fact, belong to "legal ordinances...proclaimed in the form of authoritative apodictic commands" (Weinfeld, p. 75). This case shows, again, that typical forms do not by definition indicate certain genres. Their different generic character may very well depend on other circumstances such as, for example, distinctly different settings in which they were used, and/or different functions they had in a communication. What has been said may also caution against the common assumption that laws are constituted by both a statement of the case (protasis) and a statement of the legal consequences (apodosis), whereas prohibitions stipulating no consequences cannot be considered as laws.

76. Claus Westermann, Forschung am Alten Testament, Theologische Bücherei 24 (Munich: Chr. Kaiser Verlag, 1964) 47ff.

77. Burke O. Long, "Prophetic Call Traditions and Reports of Visions," ZAW 84 (1972) 494ff.

78. Gerhard von Rad, Old Testament Theology, trans. D. M. G. Stalker (New York: Harper & Row, 1962), I, 326ff., 329; Rolf Knierim, "The Messianic Concept in the First Book of Samuel," Jesus and the Historian, ed. F. Thomas Trotter (Philadelphia: The Westminster Press, 1968) 26.

79. Von Rad, Wisdom, 38f.

rative" *(Lehrerzählung)*,[80] are examples. This does not mean, however, that the texts in which these schemes are embedded could not belong to certain generic types other than those indicated by those schemes. Therefore, the conclusion seems inevitable. Structural models can but do not have to be genres, and a tension between them is entirely possible.

3. Conversely, a genre is not always constituted by one and the same structure. For example, H. W. Wolff has defined the genre of Hosea 3 as "Memorabile." Following Jolles, he sees this genre as a basic form, in which a report and its interpretation are united.[81] The argument looks morphological. But this same basic form can be found in much of our literature other than in call-narratives or self-reports. To use the term "Memorabile" may well explain Hosea 3 on the basis of the concern or intention, regardless of the forms through which such concerns are expressed. But it contributes little toward ascertaining the basic structure of a call narrative, a prophetic *Selbstbericht,* or of "Memorabiles." In dealing with wisdom sayings, Hermisson has stressed that didactic purpose, a specific mode of thinking, or even the constitutive motifs can all play an important role in forming an expression.[82] And Long found it necessary in his study on etiology to propose that we "devise a methodology which will yield results in those cases of alleged etiological tradition where no clear formula or inferential structure is apparent. Briefly, the question is: Are there distinctive signs in this material which show it to function etiologically? ... A wider knowledge of the various marks which reveal a story's function is needed. ... "[83] The number of examples can easily be augmented.[84] One could dispense with the implications of these references if the current discussion in related fields such as, for example, literature and linguistics, would encourage us to do so. But this is not the case. In fact, there are strong tendencies to adhere to the unity or identity of structure and content in language, both on the level of *langue* and of *parole,* as well as to emphasize the dependence of structure on meaning and intention.

4. The particular problem confronting us here is that in the form-

---

80. Ibid., 46f.

81. H. W. Wolff, *Hosea,* BKAT XIV (Neukirchen: Neukirchener Verlag, 1957) 70ff.

82. *Studien zur israelitischen Spruchweisheit,* 28f., 79, 84f., 88, 93, 137ff., 189.

83. Burke O. Long, *The Problem of Etiological Narrative in the Old Testament,* BZAW 108 (Berlin: Alfred Töpelmann, 1968) 94.

84. The problem could already be demonstrated from Gunkel's various publications on the Psalms. His definitions of the genres of the Psalms in part rest ambivalently on one or two of his three major principles rather than on all of them. This ambivalence was a major reason for Mowinckel to identify the genres of the Psalms on the principle of setting, and not of structure or thought/mood, in *The Psalms in Israel's Worship* (Nashville: Abingdon Press, 1962) 81–83.

critical interpretation of Old Testament texts we often cannot expect a typical scheme to be congruent with a typical function, intention, or concern. We can observe not only that typical structures are used for varying intentions but also that typical intentions or concerns are expressed through varying structures. Therefore, if we propose that the morphological aspect be the basis for the discovery of genres, we must be aware that often this reveals nothing more than the typicality of structure. It does not necessarily reveal much about the typicality of purpose, intent, or content. Nor does it determine which of these factors dominates a text-type or a text. In other words, genre would only be a particular category within a number of typicalities of a text.

If genre is conceived in this way, we have not touched on how it relates to sociohistorical conditions. In the historical process of a society there is an inherent dialectic between communication of the typical and communication of the changing expectations of society. If types of communication are subject to the dynamics of this process, the force of the dialectic away from conventional expectations may be more of a factor in communication than fixed, conventional schemes.[85] The category of the so-called "mixed genres" (Mischgattungen) is a case in point. Their definition as mixed genres implies that they must be understood as deteriorations of "pure" genres.[86] However, it is likely that they reflect their sociohistorical conditions more typically than any pure genre could. It could be that their identity is constituted by their sociohistorical context, and not by their lack of conventional pattern. They may exist, therefore, in their own right.

For the sake of clarification, a distinction should be made between the preliminary heuristic process of recognizing a genre and the final determination of what constitutes the genre of a specific text. Preconceived models are indispensable to begin with. Recognizing traces of a schematic model may not reveal what really constitutes it, especially if the constituting factor is a typical setting or occupation of mind which could manifest itself in various forms of linguistic expressions.[87]

---

85. Hans Robert Jauss, *Literaturgeschichte als Provokation* (2d ed.; Frankfurt am Main: Suhrkamp Verlag, 1970) 144ff.

86. Martin Kessler raises the question of the understanding of "genre elements" in the context of mixed genres ("From Drought to Exile," [SBL 1972 *Proceedings*, Vol. 2, 1972] 515). The problem is difficult. One would probably have to say that while a "mixed genre" certainly consists of parts or elements of several heterogeneous genres, the presence of genre elements in a text does not yet automatically indicate a mixed genre. Mixed genre would have to be understood as a typicality of its own governing the composition of genre elements and giving the whole a typical identity. Genre elements, on the other hand, can be adduced by text-types without making mixed genres out of them.

87. Cf. Güttgemanns's discussion of the modality of literary genres (*Offene Fragen*, 180ff.).

5. Our considerations so far support suspicions. Not only does the methodological inconsistency of scholars account for the variety in criteria for identifying genres, but so also does the nature of the discipline traditionally called *Formgeschichte,* or form criticism.

To the extent that genre is by definition a "conventional structure" and a conventional structure a "form," form criticism is by definition genre criticism. However, we have seen that the discipline has had to broaden this structural notion of genre to include other factors. In its attempt to interpret specific linguistic phenomena in terms of the actual typicality which governs them, form criticism has had to resort to the categories of setting, function, intention, and occupation of mind.

There is a clear disadvantage to the identification of genre on strictly morphological grounds. It eliminates the possibility that a text may be governed by some other typicality. We have seen that there are texts governed by other typicalities. If form criticism dogmatically holds to strictly morphological criteria, it can no longer claim genre as the central category by which texts and text-types are governed and understood.

If we expand genre to include a diversity of possible typicalities by which texts can be constituted, it would be a departure from the mainstream of the form-critical tradition. We could no longer expect to determine a genre on the basis of a morphological investigation of language alone. But at the same time, we would be forced to concentrate on whatever typicality governs a text, regardless of which one it might be. This task must remain the overriding concern of form criticism whether we ultimately agree on a concept of genre or not. In view of this situation, it may be advisable to revise the form-critical method in such a way that its major traditional categories can function as heuristic tools that enable us to discover the typicality or the typicalities governing a text. Then the question can be left to eventual findings. Do these categories coincide, or are they related, in a given text? And if they are related, what is the hierarchy of their interrelationship?

Before we try to present a short outline of such a methodological design, two remarks are necessary. The first one is concerned with the relationship between oral and written texts. One of the important tenets of the form-critical method has been that the written literature is dependent on its oral tradition. This was based on the theory that the biblical literature has the life of the people as its formative matrix. One of the consequences of this assumption has been that the genres of texts were widely identified on the basis of a supposed oral language. It seemed self-evident that recognition of the oral background of a written text led automatically to understanding the literary typicality. Whatever could not be explained along that line could be assigned to the redactor and dealt with under redaction criticism.[88] We can no longer be so sure of those methodological assumptions. Not every literary typicality can be explained from an oral background. Where this is, nevertheless, the case, we have in principle to account for the probability, at least for the possibility, that written language has its own modality.[89] We have to account for the potential difference between written texts and their oral bases, a difference that may be fundamental compared with the variations oral texts of the same type have among themselves.[90] The question is no longer to what extent our texts rest on oral traditions or language, or whether oral language is more reliable than written. We must reckon with a potential qualitative difference between oral and written language. Form-critical methodology must take the literary character of our texts seriously. The literary versions are the only ones we possess. If these texts, or some of them, rest on oral traditions, then this fact must be specifically demonstrated. Furthermore, the relationship or distinctly different typicalities between written and oral versions must be explained.

Our second remark is concerned with the emphasis by form criticism on the typical, and with the individuality of texts. For not only do we possess our texts in written form, we also possess the typicalities only in individual manifestations. It has been correctly emphasized that the interpretation of text must pay attention to both their typicality and their individuality, and that both tasks stand in their own right,[91] each

---

88. This statement has not overlooked Gunkel's basic skepticism regarding the historical reliability of oral transmission which is discussed in the excellent dissertation by D. A. Knight, *Rediscovering the Traditions of Israel* (SBLDS 9; Missoula, Mont.: Society of Biblical Literature, 1973). In the passage referred to by Knight, Gunkel discusses the reliability of the transmission of oral traditions for our historical knowledge. But Knight, influenced by the perspectives of the traditio-historical literature, the history of which he wrote, did not distinguish between oral language underlying written language as its background and between oral traditions put finally into writing after a long process of growth. The extensive amount of literature as discussed by Knight shows clearly that the sociological and traditio-historical aspects in oral language (or: the form and traditio-historical questions) were constantly mixed up and that their distinction played scarcely any role for the interpretation of written texts. Knight's conclusion that Gunkel's "realization anticipates Lord by 50 years" (82) is, therefore, not correct because Lord, unlike Gunkel, did not discuss the problem of the historical reliability of oral traditions. He was interested in the relationship between texts at the stage of their oral performance and their written edition.

89. Cf. Güttgemanns's discussion in *Öffene Fragen*, 44ff., 82ff., 119ff., 154ff., and, e.g., Noam Chomsky, *Language and Mind* (New York: Harcourt, Brace & World, 1968) 100ff.

90. In view of these problems, Güttgemanns has correctly called for "a new theory of literature of the biblical genres in discussion with linguistics" (*Studia Linguistica Neotestamentica*, 145).

91. Cf. James Muilenburg, "Form Criticism and Beyond," *JBL* (1969) 88:1ff. The problem with Muilenburg's meritorious paper is that it does not show where the "rhetorical criticism" proposed by him goes "beyond" form criticism. The way he summarizes "rhetorical criticism" on p. 18 could also be part of an article on the form-critical method.

contributing in its own way to total interpretation. Through the exegesis of text-units, the identification of the text-types must be established in contradistinction to the individuality of the texts.

III

Our analysis of some of the major problem-areas of form criticism shows that the method has not been employed uniformly. Major problems implied in the method from the inception have not been sufficiently recognized. The components which comprise a text's typicality (structure/scheme/genre, setting, content/mood/function/intention) are not always unified in the same way. The interrelationship of these components is not statically fixed. They influence texts in various ways. Nevertheless, the quest for the typicalities by which the individual texts are constituted, governed, or informed remains a decisive methodological factor for their interpretation. But the actual extent to which text-types exert influence must be realistically presented in such interpretation. It is entirely possible to identify a text-type behind an individual text, for example, on the basis of some of the elements. But if this is only a partial influence on the text, one could completely misunderstand the meaning of the text as a whole. The identification of text-types behind texts is, therefore, essentially dependent on the preceding identification of texts as entities, so that both support and confirm one another. The typical behind the text and the typical in the text must coincide.

In view of the methodological diversity, it seems appropriate to conceptualize the methodology less ideologically than in the past. It is, therefore, proper to set up a framework within which the specific form-critical tools can be applied flexibly. Through such a flexible use of the tools, we could then recognize both the distinct typicalities which govern the texts and their particular interrelationships. We would also see the various ways in which the typical in the texts is related with the unique. The following outline is an attempt toward such a methodology. It will concentrate on "structure" because structural interpretation has been less developed in form criticism than have genre and setting, and because it is here that the focus of the present discussion lies.

1. Text and Structure. In the last generation we have witnessed an explosion of studies and discussions about structure. Structure has become a focus of scholarly attention in many fields.[92] In spite of its

---

This unclarity has been overcome in Roy F. Melugin, "The Typical versus the Unique among the Hebrew Prophets" (SBL Proceedings, 1972, Vol. 2) 331ff.

92. Instead of an endless bibliography, suffice it to refer to Hans Naumann, ed., *Der moderne Strukturbegriff* (Darmstadt: Wissenschaftliche Buchgesellschaft, 1973).

programmatic commitment to form-analysis and valuable contributions, Old Testament form criticism has not yet given the method of structural interpretation the attention that it deserves as a distinctive research tool in its own right. We are far from possessing either a fully developed methodology of structural research, or a comprehensive typology of structural principles, or a morphology of textual structures. However, there is no text or text-type in the Old Testament that is not structured. This fact alone is sufficient to call for a programmatic unfolding of the method of structural interpretation within form criticism.

(a) In order to establish a basis for the identification of schemes or patterns behind the texts, form criticism has to address itself first of all to the structural interpretation of the texts themselves. This has recently been advocated especially by Güttgemanns and Richter. Assuming that texts are entities, we are concerned with the factors that constitute such entities.[93] One of the main ways of finding these factors or principles is structural analysis. Form-critical understanding of structure is, therefore, different because it investigates the kind of structure that is the basis for the formation of a text and into which a text is cast. It asks for the structure of the text as *text*.

Examples chosen from the many possibilities may help to indicate the range of structural principles which may govern a text. Rhetorical or stylistic devices can govern texts: the acrostic poem, the *parallelismus membrorum*, regardless of what kind; the word association; the inversion; the meter; the chiasm;[94] and others.[95] A text-entity can be governed by certain patterns such as the decalogue (Exodus 20), the trial = *rîb* (Hosea 2; Jeremiah 9), the itinerary (Deuteronomy 1—3),[96] the messenger commission or messenger speech, the seven-day week (Genesis 1:1–2:4a), contract or covenant, ordeal (Numbers 5), ritual (Leviticus 1–7), and building blueprint (Exodus 25–27). A text can be governed by a certain kind of systematic viewpoint such as process of thought, climax and anti-climax, case and consequence (in the casuistic laws, in dynamistic and wisdom thought, in judicial and prophetic texts), a systematized creed or a central theme. This is especially true for larger compositions

---

93. This assumption points to the hermeneutical function of a unit as an integrated whole or entity, and not as an accumulation of pieces. Its modality is different from that of its parts or their summary. It has its own meaning. In it, the parts are determined by the entity, and not the entity by its parts. Such entity is based on a presupposed concept without which the parts would not be used the way they are, without which it would not exist, and which is decisive for its understanding. This insight is the decisive reason for the need of the exact delimitation of the text-units. Cf. Muilenburg, "Form Criticism and Beyond," 9; Güttgemanns, *Öffene Fragen*, 184ff.

94. Cf. Yehuda T. Radday, "Chiasm in Tora," *Linguistica Biblica* 19 (1972), pp. 12–23.

95. Muilenburg, "Form Criticism and Beyond," 88ff.

96. Cf. George W. Coats, "The Wilderness Itinerary," *CBQ* 34 (1972) 135–52.

such as Isaiah 1, Amos 7–9, Hosea 1–3, Deuteronomy 12, and Exodus 21:12–27.[97]

One of the special problem areas concerning structural analysis is that of the narrative texts. It seems as if here structural interpretation has only recently begun to make serious inroads. We have a few significant examples of the kinds of factors which may govern narrative plots. An author's arrangement of events may be dictated by an intended climax,[98] by a sequence of historical events (as perhaps in 2 Kings 9f.), by a certain synopsis of the events (as perhaps in 1 Kings 22), or a theological concern (Gen. 18:16–33), by patterns of family-relationships,[99] or by a focus on existential concerns as in some narratives in the primeval history. Research has provided us with a few examples, but not a comprehensive methodology.[100] We have not mentioned the problem of the hierarchy of structural factors present in a text. Details of structure may point up subordinate interests within the framework of the main structures.[101]

The examples given above indicate the great diversity of structural principles and their unpredictability. And they show one thing very clearly: The structure governing a text-entity can be discovered only on the basis of close textual analysis that demonstrates the inherent framework from evidence in the text itself. This does not exclude the search for patterns, types, schemes, or genres. But it makes sure that the identifiable patterns are those indicated by the structure of text-entities, and not those imposed on them by partial association. Form criticism has been interested in typical structures and has generally tended to

---

97. The often repeated qualification of such compositions as *Verschriftung* by a "Redactor" is not satisfactory. Quite apart from our revised understanding of those "Redactors," this qualification rests on the antiquated assumption that only oral texts or generically pure ones are worthy of form-critical attention. Unavoidably, however, we possess an unlimited number of literary compositions melting heterogeneous genres, genre elements, or traditions into new entities. And unless one surmises that people were thinking only when speaking, but ceased to do so when writing, one has to take these new literary, and perhaps even originally oral, entities seriously.

98. Cf. the superb interpretation in this regard of Genesis 22 by Erich Auerbach, *Mimesis*, trans. Willard R. Trask (Princeton: Princeton University Press, 1953) 3ff. Gerhard von Rad, *Das Opfer des Abraham* (Munich: Chr. Kaiser Verlag, 1971) 16–23.

99. Cf. Claus Westermann, "Arten der Erzählung," 58–89.

100. Very valuable are Klaus Koch, *Growth*, 111–58, 183–210; Wolfgang Richter, *Berufungsberichte*, 40ff., 53; idem, *Traditionsgeschichtliche Untersuchungen zum Richterbuch* (BBB 18; Bonn: Hanstein, 1963) 13, 20; Hannelis Schulte, *Die Entstehung der Geschichtsschreibung im alten Israel*, BZAW 128 (Berlin: Walter de Gruyter, 1972) 33, 60, 181–202.

101. The deficiency in Old Testament studies becomes particularly apparent in view of the research in related fields. See, for example, Jurij M. Lotman, *Die Struktur des künstlerischen Textes* (Suhrkamp: Verlag, 1973), and Erhardt Güttgemanns, "Einleitende Bemerkungen zur strukturalen Erzählforschung," *Linguistica Biblica* 23/24 (1973) 2–47, whose article I received while writing these very lines.

relegate the interpretation of the uniqueness of texts to subsequent exegesis. However, it is necessary to reverse this approach: Not only must the structural analysis of the individuality of texts be included into the form-critical method, it must, in fact, precede the analysis of the typical structure if the claim that such a typicality inherently determines an individual text is to be substantiated.[102]

(b) Text structures are typical if they show signs of supra-individuality. The typical structure can consist in formulaic language, artistic rhetorical devices, a set of colloquialisms, an institutionalized scheme, a set of ideas, and more. It can be fixed or flexible. In other words, it can appear in various guises.[103] Most of the above-mentioned examples of text-structures are, in fact, typical structures of different kinds.

Traces of typical patterns appear in texts. But we need not discuss the presence of such genre elements here, since they do not govern a text in its entirety. We must, however, pay attention to a less-recognized fact — the entirety of a text may be governed by more than one typical structure. A psalm can follow a rhetorical pattern — acrostic, strophe, verse — and at the same time the typical structure of a traditional theme, or a liturgical event. The question is, therefore, how these structural types interact. What is the hierarchy of their relations to each other? And then, which of them governs the others and ultimately the structural type of the text?

Finally, the structure of a unique text must be compared with the typical structure on which it rests. Both structures can coincide. More often, they vary. The degree of congruency or incongruency shows the degree to which the conventional influence has kept the individual expression under control, or to which the individuality created its own and often new mode of communication while availing itself of the conventional.[104]

---

102. This proposal is basically in agreement with the sequence of methodological steps proposed by Richter, *Exegese;* cf. esp. his section on form and forms, 120ff.

103. The differences in understanding the nature of "structure" would need careful analysis. Westermann's "basic forms of prophetic speech" or Baltzer's "covenant formulary" are typical structures that exist on the level of societal or institutional language. Richter's "structural model" points to a dimension behind language. And so does the notion of the structuralists, who view that dimension as a manifestation of trans-cultural thought. For them, "structure is not the model but that which expressed itself in the formula by which the model is transformed" (Paul Beauchamp, "L'analyse structurale et l'exegese biblique," VTSup 22:113–28 [1972] 121). This formula, or code, never appears in language. It can only be reconstructed through analysis of language. In view of the different concepts it seems important to assert, for the time being, that the reality of linguistic patterns on the level of social communication cannot be denied.

104. The discussion whether texts are governed either by the typical or by the unique is pointless when the alternatives are posed this way. Form critics have long known that the

2. Text, Text-type, and Genre. In view of the interrelationship of the factors that contribute to the form-critical interpretation of texts, we must acknowledge some potential distinctions between typical structure, text-type, and genre. For when we ask about the typicality of a text, we are confronted with several possibilities. The typicality of a text can consist in a typical structure. In some cases the structure is the matrix of the text-type, regardless of the varying contents as, for example, in the decalogues. The typicality of a text can also be influenced by its setting, regardless of the structure. This is the case, for example, in a sermon or an instruction. A certain concern or occupation of mind can govern the typicality of a text, regardless of both the settings and the structures through which it is expressed. The memorabilia are examples of this. The domination of a certain motif could constitute the typicality. Thus the typicality of a text, its text-type, can depend on one or another of the various factors which form criticism has regarded as representative of the typical. It depends on which factor is ultimately constitutive for the existence of a text.

These statements have consequences for the use of genre. If genre is understood as a "structural scheme," then we must account for other typicalities by which texts are governed. In this case, it would be helpful for us to distinguish between the categories of genre and of text-type. This would allow us to identify that typicality by which a given text is governed even when structure is not the dominant factor. If, however, genre is understood as that kind of typicality by which a text is governed, it would mean the same as text-type, and both terms could be used interchangeably.

In either case, our methodology should provide us with such a kind of flexibility that enables us to detect realistically those typical factors to which texts owe their existence. This does not mean that the genuine form-critical questions are discarded; it does mean that their usage will depend on the situation in a text, rather than on any preconceived methodological pattern. They will be used as tools, either separately

---

ways in which typical patterns are recognized are flexible. But it is not enough to treat this phenomenon casually. The distinctiveness of each individual occurrence of a genre is a real factor of its existence, which must be accounted for in its interpretation. Weiss, accusing Westermann for "crushing" Psalm 74 and depriving it of "its truth" (p. 98), is right when insisting that texts must be interpreted in their present form. But his statement that the traditions in texts are "nothing but raw-materials" (94) for the poet, and his complete unwillingness to even discuss typical forms and their influence on a text, is not convincing either. In spite of many good observations, especially his insistence on the priority of structure analysis, the method as outlined by him does not yet reflect a "Total-Interpretation" (cf. Meir Weiss, "Die Methode der 'Total-Interpretation,'" VTSup 22 [1972] 88–112).

or in concert, for the discovery of the typical factors, how they are hierarchically related, and how they influence individual texts.

3. Text and Setting. A few remarks are necessary in view of recent developments in the discussion of setting. Originally, setting was meant to be the oral societal origin of genres.[105] But the more one recognized that all of the Old Testament literature could not be explained on this basis, the more the understanding of setting broadened and differentiated. Richter differentiates between three sorts of setting: institutions, the style of an epoch, and literature itself.[106] "Setting" may not be the word for all of these categories, but spelling out the different connotations implied in this modified concept of setting is more important than the terminological problem.

First of all, we are now talking of settings of different sorts. True, setting can still be, and often is, the creative institutional matrix within which genres, or types, and individual texts exist. Rituals are a case in point. In these cases, the relationship between setting, on the one hand, and genre, text-type, or text, on the other, is understood genetically. This has been the genuine form-critical assumption.

The style of an epoch can also be understood as a matrix insofar as it furnishes the codes or the raw materials employed by a certain society. The characteristics of an historical period do not necessarily define any "institutional" settings within epoch, nor do they identify the types of expression which correspond to institutional settings. Nor is the style of an age necessarily the formative factor for all its units of linguistic expression. It is more the context than the cause of both types and specific units. The word "matrix" denotes in this case only the general societal background of both genres and texts. But it does not explain that kind of matrix that is the real cause of either a specific text-type or a specific text nor the reason for their existence. Such a matrix explains the function of types or texts only in terms of their general intelligibility. But it does not explain them in terms of the causes and concerns involved in their specific settings, or in terms of the intentionality of specific texts.[107]

---

105. Cf. Koch, *Growth*, 26–38.

106. *Exegese als Literaturwissenschaft*, 145ff.

107. The book by H. W. Wolff, *Amos the Prophet* (Philadelphia: Fortress Press, 1973) is a case in point. Wolff argues that Amos can best be understood on the basis of his "hereditary cultural background" (89) his *geistige Heimat*. Cf. the title of the German original: *Amos' geistige Heimat*, WMANT 118 (Neukirchen: Neukirchener Verlag, 1964). Here we have matrix-language in its genuine form-critical sense. But the background is *geistig*. This interpretation explains the general mentality and the language within which and to a certain degree the criteria upon which Amos operated. But this *geistige Heimat* neither explains the setting of Amos's prophecy nor the typically prophetic in his appearance. It does not touch upon the function or intentionality of his specific messages at all. After all, Amos appeared as a prophet and not as a wise man.

What has been said about settings of different sorts is especially true with regard to language itself. Language can be a setting of its own, so to speak, following its own rules. Language as such is a sort of setting which can be correlated with, or remain distinct from, the kinds of setting form criticism has been talking about. And it may well be that future research will discover text-types or texts whose matrix is language itself rather than certain institutions of the style of an epoch.[108] This may be the case particularly with genuine literary compositions.

Secondly, we are not only talking about different sorts of setting but also about different categories related to setting — setting of a structural scheme, of other text-types, and of texts. Settings are not only governed by and identified with typical schemes; they are not only the matrices of patterns, they can also be governed by other typicalities such as typical concerns or a typical occupation of mind, which come to expression in a variety of patterns. In this regard we have not even mentioned the question of the setting of individual texts, either in their written or their oral stage. There is reason to believe that individual texts are dependent not only on typical settings, but at least as much on the specific situations to which they owe their existence. The definition of the setting of a text-type, or a genre, is not necessarily identical with the definition of the setting of one of its unique manifestations.

Finally, it is generally known that text-types can be used in various settings. They are freely available. Hence the recognition of a text-type does not automatically reveal the setting in which it was used. Failure to distinguish between genuine and actual settings of text-types in an exegesis will lead to a distorted understanding of a text.

Therefore, when focusing on setting we must not only distinguish between various kinds of settings that are possible, and between the various ways in which those kinds may affect the same text-type or a text. We must also distinguish between the factors by which settings are governed and identified, and we must distinguish between genuine and actual settings when exegeting texts. The conclusion seems inevitable that form criticism is heading toward a typology of setting.

In such a typology, a monolithic conceptualization of setting must be avoided, and it cannot be imposed in principle on all texts for the purpose of their generic classification. Instead, setting should serve as a heuristic tool to identify the kinds of settings of genres, text-types, and texts. It should show the various functions of settings for the text-types and the degree of their interdependence with these text-types.[109]

In sum, we should be able to apply the category of setting under the

---

108. Cf. Richter, *Exegese*, 145, n.54.
109. See, concerning the problem of interdependence, what has been said under I.

dictate of the manifold situations of texts, and not under a dogmatic concept of setting to which the interpretation of texts is subjected.

The task outlined here indicates once more a multiplicity of theoretical possibilities. To outline such a multiplicity is one thing. But to employ it in the exegetical process means that we have to expect varying results. The methodological outline must, therefore, make sure that it is designed so as to avoid preempting the results.

CONCLUSION

Gunkel's program to write a history of the Old Testament literature has not been fulfilled to date.[110] On the surface it might seem as if the execution of criticism has amassed an impressive record since Gunkel. But the reasons for the failure may lie deeper than that.

What Gunkel had in mind was mainly a history of the Old Testament genres.[111] Our review of the problems inherent in the form-critical method seems to indicate that just this conceptualization of the task may not be sufficient for achieving the goal. Form criticism has employed a monolithic conception of genre and assumed the homogeneity of the typical factors inherent in it. This may, paradoxically, have been counterproductive to its own original intentions. To some extent it may have caused the discipline to lose sight of the conditions of the living process to which language and literature are subjected. The historical manifestations of typical forms, especially the interrelationship of the various typicalities in linguisitic entities, and their influence on individual texts seem to be more flexible than form criticism has been prepared to assume. This must be said at least in view of the whole of the Old Testament literature. We do not suggest that our ancient literature be exegeted on principles that the interpretation of modern literature demands. But recent progress in the methods for interpretation of language and literature does shed new light on the problems that form criticism has faced with its own texts.

In view of this, interpreting Old Testament literature and language ought to be within a context in which both appear as manifestations of communication, born by a will to communicate and functioning within such communication; that is, they include the horizon of understanding and expectation of readers and listeners and, having a historical dimension, are subject to the changing horizons in communication.

Within the concept of such a historical sociology of language, the role of form criticism would be to employ its tools heuristically. It would

---

110. Cf. Klatt, *Hermann Gunkel*, 166–192.
111. Cf. Klatt's citation of Gunkel, ibid., 170.

have to ask what, in a given text, constituted the communication event between writer and readers, between speaker and listener in a typical way. It would have to ask how the typical factors were related to one another and how the typical and the unique interact. This certainly means that answers will be found which confirm many results found in the traditional sense. But it means also that we are no longer stuck with the expectation of a distinct typicality in a text when such a typicality may never have been constitutive for its existence. The communication event in a text may be constituted by the typicality of a genre understood in a certain way or it may function through some other typicality or it may be governed by none whatsoever. We can leave such determinations to subsequent findings. Such findings may occasionally show that a text is governed by factors beyond those asked for by the form-critical method, for example, by a thematic concern or a motif.[112] Even so, the form-critical tools will be indispensable for the understanding of the texts wherever the texts are predisposed to their application. By being subservient to those factors that dominate texts rather than by dominating the texts through its own methodological system, form criticism will, probably with some kind of new face, continue to have its unique role in the concert of the exegetical disciplines.[113]

---

112. In this context, the word motif does not refer to "an elementary and distinct part of a poetic work," with the emphasis on "part" (Koch, *Growth*, 56). Rather, it refers to "leading-motif" (German: *Leitmotiv*): "any repetition that helps unify a work by potently recalling its earlier occurrence and all that surrounded it" (S. Barnet, M. Berman, and W. Burton, *A Dictionary of Literary Terms* [Boston and Toronto: Little, Brown, 1960]).

113. For assistance of various kinds I am greatly indebted to the members of the research staff of the form criticism project at the Institute for Antiquity and Christianity, Claremont Graduate School: Ms. Eleanor Beach, Antony Campbell, S.J., Michael Floyd, and Fred Tiffany.

3

The Growth of Joshua 1–12 and the Theology of Extermination

Antony F. Campbell, S.J.

"Growth of text" is certainly not the flavor of the month at the moment in exegetical circles. This essay hews closely to the contours of the present text, not attempting to go any further back into the history of the text than the pre-Deuteronomistic level represented by Joshua 2. Joshua 1 provides the introduction to the Dtr text of the book of Joshua.[1] It is a possibility worth considering that Joshua 2 provides the introduction to an earlier narrative version, with a significantly different presentation of the traditions. Identification of this possible narrative raises issues around the development of a theology of extermination.

What is argued here is a possibility that opens new avenues for understanding the text and theology of the book of Joshua. If exaggeration may be allowed to sharpen the point, the narrative begun in Joshua 2, with traces in chs. 3–4 and 6 and the substance of chs. 8–10, offers a presentation in which Joshua's Israel occupies much of the south by military or political action — with a little bit of help from God. Further developments change this presentation to one in which God's action gives the whole land to Joshua's Israel — with a little bit of help from them. This involves grafting the three sacral stories of Joshua 3–4, 6, and 7 into the narrative of the south and, simultaneously or separately, portraying a conquest of the north (within chs. 11–12). Later developments include the level of the Dtr history, the insistence on extermination of the locals, and the emphasis on the contribution and rights of the Transjordan tribes (Reuben, Gad, and the half-tribe of Manasseh). Prehistory before the "Joshua 2" level is not explored. A claim for definitive demonstration is not made. A claim is made for the possibility and legitimacy of this reading. What is explored are the avenues opened by such an understanding of the text.

---

1. V. Fritz, in the new HAT commentary on Joshua, does not represent text earlier than the basic level of the Dtr history (*Das Buch Josua* [HAT I/7; Tübingen: J. C. B. Mohr, 1994]). This essay explores the earlier "Joshua 2" level, but does not investigate the prehistory of the texts that make up this level. For a professional monograph, grappling with the puzzling contradiction of dream and reality, see G. Mitchell, *Together in the Land: A Reading of the Book of Joshua* (JSOTSup 134; Sheffield: JSOT Press, 1993).

Joshua 2 offers a picture that contrasts radically with the sacral context of the stories in chs. 3–7 in which God's action moves the world in ways that are wonderful to behold. In the narrative of Joshua 2, spies are sent out to view the land — quite unnecessary in a sacral context. The spies head for the Jericho brothel — a trifle out of place in a sacral context. The king demands the men, and the prostitute, Rahab, lies to deflect his demand — unlikely in a sacral context. Rahab bargains with the men she has saved; the men fill in the fine print of the contract. Such bargaining ill befits the sacral. Finally, the spies evade their pursuers for three days before returning to Joshua with assurances of success. This chapter has been dismissed as incompatible with the sacral stories to come.[2] It is worthwhile exploring whether it might be the other way around: the sacral stories are to be put on hold and the context of Joshua 2 retained.

My concern is to explore text, not to eliminate shameful theology and not to reconstruct events.[3] My intention is not to claim definitive interpretation but to point to possibilities.

What led me to push a little deeper into these unpleasant realms was an evening's discussion with Rolf Knierim. Knierim was waxing eloquent about that strand in the book of Deuteronomy that is insistent on the absolute purity of Israel. Did the passion that focused on the exclusive worship of YHWH, God of Israel, and on the temple in Jerusalem lead to a fanaticism that demanded the exclusion from Israel of all that did not meet a certain standard? It was only a question, but the fact of asking it implied that certain parts of Deuteronomy could possibly be traced to an unacceptable fanaticism. Suddenly Knierim stopped in his tracks. "What am I saying? I am a former student and colleague of Gerhard von Rad; I am an admirer of Gerhard von Rad. For von Rad,

---

2. J. Van Seters writes, "The story of Rahab...is not the beginning of the earliest conquest account but a later addition and fits rather awkwardly within its context" ("Joshua's Campaign of Canaan and Near Eastern Historiography," *SJOT* 4 (1990) 2/1–12, see p. 3. See also Van Seters, *In Search of History* (New Haven: Yale University Press, 1983) 325. For balance, see J. K. Hoffmeier, "The Structure of Joshua 1–11 and the Annals of Thutmose III," in A. R. Millard et al., eds., *Faith, Tradition, and History: Old Testament Historiography in Its Near Eastern Context* (Winona Lake, Ind.: Eisenbrauns, 1994) 165–79. More recently, Jacques Briend contends that Joshua 2 came into the narrative at a late date but before the Dtr redaction ("Les sources de l'histoire deuteronomique: recherches sur Jos 1–12," in A. de Pury et al., eds., *Israël construit son histoire: l'historiographie deutéronomiste à la lumière des recherches récentes* (Geneva: Labor et Fides, 1996) 343–74, see p. 357. Briend's analyses often nudge the possible beyond the necessary. He speaks, however, of "une yahvisation du récit ancien" (p. 351).

3. It would be unhelpful to discuss here issues of the emergence of Israel in Canaan. See now Diana Edelman, ed., "Toward a Consensus on the Emergence of Israel in Canaan," *SJOT* 5 (1991) 2/1–116.

Deuteronomy was the zenith of the Old Testament. Now I hear myself saying that Deuteronomy was the Old Testament's nadir."

It is appropriate that this study should be part of a volume associated with the exegetical method and theological concerns of Rolf Knierim.

THE PRE-DTR "JOSHUA 2" NARRATIVE

Joshua 2

Belonging in the "Joshua 2" narrative from this chapter are probably vv. 1–9, 12–24. An opening is needed, such as the innocuous "After the death of Moses" (1:1). The narrative has the (whole) land in view and Joshua as the leader (cf. 2:1). In the horizon of this chapter, and of this "Joshua 2" narrative, the action is focused on Joshua and Israel rather than on YHWH. Rahab confesses, "I know that the LORD has given you the land" (2:9), and the spies report to Joshua, "Truly the LORD has given all the land into our hands" (2:24); so the glory is given to the LORD. The action, however, is undertaken by Joshua and Israel. As in the case of Ehud, Jael, and Gideon (Judges 3; 4; and 7), while Israel's national deliverance may be attributed to the LORD, the acts are those of brave and courageous individuals. God is expected to go out with the armies; this is ancient Near Eastern narrative, not modern secular humanist atheism. All the more striking to realize that here, as in so many battle reports, it is Israel that is to the fore in the story, while it is YHWH who gives the victory.[4]

In the narrative, the king of Jericho is involved, with a concern that extends beyond his own city to "the land" (2:2). Rahab, described as a prostitute, is given the faith statement that "the LORD has given you the land"; the context again extends beyond Jericho and the fear expressed is of Israel ("you") rather than of the LORD (2:9). As is well known, Rahab's silence is obtained in a bargain that seems to envisage military capture and street fighting rather than a collapse of the town's walls (2:17–21).

Later than the "Joshua 2" narrative here may be 2:10–11, attributed to Dtr editing. In v. 10, Sihon and Og are mentioned together, probably an indication of later Dtr origin.[5] In v. 11b, a confession of God's nature is given that is almost identical with Deut. 4:39, a secondary Dtr text

---

4. For wide biblical echoes that may be heard in the Rahab story, see T. Frymer-Kensky, "Reading Rahab," in M. Cogan et al., eds., *Tehillah le-Moshe: Biblical and Judaic Studies in Honor of Moshe Greenberg* (Winona Lake, Ind.: Eisenbrauns, 1997) 57–68. Note also N. Winther-Nielsen, *A Functional Discourse Grammar of Joshua: A Computer-Assisted Rhetorical Structure Analysis* (Stockholm: Almqvist & Wiksell, 1995), esp. pp. 105–65. The detail of input does not generate a correlative outcome.

5. Cf. Deut. 1:4; 29:7; 31:4 — apparently later Dtr revision.

(cf. also 1 Kings 8:23). In the light of these signals, it is appropriate to attribute vv. 10–11 to Dtr editing. The reference to the Red Sea (2:10a) recurs in 4:23; the arguments for the secondary status of the crossing account may reinforce the secondary status of 2:10–11 here.

The impact of vv. 10–11 is to heighten Rahab's confessional statement, bringing it into more explicit harmony with the preceding history and the sacral stories to come.

Joshua 3–4

Belonging to the "Joshua 2" narrative from these chapters are probably 3:1; 4:10b, 13. As is well known, there is nothing about these verses that is particularly appropriate to their context. That they would belong to the beginning and end of an account coherent with the military preparations undertaken in Joshua 2 is possible. Any coherence with Joshua 3–4 can only be obtained with difficulty. If a military story of crossing followed Joshua 2, as 4:10b and 4:13 suggest, it has been suppressed in favor of the present sacral version.[6]

Later than the "Joshua 2" narrative here may be 3:2–17; 4:1–10a, 11– 12, 14–24, attributed to the sacral story of the Jordan crossing and subsequent editing. The difficulties of these chapters are legion.[7] What is clear and beyond doubt is the sacral character of the narrative.[8] The ark of the covenant is central to the action: its movement initiates the people's (3:3); its arrival at the Jordan initiates the river's stoppage (3:13–16); its emergence from the Jordan allows the river's flow to resume (4:18). The people are sanctified for the occasion (3:5). Due distance, about a kilometer, is maintained between the people and the ark (3:4). Two sanctuary explanations are associated with the narrative (4:6–7 and 20–24); also two sanctuaries (in the middle of the Jordan, 4:9; where Israel camped, 4:8 and 19). Expansions within the text are possible. For example, 3:10, with its list of seven local nations and its repeated "and Joshua said," might well be a later insertion (for this full list of seven, see also Deut. 7:1 and Josh. 24:11).

---

6. The prior element demanded by Briend for "rose early in the morning" ("Sources," 356) is supplied by ch. 2.

7. The "three days" (3:1) is scarcely one of these, despite Van Seters ("Joshua's Campaign," 3; *Search,* 325). Real time and storytelling time do not always coincide.

8. It has been argued that the idea of a liturgy here is absurd; how would the Jordan be stopped? Such an objection has never encountered Christians waving twigs and singing Palm Sunday songs. A ritual procession arriving at the unstoppable Jordan witnesses to the power of God, who alone could and did once stop these waters at the appropriate moment. Ritual and symbol are not to be confused with rational discourse or the realistic rehearsal of significant events. What is to be evoked is more the significance and less the event.

The exact nature of this text (3:2–17; 4:1–10a, 11–12, 14–24) may escape us.[9] Its original coherence with Joshua 2 is seriously doubtful. For its significance within the present text, see the discussion below, under the rubric of the "sacral stories" expansion. Subsequent editing includes the Deuteronomist (3:7–8; 4:14), the list of locals (3:10), and the reference to the Transjordan tribes (4:12).

Joshua 5

None of the verses in this chapter calls for inclusion in the "Joshua 2" narrative. In Noth's view, superseded to some extent by what is proposed here, the "collector" who had shaped and introduced Joshua 2 could be identified in 5:1 (as also in 6:27; 9:3–4aα; 10:2, 5, 40–42; 11:1–2, 16–20). The mark of the collector was, above all, the drawing together of the individual stories into a broader picture. So, in 5:1, the mention of the kings of east and west witnessed to the extent intended for the portrayal of the conquest.[10] The traditions of Joshua 5 — the circumcision after the wilderness sojourn (vv. 2–9), the observance of Passover and the end of the manna (vv. 10–12), and Joshua's encounter with the "commander of the army of the LORD" (vv. 13–15) — belong at the point of transition between the wilderness and the land.[11] They have no specific association with the narrative prepared for in Joshua 2; while they belong where they are, they seem likely to reflect later concerns.

Joshua 6

Belonging to the "Joshua 2" narrative from this chapter are probably vv. 1–2, 21–24a. The story begins with the report of siege conditions (6:1); Jericho's "king and soldiers" are to be handed over to Joshua by the LORD (6:2). What follows does not make any reference to the siege; the "king and soldiers" are not heard of again. As the start to a story of military action, vv. 1–2 are perfectly plausible. The tradition alluded to in Judg. 1:23–25 is, of course, illustrative of how a town might have been taken. The Rahab story, with its "crimson cord in the window" (2:21), evidently has a scenario in mind where a visual signal was significant

---

9. For a fuller treatment, see A. F. Campbell, *The Study Companion to Old Testament Literature* (Collegeville, Minn.: Liturgical Press, 1989/1992) 173–77. Once the military parts are eliminated, the remainder may be best understood as directions and variations for a liturgical celebration.

10. M. Noth, *Das Buch Josua* (HAT 7; 2d ed.; Tübingen: J. C. B. Mohr, 1953) 12; also p. 29.

11. The command to Joshua to remove his sandals echoes the command to Moses (Exod. 3:5); its focus is on the figure of Joshua rather than the future campaign (despite Van Seters, "Joshua's Campaign," 9–11; cf. Briend, "Sources," 353). The drawn sword suggests a military context; the command does not offer one.

for those outside the town. We would expect that v. 2 was once followed by something equivalent to v. 17 (perhaps with more detail, as in v. 21).

The placement of Joshua's instructions for the ban between his command to shout (v. 16) and the people's shout (v. 20) is odd. As noted, if the ban were important to the story, it might be expected earlier. As it stands, the instructions seem more important for the story of Achan that follows. There is no such reason to exclude vv. 21–24a. They report that the inhabitants of the city, animal and human, were put to the ban and the city burned. Joshua's orders to the two spies fit fully with the story of Joshua 2; there is no attempt to correlate the collapse of the town wall with the prostitute's house in ch. 2 and its window on the outer side of the wall (2:15; LXX lacks details but has the basics, cf. vv. 15 and 18 of LXX). These verses can belong with a story of military capture.

Later than the "Joshua 2" narrative here may be 6:3–20, 24b–27, attributed to the sacral story of the capture of Jericho and the integration of ch. 7, as well as some subsequent editing. There is good reason why this material should be seen as belonging in a sacral context and be excluded from any military narrative. There are plenty of soldiers in vv. 3–20, but they are busier processing than besieging. The "seven priests bearing seven trumpets" (vv. 4, 6, 8, 13) seem just as important. The ark of the covenant plays a central role. What makes this a sacral story, above all, is that it is not a story of military daring or skill, supported and brought to success by YHWH; it is a story of what is exclusively YHWH's action, orchestrated to coincide with Joshua's processions. As is well known, there is a tension between the noisy circuits with a trumpet blast signaling the people's shout (cf. vv. 4–5, 20b) and the silent circuits with Joshua's command signaling the people's shout (cf. vv. 10, 20a).[12]

In particular, vv. 17–19 stand out as intervening between Joshua's command and the people's shout. Verse 18 is pointing directly toward ch. 7. Verse 17 is necessary, if v. 18 is to refer to "the things devoted to destruction." While the introduction of vv. 17–18 (19) may seem clumsy, the interruption serves as a signal pointing to the subsequent introduction of the Achan episode. As to v. 19, we have no reference to any treasuries earlier than those of the kings or the temple, starting with Solomon. At some point, it would seem that Joshua could not be thought to have done less than David (2 Sam. 8:11).

The subsequent editing can be attributed to the Deuteronomist. Verses 24b–27 begin with the same reference as v. 19. The note on Rahab goes beyond v. 23 to add that "her family has lived in Israel ever

---

12. For a fuller treatment, see Campbell, *Study Companion,* 177–81.

since" (v. 25). The spies are referred to as "messengers," distinguishing this material from the preceding stories. Joshua's curse (v. 26) could
have been recorded at any time and in any context. Its attribution is im-
material to the present concerns. Joshua's fame (v. 27) fits better with
3:7–8 than with the horizon of Joshua 2.

Joshua 7–8

*Belonging to the "Joshua 2" narrative from these chapters are probably
8:1–29 (with the exception of "as before" in vv. 5 and 6).* On close inspection, the story of Achan's breach of the ban, in Joshua 7, appears
far closer to the other two sacral stories (the crossing of the Jordan and
the capture of Jericho) than it does to the story it is associated with, the
attack on Ai (Josh. 8:1–29).[13]

With the attack on Ai, the narrative moves the conquest out of the
Jordan valley and up into the hill country, but still within the territory of Benjamin. As at the start of the "military capture" of Jericho
(6:1–2), king and army are to be handed over to Joshua. The ban is mentioned early (v. 2), as might have been expected in the Jericho narrative.
The ban carried out at Jericho included "men and women, young and
old, oxen, sheep, and donkeys" (6:21). For Ai, spoil and livestock are exempted (8:2, 27). There is no mention of Achan's folly. It is as if Jericho
bore the initial symbolism of total ban, total dedication to Israel's God,
and the subsequent experiences in the narrative could be relaxed once
the high point had been established. Yet, ironically in view of what is to
come, there was a flaw in the total ban: consciously, Rahab and her family were exempted from the ban. The man who let the house of Joseph
into Bethel subsequently left the territory (Judg. 1:26). The Gibeonites
will later claim to have come from "a far country" (9:6). They live in Israel's midst by deceit. Rahab will live in Israel's midst by the conscious
commitment of the spies and of Israel.

In 8:3–9, the strategy is plotted and preparations executed; in vv. 10–
23, the successful carrying through of this strategy is narrated; finally,
in vv. 24–29, the fate of Ai and its inhabitants is reported. It is a story
of battle, Joshua's battle, with some support from the LORD. As noted
above, the strategy is twice referred back to ch. 7 ("as before" in 8:5
and 6). Within ch. 7, the strategy is not discussed; within ch. 8, the
references are not continued when the strategy is being implemented.

Several moments in the story of ch. 8 suggest that the attack on Ai is
being told for the first time. In v. 1, there is no hint that this is a second
battle. "Go up now to Ai" in the NRSV's translation has no suggestion

---

13. For Van Seters too, though with differences, Joshua 7 is an addition ("Joshua's
Campaign," 4).

that they are going up for a second time; the Hebrew — which has no "now" — is fully compatible with a first time. "See, I have handed over to you the king of Ai..." has no "this time" or anything equivalent to suggest that a defeat has just been experienced by Israel.

Later than the "Joshua 2" narrative here may be 7:1–26; the phrase "as before" in 8:5 and 6; and 8:30–35 — the first as a sacral story, the second as redactional, and the third as a late-Dtr passage. Joshua 7:1–26 is not a story of battle. Apart from the reference to the few troops needed (7:3), a report of the so-called battle is found only in 7:4 — they went up and they fled! The extent of the defeat is chronicled in v. 5. The rest of the chapter focuses on the breach in the sacral ordinance of the ban. Chapter 7 is a story where the sacral is central. The fate of a people in battle is determined by one individual's breach of sacred regulations. The atmosphere is the same as in 1 Samuel 14. Verses 6–15 are taken up with the cause of the disaster. Verses 10–15 are devoted to a speech of the LORD. Verses 16–26 are taken up with the identification and punishment of Achan, "the one who sinned against the LORD God of Israel" (v. 20).

To have a sense of the direction that such a text is taking, it is worth noting where responsibility is located. Joshua's prayer begins, "Ah, LORD God! Why have you brought this people across the Jordan at all" (v. 7). His prayer concludes, "Then what will you do for your great name?" (v. 9). The protagonist in this portrayal is YHWH. This is not action where YHWH is supporting Joshua as leader of Israel; it is action where YHWH is taking the lead on behalf of Joshua and Israel.

Joshua 7:1 reads like a summary, anticipating the story. The breach of faith is not raised in the text until the LORD's speech; Achan is not identified until v. 19; the anger of the LORD is first referred to at its end (v. 26; it is only mentioned in Joshua at 7:1, 26; 23:16). "Breach of faith" is scarcely a Dtr term (cf. Deut. 32:51 and Josh. 7:1; 22:16, 20, 22, 31). Probably 7:1 derives from the editor who inserted the sacral stories into the "Joshua 2" narrative, but only probably. The reference to transgression of YHWH's covenant in vv. 11 and 15 is strongly mirrored in Josh. 23:16.

The phrase "as before" in 8:5 and 6 is what would be expected when combining chs. 7 and 8. It is present in the strategic plotting, but not in the actual narrative of battle.

Joshua 8:30–35 is attributed by Noth to his Dtr history; the passage may be even later.[14]

---

14. M. Noth, *The Deuteronomistic History* (JSOTSup 15; 2d ed.; Sheffield: JSOT, 1991) 63–64. For M. O'Brien, Josh. 8:30–35 is later than the Dtr history (*The Deuteronomistic His-*

Joshua 9

Belonging to the "Joshua 2" narrative from this chapter are probably vv. 3–9, 11–15a, 16–17, 22–23, 25*–27a. Joshua 9:1–2 is not easily characterized. In much the same fashion as 7:1, it reads like a summary anticipating what is to come. The six-item list of locals is found here and Deut. 20:17; Josh. 11:3; 12:8; Judg. 3:5 (also five secondary occurrences in Exodus — 3:8, 17; 23:23; 33:2; 34:11; the seven-item list, including the Girgashites, is found only at Deut. 7:1; Josh. 3:10; 24:11). The list itself can scarcely be determinative of the origins of the surrounding text. The text refers to kings; the list refers to local peoples. For this reason, the list is likely to be an insertion (cf. Josh. 9:1; 11:3; 12:8). Furthermore, 9:1–2 casts its net far wider than merely Gibeon. The wider context is not present when the narrative turns to 9:3. It is worth noting that the Hebrew construction ("when they/he heard") is identical at the start of 9:1; 10:1; and 11:1; it is not the same in 9:3. Strange as it may seem, there is a reasonable probability that 9:1–2 has 11:1ff. in view. In that case, it is probably to be associated also with the list of kings in 12:7–24.

Like many of the older texts, the Gibeonite story has its own share of difficulties that need not be discussed here; they are not relevant to the present concern.[15]

Later than the "Joshua 2" narrative here may be 9:1–2, 10, 15b, 18–21, 24*, 27b. Verses 1–2 have already been discussed. Verse 10, with both Sihon and Og, is regarded as later Dtr revision. The text associated with the "leaders of the congregation" (vv. 15b, 18–21) is almost certainly late; the term is late and almost exclusively Priestly. In Joshua, Moses as God's servant is a favorite of late (Dtr) editing; the substance of v. 24 is likely to be late. The final clause of v. 27b is to be attributed to the Deuteronomist.[16] The last reference to Gibeon/Gibeonites in the Dtr history is at 1 Kings 9:2; it is likely, therefore, that their role as "hewers of wood and drawers of water" for the altar belongs in the original narrative, rather than being added later.

Joshua 10

Belonging to the "Joshua 2" narrative from this chapter are probably vv. 1–27, 42–43. The story of the Jerusalem coalition speaks of Ai, Jeri-

---

tory Hypothesis: A Reassessment [OBO 92; Freiburg, Switzerland: Universitätsverlag, 1989] 70, 79).

15. See John Gray, *Joshua, Judges and Ruth* (NCB; London: Nelson, 1967) 97–104; J. Alberto Soggin, *Joshua* (OTL; London: SCM, 1972; French original, 1970) 109–14; R. K. Sutherland, "Israelite Political Theories in Joshua 9," *JSOT* 53 (1992) 65–74; and more recently, Briend, "Sources," 344–47, 364–66. Soggin comments, "The story of the ruse itself contains evident confusions" (p. 111).

16. See Noth, *Deuteronomistic History*, 64.

cho, and Gibeon (10:1–2); it is an appropriate continuation of these stories. The five kings and their towns are named: Jerusalem, Hebron, Jarmuth, Lachish, and Eglon (vv. 3 and 5). Joshua and the army are located in camp at Gilgal (vv. 6–7, 9). The text appears to include variant versions for the storyteller. In 10:15, Joshua and all Israel return to the camp at Gilgal; all would appear to be over. In vv. 16–21, the five kings are trapped and the pursuit is still in progress; when concluded, the people (or army) return to Joshua at Makkedah. By this account, the return to Gilgal is achieved in 10:43. The text presents an unpleasantly vivid account of how partisans deal with their prisoners.[17] At the same time, God's support is regularly evident and the associated miracles have entered into folklore (10:10–14).[18] However, what occurred is explicitly dissociated from anything "before or since" (v. 14).

A conclusion to this story is found in 10:42–43. It is appropriate to the coalition story. Joshua has vanquished five kings at one stroke (v. 42); he and the army return to Gilgal, whence they had come (v. 43; cf. 10:6–7). The sequence of these verses brings out what has been the underlying tone of this narrative since Joshua 2: Joshua was successful because the LORD God of Israel fought for Israel. The protagonist is Joshua; the supporting role is played by God.

Later than the "Joshua 2" narrative here may be 10:28–41, as an expansion of the Dtr narrative. The listlike quality of these verses is evident. They deal with six southern towns: Makkedah, Libnah, Lachish, Eglon, Hebron, and Debir. Three of these figured in the Jerusalem coalition. The kings of four are reported as killed. Only the king of Hebron is listed as killed with the five (v. 23) and also in this campaign (v. 37); the other two from the coalition, the kings of Lachish and Eglon, are not mentioned (cf. vv. 32, 35). An analysis of the language used shows that the concern for *ḥerem* and extermination in these verses is denser and more marked than anywhere else.[19]

---

17. Noth attributes 10:25 to the Deuteronomist, as an embellishment of the old story (*Deuteronomistic History*, 64). The action (v. 24) requires some form of utterance to accompany it. The insertion of a single verse has to be suspect here. The pair of imperatives, "be strong and courageous," appears in almost exclusively Dtr contexts; however, here it is scarcely a commissioning. Sensitive comments on the pair are given in ch. 7 of Lori L. Rowlett, *Joshua and the Rhetoric of Violence: A New Historicist Analysis* (JSOTSup 226; Sheffield: Sheffield Academic Press, 1996) 156–80.

18. See J. H. Walton, "Joshua 10:12–15 and Mesopotamian Celestial Omen Texts," in A. R. Millard et al., eds., *Faith, Tradition, and History: Old Testament Historiography in Its Near Eastern Context* (Winona Lake, Ind.: Eisenbrauns, 1994) 181–90; B. Margalit, "The Day the Sun Did Not Stand Still: A New Look at Joshua x 8–15," *VT* 42 (1992) 466–91.

19. The language is analyzed in its "stereotyped syntagms" in K. Lawson Younger Jr., "The 'Conquest' of the South (Jos 10,28–39)," *BZ* 39 (1995) 255–64. His comment that "these syntagms function as broad sweeping statements of victory to create an image of complete conquest for ideological reasons. They overstate matters for emphasis and per-

The language of ḥerem is used for Makkedah (v. 28), Eglon (v. 35), Hebron (v. 37), and Debir (v. 39), as well as in the final summary (v. 40). Apart from 2:10 (Dtr), occurrences associated with the story of Achan (6:17, 18; 7:1, 11, 12, 13, 15), and secondary occurrences in ch. 11 (vv. 11, 12, 20, 21), the ḥerem language occurs only once in relation to Jericho (6:21), once for Ai (8:26), and once in relation to Ai and by implication Jericho (10:1). This puts 10:28–41 in a remarkably special category. Form-critically, it is a list not a story. Six towns are in the list; ḥerem language is used for four of them. Even the four occurrences in ch. 11 bear no resemblance to this density. Note also that both Lachish and Libnah are brought within the ban (ḥerem) by association with Eglon (v. 35) and Debir (v. 39) respectively. In this way, all six towns are involved.

The language of extermination is even more intense. The phrase hišʾîr śārîd is often rendered "left no one remaining." It is used for four of the six towns (Makkedah, Libnah, Hebron, and Debir), for the army of Horam of Gezer (v. 33), and in the final summary (v. 40). It is absent for Lachish and Eglon, the two towns either side of Horam's defeat.[20] Once again, association with other towns (Libnah, directly v. 32 and indirectly v. 35) paints an all-embracing picture. Otherwise, this language is used in Joshua only for the battle report at Ai (8:22) and in secondary material at 11:8. The language of "putting to the edge of the sword" is also packed densely into 10:28–41. It is used for all six of the towns (10:28, 30, 32, 35, 37, 39). Beyond these, it occurs once for Jericho (6:21) and once for the battle over Ai (8:24), and three times in ch. 11 (vv. 11, 12, 14).

What these linguistic observations spell out is what a careful reader will have realized instinctively: the list of towns in 10:28–39 is quite different from the stories earlier in the book. What the language makes unpleasantly clear is the massive emphasis on total destruction in these verses, the emphasis on annihilation or extermination. Once this passage's marked difference in language density and emphasis is noted, it is perfectly possible for it to be seen as a separate development.[21]

In contrast with vv. 42–43, vv. 40–41 have a wide vision ("the whole

suasion" (p. 261) may be helpful and right. It does not change the fact that the language here is not found with similar stereotyped density elsewhere.

20. This pattern reinforces Younger's claim for a palistrophe or chiasm in these verses, emphasizing Gezer (" 'Conquest' of the South," 260). R. David provides a valuable analysis of the elements on pp. 212–13 of "Jos 10,28–39, témoin d'une conquête de la Palestine par le sud?" ScEs 42 (1990) 209–22.

21. The comment by Rowlett can be applied with particular force to these verses: "Identity was being reasserted in the Joshua story, but it was done by adopting the violent ideology of the oppressors. The same ideology that had undermined their identity was now being used to exert their identity" (Rhetoric of Violence, 183).

land," with details), an emphasis on extermination and *ḥerem*, and a concern for God's command. Verse 41 covers the extent of the southern campaign, from Kadesh-barnea to Gibeon; the pronoun "them" binds it syntactically to v. 40. These two verses (vv. 40–41) are the conclusion to the list in 10:28–39. Verses 42–43 constitute the conclusion to 10:1–27.

Joshua 11–12

It was at quite a late stage in the preparation of this essay that my suspicions were aroused whether any of Joshua 11–12 should be seen as original and so included in the "Joshua 2" narrative. On closer inspection of the text, my suspicions were deepened, and it seemed likely that none of the material from these two chapters belonged in the "Joshua 2" narrative.

Three pointers give rise to this suspicion. Pointer number one is the absence of any reference to Joshua's whereabouts. The LORD speaks to him (11:6), and Joshua and his army — last heard of at Gilgal (10:43, MT only; LXX not since 10:6–7, 9) — "suddenly" fall on the foe at Merom, far to the north in Galilee (v. 7). Pointer number two is the vagueness of the introduction ("when Jabin heard," 11:1). Heard what? The NRSV adds an object, "of this," where the Hebrew does not have it. In this, 11:1 parallels the secondary 9:1 (where again the NRSV has added an "of this"); in 10:1, the object is mentioned, "how Joshua had taken Ai." Pointer number three is the preference given to the LORD as protagonist rather than Joshua. The case is not as clear as it is for the "sacral stories"; hamstringing horses and burning chariots are good tactics. But before this, the LORD promises to give them "slain" to Israel (v. 6, *ḥălālîm*); after it, "the LORD handed them over to Israel" (v. 8). On balance, the victory is the LORD's, with a little bit of help from Joshua and Israel.

Any one of these pointers on its own might have been dismissed or explained away. Taken together, they give rise to grave suspicion. The fact that Jabin of Hazor/Canaan figures in the Deborah/Barak story (Judg. 4:2, 23–24) may be significant, but it cannot be pursued here.

The conclusion to this account can be found in vv. 16–19 and 23. 11:3 gives the same list of six local peoples as 9:1 and 12:8b (cf. also Judg. 3:5). The list of peoples sits uncomfortably with the appeal that is sent out to kings not peoples (cf. 12:8b for similar discomfort). The emphasis and linguistic features that marked 10:28–41 recur in 11:8b–15 — no survivors remain, they were struck down with the edge of the sword, the ban is in force. It is likely that 11:8b–15 belongs on the same level with 10:28–41.

11:20 has to be a separate note. God's hardening of hearts occurs only here and in Exodus (4:21; 9:12; 10:20, 27; 11:10; 14:4, 8, 17; but cf.

Isa. 6:10).[22] The language of the ban recurs in the verse, as well as the theme of extermination; but the language of no survivors left remaining is not used. The use of těḥinnâ here for "mercy" or "favor" has only one parallel and it is late (Ezra 9:8); otherwise the meaning is "plea" or "supplication." All these signals point to the verse as a later addition.

11:21–22, as a note on the Anakim, is one of those bits of tradition that it is difficult to identify with any precision; an association with the Joshua text is possible at almost any time. Concern with the Anakim, not to be confused with "the descendants of the giants" (mentioned in 2 Sam. 21:15–21), is restricted to the books of Deuteronomy and Joshua, often in association with the fear of foes "stronger and taller than we" (Deut. 1:28). There are pointers suggesting that the verses may have been added along with 10:28–41 and 11:8b–15. First, there is the temporal note, "at that time," found above in 11:10 and otherwise in the book of Joshua only in the equally secondary 5:1 and 6:26. The concern for utter destruction (ḥerem) and those left remaining is also present (twice in v. 22, with the positive and negative language reversed).

12:1–6 are concerned with the Transjordan tribes (see below). 12:7–24 (with the exception of the later list in v. 8b) shows an interest in kings and in the total conquest, including the kings of the northern coalition. The Deuteronomist shows no interest in kings. The total conquest, including the north, betrays an interest beyond that of the "Joshua 2" narrative. The list of kings is best associated with the expansions in 11:1–8a, 16–19, and 23.

THE "SACRAL STORIES" EXPANSION

Under this rubric, we can treat the Jordan crossing, the Jericho capture, the Achan story, and the material just noted as an expansion beyond the "Joshua 2" narrative (i.e., Josh. 11:1–8a, 16–19, 23; 12:7–8a, 9–24). The so-called expansion need not have been made at the same time that the "sacral stories" were inserted into the text. Nevertheless, it is convenient to deal with both groups together.

What the addition of this material does has already been noted: it moves the emphasis of the presentation from the action of Joshua's Israel to the action of Israel's God. The sacral stories emphasize God's action by achieving ends through means that are quite inadequate in the day-to-day world of military and political action. A flowing river is stopped by the presence of the ark, as the Sea of Reeds was

---

22. According to Noth's source division, 4:21 (supplementary) and 10:20, 27 (both supplementary) are found within J; 9:12 (plague of boils); 11:10 (supplementary); and 14:4, 8, 18 (Sea of Reeds) are found within P (cf. A. F. Campbell and M. A. O'Brien, *Sources of the Pentateuch: Texts, Introductions, Annotations* [Minneapolis: Fortress, 1993]).

parted by Moses' hand. City walls collapse at a simple shout. A battle is lost because one individual broke sacred rules, as Jonathan did in 1 Samuel 14.

In the understanding presented here, the sacral stories about crossing the Jordan and capturing Jericho have replaced the bulk of the stories of military crossing and capture. Traces of the older stories remain, allowing us to realize that they had been there. The presence of haste (4:10b) and the military (4:13) are there for the crossing; the king and his soldiers (6:2) are mentioned for Jericho. It would be surprising if these traces were left by oversight or negligence; Israel knew how to keep old traditions alive.

The traditions of the northern coalition (11:1–2, 4–8a, 16–19, 23) are not smoothly integrated into the "Joshua 2" narrative. They could have been imported to complete the picture of national conquest. It is possible, but not necessary, that their inclusion occurred along with the introduction of the sacral stories.

THE DTR TEXT

What can be specifically identified as Dtr contribution within Joshua 1–12 is remarkably little and focused primarily on Joshua's role as successor to Moses. Third person reporting of Moses' role as "servant of the LORD" is restricted in its distribution and appears to be Dtr at the earliest, often late Dtr.[23] The keynote to the whole is spoken by God in the opening verses of the book: "As I was with Moses, so I will be with you" (1:5). Neither here nor in the Dtr conclusion (Josh. 21:43–45; 22:6) is there any emphasis on the extermination of the local nations or any concern for their kings.[24]

Joshua's leadership role is underlined by the Dtr addition in 3:7–8 and 4:14. 5:1 echoes the concern of 2:10. Joshua's role is echoed in his fame (6:27). A final emphasis is given with the addition of "according to all that the LORD had spoken to Moses" in 11:23. The reference to the land being tranquil without war (*šāqṭâ mimilḥāmâ*) uses language akin to the pre-Dtr framing material in Judges 3–9 and is unlikely to have originated with the Deuteronomist.[25]

---

23. The occurrences of "Moses, the servant of the Lord" are Deut. 34:5; Josh. 1:1, 13, 15; 8:31, 33; 11:12; 12:6; 13:8; 14:7; 18:7; 22:2, 4, 5; 2 Kings 18:12; 2 Chron. 1:3; 24:6.

24. Noth attributes Josh. 21:43–45 to an interpolation soon after the completion of the Dtr history, because although "so close to Dtr. in style that one could attribute it to Dtr. himself, except that, like the rest of the chapter, it comes after Josh. 11.23aβ" (*Deuteronomistic History*, 66–67). A number of developments render this judgment no longer sustainable (cf. O'Brien, *Reassessment*, p. 59 n. 41, pp. 74–75).

25. The NRSV's "the land had rest from war" here and in Judges is misleading; the Dtr "rest" is *měnûḥâ*.

To summarize the Dtr contribution. Attributed to the Josianic Deuteronomist are basically 1:1–6, 10–11; 2:10–11; 3:7–8; 4:14; 6:19, 24b–25, 27; 9:10; 11:23aβ — omitting ch. 5 from consideration. The combination of Sihon and Og occurs in 2:10 and 9:10 (as well as in 12:1–6) and may be due to later Dtr editing, as are 1:7–9 and three minor expansions within 2:11; 7:11, 15.

THE "EXTERMINATION LIST" TEXTS

What became clear in the study of the "Joshua 2" narrative is the peculiar nature of the text in 10:28–41 and 11:8b–15. These two blocks of text, relating to the southern and northern conquest respectively, are treated here as later than the Deuteronomist because of the absence in the Dtr texts of any emphasis on the extermination of the local nations.

In the "Joshua 2" narrative, the ban was applied to Jericho (in full measure) and Ai (with mitigation) and was feared by Gibeon and the coalition of five. What the texts of 10:28–41 and 11:8b–15 do is to focus with intense density on this extermination and extend it beyond a couple of towns to the whole area of Israel's conquest. What is of interest is how a narrative that smacks of standard national boasting about land seizure has been turned into a thoroughgoing theology of extermination by those who must have known it was untrue. Who, when, and why? This will be taken up briefly below.

THE TRANSJORDAN TRIBES

Mention of the tribes of Reuben, Gad, and the half-tribe of Manasseh recurs often in the book of Joshua, but always located in the text at positions that suggest later additions. The texts are 1:12–18; 4:12; 12:1–6; 13:8–32; 18:7; 22:7–9, 10–34. They seem to be late. The question raised is, What concern do they address? There would be relevance for returning exiles in quest of their "rightful" lands. The issue cannot be pursued here.

ISSUES ARISING FROM THIS EXPLORATION

Two conclusions emerge from all this discussion. One has been flagged from the outset: the possibility is there that an earlier text can be pointed to without difficulty or distortion of the present text, a text that is coherent with Joshua 2 and that presents a picture of Israel under Joshua crossing the Jordan, capturing Jericho and Ai, cutting a deal with Gibeon, and defeating a Jerusalem-led coalition. Such a text might generate about the same level of outrage as the late ninth-century Mesha stele from Moab.

Such a possibility does not address the origins and issues of texts earlier than this "Joshua 2" level; the texts now are there. Nor does it look at every possibility for later editing. What it claims is merely that such a "Joshua 2" level text is possible. This is not claimed to be the definitive understanding of the book of Joshua. It is claimed to be a possible understanding of the book's growth.

A corollary of this view is the subsequent sacralization of the Joshua account, leading to a far stronger role for God in the gift of the land to Israel. If we assume that the texts for the Jordan crossing, the Jericho capture, and the Achan episode derive from the Gilgal sanctuary, it may be possible that the sacralization of the narrative derives in some way from this sanctuary. Beyond that it is difficult to go.

The second conclusion relates to the issue of the extermination texts (10:28–41 and 11:8b–15). The limited extent of these has always been evident. It is heightened by the close study of the language involved. It is not impossible for these to have been old traditions; the distribution of the language, however, makes this unlikely.

The concern is clearly expressed in Deuteronomy (the ban: Deut. 2:34; 3:6; 7:2, 26; 13:16, 18; 20:17; no survivors: Deut. 2:34; 3:3; cf. Num. 21:35). Despite this, the concern with extermination is not given expression in the Dtr framework that sets the tone for the book of Joshua (1:1–11; 21:43–45). It is possible, therefore, that it is later.

Whatever its date, it poses problems for the history of traditions. The later Dtr revision in Joshua 23 insists that there were survivors and that Israel was not to worship their gods or intermarry with their women (23:7, 12). Furthermore, there are three passages early in the book of Judges, all potentially secondary, that seek to explain the presence of the surviving nations. According to Judg. 2:1–5, the locals are to be Israel's adversaries and their gods a snare to Israel. According to Judg. 2:20–23 and 3:4, the locals were left as a test of Israel's fidelity; and, as far as 3:5–6 was concerned, Israel failed the test. According to Judg. 3:1–3, the locals were left so that the inexperienced in Israel might be tested in war.

There are texts in Deuteronomy that speak of purging the evil "from your midst" or "from Israel" (Deut. 13:6 [NRSV, 5]; 17:7, 12; 19:19; 21:21; 22:21, 22, 24; 24:7). There is no direct link in the language used in these texts with the extermination texts in Joshua. The mindset, however, is close. If there is evil within Israel, purge it. Similarly, if there are local peoples in the country, purge them. One is an evil within Israel that is to be put without; the other is viewed as an evil outside Israel that is to be kept out. The mindsets may be close; the language expressing them is not. Thematic association is possible; linguistic association is not.

Linguistic association emerges in Deut. 13:13–19 (NRSV, 12–18), a passage related to Deut. 13:6 (NRSV, 5). If the inhabitants of a town have been led astray by those saying, "Let us go and worship other gods" (13:14, NRSV, 13; cf. 13:3, 7–8, NRSV, 2, 6–7), they shall be put to the edge of the sword and the ban shall apply to them and to their goods. Missing is only the "no survivors" language. The appalling nature of such a text has long been recognized.[26]

These texts are operating in a world that to many today is largely incomprehensible. Are the extermination texts in Joshua another attempt to come to terms with the locals by affirming that none survived? Joshua's generation alone is proclaimed as faithful to the LORD (Josh. 24:31; Judg. 2:7). Deuteronomy 7:1–4 makes clear the LORD's will for the locals: extermination. Therefore, despite texts to the contrary, Joshua's generation must have done it and it is to be recorded in the book of Joshua. Early or late, widespread or isolated, these texts pose problems for the history of traditions. Late and isolated looks more likely; even as such the origins of the theology of extermination remain obscure. Why, for God's sake, are the heights and depths so dangerously close?

---

26. The comment on Deut. 21:18 is valid for both 21:18 and 13:13–19 (NRSV, 12–18): "A Sage of the Talmud flatly declared that the conditions which would cause a court to decree the death penalty 'never occurred and never will occur.'" See W. Gunther Plaut, ed., *The Torah: A Modern Commentary* (New York: Union of American Hebrew Congregations, 1981) 1484; cf. pp. 1431, 1435, 1489. "The sole purpose of the warning is that it might be studied and that one might receive reward for such study" (p. 1435).

4

The Identity of the People
in 2 Kings 17:34–41

Sok-chung Chang

TRANSLATION

[34]*To this day*[1] *they do*[2] according to the former manners. *They do not fear*[3] YHWH, and they do not follow *their statutes*[4] or *their ordinances*[5] or the law or the commandment which YHWH commanded the descendants of Jacob, whom he named Israel. [35]YHWH made a covenant with them, and commanded them, "You shall not fear other gods or bow yourselves to them or serve them or sacrifice to them; [36]but you shall fear YHWH, who brought you out of the land of Egypt with great power and with an outstretched arm; to him you shall bow yourselves, and to him you shall sacrifice. [37]And *the statutes*[6] and *the ordinances*[7] and the law and the commandment which he wrote for you, you shall always be careful to do. You shall not fear other gods, [38]and you shall not forget the covenant which I have made with you. You shall not fear other gods, [39]but you shall fear YHWH your God, and he will deliver you out of the hand of your enemies."

---

1. This phrase indicates that a certain period had passed since foreigners launched their syncretistic cultic practice in the land. At the same time, we need to respond to the question, What date does it refer to?

2. By using the participial form, the writer does not clarify the subject of the sentence. It is because the writer is still talking about those foreigners whom he mentioned in the previous unit (vv. 24–33).

3. Again the participial form of the verb is used, which does not reveal the subject clearly. Therefore, the writer is also talking about those foreigners here. Some scholars and translations (RSV and NRSV) divide v. 34 into two at this juncture and regard the latter, which begins with "they do not fear," as the report about Israelites (except for v. 41). However, my study shows that vv. 34–41 are about those foreigners without interruption. This is also supported by the translation of NJPS, where vv. 24–41 are grouped together. Furthermore, NJPS translates this phrase, "they do not worship the LORD [properly]." This shows that the writer now gives his comment on foreigners' syncretistic cultic practice. His comment should be distinguished from his report of their practice in the previous verse, "they feared YHWH but also served their own gods" (v. 33).

4. The 3m.pl. suffix is too significant to ignore in translation, because it means that the statutes are not YHWH's but foreigners'. YHWH's statutes are normally referred to as "his statutes" or "my statutes."

5. The same argument as in the case of "their statutes" can be made here.

6. Here the writer refers to YHWH's statutes that Israel should follow. The writer deliberately does not use the 3m.pl. suffix, to show that these are not foreigners' statutes.

7. The same argument as in the case of "the statutes" can be made here.

[40]However they would not listen, but they did according to their *former*[8] manners. [41]So these nations feared YHWH, and also served their graven images; their children likewise, and their children's children — as their fathers did, so they do to this day.

ANALYSIS

The identity of the people and the location in which they were living at the time of the writer have attracted the attention of scholars. They were the imported foreigners in Samaria (Gray, Würthwein, Viviano, Long[9]), the Israelite remainees in Samaria after the fall (Talmon), the Israelites in exile (Cogan), the inhabitants in the land (Noth), or just the Israelites with no specific location mentioned (Cogan and Tadmor). Hoffmann says that vv. 34–41 concern the religious situation in Samaria. The criteria of these scholars for their arguments will be discussed in the following section. A diagram of the structure of vv. 34–41 can be illustrated as follows:

I. They[10] stick to the former manner	34–40
A. Their former manner	34a
B. They do not fear YHWH	34b
C. The covenant with YHWH	35–39
1. Covenant making	35a
2. The content of the covenant	35b–39
a. What you shall not do	35b
b. What you shall do	36
c. Obeying the law and not fearing other gods	37
d. Not forgetting the covenant and not fearing other gods	38
e. Command to fear YHWH and His protection	39
D. Their disobedience and former manner	40
II. Nations' ongoing syncretistic cult practice	41

Verse 34a reads, "they are acting according to former מִשְׁפָּט," which also appears in v. 40. "To this day" in v. 34 refers to the time the writer wrote this chapter. This *Wiederaufnahme* can be linked to the one in v. 23. According to our analysis, vv. 24–33 are inserted, but not necessarily at a later time, by a different editor, between v. 23 and vv. 34–40. Verse 34 states that they do not fear YHWH, and that they do not act according to the statutes or the ordinances or the law or the commandment. The participial forms of the verbs (עֹשִׂים) indicate the writer's intention to

---

8. The MT reads הראשׁון (m.sg.) instead of הראשׁנים (m.pl.).

9. Long uses the term "non-Israelite Samarians" in 2 *Kings* (FOTL 10; Grand Rapids: Eerdmans, 1991) 187.

10. According to the MT these people could be either the Israelites or the foreigners, but according to the LXX they are clearly the foreigners.

show the contemporary situation of these people. There is a shift in the people's cultic practice from "fearing YHWH" (vv. 32–33) to "not fearing YHWH" (v. 34). Verse 40 also ends with the participial form of the verb. Two modifying clauses are used in v. 34: the commandment *which* (אֲשֶׁר) YHWH commanded the sons of Jacob, *whom* (אֲשֶׁר) he named Israel.

This shift in the foreigners' cultic practice from v. 33 and v. 34 attracts my attention. The LXX has a very different reading in v. 34 and will be dealt with later in this section. The apparent shift in the MT can be understood by distinguishing between the writer's report of an event and his comment on it. The writer's report on the imported foreigners begins with v. 24 and ends with v. 34a, followed by his comment beginning in v. 34b, and the reason for his comment in the following verses up to v. 39. Then another report follows in v. 40.[11] Finally, his concluding report is given in v. 41. "These nations" in v. 41 makes it certain that the writer has been speaking of those imported foreigners without interruption since v. 24. The 3m.pl. subject in v. 32 clearly refers to those nations and it controls all the 3m.pl. subjects of sentences up to v. 40. However, this understanding of the shift in vv. 33–34 concerning the foreigners' cultic practice is a possibility, not an absolute certainty. The LXX text in those verses is very different from that of the MT. In the case of the LXX, I prefer not to explore this possible interpretation, because there is no shift in the LXX.

Why does the writer use "the sons of Jacob"? The answer would be twofold. First, the history of Israel begins with the sons of Jacob in the writer's mind. That is, Israel's sojourning in Egypt is what he refers to here. Second, that the term "Israel" began with Jacob needs to be remembered. The writer makes sure that the readers know that he is talking about the commandment that was given to Israel, implying Israel as the entity of the people before the monarchy.

Before I begin analysis of individual verses in this unit, I would like to focus on the YHWH speech that most scholars identify in vv. 35aβ–39.[12] I agree with the argument that a YHWH speech begins in v. 35aβ after לֵאמֹר. However, it ends in v. 35b. The writer's own word concerning fearing YHWH begins with v. 36 and continues up to v. 39. First of all, in v. 36 the text says, "you shall fear YHWH" instead of "you shall fear me." The first person objective is not used although it is required in a YHWH speech. Second, in that same verse the text reads, "you shall bow yourselves *to him*, and *to him* you shall sacrifice" (וְלוֹ תִשְׁתַּחֲווּ וְלוֹ תִזְבָּחוּ). If

---

11. The 3m.pl. subject that was used in vv. 32–34 reappears in v. 40.

12. J. Gray (*I and II Kings: A Commentary* [rev. ed.; OTL; Philadelphia: Westminster, 1970] 655); T. R. Hobbs (*2 Kings* [WBC 13; Waco, Tex.: Word, 1985] 222); M. Cogan and H. Tadmor (*II Kings* [AB 11; Garden City, N.Y.: Doubleday, 1988] 209). The RSV and NRSV read YHWH speech in vv. 35aβ–39.

it were part of a YHWH speech, "to me" would have been used. Third, in v. 37 the expression "the commandment which *he* wrote for you" (והמצוה אשר כתב לכם) indicates that it is the writer's speech instead of a YHWH speech. Finally, in v. 39 the text says, "you shall fear YHWH your God, and *he* will deliver you" (והוא יציל אתכם). All of these evidences support that vv. 36–39 are the words of the writer, not part of a YHWH speech. Also, כי אם and the usage of YHWH in vv. 36 and 39 indicate that vv. 36–39 have syntactical coherence, according to Frevel.[13]

The only problem with the MT in arguing this way is the 1c.sg. subject in v. 38 in the expression והברית אשר־כרתי. The LXX and the Vulgate read a 3m.sg. subject here. In my opinion, the reading of a 3m.sg. subject is preferable because of the overwhelming evidences listed above. The next question would be, How do we interpret this observation in vv. 35–39? Why did the writer put his own words right after a YHWH speech?

Our analysis concludes that a YHWH speech appears in vv. 35aβ+b and that the content of YHWH's commandment is "not fearing other gods." The writer's interpretation of this commandment follows in vv. 36–39, that is, Israel should fear YHWH. The commandments of *not fearing other gods* and of *fearing* YHWH should be combined in order to produce the commandment "you shall fear YHWH alone." The former (not fearing other gods) could mean that Israel's not fearing YHWH is possible. The latter (fearing YHWH) could mean that Israel's fearing other gods as well as YHWH is possible. Therefore, we are led to conclude that the original of YHWH's commandment to Israel was "fearing YHWH alone."

Verse 35 introduces the concept of covenant. YHWH's command in the covenant between YHWH and Israel is exclusively emphasized. The content of his command in vv. 35–36 is *not to fear other gods* but *to fear* YHWH. Our text does not say only that Israel should fear YHWH. It always states that Israel should not fear other gods, but fear YHWH. Why is this?

First, if there is only the command to fear YHWH (without the word "alone"), it may assume that there is no other god but YHWH. Second, if there is only the command to fear YHWH exclusively, it assumes the existence of other gods or objects of fearing. Third, if the command is to fear YHWH and not to fear other gods, it still assumes the existence of other gods. The great possibility of Israel's fearing other gods caused

---

13. Frevel also notes that there is disunity in vv. 34–40: "Der Abschnitt vv. 34–40 ist nicht einheitlich, denn die in v. 35 begonnene JHWH-Rede, die in v. 38 eindeutig in der 1. Pers. Sg. gehalten ist, wird durch die Rede über JHWH in der 3. Pers. Sg. zweimal durch den Einsatz mit [כי אם] in vv. 36.39 in der syntaktischen Kohärenz gestört" (19, 25). See Christian Frevel, "Vom Schreiben Gottes: Literarkritik, Komposition und Auslegung von 2 Kön 17, 34–40," *Biblica* 72 (1991) 25.

the writer, whenever it was possible, to repeat the command not to fear other gods together with the command to fear YHWH.

Actually, a particular aspect of the covenant is given in vv. 35–36. Then the question becomes, Where do we have this kind of covenant in the OT? Is the aspect of the covenant emphasized in vv. 35–36 merely one of the many components of the content of covenant? If the answer is yes, there must be a reason why only one of many components in the content of covenant is exclusively required here, that is, fearing YHWH and not fearing other gods. Traditio-historical research is absolutely required.

Another aspect to be fleshed out in vv. 35–36 concerns what they should and should not do.

V. 35: You *shall not*	(1) fear other gods
	(2) bow yourselves to them
	(3) serve them
	(4) sacrifice to them
V. 36: You *shall*	(1) fear YHWH
	(2) bow yourselves to him
	(3) sacrifice to him

The list of what Israel should not do has one more item than the list of what Israel should do: Israel shall not *serve* other gods. Why did the writer not add the command that Israel shall serve YHWH? The verb עבד ("to serve") is applied to the foreigners who are resettled in the land: they served their own gods and graven images (vv. 33, 41), while they feared YHWH. We know that the verb עבד has been frequently applied to YHWH throughout the OT. However, if we collect the examples from the Deuteronomic History, we may find certain conditions under which this verb is used. Further research is needed to flesh out this issue.

The flashback concerning the past deeds of YHWH in v. 36 is certainly noticeable due to its unique expression: YHWH who brought you out of the land of Egypt *with great power and with an outstretched arm.* This expression has been used in three other verses (Deut. 9:29; Jer. 27:5; 32:17), and only Deut. 9:29 implies YHWH's liberating Israel from Egypt. The other two concern YHWH's creation of the universe. Only in DH is this expression used to denote YHWH's liberating his people from Egypt. Even the flashback concerning the past deeds of YHWH in v. 7 does not have this image of the powerful YHWH. Could this have a particular significance?

The list of stipulations in v. 37 has the same order as the one in v. 34. At the end of v. 37 the writer adds, "You shall not fear other gods."

Verse 38 stipulates that Israel should not *forget* the covenant ("covenant" having a definite article, הברית), instead of stipulating that Israel should *remember* the covenant. Even though they are two sides of the same coin, the aspect of forgetting is underscored. Then at the end of v. 38 the writer again adds the same sentence as the one in v. 37, "You shall not fear other gods." Why did the writer use the expression verbatim in two consecutive verses?

Verse 39 starts with a clause introduced by כי אם that emphasizes that YHWH will do something good for Israel if Israel fears YHWH. The protasis is that Israel will fear YHWH, and the apodosis is that YHWH will deliver Israel from all enemies. If we consider vv. 38–39 as a unit concerning the covenant, the content of the covenant would be this: if Israel fears YHWH and does not fear other gods, YHWH will rescue Israel from all enemies. The conditionality in the covenant between YHWH and Israel is underscored. Then the oddly repeated sentence of vv. 37–38, "you shall not fear other gods," can be understood because v. 37 is separated from vv. 38–39, that is, they belong to different units.

The ensuing question is why suddenly at the end of the chapter the writer depends upon this conditional covenant. The reward for Israel's fearing YHWH is given in v. 39. Yahwism as a weak religion in a syncretistic environment may be indicated here. Or the writer may want to emphasize Israel's disobedience by introducing YHWH's promise in the covenant to protect Israel from enemies. The idea that YHWH will deliver Israel from their enemies is not found in this chapter, but it dominates in 2 Kings 18–19.[14]

Verse 40 closes with the remark that Israel would not listen and kept doing according to their former manner.[15] This sentence is very similar to the one in v. 34, and thus the unit comprised by vv. 34–40 begins and closes with the same expression emphasizing that Israel still sticks to sinful behavior in the eyes of YHWH.

Verse 41 describes what the foreigners introduced in vv. 24–33 did: fearing YHWH and serving their graven images to this day, that is, to the era of the writer. Rather than emphasizing the nations'/foreigners' syncretistic religions in the land, the writer wants to underscore that *even these nations feared* YHWH for many generations. Of course, what the foreigners did was not exactly "fearing YHWH" according to the criterion of YHWH worshipers. But they are foreigners, not the Israelites. Did the writer expect them to convert to Yahwism? Or was he interested in guiding Israel to fear YHWH and eventually bringing them back to their

---

14. See Pauline A. Viviano, "2 Kings 17: A Rhetorical and Form-Critical Analysis," *CBQ* 49 (1987) 555.

15. Verse 40 of the LXX is very different from that of the MT.

land? The last resort of the writer is to emphasize in v. 41 that these foreign nations feared YHWH. Therefore, even though this verse is about the foreign nations' syncretistic cultic practice, it is added to call Israel's attention to fearing YHWH as the people of the covenant, which requires them to worship YHWH exclusively.

One question can be raised. Certain units might have been written by exilic editors, or the whole chapter might have been written in the exilic period.[16] Whether insertion or addition took place or not, all units within this chapter have their roles to play in the unity of the extant text. What are their roles? In other words, all the reports and comments of diverse origins are intermingled in this chapter in a presumably systematic way under a unifying concept. The interesting as well as crucial research to identify this overarching concept within the text requires another, much longer paper.

The structural analysis of 2 Kings 17 of the MT indicates two complementary elements at work: Israel and the land.

> I. vv. 1–23   Israel + in the land
> II. vv. 24–33, 41 foreigners + in the land
> III. vv. 34–40   foreigners/Israel + in the land/in exile

We may argue that two parentheses in III can be filled out with various elements because the reading of the MT text is not clear.[17] However, the LXX gives us a rather clear picture concerning III that will be reviewed later in this essay.

The main focus in 2 Kings 17 may seem to be Israel's being removed from their land, not their being conquered by the Assyrians. This is because in vv. 7–23, especially vv. 18–23, Israel's being carried away from the land is repeatedly emphasized (18, 20 including Judah, 23). Two concepts are introduced in vv. 4–6: the fall of Israel and the exile. In the transmitted sources, which were presumably in the form of the Chronicles of Israel, the exile might be subordinated to the fall (vv. 1–6). However, when vv. 7–41 were written, the exile (being removed from the land) became the dominating concept in this chapter. The concept

---

16. H.-D. Hoffmann (*Reform und Reformen: Untersuchungen zu einem Grundthema der deuteronomistischen Geschichtsschreibung* [ATANT 66; Zurich: Theologischer Verlag, 1980]) and Viviano ("2 Kings 17") posit that 2 Kings 17 was written in the preexilic era, while S. Talmon ("Polemics and Apology in Biblical Historiography — 2 Kings 17:24–41," in R. E. Friedman, ed., *The Creation of Sacred Literature* [Berkeley: University of California Press, 1981] 57–75; "Polemics and Apology in Biblical Historiography — 2 Kings 17:24–41," in *Literary Studies in the Hebrew Bible: Form and Content, Collected Essays* [Jerusalem: Magnes Press] 134–59) argues that it was added to the book of Kings in the postexilic era.

17. As already noted, several options for III have been suggested by a number of scholars.

of the exile has to be understood in the light of the concept of the land. Therefore, the concept of the land is the dominating concept throughout this chapter.

Being conquered by Assyria is only the preliminary stage that opens the door for the main stage of the exile, that is, the removal of the Israelites from the land that YHWH promised to them and the importation of foreigners into YHWH's land. These two stages or concepts have to be distinguished because there can be a conquest without an exile, while an exile cannot exist without a conquest. They are two separate events. Then we can also understand why vv. 24–33 of the MT text, the report on the immigrating foreigners, must be situated in this chapter. The sole concept of the exile can be emphasized by introducing a case that happened to the immigrating foreigners into the land of YHWH, even though it happened to foreigners and not to Israelites. The land is what the writer cares about most in this chapter, even though the fall of Israel seems to be more important to some readers.

The macrostructure of vv. 1–41 of the MT follows:

I. Regnal formula	1–2
II. Report on the fall and the exile of Israel	3–6
III. The commentary on Israel's exile	7–18
IV. Judah's sin	19
V. The exile of Israel	20
VI. Summary of Israel's exile	21–23
VII. Report of the immigrants in the land	24–33+41
VIII. They[18] stick to the former manner	34–40

EXCURSUS: ACTANTS

If "they" in v. 34 refers to Israel, the writer did not have to use the phrase "the children of Jacob, whom he named Israel." He could have used "YHWH commanded *them*." Or v. 34 should start with "to this day Israel does according to. . . . " Then we can pursue the other possibility that v. 34 is the description of foreigners and not Israel.

> *They* do not fear YHWH and *they* do not follow the statutes or the ordinances or the law or the commandment which YHWH commanded *the children of Jacob,* whom he named *Israel.*

Verse 34a is the writer's *report* of what foreigners were doing in the land. Verse 34b is the writer's *comment* on what those foreigners had been doing to that day. In this comment the writer is criticizing them

---

18. Here we regard them as the people (possibly the Israelites) other than those deportees. However, if we regard them as those deportees, VIII could be included in VII.

because they did not fear YHWH properly in the land. Verse 35 begins with the explanation of YHWH's making a covenant with Israel and v. 40 ends with a report that Israel did not observe the covenant. Verses 35–40 are a reference about Israel and its covenant with YHWH, but they are not describing what the remaining or exiled Israel was doing. Verse 41 picks up the writer's report on what the foreigners were doing in the land to that day. The composition analysis of vv. 34–41 of the MT shows that the writer is still talking about those foreigners by using some covenant themes that are familiar to Israel. The report and the comment of the writer are constantly shifted within the text. These frequent shifts cause much confusion to readers today.

THE LXX EVIDENCE OF 2 KINGS 17:34–41

In this section the relationship between v. 34 and v. 40 is very important in determining the identity of the people described in vv. 34–40.

[34]ἕως τῆς ἡμέρας ταύτης αὐτοὶ ἐποίουν κατὰ <u>τὸ κρίμα</u> αὐτῶν·   αὐτοὶ φοβοῦνται καὶ αὐτοὶ ποιοῦσιν κατὰ τὰ δικαιώματα αὐτῶν καὶ κατὰ <u>τὴν κρίσιν</u> αὐτῶν καὶ κατὰ τὸν νόμον καὶ κατὰ τὴν ἐντολήν, ἣν ἐνετείλατο κύριος τοῖς υἱοῖς Ιακωβ, οὗ ἔθηκεν τὸ ὄνομα αὐτοῦ Ισραηλ.

Until this day they did according to their <u>manner</u>; *they fear* [. . .], and they do according to *their* customs, and according to *their* <u>manner</u>, and according to the law, and according to the commandment which the Lord commanded the sons of Jacob, whose name he made Israel.

According to the MT, one of the crucial points for identifying the people in vv. 34–40 would be v. 34, because there is a sudden change in people's cultic practice: from fearing YHWH to not fearing YHWH. This could be the sign for separating the foreigners in vv. 24–33 from the Is-raelites in vv. 34–40. However, the LXX shows a different reading. There is no change in people's cultic practice in the LXX reading: "they fear, and they act according to their customs. . . . " The negative marker used in the MT is missing in the LXX.

The LXX does not have the object "the Lord" (τὸν κύριον) for the verb φοβοῦνται in the beginning of v. 34. The LXX does not say whom they feared. This may mean that they feared their own gods. The LXX does not differentiate the people in vv. 24–33 and 34–40.

These people are the foreign nations resettled in the cities of Samaria. Then v. 41, which talks about the nations ("they feared YHWH and served their graven images"), goes together perfectly with vv. 24–40. But there is a problem to be solved. What about those images that are pertinent only to the Israelites: the covenant, the liberating from Egypt? We can suggest that vv. 35–40 is a modifying paragraph for "Israel, the sons of Jacob." The writer wants to show the right way of fearing YHWH by using Israel's historical events.

Because v. 34 says that they fear (no object for the verb "fear"; YHWH is the object in the MT), and they act according to their customs, the LXX seems to have an understanding of the identity of the people in vv. 34–40 different from the one of the MT. According to the MT, which says that "they do not fear and do not act," v. 34b seems to talk about the Israelites, who did not depart from evil. However, the LXX treats the same foreigners as in vv. 24–33 here in vv. 34–41. "The Lord commanded *the sons of Jacob*" in v. 34 should have been "the Lord commanded *them*" if the writer of the MT wanted vv. 34ff. to be about the Israelites. By using the images that are relevant only to the Israelites, the writer clearly distinguished these foreigners who feared YHWH and the Israelites who were not supposed to fear other gods but to bow down to YHWH. For foreigners the exclusive fear of YHWH is not required. They could fear YHWH and serve their own gods at the same time. While the writer of the MT is still talking about these foreigners from v. 24, he used the Israelite images in vv. 34–40 to differentiate them from the Israelites.

As already noted, the MT reads in v. 34b, "they do not fear YHWH, and they do not follow the statutes. . . . " This reading causes exegetes to divide v. 34 into two parts: 34a and 34b. Also, this MT reading could make vv. 34–40 into the passage about the Israelites. However, the LXX reading does not need to divide v. 34 into two parts. "Until this day they did according to *their* κρίμα, that is, they fear [YHWH] and they do according to *their* δικαιώματα [they serve their gods], *their* κρίσιν,[19] the law (νομον) and the commandment (ἐντολην) which YHWH commanded the sons of Jacob, whose name he made Israel," reads v. 34 of the LXX.

One of the striking phenomena in the LXX and the MT is the use of the word αὐτῶν ("their") to modify the words κρίμα, δικαιώματα, and κρίσιν.[20] All three words can be translated with "judgment."[21] To the contrary, αὐτῶν is not applied to the words "law" and "commandment." This can be a clear evidence for the LXX and the MT to identify whom the text is talking about in vv. 34–40. First of all, αὐτῶν, which obviously means "the foreigners'," cannot be used for "law" and "commandment," because they are YHWH's law and commandment to Israel. The foreign settlers cannot claim that these are theirs by any means. The modifying clause "which YHWH commanded the sons of Jacob, whose name he made Israel" (LXX; MT: "whom he named Israel") even more

---

19. The Greek word κρίσις" means "judgment, justice."

20. In the MT we also have their statutes (מֹשְׁפָּט) and their ordinances (חֻקֹּת). However, the NRSV translates these words as "statutes" and "ordinances" without considering their suffix (3m.pl.).

21. The word δικαιώματα can also be translated "ordinances."

clarifies that "law" and "commandment" are not given to the foreigners. Second, in v. 8 Israel "walked in the ordinances [δικαιώμασιν] of the nations." Κρίμα, δικαιώματα, and κρίσιν are these foreigners', as the texts say. According to *their own* judgment and ordinances and decision they do and fear (YHWH), but they do according to *Israel's* law and commandment. Therefore, by using αὐτῶν in v. 34, the LXX clarifies the possible confusion of the MT text. The LXX deals consistently with the foreigners in the land of Israel throughout vv. 24–41. Then v. 41 neatly goes together with vv. 34–40.

Furthermore, the MT reads in v. 34a and v. 40 the expression "they do according to the former manners." No possessive pronoun is given to "the former manners." However, the LXX reads τὸ κρίμα αὐτῶν (v. 34) and τῷ κρίματι αὐτῶν (v. 40). In both verses the LXX reads *"their* judgment" instead of "the *former* manner/judgment." The Hebrew ראשנים or ראשון ("former") does not have a corresponding Greek word in the LXX text. By using the possessive pronoun "their," the LXX tries to identify the people in the text (vv. 34–41), while the word "former" in the MT does not tell us whose former manner the writer is talking about in the text. According to the LXX, they are the imported foreigners, not the Israelites, as we already noted above, by the use of αὐτῶν in v. 34b.

Why did this difference between the MT and the LXX arise concerning the words "former" and "their" in vv. 34 and 40? When the word "former" is used, it means that the current status, practice, or situation had already changed. Things are different from the former time. The foreigners' worship of their own gods had not been changed at all. They just added one deity, YHWH, to their deity list when they learned how to fear YHWH. The MT reading might have confused the reader and given the impression that the foreigners changed their cultic practice and really worshiped YHWH alone at one point, and then turned back to the former manner. According to the LXX, they never changed their basic attitude of cultic practice: syncretistic worship. The phrase "their manner" emphasized their unchanged worship and "otherness" of the cultic practice. It is not the Israelite manner of cultic practice by any means according to the LXX reading.

Now let us look at v. 40 of the MT and the LXX carefully, because v. 40 might be a clue to understanding the section of vv. 34–41 or even vv. 24–41.

MT
V. 34: To this day they *do* according to the *former* manners/customs.[22]
They *do not* fear YHWH, and they *do not* follow the statutes or the ordi-

---

22. The NRSV translates משפטים, "their (former) customs," while the RSV translates it, "the (former) manner." NRSV regards it as the plural form with 3m.pl. suffix, while the RSV

nances or the law or the commandment which YHWH commanded the sons of Jacob, whom he named Israel.

V. 40: However, *they* would not listen, but they did according to *their former* manners.

LXX
V. 34: To this day they *did* according to *their* manner.

They *fear* [. . .], and they *do* according to *their* custom, *their* manner, the law, and the commandment which YHWH commanded the sons of Jacob, whose name he made Israel.

V. 40: Yet *you* shall not listen to *their* manner, which they practice.

The MT emphasizes that their manner is the same as the former one. Their former sinful manner is remembered and compared to the present manner. In the MT v. 34 has to be connected with v. 40 to accuse Israel of what they have done and continue doing until this day. Verse 34 is an opening accusation of Israel and v. 40 is a closing one. On the contrary, according to the LXX, v. 34 is an explanatory statement of what the imported foreigners have been doing, while v. 40 is a part of the content of Israel's covenant with YHWH that began in v. 35. Therefore, in the LXX vv. 35–40 is a unit that is inserted between v. 34 and v. 41, which both are explanatory statements of what the imported foreigners have been doing in the cities of Samaria.

MT	LXX
1. v. 34, Israel/nations	1. v. 34, the nations
2. vv. 35–39, Israel	2. vv. 35–40, Israel as a reference
3. v. 40, Israel	3. v. 41, the nations
4. v. 41, the nations	

Based on this chart comparing the MT and the LXX, v. 41 in the MT seems unrelated to the rest of vv. 34–40. However, v. 41 in the LXX goes together well with vv. 34–40, because they deal with the same people, the imported nations. A diagram of the structure of vv. 34–41 of the LXX follows:

I. Summary statement: nations' deeds	34
A. Their manner as a whole	34a
B. Their manner in detail	34b
1. Fear (. . .)	34bα
2. Criteria of their doing	34bβ
II. Content of Israel's covenant with YHWH	35–40
III. Nations' ongoing syncretistic worship	41

does not read any suffix here. I regard this word as the plural form without a suffix. My translation would be, "the (former) customs."

V. 40: καὶ οὐκ ἀκούσεσθε ἐτὶ τῷ κρίματι αὐτῶν, ὃ αὐτοὶ ποιοῦσιν.

V. 40: And you [pl.] shall not listen to their practice/judgment again, which they follow.

Verse 40 of the LXX has a clearly different understanding from that of the MT. The subject of v. 40 of the LXX is "you" (pl.) which is the continuing subject in vv. 35–39. The translation of v. 40 of the LXX would be this: "Yet *you* shall not listen [obey] to their manner [judgment], which they practice." This is a part of Israel's covenant with YHWH, which is described in vv. 35–39. However, the MT reads v. 40 thus: "However, *they* would not listen, but they did according to their *former* manner." Verse 40 of the MT cannot be a part of Israel's covenant with YHWH, because it states how they (possibly Israel) responded to the covenant.

The LXX understands vv. 35–40 as a section that explains the content of Israel's covenant with YHWH. This explanatory section is necessary because v. 34 mentions the law and the commandment of YHWH that were given to the sons of Jacob, that is, Israel. Because of the benefit from obeying the law of YHWH, namely, being delivered from enemies, the nations fear YHWH even though they also served their own gods. After explaining the content of the covenant, v. 41 recapitulates what the nations do to this day: they fear YHWH and serve their gods at the same time. Therefore, if we follow the reading of the LXX, the identity of the people in vv. 34–40 is not a problem anymore. They are the sons of Jacob, the Israelites who made covenant with YHWH. They are introduced here as a historical reference because the writer wants to explain their covenant with YHWH. They do not have any relationship with the current syncretistic situation in the cities of Samaria. The writer of the LXX text speaks about those imported foreigners who feared YHWH and served their own gods in Samaria until this day in vv. 34–41 (even in vv. 24–41). This is a clearly different picture from that of MT, where the identity of the people in vv. 34–40 causes many unsolved problems for exegetes.

BIBLIOGRAPHY

Cogan, Mordechai. "Israel in Exile — the View of a Josianic Historian." *JBL* 97 (1978) 40–44.

————. "For We, Like You, Worship Your God: Three Biblical Portrayals of Samaritan Origins." *VT* 38 (1988) 286–92.

————. "Judah under Assyrian Hegemony: A Re-examination of Imperialism and Religion." *JBL* 112 (1993) 403–14.

Cogan, Mordechai, and Hayim Tadmor. *II Kings.* AB 11. Garden City, N.Y.: Doubleday, 1988.

Frevel, Christian. "Vom Schreiben Gottes: Literarkritik, Komposition und Auslegung von 2 Kön 17, 34–40." *Biblica* 72 (1991) 23–48.

Gray, John. *I and II Kings: A Commentary.* Rev. ed. OTL. Philadelphia: Westminster, 1970.

Hobbs, T. R. *2 Kings.* WBC 13. Waco, Tex.: Word, 1985.

Hoffmann, Hans-Detlef. *Reform und Reformen: Untersuchungen zu einem Grundthema der deuteronomistischen Geschichtsschreibung.* ATANT 66. Zurich: Theologischer Verlag, 1980.

Knoppers, Gary N. " 'There Was None Like Him': Incomparability in the Books of Kings." *CBQ* 54 (1992) 411–31.

————. *The Reign of Solomon and the Rise of Jeroboam.* Vol. 1 of *Two Nations under God: The Deuteronomistic History of Solomon and Dual Monarchies.* HSM 52. Atlanta: Scholars Press, 1993.

————. *The Reign of Jeroboam, the Fall of Israel, and the Reign of Josiah.* Vol. 2 of *Two Nations under God: The Deuteronomistic History of Solomon and Dual Monarchies.* HSM 53. Atlanta: Scholars Press, 1994.

Long, Burke O. *The Problem of Etiological Narrative in the Old Testament.* BZAW 108. Berlin: Verlag Alfred Töpelmann, 1968.

————. *1 Kings: With an Introduction to Historical Literature.* FOTL 9. Grand Rapids: Eerdmans, 1984.

————. "Historical Narrative and the Fictionalizing Imagination." *VT* 35 (1985) 405–16.

————. "Framing Repetitions in Biblical Historiography." *JBL* 106 (1987) 385–99.

————. *2 Kings.* FOTL 10. Grand Rapids: Eerdmans, 1991.

Talmon, Shemaryahu. "Polemics and Apology in Biblical Historiography — 2 Kings 17:24–41." In *The Creation of Sacred Literature,* ed. R. E. Friedman, pp. 57–75. Berkeley: University of California Press, 1981.

Viviano, Pauline A. "2 Kings 17: A Rhetorical and Form-Critical Analysis." *CBQ* 49 (1987) 548–59.

von Waldow, Hans Eberhard. "Israel and Her Land: Some Theological Considerations." In *A Light unto My Path: Old Testament Studies in Honor of Jacob M. Myers,* ed. H. N. Bream, R. D. Heim, and C. A. Moore, pp. 493–508. Philadelphia: Temple University Press, 1974.

Würthwein, Ernst. *Die Bücher der Könige: 1 Kön. 17–2 Kön. 25.* ATD 11/2. Göttingen: Vandenhoeck & Ruprecht, 1984.

5

Divine Action and Human Action: A Comparative Study of Deuteronomy 26:1–11 and Haggai 2:10–19

Keith L. Eades

INTRODUCTION

This essay will address two critical tasks for biblical exegesis and interpretation. First, it is vital to understand to the best of our ability not only what a text says, but also the conceptual world that was the matrix within which the text was formed and that the text addressed. Second, interpretation, especially interpretation of texts as Scripture, as the foundation for the faith and practice of a faith community, must explain the relationships among texts that may reflect differing conceptualities.[1] The importance of these tasks will be illustrated by a comparative study of Deut. 26:1–11 and Hag. 2:10–19, texts that in their own ways address the relationship of God's saving and blessing activity to Israel's actions in public worship (or cult).[2] The following discussion of Deut.

---

1. These tasks, which have always had their place in the work of Professor Rolf P. Knierim as a pastor, teacher, and scholar, have been described in programmatic ways in his recent publications. The relationship of a text to its conceptual matrix is addressed in *Text and Concept in Leviticus 1:1–9: A Case in Exegetical Method* (FAT 2; Tübingen: J. C. B. Mohr, 1992). The issue of interpreting the relationships among texts exhibiting differing conceptualities and the relationship of the differing theological concepts to be found within the OT as the task of OT theology is the subject of "The Task of Old Testament Theology" (*HBT* 6 [1984] 25–57), responses by Walter Harrelson, W. Sibley Towner, and Roland E. Murphy (*HBT* 6 [1984] 59–80), and Knierim's rejoinder "On the Task of Old Testament Theology: A Response to W. Harrelson, S. Towner, and R. E. Murphy" (*HBT* 6 [1984] 91–128). This series of essays, originally appearing in *Horizons in Biblical Theology*, has been reprinted with some modification in Knierim's *The Task of Old Testament Theology: Substance, Method, and Cases* (Grand Rapids: Eerdmans, 1995) 1–56. Citations here will be to the essays as they appear in this volume. Those who are familiar with Professor Knierim's work will recognize my indebtedness to my teacher.

2. Claus Westermann has argued that OT theology should not be a discussion of the concepts of the OT, which he argues would not do justice to the historical and theological diversity of the texts, but rather should be a discussion of the dynamic relationship between God's actions on the one hand, and those of Israel and the world on the other. He says, "If we wish to inquire concerning these broad lines determining the whole way in

26:1–11 and Hag. 2:10–19 will attempt to clarify aspects of the conceptual worlds and unwritten assumptions of these texts and to describe their differing conceptions of the relationship between divine actions and human actions.

DEUTERONOMY 26:1–11

Exegetical Discussion

The book of Deuteronomy is cast as the testament of Moses to Israel, his final speeches made in the plains of Moab before the crossing of the Jordan, speeches that were intended to instruct a new generation of Israel on the application of God's law to their future life in the land. The speeches seek to persuade that generation both to be faithful in obedience to the law themselves and to be faithful in transmitting their heritage to future generations.[3] Appended to the testament of Moses is the account of his death and burial in an unknown tomb and the evaluation of Moses as a man like no other before or since.

Deuteronomy 26:1–11 is one of two casuistically formulated laws

which the Old Testament speaks about God and yet not overlook the many forms in which it occurs, we shall therefore have to start from *verb structures*. This demands a complete change in our way of thinking. The story told in the Old Testament is then not a salvation history in the sense of a series of God's salvation events, but rather a history of God and man whose nucleus is the experience of saving" (*Elements of Old Testament Theology* [trans. D. W. Stott; Atlanta: John Knox, 1982] 10–11). Israel came to know God through his saving acts, and came to reflect upon God's blessing acts. Israel responded to God's acts in the basic forms of praise and lament (Westermann, *Elements*, 9–34). The "systematic" aspect of OT theology for Westermann is historical and descriptive. In this sense his position seems to be similar to Eichrodt's understanding of the "systematic" aspect of OT theology ("Hat die Alttestamentliche Theologie noch selbständige Bedeutung innerhalb der Alttestamentlichen Wissenschaft?" ZAW 47 [1989] 83–91; ET, "Does Old Testament Theology Still Have Independent Significance within Old Testament Scholarship," in B. C. Ollenburger, E. A. Martens, and G. F. Hasel, eds., *The Flowering of Old Testament Theology* [SBTS 1; Winona Lake, Ind.: Eisenbrauns, 1992] 30–39). Eichrodt held that questions of truth or validity belonged to systematic or dogmatic theology, not to OT studies, though he allowed that the interrelatedness of the theological disciplines might account for the interest or ability of individuals to cross the boundaries of the disciplines (pp. 38–39). For others, such as Eissfeldt ("Israelitisch-jüdische Religionsgeschichte und Alttestamentliche Theologie" ZAW 44 [1926] 1–12; ET, "The History of Israelite-Jewish Religion and Old Testament Theology," in Ollenburger, Martens, and Hasel, *Flowering*, 20–29) and Knierim ("The Task" and "On the Task"), the OT texts, especially in their diversity, demand a consideration of their claims to truth or validity.

3. The starting point for this investigation will be the Masoretic text. This is not to ignore the question of the literary history of the book of Deuteronomy or its legal traditions. Any information on the growth and development of the material, however, is gained through an encounter with the canonical text. The presence of tensions raised by features within the canonical text drive investigations of literary and tradition history, but the starting point is the canonical text.

coming at the end of the legal material in chs. 12–26.[4] Each of these
laws includes a declaration to be made by the head of the Israelite fam-

---

4. Neither the question of the relationship of this unit to the rest of the book and the
problem of the literary and tradition history of Deuteronomy nor the history of the interpretation of Deut. 26:1–11 can be treated extensively here. A. D. H. Mayes attributes Deut.
26:1–11 and 12–15 to the second Deuteronomist. He finds their present placement puzzling
because the subjects treated in these units were already dealt with in the Deuteronomic
law (14:22–29). He concludes that 26:1–15 provides a historical-theological foundation for
the ancient custom of offering firstfruits and tithes (*Deuteronomy* [NCBC; Grand Rapids:
Eerdmans, 1979] 331–32).

Gerhard von Rad saw in this text an ancient "credo" that guided the Yahwist in combining materials on various themes to give the decisive theological shaping to the traditions
of the Hexateuch in a period of Solomonic enlightenment (see "The Form-Critical Problem
of the Hexateuch," in *The Problem of the Hexateuch and Other Essays* [trans. E. W. Trueman
Dicken; London: SCM, 1984] 1–78). The articles of Leonhard Rost ("Das kleine geschichtliche Credo," in *Das kleine Credo und andere Studien zum Alten Testament* [Heidelberg: Quelle
& Meyer, 1965] 11–25); Wolfgang Richter ("Beobachtungen zur theologische Systembildung in der alttestamentlichen Literatur anhand des 'kleinen geschichtlichen Credo,'"
in *Wahrheit und Verkündigung* [FS M. Schmaus; vol. 1; Munich: Ferdinand Schöningh, 1967]
175–212); C. Carmichael ("A New View of the Origin of the Deuteronomic Credo," *VT*
19 [1969] 273–89); Norbert Lohfink ("Salvation History: The Theology, Exemplified in a
Salvation-Historical Exhibition of Recent Decades," in *Great Themes from the Old Testament*
[trans. Ronald Walls; Edinburgh: T. & T. Clark, 1982] 77–93; "Zum 'kleinen geschichtlichen
Credo' Dtn 26,5–9," *TP* 46 [1971] 19–39); R. Rendtorff ("The 'Yahwist' as Theologian? The
Dilemma of Pentateuchal Criticism," *JSOT* 3 [1977] 2–10; "Pentateuchal Studies on the
Move," *JSOT* 3 [1977] 43–45); R. N. Whybray ("Response to Professor Rendtorff," *JSOT* 3
[1977] 11–14); John van Seters ("The Yahwist as Theologian? A Response," *JSOT* 3 [1977]
15–19); Norman E. Wagner ("A Response to Professor Rolf Rendtorff," *JSOT* 3 [1977] 20–
27); George W. Coats ("The Yahwist as Theologian? A Critical Reflection," *JSOT* 3 [1977]
28–32); H. H. Schmid ("In Search of New Approaches in Pentateuchal Research," *JSOT*
3 [1977] 33–42); and R. N. Whybray's *The Making of the Pentateuch: A Methodological Study*
(JSOTSup 53; Sheffield: Sheffield Academic Press, 1987) introduce the reader to the reversal of scholarly opinion not only on the age of the credo, but also on the date of the
uniting of the themes of the Pentateuch by a Yahwist (and even on the existence of a Yahwist or a Yahwistic document). That scholarship has been in search of a new consensus is
indicated by these works and by the formation of the seminar on the "Tradition History
of the Pentateuch" in the Society of Biblical Literature in 1985.

The tendency in the works cited here is to date the pulling together of the pentateuchal
traditions to the Deuteronomic period at the earliest, which is also the same period to
which the credo is being assigned. This raises a set of questions. If the credo is considered
as an abstraction from the whole, a "canon within a canon," must we assume that there
was no guiding factor in the gathering and ordering of the pentateuchal traditions? If we
see the gathering of the traditions motivated by theological as well as historical concerns,
must we not assume that what were understood to be the central elements of theological
concern must have shaped the way the traditions were presented? If von Rad's thesis
about the antiquity of the credo must now be rejected, is it not an oversimplification to
regard the credo merely as an abstraction, without considering the manner in which a
people's understanding of themselves and their world would influence the way in which
that people would present their traditions about themselves? Can a society be imagined
that worships a god and produces literature about itself and its god without some kind of
written or unwritten credo?

The issue would seem to be rather like the question "Which came first, the chicken

ily who is to carry out the required action.[5] The structure of the laws is indicated by the outline on the following page. Part I indicates the temporal, geographical, and socioeconomic conditions presupposed for the laws requiring the offering of the firstfruits (part II, Deut. 26:2–11) and the distribution of the tithe of the third year (part III, Deut. 26:12–15).[6] Verse 1 indicates that these laws are meant to be understood as applying to the future, "When you have entered the land that the LORD your God is giving to you as an inheritance and you possess it and dwell in it."[7]

Part II (Deut. 26:2–11) instructs the worshiper about preparation for and pilgrimage to the sanctuary (v. 2) and about the actions and speeches that were to accompany the offering of the firstfruits at the sanctuary (vv. 3–11). The law describes steps that follow one after the other. The worshiper is to approach the priest and offer the appropriate recitation (v. 3). The mediating activity of the priest (v. 4) seems to be intrusive. The statement that the *priest* will set the basket containing the worshiper's offering before the *altar* of Yahweh is in tension with the instruction in v. 10b for the *worshiper*, at the conclusion of his speech, to set the offering before *Yahweh*. This tension raises the question of the literary history of the text. Might there have been an earlier form of this law, which could be reconstructed from vv. 1–3 and 10–11 and which would correspond more closely in form to the law in Deut. 26:12–15, in which the role of the priest, if any, would have been quite different?[8]

---

or the egg?" To speak either of a credo shaping traditions, or of a credo that is merely abstracted from traditions, is to oversimplify a complex relationship.

See also such works as B. S. Childs, "Deuteronomic Formulae of the Exodus Tradition," *VT* 16 (1967) 30–39; J. P. Hyatt, "Were There an Ancient Historical Credo in Israel and an Independent Sinai Tradition?" in H. T. Frank and W. L. Reed, eds., *Translating and Understanding the Old Testament* (Nashville: Abingdon, 1970) 152–70; Georg Braulik, *Sage, was du glaubst. Das älteste Credo der Bibel: Impuls in neuester Zeit* (Stuttgart: Katholisches Bibelwerk, 1979); and François Dreyfus, "L'Araméen voulait tuer mon père': l'actualisation de Dt 26,5 dans la tradition juive et dans la tradition chrétienne," in Maurice Carrez, J. Doré, and P. Grelot, eds., *De la Tôrah au Messie, études d'exégèse et d'herméneutique bibliques offertes à Henri Cazelles pour ses 25 années d'enseignement à L'institut Catholique de Paris* (Paris: Desclée, 1981) 147–61.

5. The prescribed declarations have led to the identification of these texts as "liturgical confessions" (W. S. LaSor, D. A. Hubbard, F. W. Bush, et al., *Old Testament Survey: The Message, Form, and Background of the Old Testament* [2d ed.; Grand Rapids: Eerdmans, 1996] 113).

6. This law is to be understood as expanding on the law in Deut. 14:28–29.

7. The force of these temporal clauses continues through the remainder of the law of firstfruits (Deut. 26:1–11) and the law of the tithe of the third year (Deut. 26:12–15). See the outline indicating the structure of the passage.

8. The reconstruction suggested here differs slightly from that suggested by Yoshihide Suzuki ("The 'Numeruswechsel' in Deuteronomy" [Ph.D. diss.; Claremont Graduate School, 1982] 119–20). Suzuki retains v. 4 in his reconstruction, which maintains the tension between v. 4 and v. 10. Suzuki seems to have come closer to the solution to the problem of the history of the growth of this text than most other proposals. It has been

Laws for Offering Firstfruits and the Tithe of the Third Year —
Deuteronomy 26:1–15

---

proposed by Lohfink ("Zum kleinen Credo," 22–34; "Salvation History," 81); Braulik (*Sage,* 27–35); and Mayes (333) that the first stage of the recitation to accompany the offering of the firstfruits was composed of $5a\alpha^2$ + 10a: "My father was a wandering Aramaean — but see, here I bring the first fruits of the land that you, Yahweh, have given me" (Lohfink, "Salvation History," 81).

Lohfink ("Zum kleinen Credo," 33–34) is certainly correct to call attention to the contrast between the landless ancestor and the worshiper who offers the fruit of the fields Yahweh has given him. This is an important aspect of our text (as will be seen below). However, the close relationship between the three-word sentence of v. $5a\alpha^2$ and the triadic patterning of vv. $5a\alpha$–9, which Lohfink has also seen, however, may indicate a closer connection between the two than the connection that the three-word sentence of v. 5aa2 suggested as the pattern for the composition of the remainder of vv. 5aa–9. Lohfink's conclusion that v. $5a\alpha^2$ must be considered as a preexisting unit that guided the composer of vv. 5a–9 and not also a product of the same composer is not persuasive. Besides the close connection exhibited by the literary artistry of vv. $5a\alpha^2$ and $5a\alpha$–9, the aesthetic dissimilarity between v. $5a\alpha^2$ and v. 10 must be considered. A person wishing to contrast the circumstances of the ancestor with those of the worshiper and capable of the literary artistry of v. $5a\alpha^2$ could be expected to have produced something more aesthetically pleasing than v. 10.

1 וְהָיָה֙ כִּי־תָב֣וֹא אֶל־הָאָ֔רֶץ אֲשֶׁר֙ יְהוָ֣ה אֱלֹהֶ֔יךָ נֹתֵ֥ן לְךָ֖ נַחֲלָ֣ה וִֽירִשְׁתָּ֑הּ וְיָשַׁבְתָּ֖ בָּֽהּ׃

2 וְלָקַחְתָּ֞ מֵרֵאשִׁ֣ית ׀ כָּל־פְּרִ֣י הָאֲדָמָ֗ה אֲשֶׁ֨ר תָּבִ֧יא מֵֽאַרְצְךָ֛ אֲשֶׁ֨ר יְהוָ֧ה אֱלֹהֶ֛יךָ נֹתֵ֥ן לָ֖ךְ וְשַׂמְתָּ֣ בַטֶּ֑נֶא וְהָֽלַכְתָּ֙ אֶל־הַמָּק֔וֹם אֲשֶׁ֤ר יִבְחַר֙ יְהוָ֣ה אֱלֹהֶ֔יךָ לְשַׁכֵּ֥ן שְׁמ֖וֹ שָֽׁם

3 וּבָאתָ֙ אֶל־הַכֹּהֵ֔ן אֲשֶׁ֥ר יִהְיֶ֖ה בַּיָּמִ֣ים הָהֵ֑ם וְאָמַרְתָּ֣ אֵלָ֗יו הִגַּ֤דְתִּי הַיּוֹם֙ לַיהוָ֣ה אֱלֹהֶ֔יךָ כִּי־בָ֙אתִי֙ אֶל־הָאָ֔רֶץ אֲשֶׁ֨ר נִשְׁבַּ֧ע יְהוָ֛ה לַאֲבֹתֵ֖ינוּ לָ֥תֶת לָֽנוּ׃

10 וְעַתָּ֗ה הִנֵּ֤ה הֵבֵ֙אתִי֙ אֶת־רֵאשִׁית֙ פְּרִ֣י הָאֲדָמָ֔ה אֲשֶׁר־נָתַ֥תָּה לִּ֖י יְהוָ֑ה וְהִנַּחְתּ֗וֹ לִפְנֵי֙ יְהוָ֣ה אֱלֹהֶ֔יךָ וְהִֽשְׁתַּחֲוִ֔יתָ לִפְנֵ֖י יְהוָ֥ה אֱלֹהֶֽיךָ׃

11 וְשָׂמַחְתָּ֣ בְכָל־הַטּ֗וֹב אֲשֶׁ֧ר נָֽתַן־לְךָ֛ יְהוָ֥ה אֱלֹהֶ֖יךָ וּלְבֵיתֶ֑ךָ אַתָּה֙ וְהַלֵּוִ֔י וְהַגֵּ֖ר אֲשֶׁ֥ר בְּקִרְבֶּֽךָ׃

The mediation by the priest depicted in v. 4 provides a transition to v. 5aα[1] and to the recitation of Israel's *Heilsgeschichte*, which begins the worshiper's response (vv. 5aα²–10a) and perhaps also some clues to the historical development of our text. The worshiper's response involves both declarations (v. 3b and vv. 5aα²–10a) and actions (v. 11). The worshiper's declarations concern both his past (v. 3b and vv. 5aα²–9) and his present (v. 10a).

The recitation of Israel's history and God's gracious acts toward the nation (vv. 5aα²–9) highlights God's graciousness and the goodness of Yahweh's gifts as well as Israel's utter dependence upon Yahweh. This declaration of thanksgiving has poetic features, is filled with stock phrases, and should be considered as liturgical prose. The recitation is in five "movements," in each of which Israel "moves" from a less favorable state to a state that is in some way more favorable.[9] The first movement (v. 5aα²–β) is from Canaan, where Israel (Jacob and his family) was on the verge of perishing[10] because of a famine, to Egypt (where

---

It appears much more compelling to consider an original law for offering the firstfruits in which the worshiper in his declaration connects his giving of the firstfruits with Yahweh's giving of the land. This was later expanded upon and the expansion introduced several sets of contrasts (see below).

9. Peter Craigie divides the recitation of the history of Israel into three parts: (1) Jacob in Canaan and the journey to Egypt; (2) the stay in Egypt and the exodus; and (3) the bringing of the people to the land (*The Book of Deuteronomy* [NICOT; Grand Rapids: Eerdmans, 1976] 322). Lohfink ("Salvation History," 82–83) divides it into five parts: (1) the Aramaic ancestor (v. 5); (2) journey to Egypt and becoming a nation (v. 5); (3) oppression in Egypt (v. 6); (4) lamenting and being heard in Egypt (v. 7); (5) Yahweh's redemptive act (exodus, entry, gifts of the land) (vv. 8ff.). Lohfink interprets parts 1 and 2 as preparatory in nature to the cycle of common distress, common lament, the transcending experience (Yahweh hears the cry, sees the distress), and Yahweh's saving intervention, which is seen in parts 3 through 5 ("Salvation History," 85–89; "Zum kleinen Credo," 34–39).

Lohfink also draws attention to the triadic patterning that can be seen in the three verbs in v. 5aβ–b, and three verbs in v. 6 (see "Zum kleinen Credo," 24–25). With v. 7, however, the triad is not verbal but is subordinated to the second of two verbs having Yahweh as the subject. The pattern of triads is important in the text, but the dominant structural signals appear to highlight the contrasts between differing conditions for existence.

10. The AV and RV translate אבד in the sense of "perishing," as does S. R. Driver (*A

there was grain). There is irony in this movement because while the second state was more favorable on the surface, there was potential danger. The second movement (v. 5aγ–b) is from a small family to a teeming nation (again with potential danger). The danger that was in the shadows in the first two movements comes to light in the third movement (vv. 6–7a), where the less favorable state is Israel's oppression at the hands of the Egyptians. Three verbs are used to express the Egyptian oppression. The more favorable state to which Israel moves is that of crying out to Yahweh, the God of the ancestors. In this case the improvement of Israel's lot lies under the surface. The fourth movement (v. 7b) is very closely related to the third. The third movement ends with Israel's cry to Yahweh, and the fourth begins with Yahweh's attention to Israel's cry. This is a favorable state in itself, but the recitation moves to the even more favorable state of Yahweh's active investigation. Yahweh sees Israel's affliction, trouble, and oppression. The fifth movement (vv. 8–9) is from the state of Israel's being brought out of Egypt by Yahweh's power (which again is favorable) to the even more favorable state: Israel's being brought to Canaan and given possession of the land.

In the first three movements, humans are the actors, at least on the surface. They are the subjects of the verbs. Yahweh is the subject of the verbs in the last two movements and may be assumed to have been at work behind the human actors in the first three movements.[11]

A different kind of statement follows this recitation, which would seem, on the basis of style and logic, to continue the declaration of the worshiper begun in v. 3b.[12] The "now" (ועתה) draws a contrast between the time before Israel was in possession of the land and the worshiper's socioeconomic setting as one who has "come into the land" that provided his livelihood. This declaration is addressed directly to Yahweh. (There is little tension between v. 10 and v. 3bα¹, since the declaration said to be made to the priest is made *before* Yahweh.) When the declaration is completed, the worshiper is to present the offering to Yahweh (in tension with v. 4) and prostrate himself before Yahweh. Then the

Critical and Exegetical Commentary on Deuteronomy [ICC; New York: Scribner, 1903] 289). Craigie translates it as "ailing" and preserves some of the alliteration of the original and notes that "perishing or ailing" provides the better sense. The RSV translates it as "wandering," as does Mayes, who also notes "ready to perish" as an alternative (*Deuteronomy*, 334).

11. François Dreyfus has explained that ancient Jewish and Christian interpreters understood Deut. 26:5aα² to mean "the Aramaean wanted to kill my father," and thus understood Deut. 26:5–9 to refer to two acts of divine deliverance: Yahweh had acted to deliver Israel when Israel was small, and Yahweh had acted to deliver Israel when Israel had become a great nation ("L'Araméen," 147–61).

12. See n. 8 above. G. von Rad noted the change in style between v. 9 and v. 10, and took them as belonging together in the scheme of the individual psalm of thanksgiving (*Deuteronomy: A Commentary* [OTL; Philadelphia: Westminster, 1966] 158–59).

worshiper and his family (here one sees most clearly that this text is addressed to the male head of a household), along with the Levite and the alien, are to rejoice together in the good that Yahweh has given to the worshiper and his family (v. 11).

Theological Evaluation

The laws in Deut. 26:1–11 and 12–15 operate on the basis of the qualitative contrast between the socioeconomic condition described in part I (v. 1) — the setting assumed for the laws in parts II and III — and those conditions described in the recitation of Israel's history before the settlement in the land. The text also operates on the basis of contrasts between quantitatively delimited concepts. The concept of the status of the alien is contrasted with the status of the citizen.[13] The worshiper addressed in the text is a citizen, the head of a family, a landowner, a full participant in the socioeconomic system. He plants and harvests his crops, and participates in the cult.[14]

Another contrast is between the realm of that which is possible as a result of human action and that which comes as the result of divine action. Human beings go down to Egypt, suffer oppression at the hands of other human beings, and cry out in distress; but it is Yahweh who brings them out of Egypt. Human beings can bring in the yearly harvest, but it is Yahweh who gives possession of the fertile land.

The laws requiring the bringing of the firstfruits and the third-year tithe (Deut. 26:1–15) link these cultic actions of the Israelites to the saving and blessing actions of Yahweh. The declarations prescribed for both offerings explicitly acknowledge Yahweh's gift of the land to Israel and the productivity of the land (Deut. 26:3, 8–10a, 15). The declaration required for the offering of the firstfruits includes an expression of thanksgiving that recalls the main elements of God's provision for Israel from the patriarchal period to the settlement in the land of Canaan.[15] In

---

13. Craigie also notes the differing economic status of the worshiper as compared with the resident alien or the Levite (*Book of Deuteronomy*, 322).

14. Mayes also recognizes the importance of the contrast between the status of the ancestors and that enjoyed by the worshiper for the meaning of the text (*Deuteronomy*, 333). Craigie contrasts Jacob's alien status in Egypt with the citizen status of the worshiper (*Book of Deuteronomy*, 321).

15. This text and Deut. 26:12–15 are laws requiring offerings that are to be accompanied by oral declarations. The generic nature of the declaration prescribed in this text, esp. vv. 5aα²–9, needs further discussion. Gerhard von Rad said of these verses, "The whole might be called a confession of faith, or rather an enumeration of the saving facts which were the constitutive element of the religious community" ("The Form-Critical Problem," 4–5). He went on to say, "Deut. xxvi.5ff is a creed with all the characteristics and attributes of a creed" ("The Form-Critical Problem," 5). R. Knierim calls 26:5–11 a תודה, "a statement of individual thanksgiving" ("Cosmos and History in Israel's Theology," *HBT* 3 [1981] 97–99). A personal song of thanksgiving may have the following elements:

their canonical literary context, the requirements of the laws look forward to the time when Yahweh's promise to give the land of Canaan would have been fulfilled, the climax of what Westermann would describe as the foundational saving action of Yahweh in the history of Israel. In the conceptual world of this text the requirements of these laws presuppose the blessing activity of God that Westermann would associate with the biblical theme of creation. Neither firstfruits nor tithes could be offered if the land that Yahweh had given to Israel was not productive.[16] These laws present human action in worship as a response of gratitude and praise for God's saving and blessing actions on Israel's behalf. The *Sitz im Leben* of this text (throughout its development) would have been among those groups of cultic personnel whose responsibility it was to prepare the laypeople for those aspects of cultic ritual that required specific acts or recitations. Different groups of persons might have had this responsibility at different periods in Israel's history that might correspond with those periods when new elements were added to the text.

---

1. A call to sing or give thanks
2. An account of trouble and salvation
3. Praise of Yahweh the savior
4. An announcement of sacrifice
5. A blessing upon the participants
6. Hymnic elements.

The genre of the song is understood to have originated in a *Sitz im Leben* in which individuals offered psalms of complaint when facing a specific threat, and offered psalms of thanksgiving when the threat was removed. The individual psalm of thanksgiving was bound — at least in its origin — to one specific historical moment when a threat had been removed, and not to a recurring celebration as part of the cultic calendar. See Erhard Gerstenberger, "Psalms," in John H. Hayes, ed., *Old Testament Form Criticism* (TUMSR 2; San Antonio: Trinity University Press, 1974) 200–205; and *Psalms: Part 1, with an Introduction to Cultic Poetry* (FOTL 14; Grand Rapids: Eerdmans, 1988).

The declaration in Deut. 26:5aα²–9 shares some of the formal characteristics of the personal song of thanksgiving, but in its present context is bound to the annual cultic offering of firstfruits. It may be spoken of as a personal statement of thanksgiving, a תודה, in a cautious manner, understanding that the goal of the recitation was for the worshiper to reexperience the trouble faced by his people — not only the oppression in Egypt, but the lack of the means of sustenance implied in the phrase ארמי אבד אבי (see the discussion of the text below) — and Yahweh's gracious deliverance from oppression and the gift of a fruitful land. This recitation can be compared with those accompanying the Passover Seder. It could be called haggadah.

It was von Rad's understanding of the closeness of the concepts of praise and confession that suggested the term "credo," which continues to appear in the literature (see *Old Testament Theology*, vol. 1 [trans. D. M. G. Stalker; New York: Harper & Row, 1962] 356–70).

16. See Knierim, "Cosmos and History," 59–123. However, Elmer A. Martens understands the text to recognize "Yahweh not so much as creator, but as deliverer" (*God's Design: A Focus on Old Testament Theology* [3d ed.; N. Richland Hills, Tex.: BIBAL, 1998] 135).

HAGGAI 2:10–19

Exegetical Discussion

The oracles of the prophet Haggai also relate Israel's material or socio-economic conditions to cultic actions in worship, and offer a different perspective on that relationship than was seen in Deut. 26:1–11. The difference can be clearly seen in Hag. 2:10–19. The interpretation that follows is based upon the MT.

Report of Prophetic Activity — Haggai 2:10–19

I. Introduction	10
II. Report proper	11–19
A. Commanded Torah-inquiry	11–13
1. Messenger formula	11a
2. Two Torah-inquiry cycles	11b–13
a. First cycle	11b–12
1) Command to inquire (compliance assumed)	11b–12a
2) Priests' declaration of Torah	12b
b. Second cycle	13
1) Haggai's question to the priests (command assumed)	13a
2) Priests' declaration of Torah	13b
B. Deliverance of Yahweh's words	14–19
1. Introductory formula	14aα^1
2. Yahweh's words	14aα^2–19
a. Declaration of uncleanness	14aα^2–b
b. Oracle of salvation	15–19
1) Reference to the past	15–17
a) Report of a Yahweh speech	15–17bα
(1) Call to consider	15
(2) Object for consideration	16–17bα
(a) Former condition	16
(b) Reason for condition	17a–bα
b) Oracular formula	17bβ
2) Promise for the future	18–19
a) Call to consider	18
b) Object for consideration	19
(1) The condition of the past	19a
(2) The condition of the future	19b

Haggai 2:10–19 is a report of Haggai's prophetic activity on the twenty-fourth day of the ninth month of the second year of Darius the king. This was in December 520 B.C.E. The text as we have it is the product of a tradition of editing or redacting, and the resulting tensions seen within the MT of Haggai (in addition to a critical historical in-

terest) lead many commentators to reconstruct and rearrange the text.[17] This interpretation will regard the editing and redacting efforts as purposeful and will attempt to discern the purpose of the redactors. The introductory formulae for this unit and the unit that follows (v. 10 and v. 20) clearly indicate the redactor's intention for vv. 10–19 to be seen as a unit.[18]

The report of Haggai's activity in 2:10–19 has two parts: the introduction (v. 10) and the report proper (vv. 11–13). The introduction dates the activity and shows that the major focus of his activity is the deliverance of a divine word. The report proper includes a commanded Torah-inquiry (vv. 11–13) and Haggai's delivery of Yahweh's words (vv. 14–19).

The fact that the commanded Torah-inquiry is introduced by the messenger formula and not a narrative formula illustrates a tension in the structural signals of the text and points to the importance of Yahweh's word. The commanded Torah-inquiry involves two cycles that presuppose three elements: (1) Yahweh's command that Haggai ask the priests a question, (2) Haggai's compliance with that command, and (3) the priests' answer to the question cast as a declaration of Torah. Neither cycle reports all three of the steps assumed, but these steps are clearly evident from the report of both cycles together.[19] In the first cycle Yahweh commands Haggai to ask, "If a person carries meat that is holy in the skirt of his garment, and should touch with the skirt of his garment bread, or stew, or wine, or oil, or any food, would it make it holy?" Haggai's compliance is to be assumed because the priests answer, "No!" In the second cycle, Haggai asks, "If one who is unclean

---

17. See, for example, the commentaries of Samuel Amsler, *Aggée; Zacharie 1–8* (CAT 11c; Neuchâtel and Paris: Delachaux & Niestlé, 1981) 13–42; Wilhelm Rudolph, *Haggai, Sacharja 1–8, Sacharja 9–14, Maleachi* (KAT 13/4; Gütersloh: Gütersloher Verlagshaus Gerd Mohn, 1976); and H. W. Wolff, *Dodekapropheton 6, Haggai* (BKAT 14/6; Neukirchen-Vluyn: Neukirchener, 1986); ET, *Haggai: A Commentary* (trans. Margaret Kohl; Minneapolis: Augsburg, 1988).

18. So also, B. S. Childs, *Introduction to the Old Testament as Scripture* (Philadelphia: Fortress, 1979) 467. Ralph L. Smith takes 10–14 and 15–19 together as a unit, apparently only on the basis of the dates. He says, "20:10–19 is made up of two parts which seem to be unrelated" (*Micah–Malachi* [WBC 32; Waco, Tex.: Word, 1984] 159). Hinckley G. Mitchell takes 2:10–19 as a unit in "A Critical and Exegetical Commentary on Haggai and Zechariah," in *A Critical and Exegetical Commentary on Haggai, Zechariah, Malachi and Jonah* (ICC; New York: Scribner, 1912) 66–76. David L. Petersen (*Haggai and Zechariah 1–8: A Commentary* [OTL; Philadelphia: Westminster, 1984]) follows K. Koch ("Haggais unreines Volk," *ZAW* 79 [1967] 52–66) in taking 2:10–19 as a unit. Richard Wolff also sees 2:10–19 as a unit (*The Book of Haggai: A Study Manual* [SBSO; Grand Rapids: Baker, 1967] 17). Carol Meyers and Eric Meyers (*Haggai; Zechariah 1–8* [AB 25B; Garden City, N.Y.: Doubleday, 1987] xlviii–l) take vv. 10–19 as a unit. Pieter A. Verhoef (*The Books of Haggai and Malachi* [NICOT; Grand Rapids: Eerdmans, 1987] 20–25, 110–37) also interprets 2:10–19 as a unit.

19. So also Amsler, *Aggée; Zacharie 1–8*, 36.

by reason of a corpse should touch any of these, would it become unclean?" The divine command is assumed. The priests answer, "It would be unclean!"

The remainder of the unit is to be understood as Haggai's deliverance of Yahweh's word (vv. 14–19) in response to these pronouncements of the priests (v. 14, ויען חגי ויאמר as opposed to ויאמר חגי in v. 13). "So is this people, and so is this nation before me...and so are all the works of their hands! And whatever they offer there — it is unclean!" This is Yahweh's first response to the priests' pronouncement of Torah (vv. 14aα²–b). There have been two different identifications of the "unclean nation." Some interpreters have understood this to refer to the Samaritans who wanted to assist in rebuilding the temple,[20] but the text of Haggai offers little to suggest that. The other interpretation offered is that Yahweh regarded the Judeans as unclean.[21] The uncleanness would seem to have been centered in the cult,[22] and to have spread from the cult to every other aspect of their lives.

Yahweh's second word for the people, however, is an oracle of hope (vv. 15–19). It begins with an analysis of their past conditions and the reason for those conditions (vv. 15–17). Their economic situation had been dismal because Yahweh had smitten them.[23] Yahweh had apparently hoped that the dismal economic outlook would cause the people to turn to their God, but it did not.[24] The hope for the future (vv. 18–19) is based upon the fact that something had happened. The people had laid the foundation for the rebuilding of the temple, and from that day forward, things were going to be different. It would appear to be possible to read the MT of v. 19a as, "Was the seed still in the storehouse? And even the vine and the fig tree and the pomegranate tree and the olive tree did not bear!" This reading would understand the first question to be answered in the negative. The seed had not remained in the storehouse. It had been planted. The people had done their tilling and sowing, but their harvests had been dismal. The vine,

---

20. So Rudolph (*Haggai*, 44–52) following J. W. Rothstein, *Juden und Samaritaner. Die grundlegende Scheidung von Judentum und Heidentum: Eine kritische Studie zum Buche Haggai und zur jüdischen Geschichte im ersten nachexilischen Jahrhundert* (BWANT 3; Leipzig: J. C. Hinrichs, 1908), and more recently, H. W. Wolff (*Dodekapropheton 6, Haggai*, 92–94).

21. So Amsler, *Aggée; Zacharie 1–8*, 36–39; Petersen, *Haggai and Zechariah 1–8*, 79–85; Verhoef, *Haggai and Malachi*, 118–20; Smith, *Micah–Malachi*, 161; as well as Meyers and Meyers, *Haggai; Zechariah 1–8*, 57–58.

22. Petersen's thesis that the impurity was the result of not having performed the proper cleansing ceremony (*Haggai and Zechariah 1–8*, 79–85) would support this argument.

23. Petersen notes the similarity of 2:17 with Amos 4:9. He takes 2:17 to refer to Yahweh's action against crops in the field rather than as the reason for the misfortunes discussed in v. 16, diminishing stores (*Haggai and Zechariah 1–8*, 90–93).

24. It had not worked earlier either, as Amos had reported. Cf. Petersen, *Haggai and Zechariah 1–8*, 90–93.

fig tree, pomegranate tree, and olive tree did not require planting year
after year (pruning was necessary, of course), but even these plants that
had lived year after year did not bear. The future "from this day on"
will be different because of Yahweh's promise, "I will bless you!"

Theological Evaluation

Two kinds of contrasting concepts that relate to the quality of God's
relationship to the universe can be seen in Hag. 2:10–19. The first is
the contrast between what is *holy* (קדשׁ), or set apart for Yahweh and
cultic use, and what is *unclean* (טמא), that which cannot at all be used
for the cult. The contrast thus drawn is a radical one since קדשׁ ("holy")
is usually paired with חל ("profane"), as in Lev. 10:10; 1 Sam. 21:5; and
Ezek. 22:26; 42:20; 44:23; and טמא ("unclean") is usually contrasted with
טהור ("clean"), as in Lev. 10:10; 11:47; 14:57; 20:25; Num. 19:19; Deut.
12:15, 22; 15:22; Job 14:4; Eccl. 9:2; Ezek. 22:26; 44:23.[25]

The second contrast that is drawn is between the *dismal* economic
condition associated with the crops that have been smitten by Yahweh
(vv. 16–17) and the *better* crops and economic conditions that Yahweh
promises (v. 19b).

There are also two contrasting sets of concepts that delimit the qual-
ities highlighted in the text. The first is the contrast between the *realm
of the cult*, which is indicated by the references to בשׂר־קדשׁ (v. 12),
ואשׁר יקריבו שׁם (v. 14), בהיכל יהוה (v. 15), יסד הכל־יהוה (v. 18), and the
wider realm of life, especially agriculture indicated by such terms as
כל־מאכל (v. 12), כל־מעשׂה ידיהם (v. 14), כל־מעשׂה ידיכם (v. 17), and הזרע,
הרמון, התאנה, הגפן, and עץ הזית (v. 19).
The second is the contrast between the temporal realm of the *past*
(מטרם שׁום־אבן אל־אבן בהיכל יהוה, v. 15) and that of the *future* (מן־היום הזה
ומעלה, vv. 15, 18).

In the conceptual world of this text, improper cultic activity is *uncleanness* and adversely affects every other sphere of the people's life
(their agricultural yields had been poor because Yahweh had smitten
them), but proper cultic activity is *holy* and leads to Yahweh's blessing
(which is also understood in agricultural and economic terms). This is
shown both in Yahweh's declaration of the uncleanness of the people
(v. 14aα²–b) and in the description of the turning point in the fortunes
of the people (vv. 15–19). This turning point that ends the dismal agricultural and economic situation of the *past* and marks the beginning of
Yahweh's blessing for the *future* is the day of a cultic act — the founding

---

25. Petersen's discussion of the terms is helpful (*Haggai and Zechariah 1–8*, 71–80). Modern readers must remember that "profane" as a translation for חל is imperfect because
modern conceptions of "sacred" or "holy," as opposed to "secular" or "profane," reflect a
different understanding of our world than the ancients had.

of the temple. In this text Yahweh's blessing (or smiting) is dependent upon the cultic actions of the people.[26]

In Hag. 2:10–19 Israel's proper cultic action is shown to be the necessary precondition for Yahweh's provision. The same relationship between cult and blessing is seen consistently in the book of Haggai.[27] We have come to the theological problem presented by the ex-

---

26. Klaus Koch draws attention to the prophet's understanding of the act-destiny correlation (דרך). He says, "Yahweh only intensifies with his own actions what human beings have begun. The strict correspondence here between the acts of God and the acts of man suggests that we should avoid talking about retaliation as a preeminently motivating force." He goes on to say, "Only the holy presence of God makes it possible for people to be liberated from the correlation of misdeed and calamity, which paralyses the doer of the deed, and entangles sinners more and more as time goes on; for it is the curse of the evil act that from the moment when it is committed, evil is forced to go on bringing forth evil. But the foundation stone of the temple represents the first efficacious token of the divine presence, so it can be the place of an atonement which liberates the cultic community from the guilt which clings to it and which has been imposed in the course of history (Zech. 3.9)" (The Prophets, vol. 2 [Philadelphia: Fortress, 1982] 161, 162). A similar understanding can be seen in the older work by Mitchell: "Their great fault in his [Haggai's] eyes was that they had neglected to rebuild the temple and thus prevented the return of Yahweh and the introduction of the Messianic era" (Haggai, Zechariah, Malachi, and Jonah, 68–69). Even the concept of an act-destiny correlation does not change the fact that the laying of the foundation stone, as the necessary prerequisite for Yahweh's blessing presence in the community, is a human deed. The focus of Hag. 2:10–19 is on human action as the precondition for blessing. See also Paul D. Hanson, "Haggai and Zechariah: The Hierocratic Temple Program Receives Prophetic Legitimation," in The Dawn of Apocalyptic: The Historical and Sociological Roots of Jewish Apocalyptic Eschatology (rev. ed.; Philadelphia: Fortress, 1979) 240–62. Of Haggai's message he says, "The human endeavor of rebuilding the temple becomes the condition for the arrival of the messianic kingdom" (p. 248).

27. It can be seen in the overall structure of the book. Those who see the book of Haggai as made up of four reports of prophetic speech (and/or activity) are correct (so James D. Newsome Jr., The Hebrew Prophets [Atlanta: John Knox, 1984] 160; H. W. Wolff, Dodekapropheton 6, Haggai, 17; and Verhoef, Haggai and Malachi, 39, but note below the different understanding of the structure of Haggai that Verhoef presents on pp. 20–25!). These four reports are found in 1:1–15 (the place of 1:15b is disputed), 2:1–9, 2:10–19, and 2:20–23. Neither Newsome nor H. W. Wolff explicitly discusses the relationship of these units to one another — the structure of the book of Haggai (although Wolff addresses the question of the relationship between 2:10–14 and 2:15–19 as intended by the redactor who gave the text its present shape [Dodekapropheton 6, Haggai, 67]).

Verhoef and Meyers and Meyers offer essentially the same structure for the whole book, Verhoef in the form of an outline (Haggai and Malachi, 20–25):

> A. First Section
> 1. The Command to Rebuild the Temple   1:1–11
> 2. The People's Favorable Response   1:12–15a
> B. Second Section
> 1. The Promised Glory of the New Temple   1:15b–2:9
> 2. Blessings for a Defiled People   2:10–19
> 3. Zerubbabel, the Lord's Chosen Signet Ring   2:20–23

Meyers and Meyers do not present their structure in the form of an outline, but it differs little from that presented by Verhoef. Their first section is "Restoration of the Temple (1:1–15)," which has the two subsections, "Prophetic call to work on the temple (1:1–11)" and

istence within the canon of the OT of texts with conflicting theological assumptions.

THE THEOLOGICAL PROBLEM

The goal of biblical exegesis is to allow the texts to speak for themselves. Exegesis reveals the distinct messages of texts from different authors in different times, places, and situations — messages that are not always easy to relate to one another. For Deut. 26:1–11, Israel's cultic actions are a response that presupposes Yahweh's gracious provision of the land that provides Israel's livelihood. For Hag. 2:10–19, Israel's cultic actions are the precondition for either Yahweh's smiting of the sources of Israel's livelihood or the blessing of those sources.[28] How may these two conceptions of the relationship between human action and divine action be related to one another?

In his book *The Diversity of Scripture,* Paul Hanson argues that the diversity of the voices raised and the theological understandings presented in the OT serve to enrich the life and understanding of the communities that use the Scripture as canon. The contrasting viewpoints confront us and make us think critically about our own theology. He discusses two polarities formed by contrasting viewpoints in the OT (the form/reform polarity and the visionary/pragmatic or vision/revision polarity), illustrates their function in the history of Israel,

---

"Response of leaders and people (1:12–15)." Their second section, "Oracles of Encouragement (2:1–23)," has the three subsections, "Assurance of God's presence (2:1–9)," "Priestly ruling with prophetic interpretation (2:10–19)," and "Future hope (2:20–23)" (see *Haggai; Zechariah 1–8,* xlviii–l). Their suggestions are unsatisfactory because 2:10–19 returns to the issue of the rebuilding of the temple as the necessary precondition to Yahweh's blessing.

The book of Haggai is made up of two similarly constructed parts, each beginning with a section focusing on the rebuilding of the temple as the necessary precondition for blessing, followed by a section characterized by Yahweh's message of encouragement:

Haggai

I. Two reports of prophetic activity	1:1–2:9
A. Activity focused on the rebuilding of the temple as the precondition for Yahweh's blessing	1:1–15
B. Activity focused on Yahweh's message of encouragement	2:1–9
II. Two reports of prophetic activity	2:10–23
A. Activity focused on the rebuilding of the temple as the precondition for Yahweh's blessing	2:10–19
B. Activity focused on Yahweh's message of encouragement	2:20–23

28. The addition of an explicit reference to the exodus and covenant in 2:5aα did not remove this theological problem from the book of Haggai. It raises the tension within the book itself.

and discusses how the same polarities ought to function in our own religious communities. While he thus embraces the polarities in the OT, he also relates their function to what he calls the heart of the OT message: God's ongoing work toward the goal of creation, a kingdom wedding peace (*shalom*) and righteousness. In light of this goal and God's continuing work, the *reform* and *vision* sides of the polarities are especially important, as the vision of the ultimate goal and reforms are necessary to the attainment of the goal. Hanson thus relates the diverse viewpoints represented by the polarities he discusses to the One God of the OT and God's goal for creation. He shows the diversity to be subordinate theologically to God's goal for creation. He says, "It is of course clear that not every symbol will be appropriate to every situation. But our basis for choice at least should reach beyond our narrow self-interests to a sense of God's purpose embracing broadly all of creation."[29]

In his book *Theological Diversity and the Authority of the Old Testament,* John Goldingay classifies four types of "contradictions" with which interpreters must cope: formal, contextual, substantive, and fundamental. Formal contradictions involve differences at the level of words, but not at the level of meaning. He argues that the OT's assertions that God repents or changes his mind and that God does not change his mind (both of which can be found in 1 Samuel 15) work together to demonstrate the nature of God's interaction with real people. To illustrate contextual contradictions, Goldingay points to the contrasting messages about Jerusalem given by Isaiah in the eighth century and by Jeremiah in the sixth. The messages were different because the situations were different. The completely differing theological assumptions of Elijah and the worshipers of Ba'al, or between Jeremiah and the Judeans who were devoted to the Queen of Heaven, are examples of what Goldingay terms fundamental contradictions. Perhaps the most difficult type of contradiction Goldingay discusses is the substantial contradiction. This is seen in texts that may be contemporary, but express radically different understandings of God's message to the people, such as the contrasting views of Israel's relationship to the nations in Ezra and Nehemiah on the one hand and in Jonah and Ruth on the other.[30] He discusses and illustrates three approaches to the diverse texts and concepts of the OT. His first approach seeks to understand the diverse concepts on the basis of their historical contexts,[31] and he illustrates this with a discus-

---

29. Paul D. Hanson, *The Diversity of Scripture: A Theological Interpretation* (OBT 11; Philadelphia: Fortress, 1982) 102.

30. John Goldingay, *Theological Diversity and the Authority of the Old Testament* (Grand Rapids: Eerdmans, 1987) 15–25.

31. Goldingay, *Theological Diversity,* 29–58.

sion of the Bible's varying conceptions of what it means to be the people of God.[32] He notes that certain contexts allow a given concept to attain a deeper expression than other contexts, and describes an evaluative approach that would place the differing conceptions on a scale from those that reflect God's word more clearly to those that reflect it less clearly.[33] He illustrates this approach with a discussion of the teaching of Deuteronomy.[34] The third approach he discusses he calls a unifying or constructive approach, which interrelates concepts without involving judgments about what is foundational and what is subordinate.[35] He illustrates this approach by discussing the themes of creation and salvation in the OT.[36] Goldingay's book is a valuable contribution to the discussion of the contrasting and conflicting theological concepts found in the OT. Goldingay's stress on looking for the positive contribution of concepts that may be considered as less reflective of God's word than others is welcome; however, if all three approaches are used — as he seems to suggest they should be — it is not certain whether the interpreter finally is to make evaluative judgments or resist evaluating the differing concepts.

Understanding the interrelationship of such "contradictions" or "theologies" within the OT is the essential task of OT theology for Rolf Knierim, who says that OT theology is to be "concerned with criteria by which the various theologies can be correlated in terms of theological priorities, including the ultimate priority governing all others. . . . Under theological priorities discerned from within the Old Testament, it systematizes the plurality of theologies analyzed by exegesis, summarily described in the conclusions of or appendices to exegetical works, and provides the criteria for the accountability of what ought to be confessed."[37] As criteria for systematizing the theologies of the OT, Knierim proposes the "universal dominion of Yahweh" as the ultimate quantitative expression of the extent of Yahweh's relationship to reality, and "justice and righteousness" as the ultimate OT expression of the quality of God's relationship to the universe.[38] Knierim argues that every interpreter, every pastor, every Bible reader, operates on the basis of a "canon within the canon," whether consciously or not, and that this "canon within the canon" should become the subject of critical reflec-

---

32. Goldingay, *Theological Diversity*, 59–96.
33. Goldingay, *Theological Diversity*, 97–133.
34. Goldingay, *Theological Diversity*, 134–66.
35. Goldingay, *Theological Diversity*, 167–99.
36. Goldingay, *Theological Diversity*, 200–239.
37. "The Task of Old Testament Theology," 17–18.
38. "The Task of Old Testament Theology," 10–15.

tion. This involves determining the concepts that are foundational and relating the other different or conflicting concepts to them.[39]

CONCLUSION

Certainly the OT affirms that Yahweh responds to human action; but would not an understanding of Yahweh as the creator of the universe, and human beings as created beings, imply an understanding that divine action is foundational and humans respond to it? If so, Deut. 26:1–11 would represent a more foundational understanding of the relationship of divine action and human action than Hag. 2:10–19.

This is not to conclude that Hag. 2:10–19 has nothing to say that would be of theological value. Haggai's use of the concept "holy" would certainly point to the distinction between God and humans, and the text does point to the human relationship with God and to the demand for the "holiness" of human actions as matters of concern. With regard to the way human action or worship is related to divine blessing and provision for life, however, Haggai's message would have to be interpreted in light of the more foundational message of Deut. 26:1–11. It should also be noted that although Deut. 26:1–11 witnesses to the foundational nature of God's gracious provision, the text is patriarchal and perhaps nationalistic, and that the kind of theological tension or contrast seen between Deut. 26:1–11 and Hag. 2:10–19 could also be seen if one compares Deut. 26:1–11 with Deuteronomy 28.[40]

One might even assume that if pressed to reflect on the matter somewhat differently, Haggai and his redactors would no doubt say, "Of course even proper cultic action itself is dependent upon and responds to Yahweh! We know that!"[41] The first step in our understanding of the text, however, must be to determine what it actually says and not what it should say or what it "means." The prophet could have used other approaches to motivate the people to rebuild the temple. The answer to the people's objection that the time to rebuild the temple had not yet

---

39. See Knierim, "The Task," 16 n. 14; the responses of Harrelson, Towner, and Murphy (*HBT* 6 [1984] 59–80); and Knierim's reply, "On the Task," 44–45.

40. See von Rad, *Old Testament Theology*, 1:230; Ralph L. Smith, *Old Testament Theology: Its History, Method, and Message* (Nashville: Broadman and Holman, 1993) 126–27.

41. So H. W. Wolff's comment, "The conditions for the change are worthy of note. At first sight, human decision is determinative — the decision on this day 'to place stone to stone on Yahweh's temple' (2:15b; cf. 18bb). Without a particular human act, nothing would change. But this act is an act of obedience to the prophetic demand (1:8a), and springs from the divine influence on human will (1:12–14). The obedience is a festal act rather than a human achievement. So it is not the act as such that brings about the new era: it is the recognition of God's judgment (1:9–11) and trust in God's promise (1:8b)" (67).

come (Hag. 1:2) presupposes God's blessing action to provide for the fertility of the land. Even though economic conditions had not been the best, some progress had been made toward the renewal of Jerusalem and the surrounding area. The prophet might have said, "God has blessed you with paneled houses! Are these ruins an appropriate response to God's blessings?"[42] The prophet did not say that. The paneled houses of the people are not described as the result of Yahweh's provision, but of the people's concern for their own houses. Speaking for Yahweh, Haggai condemned the people and commanded them to rebuild the temple, and it is not until after the text reports that the leaders and the people obeyed and feared the Lord that it reports that the prophet brought this word from the Lord: "I am with you" (Hag. 1:13).[43]

In his message of encouragement to the leaders of the people on the twenty-first day of the seventh month, Haggai used that phrase אני אתכם again (2:4bα). This would connect with the participial clause ורוחי עמדת בתוככם in v. 2:5aβ, if it were not for the awkward construction את־הדבר אשר־כרתי אתכם בצאתכם ממצרים in 2:5aα. This is obviously a reference to the exodus and the covenant at Sinai, and is widely considered to be a gloss.[44] But what was the reason for the gloss? Was it the random comment of a tradent who heard an echo of the covenant language in vv. 4–5, or did a tradent who was disturbed by the surface implication of Haggai — that proper cultic response would guarantee God's blessing — want to make explicit what was at best only implicit, and to put the demand of Haggai for proper cultic action in the context of a covenant that presupposed Yahweh's blessing? Did the theological assumptions of the book of Haggai need to be brought into line with theological assumptions more like those seen in Deut. 26:1–11?

For the interpreter's task to be complete, both of these texts would have to be related to the other theological concepts from the biblical tradition and from the heritage of the interpreter's community of faith. We cannot extensively explore the relationship of the theological concepts of these texts to all the theological concepts of the biblical tradition and

---

42. Cf. 2 Sam. 7:1–3.

43. Gerhard von Rad says that Haggai's message, with its implication that "the rebuilding of the Temple is actually the necessary precondition of Jahweh's advent and of his kingdom," must be understood in relation to a "completely different spiritual condition of the people" than that faced by the earlier prophets (*Old Testament Theology*, vol. 2 [trans. D. M. G. Stalker; New York: Harper & Row, 1965] 281). I have tried to show that Haggai could have argued in a different way than he did. The difference was not just in the spiritual attitude of the people. It was also in the theological assumptions of the prophet and the redactors of his book.

44. So, for example, Joyce G. Baldwin, *Haggai, Zechariah, Malachi: An Introduction and Commentary* (TOTC; London: Inter-Varsity, 1974) 47; Petersen, *Haggai and Zechariah 1–8*, 66; Smith, *Micah–Malachi*, 156; Amsler, *Aggée; Zacharie 1–8*, 32; Rudolph, *Haggai*, 40.

the heritage of either the church or the synagogue, but some proposals for the hermeneutical appropriation of these texts can be offered.[45]

Deuteronomy 26:1–11 is addressed to individual members of a privileged group of people. It is a law requiring the offering — in an appropriate manner — of part of the bounty with which the individual has been blessed. While making the offering, the individual is to recite a declaration that recalls both the nature of the blessings received from Yahweh, and the conditions of economic and sociopolitical deprivation and oppression suffered by the forebears of the worshiper (with whom the worshiper identifies) before they experienced Yahweh's liberation and blessing provision. In making the offering, the worshiper is to make it possible for others — persons who do not share his privileged position — to join in rejoicing in Yahweh's blessings. This text, read in the context of the Judeo-Christian tradition, would point to the obligation of privileged persons (1) to remember their own dependence upon God's grace and provision, (2) to identify themselves with those persons who are not privileged, (3) to seek the removal of structures that deprive and oppress some people while granting privilege to others, and (4) to seek the establishment of a just order in the world in which all persons have the opportunity to fulfill their potential. The text would indicate that the goals to be sought (3 and 4) require human participation and cooperation in God's liberating and blessing actions.

Haggai 2:10–19[46] reports a prophetic confrontation with a group of people who have experienced disappointment in the economic and sociopolitical realms, but who are nevertheless considered to be capable of acting in their own interests. The prophet uses an accepted understanding of the difference between what is acceptable as an offering to God and what is utterly unacceptable to demonstrate the unacceptability of a lifestyle that forgets one's obligation to remember God's blessing and respond properly. The prophet promises that a brighter future will be the result of the changed lifestyle of the people, demonstrated in their proper cultic action. All human religious action ought to be understood as a response to the experience of God's action. This text points to the obligation of those who have experienced God's grace to respond in a way that takes cognizance of God's grace and God's holiness.

---

45. For another hermeneutical appropriation of Deut. 26:5–9, see Braulik, *Sage.*

46. The text will be interpreted here in light of the more fundamental, or foundational, understanding of the relationship between God's actions and human religious actions provided by Deut. 26:1–11.

Selected Bibliography

Campbell, Antony F., S.J. "Structure Analysis and the Art of Exegesis." In *Problems in Biblical Theology: Essays in Honor of Rolf P. Knierim*, ed. Henry T. C. Sun, Keith L. Eades, James M. Robinson, and Garth I. Moller, pp. 76–103. Grand Rapids: Eerdmans, 1997.

Goldingay, John. *Models for Interpretation of Scripture*. Grand Rapids: Eerdmans; Carlisle: Paternoster, 1995.

————. *Theological Diversity and the Authority of the Old Testament*. Grand Rapids: Eerdmans, 1987.

Hanson, Paul D. *The Diversity of Scripture: A Theological Interpretation*. OBT 11. Philadelphia: Fortress, 1982.

Knierim, Rolf P. *The Task of Old Testament Theology: Substance, Methods, and Cases*. Grand Rapids: Eerdmans, 1995.

————. *Text and Concept in Leviticus 1:1–9: A Case in Exegetical Method*. FAT 2. Tübingen: J. C. B. Mohr, 1992.

Martens, Elmer A. *God's Design: A Focus on Old Testament Theology*. 3d ed. N. Richland Hills, Tex.: BIBAL, 1998.

Mayes, A. D. H. *Deuteronomy*. NCBC. Grand Rapids: Eerdmans, 1979.

Meyers, Carol, and Eric Meyers. *Haggai, Zechariah 1–8*. AB 25B. Garden City, N.Y.: Doubleday, 1987.

Petersen, David L. *Haggai and Zechariah 1–8: A Commentary*. OTL. Philadelphia: Westminster, 1984.

Rost, Leonhard. "Das kleine geschichtliche Credo." In *Das kleine Credo und andere Studien zum Alten Testament*. Heidelberg: Quelle & Meyer, 1965.

von Rad, Gerhard. "The Form-Critical Problem of the Hexateuch." In *The Problem of the Hexateuch and Other Essays*. Trans. E. W. Trueman Dicken. London: SCM, 1984.

Westermann, Claus. *Elements of Old Testament Theology*. Trans. D. W. Stott. Atlanta: John Knox, 1982.

Wolff, H. W. *Dodekapropheton 6: Haggai*. BKAT 14/6. Neukirchen-Vluyn: Neukirchener, 1986. ET *Haggai: A Commentary*. Trans. Margaret Kohl. Minneapolis: Augsburg, 1988.

6

Leviticus 15:
Contrasting Conceptual Associations
Regarding Women
Deborah Ellens

INTRODUCTION

Two sets of contrasting conceptual associations comprise the author's conceptualization of women in Leviticus 15, where the primary concern is the mediation of the impurity of the genital discharges of both men and women.

The first set of conceptual associations is suggested by point of view, language depicting the sex act, and a single vocabulary word signifying the menstruant at the end of the chapter. These features suggest a concept of woman as marginalized, objectified, and periodically unhealthy. Her agency is curtailed and her normal menstrual flow is associated with illness. The same features in Leviticus 15 suggest a concept of man as central, subject, and never unhealthy on account of his normal seminal emissions.

A second set of conceptual associations is suggested by the structure of Leviticus 15, that is to say, the larger organizing principles operative in the chapter. The structure pictures the woman equal to the man. She, a member of the community like the man, is as responsible as he for maintaining the laws of purity with respect to genital discharge. Her status as agent in this respect is equivalent to his. In addition, mediation of impurity caused by her genital discharge is equivalent, in its significance, to mediation of impurity caused by his genital discharge. Likewise, jeopardy of her purity by genital discharge from the man or from herself is equivalent to jeopardy of his purity by the same. In this way, her flow is typologically equivalent to his.

Thus, contrasting, if not opposing, conceptual associations comprise the author's conceptualization of women in Leviticus 15.

This essay is a revision of a portion of my dissertation, "A Comparison of the Conceptualization of Women in the Sex Laws of Leviticus and in the Sex Laws of Deuteronomy" (Ph.D. diss., Claremont Graduate University, 1998).

DISCUSSION

The First Set of Conceptual Associations

Point of View

The point of view of Leviticus 15 is apparent in the first verse of the chapter. YHWH instructs Moses and Aaron to address בני ישראל, a male collective. Thus, the first two groups of laws begin respectively with איש איש (v. 2b) and ואיש (v. 16). However, the next two groups of laws begin with ואשה (vv. 19 and 25). These latter two groups of laws pertain to the uncleanness derived from the bodily emissions of women. Explicit reference to the man in these two groups of laws occurs only in v. 24. The emphasis on the man, created by his appearance as the initial character in that verse, is mitigated by two factors: (1) his explicit appearance elsewhere in the two units is nonexistent; and (2) v. 24 is merely the final rule in a section emphasizing and pertaining to women.

The content of these latter two groups of laws in vv. 19–30 and the absence in the chapter as a whole of a male character who relays the information of vv. 19–30 to the woman suggest that בני ישראל addresses a male collective in the midst of which stand women who are also listening to Moses and Aaron. Nevertheless, the men are the ones named. They are the ones to whom the narrator/author speaks explicitly. Women are only implicit addressees. As such, they are marginalized to the background.

Another feature in the text perhaps related to point of view supports this marginalization. Although the author inserts no explicit male character between Moses and the woman in order to mediate her instruction, mediation is apparent in the ritual for presentation of offerings. Men bring their offering to YHWH at the door of the tent of meeting, while women bring it to the priest at the door of the tent of meeting. Men and women bring the same offering; both go to the "door of the tent of meeting"; and the priest propitiates לפני יהוה on behalf of both of them. Nevertheless, the man approaches YHWH and the woman does not.

Thus, point of view in Leviticus 15 marginalizes woman.

Language Depicting the Sex Act

The language depicting the sex act in Leviticus 15 offers an even more pronounced denigration. It consistently places the man in the dominant position as subject. The woman is always object. In vv. 18 and 24 she is the direct object. In v. 33b she is the object of a preposition. In the sex act she is never initiator, never actor. She is only the receptor of the man's actions.

Furthermore, the description of the sex act is designated by a function that occurs with respect to the male body (שכבת־זרע) and not with respect to anything specific to the female body. In v. 18 this subject/object polarity is mitigated somewhat by the emphasis of the proleptic referent. Nevertheless, the objectification of woman created by language depicting the sex act is pronounced.

In fact, her grammatical placement in the chapter as a whole is consonant with her placement in the sex verses (vv. 18, 24, 33b) where the sex act is depicted. In the chapter as a whole, she is subject only with respect to inanimate objects and with respect to remediation of her own impurity.

Thus, language depicting the sex act in Leviticus 15 objectifies woman.

Vocabulary Signifying the Menstruant: דוה

The use of דוה to signify the menstruant in v. 33 coincides with the denigrating impulses of point of view and language depicting the sex-act. דוה polarizes the genital discharge, since the use of similar vocabulary signifying the man's discharge is absent from the chapter.

דוה is used only once in Leviticus 15, in the summary. Both the cognate associations of דוה and its metaphorical and literal applications in other parts of the Hebrew corpus[1] seem to suggest the connection of menstruation with illness.

Milgrom emphasizes the illness connection by way of the cognate associations of דוה in Lev. 15:33:

> her . . . infirmity (děwōtāh). An infinitive construct — not a plural noun — of the verb dāwâ (Lam 5:17; Keter Torah), which also appears as an adjective, dāweh (15:33; 20:18), dawwāy (Isa 1:5; Jer 8:18) and as a noun, děwāy (Ps 41:4), dāwâ (Isa 30:22), a menstruous garment (cf. b. Nid. 9a), and madweh (Deut 7:15; 28:60). The cognates, Akk. dawû "be sick, stagger" (AHw) and Ug. dwy "sickness" (KTU 1.16 — CTA 16.6 [127] 35, 51) conform to and confirm the contextual connotation of the biblical root "be sick, infirm." Interestingly, in Hittite, "the linguistic form of the word for moon, arma- is not only associated with conception, pregnancy, and menstruation but also with weakness and sickness" (Moyer 1969: 70). Thus philology confirms experience: menstruation is associated with sickness. Hence, niddâ and dāwâ are related.[2]

Milgrom states that the expression using דוה in Lev. 15:33 is an idiom borrowed from Lev. 12:2, where the impurity of birth is mediated.[3]

---

1. Deut. 7:15; 28:60; Isa. 1:5; 30:22; Jer. 8:18; Ps. 41:4; Job 6:7; Lam. 1:13, 22; 5:17.
2. Jacob Milgrom, Leviticus 1–16 (AB 3; New York: Doubleday, 1991) 745–46.
3. Milgrom, Leviticus, 947.

While the illness connection is not conclusive in Leviticus 12 or Leviticus 15 by themselves, it is clearly apparent in other instances within the Hebrew corpus. Lamentations 5:17 states that, on account of our sins, "our heart has become דוה; our eyes have grown dim," a parallelism aligning דוה with a bodily weakness, loss of eyesight. Ps. 41:4 establishes a parallel between דוי and illness (חלי), as does Isa. 1:5. מדוה is used twice in Deuteronomy (Deut. 7:15; 28:60) to refer to the diseases of Egypt. Other occurrences of the root, lacking such clear-cut signification of illness, nevertheless refer to something negative in association with things like desolation (Lam. 1:13), defilement and scattering (Isa. 30:22), tasteless food (Job 6:7), a desperate future on account of past sins (Jer. 8:18), and despair on account of past rebellion (Lam. 1:22). At most, the illness association and, at least, the negative association of דוה are difficult to avoid.

The lack of such associations with normal seminal emission suggests that woman's impurity from genital discharge is tied to her gender, whereas the corresponding impurity for man is not. Milgrom suggests that the expression הדוה בנדתה is used instead of נדתה in v. 33 so as to distinguish the woman's "menstrual infirmity from the other genital infirmities she experiences, as a parturient (ch. 12) and as a zābâ (ch. 15)."[4] Such may be the case. The fact remains that a word associated with illness was selected to describe the woman's normal condition and no such word was selected to describe the man's normal condition.

Perhaps the illness association reflects the real experience of many women at menses.[5] Nevertheless, such association, regardless of its source, brands the woman's normal genital discharge as necessarily unhealthy and perhaps, therefore, dangerous, as compared to the man's genital discharge.

Thus, vocabulary signifying the menstruant in Leviticus 15 qualifies woman's discharge negatively in comparison to the man's discharge.

Summary

This negative qualification of the woman's genital discharge, along with her marginalization and objectification, by way of point of view and language depicting the sex act, make the statement presented by the

---

4. Milgrom, *Leviticus*, 746.
5. See Penelope Shuttle and Peter Redgrove, *The Wise Wound* (New York: Grove Press, 1978) 41–42. Whether or not this experience is shaped by, derives from, or is a function of gender bias inherent in and reaching across a variety of cultures, including that of ancient Israel, rather than hormonal or other bodily changes is a question outside the purview of this essay. See also Karen E. Paige, "Women Learn to Sing the Menstrual Blues," *Psychology Today* (September 1973) 41–46.

organizing principles of the chapter, that is, the structure, all the more stunning.

The Second Set of Conceptual Associations

Milgrom states categorically that "menstruation is associated with sickness."[6] However, he also states categorically that "menstruation is a normal condition and is, therefore, not to be compared with abnormal genital discharges (vv. 13–15, 28–30)."[7] These two statements taken together may seem contradictory, but in fact they are the truth of the text. The author uses a vocabulary word signifying the menstruant that reflects one set of conceptual associations. He organizes his text to reflect another.

Structure

The structure of the text, which pairs seminal emission with menstrual flow, vis-à-vis the category of anomalous flow, makes a conceptual statement that diverges from the conceptual effects of point of view, language depicting the sex act, and vocabulary signifying the menstruant. Seminal emission is a normal condition decidedly not associated with illness. So also, according to the structure, is menstruation.

The macrostructure of Leviticus 15 is shown in the chart on the following page.

The conditionals introducing each of the four major sections of the "Main Body of Speech," which contains the bulk of the author's discussion, are as follows:

1. A man: if his flow is flowing from his flesh

2. A man: if an emission of semen goes out from him

3. A woman: if she is flowing, blood is her flow from her flesh

4. A woman: if a flow of her blood is flowing

Each conditional identifies the topic of its respective section, one of four kinds of genital flow. Each section treats the mediation of the impurity of its particular flow. The "Summary," underscoring the same concern, begins with an adjuration to separate the Israelites from their uncleanness and then states, "This is the law of the one flowing...." Thus the chapter, structured according to a taxonomy of genital flows, instructs the reader in the science of the mediation of the impurity of

---

6. Milgrom, *Leviticus*, 746.

7. Milgrom, *Leviticus*, 935. See also Baruch A. Levine, *Leviticus* (Philadelphia: Jewish Publication Society, 1989) 92. Julius Preuss notes, "The *zaba*, or woman with a flux, is fundamentally different from the normal menstruating woman" (*Biblical and Talmudic Medicine* [trans. and ed. Fred Rosner; New York: Sanhedrin Press, 1978] 375).

---

8. The organizing structural signals used for this structure follow the precedent set by the Forms of the Old Testament Literature (FOTL) commentary series, edited by Rolf P. Knierim and Gene M. Tucker, published by Eerdmans.

these flows. In each case the intent is to "map" the way from impurity of genital flow to purity for the sake of the individual and the
community.

Two of the four major sections conclude with one of the three sex
verses (vv. 18, 24, 33b) in the chapter. Verse 18, a conditional signaled
by אִישׁ, and v. 24, a conditional signaled by אִם, conclude the men's and
women's nonanomalous sections respectively. The third verse, 33b, concludes the summary of the entire chapter. The placement of 18 and 24,
each at the conclusion of the nonanomalous sections, supports the chapter's structural symmetry. Even the placement of 33b, in the summary
rather than in the main body of the speech, may be a deliberate attempt
by the author/redactor to protect the symmetry, gender or structural,
of the chapter.[9] The four major sections, within which the sex verses are
strategically placed, fall into two larger divisions, which constitute the
main body of the YHWH speech. These larger divisions divide according
to gender. Thus, structural symmetry constitutes gender symmetry.

The first larger division concerns male genital discharge, and the
second, female genital discharge.[10] The two divisions each consist of
an anomalous and a nonanomalous subunit. Altogether, these are the
four major sections. Each anomalous section divides into two units: one
concerning purity, the other impurity. The anomalous/nonanomalous
subunits of the divisions are reversed from one another, producing a
chiasm of the form ABBA.

These two divisions are, thus, schematic reverse images. These structural correspondences between the male and female sections are the
most apparent indication of gender symmetry with respect to purity.
They suggest that the concerns and categories addressed for both sections, and therefore for both genders, are the same.[11] Differences that

---

9. See Judith Romney Wegner, *Chattel or Person* (New York: Oxford University Press,
1988) 165. A failure to understand the nature and placement of v. 33b gives rise to statements similar to the following statement from Wegner: "Scripture applies the rules of
contamination to '*anyone, male or female, who has a discharge, and* also the man who lies
with a cultically unclean woman' (Lev. 15:33, emphasis added). A woman who has intercourse with a cultically unclean man is not mentioned because the only pollution that
matters is contamination of male by female. Mishnah, following Scripture, worries about
woman's cultic purity only as it affects their male contacts. The woman is a polluting *object*, the man is a *person*." In fact, this statement reveals a misunderstanding of the nature
of v. 33b, its place in the structure and the structure as a whole. See the discussion below.

10. See Karl Elliger, *Leviticus* (HAT 1/4; Tübingen: J. C. B. Mohr, 1966) 192–93; Walter
Kornfeld, *Levitikus* (Würzburg: Echter Verlag, 1983) 59–62; Levine, *Leviticus,* 93–98; Mil-
grom, *Leviticus,* 904; Martin Noth, *Leviticus* (OTL; Philadelphia: Westminster, 1977) 113;
Gordon J. Wenham, *Leviticus* (NICOT; Grand Rapids: Eerdmans, 1979) 216.

11. The following scholars make similar statements: Howard Eilberg-Schwartz, *The
Savage in Judaism* (Bloomington: Indiana University Press, 1990) 181; Lawrence A. Hoffman, *Covenant of Blood* (Chicago: University of Chicago Press, 1996) 148; Shaye J. D. Cohen,

do occur between the two divisions are a function of gender-neutral factors.[12]

The Sex Verses

A close reading of the three sex verses (vv. 18, 24, 33b) supports these assertions. Cross-gender contamination is particularly acute during sexual intercourse. The three sex verses are, therefore, especially revealing for the conceptualization of women in the chapter. Analysis of their content and their placement in the chapter is key to understanding the author's organizing principles, his primary concern, and by extension, therefore, his second set of conceptual associations regarding women.

Verse 18. The structure of v. 18 can be understood in at least one of two ways. The first possibility is that אשר is a conjunction translated "if"[13] and אשה is a *casus pendens* construction as well as the proleptic referent to the accusative pronominal suffix. The second possibility is that אשר is a relative and אשה is again the proleptic referent to the accusative pronominal suffix. In this case, all of 18a is the *casus pendens* construction.[14] Either way, the verse is a conditional.

With neither of these two possibilities is the woman, as Milgrom suggests, the grammatical subject of the verse.[15] In 18a the subject is the man not the woman. In 18b the verbs designate the plural subject. Undeniably, as proleptic referent, the woman receives special emphasis. But she is not the subject of 18a, and *she alone* is not the subject of 18b. Both the man and the woman become unclean during intercourse. Both are unclean only until evening. And both must cleanse. The content and syntax as well as the structure of the verse demonstrate that, with respect to purity issues related to sexual intercourse, the author treats the man and woman equally.[16]

"Menstruants and the Sacred in Judaism and Christianity," in Sarah B. Pomeroy, ed., *Women's History and Ancient History* (Chapel Hill: University of North Carolina Press, 1991) 276, see also 291.

12. See the discussion below.

13. See Richard Whitekettle, "Leviticus 15.18 Reconsidered: Chiasm, Spatial Structure and the Body," *JSOT* 49 (1991) 35.

14. אשה might be understood as a *casus pendens* within a *casus pendens*. See Bruce K. Waltke and M. O'Connor, *An Introduction to Biblical Hebrew Syntax* (Winona Lake, Ind.: Eisenbrauns, 1990) 76–77, no. 5. See Waltke and O'Connor for the function of a relative in connection with a *casus pendens* construction.

15. Milgrom, *Leviticus*, 930. Whitekettle writes, "The word *'ašer* is of course most commonly read as a relative pronoun. This reading, however, would indicate that the subject of the verse is the woman, a reading ruled out by the plural subject of the verse's apodosis" ("Leviticus," 35). While Whitekettle is correct when he says that woman is not the subject, his latter description is inaccurate. אשה is a *casus pendens* construction related to a resumptive pronoun in the accusative case whether or not אשר is a relative or a conjunction (see Waltke and O'Connor, *Biblical Hebrew*, 76–77, no. 5).

16. Several scholars have recently posited that the menstrual taboo exemplified in the

Verse 24. Verse 24 is a conditional, as well, signaled by אִם. The protasis consists of two situations, which must be true for the circumstances
of the apodosis to take place. First, the man must lie with the woman.
Second, "her impurity" must be upon him.[17] The apodosis, which begins at 24aγ,[18] describes the extent of the impurity and also consists
of two parts. The first part states the duration of the man's impurity.
The second part describes the contagious effects of his impurity. Like in
v. 18, the man is the subject and the woman is the object. Unlike in v. 18,
the woman appears only in the pronominal suffix. While mediation of
her impurity is noticeably absent in v. 24, vv. 19–23 address that issue in
detail. Since the impurity of menstruation is more severe than the impurity of simple intercourse, the stipulations of vv. 19–23 are more than

---

Bible is ultimately responsible for the subsequent isolation of women and their exclusion
from religious practice in Judaism: Léonie J. Archer, "Bound by Blood: Circumcision and
Menstrual Taboo in Post-Exilic Judaism," in Janet Martin Soskice, ed., *After Eve: Women,
Theology and the Christian Traditions* (London: Marshall Pickering, 1990) 45; idem, "The Role
of Jewish Women in the Religion, Ritual and Cult of Graeco-Roman Palestine," in Aviril
Cameron and Amélie Kuhrt, eds., *Images of Women in Antiquity* (Detroit: Wayne State University Press, 1983) 275; Cohen, "Menstruants," 273–99; Eilberg-Schwartz, *The Savage,* 171,
177–94; Hoffman, *Covenant,* 146–54, 171–72, 190–91; Wegner, *Chattel,* 162–66. Such developments in connection with the menstrual taboo are outside the bounds of this essay.
This development, as well as the broader implications of fluid symbolism, as described by
people like Eilberg-Schwartz and Hoffman, does not define the conceptuality of Leviticus
15. Leviticus 15, in fact, does not exhibit this isolation and exclusion. Rather, it demonstrates considerable equity in the treatment of men and women with respect to the
purity issues of concern, as even scholars like Eilberg-Schwartz and Hoffman recognize
(Eilberg-Schwartz, *The Savage,* 147; Hoffman, *Covenant,* 181–82).

17. Milgrom, *Leviticus,* 940. See Milgrom's discussion of the possibilities for deciding
whether v. 24 refers to the deliberate act of copulating with a menstruant or whether it
refers to a situation of happenstance.

18. Milgrom, *Leviticus,* 940–41. Milgrom maintains that clause 24aβ is also part of the
apodosis. He writes concerning 24aβ, "But as part of the protasis this clause should begin
wĕhāyĕtâ; MT's *ûtĕhî* rather indicates a consequence, hence it belongs with the apodosis"
(p. 941). In addition, Milgrom states that since the antecedent of אֹתָהּ is the menstruating
woman, the blood flow is not something that happened accidentally during intercourse.
Intercourse, in the context of menstruation, is intentional. Thus, "her impurity upon him"
is not one of the contingencies of the protasis. Rather, it is one of the sure results of
the case. Therefore, it is a consequence. Thus, 24aβ is part of the apodosis. Milgrom's
error is in assuming that the protasis of such a conditional will not have within it one
situation (i.e., "her impurity is upon him") that is a certain and sure consequence of a
prior situation described in the same protasis (i.e., "a man lies with a mensturant"). Such
a "consequence," according to Milgrom, can only be in the apodosis. But, in fact, the
author might include such a consequence in the protasis for the sake of emphasis. Such a
reading would translate as follows: "If a man lies with her so that her impurity is upon
him, then he shall be unclean." Milgrom's final point is this: "Finally, the structure of
the pericope — v. 24 is a collapsed version of vv. 19b–20a; because 24b parallels v. 20a,
v. 24a must correspond to v. 19b — shows that this clause deals with the *consequence* of
intercourse with a menstruant. The conclusion is therefore inescapable: (2) this clause is
part of the apodosis." The same critique applies to this statement. In addition, I would
simply disagree that v. 24 is a collapsed version of vv. 19b–20a.

adequate to cover the woman's impurity for the situation of v. 24. Both the man and the woman are unclean seven days. Stipulations for ablutions are absent for both. Both transfer their impurity to objects around them. Again, with respect to purity issues related to sexual intercourse, the author treats the man and woman equally.

Verse 33b. The complete sentence to which v. 33b belongs consists of vv. 32–33, the summary to the YHWH speech. This unit begins with "this is the law of" followed by a taxonomy of flow cases. The taxonomy makes sense until the reader comes to v. 33b, which initially looks like a reference to v. 24.[19] However, such referencing in the summary, which includes v. 24 and excludes v. 18, is problematic in a text that otherwise pays close attention to thematic and structural balance. Furthermore, the structure of 33aγ–33b seems to suggest that the category implicit in 33b is typologically the same as the categories implicit in 33aγ. If 33b refers to 24, then the structure belies the content.

The structure itself is the key to this dilemma. Verses 32–33 divide according to the components of a single, non-verbal clause.[20] הזב in v. 32a refers to all flows treated in chapter 15.[21] The *waw* at the beginning of 32b is an epexegetical *waw*,[22] and 32b–33b is a delineation of this הזב. The first half of the delineation, 32b–33aα, refers to nonanomalous flow.[23] The topic of the second half, 33aβ–33b, is more ambiguously expressed and its reference, therefore, difficult to identify. Either it refers to all flows and הזב means the same thing as the הזב in 32a, or it refers to only anomalous flow and, thus, means something different from the initial הזב. The categories of 32b–33b are as follows:

1. man with issue of semen (32b)
2. menstruant (33aα)
3. הזב (33aβ–33b)
   a. male (33aγ₁)
   b. female (33aγ₂)
   c. man who lies with impure woman (33b)

The *lamed*s indicate that the writer perceived a, b, and c to be equally weighted and on the same level. If הזב of 33aβ refers to all flows, then 3 recapitulates the categories of the chapter, including the ones listed

---

19. Milgrom, *Leviticus*, 948.
20. See the structure above.
21. See Milgrom (*Leviticus*, 905, 945–48) for an excellent discussion of the difficulties of this unit and for a solution different from my own.
22. Waltke and O'Connor, *Biblical Hebrew*, 652–53.
23. שכבת זרע indicates v. 32b refers to the nonanomalous issue from the man's body. The time designations associated with נדתה in vv. 19 and 25, as well as the comparisons made in vv. 25–26 to the nonanomalous sections, demonstrate that the flow, which comes during the monthly cycle, is what is meant unambiguously by נדתה.

in 1 and 2. However, such recapitulation is incomplete and somewhat halfhearted in an otherwise highly systematized chapter. On the other hand, if הזב of 33aβ refers only to anomalous flow, then 32b–33aα refers to nonanomalous flow and 33aβ–33b to anomalous flow. The taxonomy of the summary is then concise and complete.

This latter solution is stymied, however, by the fact that 33b seems to refer to v. 24, which concerns *nonanomalous* flow.[24] Perhaps this latter assumption is mistaken. All three categories of 33aγ–33b involve individuals who are flowing. Technically, a and b could cover the situation of c. Even though this is the case, the author includes c. He must have a reason.

If 33aβ–33b has to do with only anomalous flow, then 33b refers to the only situation of double flow involving intercourse not delineated in the main body of the speech: intercourse between a woman with anomalous flow and a man with or without anomalous flow.[25] Verse 25bβ, concerning anomalous flow, underscores this connection: "she is טמאה." Verse 33b states that the man lies "with a טמאה." Thus the writer of the summary wants this particularly noxious situation emphasized. The question remains, Why does the author reference it in the summary and not in the main body of the text? Redaction is one plausible explanation. Another, and perhaps complementary, explanation is that the author/redactor wants to preserve the symmetry of the chapter.

If the same situation occurred in the main body of the text, it would be in the woman's anomalous section. However, the corresponding situation (intercourse between a woman without flow and a man with anomalous flow) is absent in the men's anomalous section. The most we can say about this latter exclusion is that the writer considered the impurity that obtained and the stipulations that prevailed in such a situation to be evident from other portions of the text.[26] Furthermore, since it did not involve *double* flow, the author was not concerned to emphasize it in the summary.[27] Double-flow intercourse always involves

24. Milgrom, *Leviticus*, 948.

25. The woman's anomalous flow qualifies this situation as anomalous whether or not the man's flow is anomalous.

26. Perhaps they are evident in vv. 18 and 7. The situation of lesser and equal impurity can be understood to be the least that would apply to the situation of equal or greater impurity. See Milgrom, *Leviticus*, 914.

27. David P. Wright writes, "A question in regard to the *zāb* may be brought up at this point. If it seems logical to apply the pollution that sexual intercourse with a menstruant causes to the case of the *zābâ*, is it not logical to apply it also to the case of the *zāb*? I do not think this question can be decided. On the one hand, the pollution effect of all three cases otherwise is very similar. This may suggest that intercourse with a *zāb* brings pollution as in the case of the menstruant. On the other hand we noticed earlier…that the pollution of the *zāb* may be considered slightly less severe (in some way) than that of

blood. The impurity of blood was of special concern.[28] Since such a stipulation concerning woman without flow and a man with anomalous flow was not included in the men's anomalous section, a corresponding stipulation included in the woman's anomalous section would have upset the schematic, structural symmetry of the chapter. Thus, the author/redactor left it out of the main body of the text. However, he could not release the summary and the chapter until he named outright this one situation of intercourse involving double flow and thus blood, which was up to that point unnamed.[29]

If this scenario concerning 33b is accurate, then the author made a special effort to preserve the schematic, structural symmetry of the chapter. In Leviticus 15, which divides into male and female sections, this amounts to an effort to preserve gender symmetry with respect to purity issues related to genital flow in general and sexual intercourse in particular. However, the nomenclature used to designate the man and woman in 33b seems diametrically opposed to this effort.

Within this chapter, two terms used to designate the flowing woman or her flow have a necessary connection to the pejorative word field of impurity (טמא). The male nomenclature lacks such a necessary connection. As explained above, טמאה in v. 33b is a reference to the טמאה in v. 25. While v. 33b is unbalanced in its gender nomenclature, the same is not true for the anomalous sections from which טמאה comes. Just as טמאה הוא occurs in the woman's section, so also טמא הוא occurs in v. 2 of the men's section. Thus, within the chapter the author gives at least one formula of equivalence for the man and for the woman, aligning each with the pejorative word field of impurity. He highlights only the female nomenclature in v. 33b because only "intercourse in the context of double flow" is his concern and the impurity nomenclature of the woman in conjunction with ישכב is sufficient to identify that situation. The impurity nomenclature of the man is insufficient because it leaves out the blood factor. Furthermore, the איש of 33b refers to a man with or without anomalous flow. טמא would have said less than the author

---

28. the menstruant and zābâ. If this is so, then perhaps the prescriptions may not intend that a zāb can pollute like a menstruant by sexual intercourse" (Disposal of Impurity [Atlanta: Scholars Press, 1987] 195).

28. Evidently, blood has greater impurity than men's anomalous or nonanomalous flow. Wright states, "It may be that the editor perceived the impurity of an abnormal discharge in a male to be less severe in some way than that of a blood flow — normal or irregular — in a woman" (Disposal, 187).

29. The typological kinship of the components of 33aγ–33b derives from the anomalous-flow qualification present in each. This is enough to warrant the lameds even though 33b, unlike 33aγ1 and 33aγ2, names a situation involving individuals rather than naming simply individuals.

wanted. Thus, the factor governing the nomenclature of v. 33b is the gender-neutral blood factor.[30]

Again, with respect to purity issues the author treats the man and woman equally.

The Challenge

Introverted Structure. The most significant challenge to the above interpretation is the structural solution that Milgrom and Whitekettle propose for the perceived syntactic and conceptual problems of v. 18. This solution posits an introverted structure[31] for Leviticus 15. Verse 18 is the center of the structure, belonging to neither the male nor female sections. While this structure demonstrates gender symmetry with respect to genital flow,[32] gender symmetry with respect to sexual intercourse is at least potentially compromised.[33] The male nonanomalous section lacks a verse corresponding to v. 24 in the female section. One might assert that v. 18, even as an independent unit, provides the balance. But v. 18 as an independent unit carries a different message than v. 18 as an integral part of 16–18.[34] The chapter then structurally and thematically appears to be biased, protecting the man against the impurity of the woman.

These comments, however, only beg the question if they are used to discredit the chiastic structure. Such discredit must stand on more solid ground.

Syntactic Difficulties: Milgrom. One of the major syntactic puzzles of v. 18 is the initial placement of אשה, which emphasizes the woman where one would expect emphasis to remain with the man.[35] Milgrom's solution to this puzzle suggests that v. 18 is an inverted "hinge," an independent connecting unit between two texts. A preceding word

---

30. See below for discussion of the gender of the blood.

31. For the use of this term, see Isaac M. Kikawada, "The Shape of Genesis 11:1–9," in Jared J. Jackson and Martin Kessler, eds., *Rhetorical Criticism* (Pittsburgh: Pickwick Press, 1974) 23.

32. See Hoffman, *Covenant*, 147–50. Hoffman uses this structure to demonstrate that the taxonomy of genital impurity is not gender based. Rather, it is based on the normal/abnormal polarity.

33. Hoffman (*Covenant*, 149) fails to notice this structural asymmetry in Leviticus 15.

34. In fact, Whitekettle argues for the distinctive import of v. 18 as an independent center, which leads him finally to conclude that the primary concern of the chapter is "ideal physiological functioning of the reproductive system" ("Leviticus," 37). At the very least, the chiastic structure fails to account for the deliberate placement of a sex verse as the conclusion of each nonanomalous section. Such placement underscores the fact that no special danger comes from intercourse because of the *gender* of the flow.

35. The פתחחה preceding v. 18 indicates that the Masoretes also puzzled over this placement. See Milgrom, *Leviticus*, 930. Milgrom observes that the woman is the subject of the verse. As I have argued above, the woman is not the subject. However, the question remains concerning the pronounced emphasis given to her within the men's section.

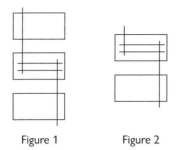

Figure 1   Figure 2

(אשה), within the hinge, echoes the text following; and a following word (איש) echoes the text preceding (see fig. 1).[36] This inverted hinge is the foundation of Milgrom's introverted structure.[37] Milgrom cites Parunak as the source of his hinge model.[38] Of the several literary connectors Parunak describes, the inverted hinge is certainly the closest approximation to what we have in the text.[39] However, Parunak does not claim, nor can we assume, that he has described every type of linking structure that is either possible or that ever occurs. If v. 18 functions as a hinge, it follows a pattern that Parunak has not addressed.

That v. 18 contains reverse echoes of preceding and following text is undeniable. However, as a hinge it is asymmetrically placed, embedded in one side of the structure. Call it an "inverted hanging hinge": Aba/B (see fig. 2). This placement accounts for two features of the text that Milgrom's structure ignores: the similar subject matter — semen — of v. 18 and vv. 16–17, and the symmetry created by the conclusion of each non-anomalous section with a verse on intercourse. Thus, while v. 18 may indeed function as an inverted hinge, such a function does not necessarily designate it as a separate case, as Milgrom suggests. Nor does it entail chiasm as the fundamental structure of the chapter.[40] The fact

---

36. Milgrom, *Leviticus*, 905, 930–31. See H. Van Dyke Parunak, "Transitional Techniques in the Bible," *JBL* 102 (1983) 541.

37. Milgrom, *Leviticus*, 905.

38. Milgrom, *Leviticus*, 930–31.

39. Parunak, "Transitional," 541. He writes, "The inverted hinge, on the other hand, offers the pattern A/ba/B and reverses the order of the joining elements from that of the larger blocks of text."

40. Milgrom, *Leviticus*, 930–31. Milgrom also refers to Lev. 4:1–35 and Gen. 11:5 as examples in which אשר is used "as both a pivot and a marker to indicate the transition to a new category within the same unit." While I have no quarrel with the idea that אשר might be used as a pivot and a marker, I do quarrel with the idea that this usage in Leviticus 15 is at the center of a chiasm. Milgrom also cites Kikawada's analysis of Genesis 11 (Kikawada, "The Shape," 18–32). Interestingly, Kikawada finds at least two "pivots" in his text: v. 5 and v. 8. However, only one of these, v. 5, functions as the center of a chiasm (see pp. 23–24).

that Milgrom offers two structures even while calling the introverted structure a "more meaningful division" supports this observation.[41]

Conceptual Difficulties: Whitekettle. The conceptual difficulty in v. 18 has to do with this question: Why does emission of semen or sexual intercourse, which is necessary to obtain something so highly valued as progeny, cause impurity?[42] Whitekettle's study ultimately attempts to answer this question. As part of his argument, which concludes that the functional ambiguity of the penis is the source of impurity,[43] he posits the structural and thematic independence of v. 18 and, thus, the "interlocking pivotal structure"[44] for the chapter. A related conclusion is that the primary concern of Leviticus 15 is the "ideal physiological functioning of the reproductive system" rather than mediation of impurity caused by genital discharge.[45]

Whitekettle posits structural independence based on two prior suppositions: (1) אשר in v. 18 necessarily demarcates a distinct legal unit;[46] and (2) the noncontagious impurity of v. 18 indicates that it is not a subcase and is, therefore, independent of vv. 16–17.[47] These suppositions are erroneous.

Whitekettle has failed to notice the use of the אשר construction throughout the chapter. It occurs similarly in other clauses (vv. 4a, 4b, 9, 11, 12a, 20a, 20b), which Whitekettle himself would not identify as distinct legal units. The difference between them and v. 18 is that they can be read more easily as relatives than v. 18, since the subjects and verbs of their protases and apodoses agree in number. Nevertheless, like v. 18, they can also be read as conditionals with *casus pendens.*[48] The similarity is not accidental.

Whitekettle's conclusion that v. 18 is the independent center of the chapter because it is not a subcase of vv. 16–17 is also misguided. However, the literary phenomenon on which he bases his conclusion is real. The law on sexual intercourse concluding the men's nonanomalous section is a separate case, whereas in the women's nonanomalous section,

---

41. Milgrom, *Leviticus,* 904–5.

42. Whitekettle, "Leviticus," 31; also Wenham, "Why Does Sexual Intercourse Defile (Lev 15:18)?" *ZAW* 95 (1983) 432. See also Eilberg-Schwartz, *The Savage,* 186; Milgrom, *Leviticus,* 933–34.

43. Whitekettle, "Leviticus," 43–44.

44. Whitekettle, "Leviticus," 37. This is his name for the introverted structure.

45. Whitekettle, "Leviticus," 36–37.

46. Whitekettle, "Leviticus," 35.

47. Whitekettle, "Leviticus," 35–36.

48. See Waltke and O'Connor, *Biblical Hebrew,* 77, no. 5. See their example of a relative, very similar to the ones used in Leviticus 15, under the discussion on the nominative absolute (i.e., *casus pendens*).

that concluding law is a subcase of the case that begins the section.[49] In fact, this construction — two separate but related cases — in the men's section is unique in the chapter.

Whitekettle, however, suggests more than this. Not only is v. 18 not a subcase, but it is also an independent unit. He bases this assumption on the conclusion that whereas the impurity of the other sections is contagion, the impurity of v. 18 is not. Whitekettle notes that the subject of v. 18 is not singular, that a phrase analogous to "and her monthly flow touches him" (from v. 24) is absent, and that the man is explicitly mentioned even though we know already from vv. 16–17 that he is unclean during intercourse. Since these three factors occur, he concludes that the impurity of v. 18 is not contagion.[50]

However, the plural subject and explicit mention of the man are present for emphasis: *both* man and woman become impure during the desirable act of intercourse. Verse 24 lacks the same emphasis because vv. 19–23 unambiguously describe the woman's impurity already. Verse 24 emphasizes that the man contracts the same level of impurity as the woman. The lack of the "analogous phrase" in v. 18 is a function of the number of discharges involved. In v. 18 only one discharge is involved. Thus, the reader knows without a doubt that the prescription applies to seminal discharge. In v. 24 two discharges of differing severity are involved: semen and blood. The author wants unambiguously to state that in v. 24 *blood* is the cause of the impurity. Thus, ותהי נדתה עליו occurs in v. 24 and no such phrase occurs in v. 18.

In fact, contrary to Whitekettle's contention, 18b indicates that contagion is at work: וטמאו עד־הערב. Nothing could be plainer. Even Whitekettle's final answer concerning the source of impurity of v. 18 must admit contagion because of v. 18b.[51] Thus, the men's nonanomalous section is unique not because contagion is lacking but because the "physiology" of that section in connection with impurity is open to confusion and misunderstanding.

The writer foresaw that if he allowed vv. 16–17 to encompass the situation of v. 18, analogously to the woman's nonanomalous section, or if he framed v. 18 as he framed v. 24, confusion would arise. Who can believe that sexual intercourse, necessary for the production of progeny, defiles? Not even twentieth-century scholars believe that the ancient writers believed it. The fact that they have taken the impurity caused by emission of semen during intercourse to be such a puzzle demonstrates this writer's remarkable foresight. The "desirability" and

---

49. Whitekettle, "Leviticus," 35. See the structure above.
50. Whitekettle, "Leviticus," 36.
51. Whitekettle, "Leviticus," 44.

"normalcy" of intercourse creates the potential for misunderstanding and confusion. Thus, the writer includes an explicit stipulation to dispel the potential confusion. He wants it understood that, contrary to what we might consider to be common sense, emission of semen causes impurity to both man and woman under *any* circumstance, even the desirable circumstance necessary for the production of progeny — sexual intercourse.

Whitekettle's argument for the *thematic* independence of v. 18 is from another direction. He bases it on the supposition that the following do not cause the impurity of v. 18:[52] loss of life liquids, that is, crossing boundaries, emission of semen per se, sexual intercourse per se.[53] Indeed, sexual intercourse per se is not the source of impurity. Emission of semen is.[54] Whether or not the power of the impurity of semen draws on a conceptuality concerning loss of life liquids or crossing boundaries is open to question.[55] The author mentions שכבת־זרע, a seeming repetition, because he wants no confusion to arise over the fact that specifically this genital discharge causes impurity.

Thus, Whitekettle's suppositions concerning structural and thematic independence cannot be sustained. Furthermore, genital discharge, not the woman, not the man, not intercourse, not the functional ambiguity of the penis, is the source of the impurity of v. 18.[56] The construction of v. 18 is a result of the writer's concern to emphasize that during the "desirable" act of intercourse, which every married couple was expected to perform, impurity necessarily occurs to both individuals.

The logic of the impurity of genital discharge rules the chapter without exception, not even the exception of intercourse. The operative question is not, Why does semen or intercourse defile? Rather, it is, Why does genital discharge defile? And this is a question that we must put to the entire chapter, not to just v. 18.

Conclusion. The arguments that support the introverted structure from both Milgrom and Whitekettle are unfounded. While awkwardness and idiosyncrasies may characterize v. 18, far simpler solutions

---

52. Whitekettle does not explicitly state the basis for his assertion concerning thematic independence. The summary given here is my interpretation of the inferences he seems to be drawing.

53. Whitekettle, "Leviticus," 33, 36.

54. For the practice of sexual intercourse without emission of semen, see Mantak Chia, *Taoist Secrets of Love: Cultivating Male Sexual Energy* (Santa Fe: Aurora Press, 1984) 113–39.

55. Whitekettle's argument ("Leviticus," 33) that the boundaries of "one flesh" are constitutive during intercourse rather than the boundaries of the individual body is highly speculative, regardless of Gen. 2:24.

56. Milgrom writes, "It is the discharge that contaminates, not the person. Hence, objects that are underneath him — bed, seat, saddle — but no others are considered impure" (*Leviticus*, 44).

than that of the introverted structure explain them. The two-part structure, which demonstrates gender symmetry, with respect to purity issues related to genital discharge in general as well as sexual intercourse in particular, is a more accurate rendering.

Two Additional Challenges

Two additional challenges might be suggested as potentially undermining the description of structural symmetry, and therefore gender symmetry, just given. The first is the absence of several items in the woman's section that are present in the man's section. The second is the nature of the blood and, by extension, the import of the difference in time for purification from the nonanomalous discharge of men and women.

Shorthand Technique. The first challenge is easily met if Milgrom's assessment of the matter is correct.

Mediation of the woman's impurity is noticeably absent from v. 24. Prescriptions for ablutions for the man in that verse are lacking as well. In fact, ablutions are absent from the entire women's section. Milgrom suggests that this asymmetry is a function of what I call the "shorthand technique."[57] This technique, described by Milgrom, is a gender-neutral feature of the text.[58]

In Leviticus 15 the technique works in at least two ways. First, the author allows one section of text to rely upon another section for the completion of its prescriptions.[59] Second, the author allows one phrase to signify more than it denotes at face value.[60] The absence of ablutions in vv. 9–30 is a function of both forms of this technique.[61]

---

57. Milgrom, *Leviticus.* See the following pages for specific instances of the application of this technique: 905, 914, 919, 923–24, 934–37, 939–41. Wright, *Disposal*, 191.

58. It might be argued that beginning the text with the men's section was a decision based on gender. This may be so. But that choice having been made, the shorthand literary technique by which the woman's section depends on the prior men's section for completion is gender neutral. The same dynamic is at work internally to the woman's section.

59. Milgrom, *Leviticus*, 905, 923–24. Milgrom states that the second half of the chapter is "wholly dependent on the language and content of the first half" (p. 905). He writes, "The menstruant and the *zābâ* . . . abbreviate their contamination rules because they are derivable from the *zāb*" (p. 924). See also pp. 934–35; Levine, *Leviticus*, 97; Wright, *Disposal*, 181–96.

60. Milgrom, *Leviticus*, 919. Milgrom has argued concerning *yitmā' 'ad-hā'āreb*, "Bathing is always assumed by this expression, for it is a basic requisite for all purifications."

61. Milgrom writes, "There is no mention of ablutions for the menstruant or for the woman with chronic discharges (v. 28). Still, all statements regarding the duration of impurity automatically imply that it is terminated by ablutions. . . . Besides, if a minor impurity such as a seminal discharge requires ablutions (15:16), all the more so the major genital discharges" (*Leviticus*, 934–35).

So also is the absence of mediation of the woman's impurity in v. 24.[62]

Other similar asymmetries, which might be thought of as belying the structural symmetry of the chapter, are due to this technique as well.

Blood. The second challenge is more difficult.

Several scholars have suggested that the blood of menstruation pollutes because of the *gender* of the blood.[63] If this is so, then the difference in time for purification from nonanomalous discharge is a function of gender, and the structural symmetry as described above is compromised.

In fact, the blood of menstruation in Leviticus 15 does not pollute because of the gender of the blood. In Leviticus 15 the blood of menstruation is a gender-neutral factor that pollutes for the same reason semen pollutes: its association with the potential or capacity to create life. As a gender-neutral factor it fails to overrule the deliberate equivalence set forth by the structure.

A review and critique of some of the salient points of Eilberg-Schwartz's theory of the pollution of bodily fluids[64] illustrates the major concerns in the discussion of such matters. It also serves as a springboard for my own explanatory preference concerning such pollution.

Eilberg-Schwartz suggests at least three polarities, each, to a greater or lesser degree, having the capacity to explain the pollution of bodily fluids: the gender polarity,[65] the controllability/uncontrollability polarity,[66] and the life/death polarity.[67] I will discuss each in the order I have listed them.

Eilberg-Schwartz himself refutes the gender polarity as an adequate

---

62. Verse 24 relies on vv. 19–23 for completion of instructions regarding the woman's impurity.

63. See Eilberg-Schwartz, *The Savage*, 174, 179–81, 186. Eilberg-Schwartz states, "The difference between semen and menstrual blood might also be part of the symbolic domination of women. Although the loss of both fluids represents a missed opportunity for procreation, menstrual blood is more contaminating simply because of its gender" (p. 186). See also Hoffman, *Covenant*, 136–54; Archer, *Her Price Is Beyond Rubies* (Sheffield: JSOT Press, 1990) 37; idem, "Bound," 38–61. This conclusion is drawn by Eilberg-Schwartz and other scholars who compare the blood of menstruation with the blood of circumcision. They see circumcision and menstruation functioning as a polarity that ultimately has deleterious effects for women. However, I am concerned not with the larger context — literary or historical — but with Leviticus 15 in particular. Both Eilberg-Schwartz (*The Savage*, 181) and Hoffman (*Covenant*, 147–48) themselves note that the gender polarity does not govern the fluid symbolism of Leviticus 15 asymmetrically. See also Mary Douglas, *Implicit Meanings* (London: Routledge & Kegan Paul, 1975) 69.

64. Eilberg-Schwartz, *The Savage*, 179–82.

65. Eilberg-Schwartz, *The Savage*, 182–86.

66. Eilberg-Schwartz, *The Savage*, 186–91.

67. Eilberg-Schwartz, *The Savage*, 182–86.

explanation for the impurity of the blood in Leviticus 15. Speaking of Leviticus 15, he writes,

> The signification of women's bleeding thus depends upon the context in which it is viewed. When contrasted with the blood of circumcision, a contrast suggested by the proximity of circumcision to the bleeding associated with birth, female blood is a symbol of women's exclusion from the covenant. But this contrast disappears when menstrual blood is treated among other bodily emissions.[68]

In other words, even if the *gender* of the blood determines the impurity or purity of blood in the wider literary context, which includes texts on circumcision, or in the larger historical context, which includes the subsequent isolation of women, in the context of Leviticus 15 it does not. The gender polarity cannot explain the pollution of Leviticus 15.

Hoffman suggests even more strongly than Eilberg-Schwartz "that the key to body-fluid pollution should be sought in the issue of control."[69] Hoffman's concern is less to explain the pollution of the biblical text than to explain subsequent rabbinic treatment of body fluids. His critique of Eilberg-Schwartz's version of the controllability theory is nevertheless relevant.

> Why should the Rabbis have overlooked the fact that at the moment prior to ejaculation a man has no more control over semen than a woman has over menstrual blood? Or that nocturnal emissions are even more unpredictable than the average woman's period, which at least is expected around a given time? Moreover, why should we believe that tears are controllable? or breast milk? or earwax? or mucus that escapes in a "runny nose"? True, our own culture cleans up the human body in such a way that we like to imagine we have control over all such emissions. We cough involuntarily, and turn our faces away from an observer who pretends not to observe until we finish wiping our noses and mouths with a tissue. We keep our ears well-groomed. We "fight back tears," even though we know of times when "tears well up and overwhelm us," for which we

---

68. Eilberg-Schwartz, *The Savage*, 182.

69. Hoffman, *Covenant*, 154. See also Eilberg-Schwartz, *The Savage*, 186–89. Archer suggests something similar in connection with the nature/culture construct: "Within this scheme of thought, anything which cannot be controlled is labelled dangerous and marginal, particularly when society is working to preserve its unity and to develop more sophisticated systems of self-definition, as was the case for the Jewish community in Palestine following the exile. The blood of childbirth and menstruation, which follows a passive and unstoppable cycle, can be construed (by the powers that be) to fall within this category, and so it is required that cultural regulation step in with restrictive legislation. That cultural regulation, as we have seen, is controlled by men, for (and this brings me to the third point) within this scheme of thought, woman herself is placed more fully within the realm of nature than man in consequence of the fact that more of her time and her body are seen to be taken up with the natural processes surrounding reproduction of the species" ("Bound," 51).

may even dutifully apologize. Adults should not be "cry-babies." But all of that is our own cultural imagination at work, tidying up the untidy facts of bodily substances that defy our will more than they obey it.[70]

Thus, the uncontrollability/controllability polarity as an explanation of body-fluid pollution is limited. Hoffman offers a refinement of Eilberg-Schwartz's theory, maintaining that the issue of control is less a "biological phenomenon" than a "social one."[71]

> The binary opposition obtains between men, who are in control of their blood, so of themselves, and therefore of society; and women who, lacking control of blood and therefore of self, are thus denied control of society as well.[72]

While his refinement may account for the pollution of body fluid in the literature of rabbinic Judaism, it is more difficult to apply to Leviticus 15. Given that the lack of gender polarization as a structuring factor in the chapter is admitted by Hoffman[73] and Eilberg-Schwartz,[74] and given that Hoffman questions the nature of control over semen versus menstrual blood, exactly how, then, does Leviticus 15 demonstrate the binary opposition he describes? In other words, Hoffman has admirably discredited the controllability/uncontrollability polarity as presented by Eilberg-Schwartz, offering in its stead a refinement, which suits the rabbinic literature but not Leviticus 15.

The life/death polarity holds more promise, although Eilberg-Schwartz considers its explanatory power to be limited, and Hoffman dismisses it on the basis of "anomalies" for which he believes it is unable to account.[75]

Before critiquing these "anomalies," however, I must respond to Eilberg-Schwartz's contention that since only some kinds of blood contaminate, "the prohibitions on the menstruous woman have nothing to do with the inherent quality of blood,"[76] contrary to the implications of the life/death polarity. Early in his argument, he dismisses the "horror of the blood" (Gen. 9:4; Lev. 17:11–14; Deut. 12:23) as a factor explaining this severity.[77] He argues,

> Indeed, there is warrant for arguing that the latter view in fact explains the menstrual taboo in Israelite religion, since Scripture states unequivocally that blood carries the essence of life (Gen. 9:4; Lev.17:11–14; Deut.

70. Hoffman, *Covenant*, 154.
71. Hoffman, *Covenant*, 151–54.
72. Hoffman, *Covenant*, 154.
73. Hoffman, *Covenant*, 147–48.
74. Eilberg-Schwartz, *The Savage*, 181.
75. Eilberg-Schwartz, *The Savage*, 185–86; Hoffman, *Covenant*, 151–52.
76. Eilberg-Schwartz, *The Savage*, 179.
77. Eilberg-Schwartz, *The Savage*, 179.

12:23 [Feldman 1977, 37; Patai 1959, 152]). But the contrast between menstrual blood, which is contaminating, and the blood of circumcision or sacrifice, which is positively marked, indicates that only some kinds of blood are contaminating.... Blood has different meanings depending upon how it originates and from whom it comes. Significantly, the familiar Israelite idea that "life is in the blood" appears only in contexts related to the slaughter of animals or murder, that is, acts in which a living being dies. Some blood is symbolic of life; other kinds of blood are not.[78]

In reply to Eilberg-Schwartz, it can be suggested that even if only some kinds of blood contaminate, it may still be the case that "life is in the blood" is true for all contexts. Life may be in all blood under all circumstances at the same time that "life" is at risk in only certain contexts or spillings, such as slaughter, murder, and menses.[79] The factor constitutive for the risk of these situations is that life, manifested as a potential or actual living creature, is aborted by the spilling.[80]

In fact, two primary qualifications might be said to constitute the impurity of bodily fluids: (1) whatever kills life (blood spilled in murder), whatever represents missed opportunity for life (spilled semen), whatever represents a compromise in the process of making life, or whatever actually does compromise the process of making life;[81] (2) whatever is essential for life or for creating life, even if it is only part of the process of creating and does not ultimately become that life (semen, menstrual blood, lochial discharge).[82]

Objection to "horror of the blood" as a source of impurity is not the only problem Eilberg-Schwartz has with the life/death polarity as an explanation. He and Hoffman offer a list of anomalies for which they believe the polarity cannot account.[83] A critique of the three primary "anomalies" provides a model by which others might also be dismissed. These three "anomalies" can be posed in the form of the following questions.

---

78. Eilberg-Schwartz, *The Savage*, 179.

79. For example, life or life potential is not at risk when someone scrapes a knee.

80. Wenham, "Why," 434; Whitekettle, "Leviticus," 33. Tikva Frymer-Kensky states, "Another element is present — blood and its associations with death — for contact with death also results in a week-long impurity" ("Sex in the Bible," in *In the Wake of the Goddesses* [New York: Fawcett Columbine, 1992] 189 n. 12).

81. For example, nonseminal discharge or anomalous female blood flow may indicate conditions that jeopardize the ability to conceive or to conceive a healthy, "whole" child.

82. Kirsten Hastrup writes, "It is not difficult to understand the danger of menstrual blood, since this is associated with 'a child not to become', with death, and as both part of the woman and not so" ("The Sexual Boundary-Danger: Transvestism and Homosexuality," *JASO* 6 [1975] 52).

83. Eilberg-Schwartz, *The Savage*, 185–86; Hoffman, *Covenant*, 151–52.

1. Why does nonseminal discharge pollute more than seminal discharge if spilling of seminal discharge represents "life wasted" while nonseminal does not?

2. Why does the blood of birth pollute if that blood represents creation of new life?

3. Why does semen pollute during intercourse if this is the very act necessary for the creation of new life?

For the most part, discernment of what in the actual life of a community pollutes or cleanses is relatively simple.[84] This is one level of alignments in the purity system. A second level is the association of the life/death polarity, or some other construct, with the purity/impurity polarity. This second level of alignments is more difficult to discern. Its truth or value depends upon its capacity to explain all elements of the first level. The third level of alignments is even more difficult to discern. This level has to do with *how* the second level explains the first level. My critique of Eilberg-Schwartz and Hoffman is a critique of their perceptions of what is going on at this level. They believe that the life/death polarity cannot explain all the elements at the first level. I believe it can.

Examination of the three "anomalies" will demonstrate what I mean. The first "anomaly" suggested by Eilberg-Schwartz and Hoffman is, Why does nonseminal discharge pollute more than seminal discharge if spilling of seminal discharge represents life wasted or "abortion of life potential" while spilling of nonseminal discharge does not? Eilberg-Schwartz and Hoffman assume that since nonseminal discharge does not create life and since seminal discharge does, spilling of nonseminal discharge cannot be aligned with "life wasted" or "abortion of life potential." Therefore, it cannot be aligned with the pole opposite life, namely, death. Therefore, it cannot be aligned with impurity. But Leviticus 15 does align it with impurity. Thus, life/death cannot explain the pollution of nonseminal discharge.

Their conclusion concerning the alignment of life/death, and thus purity/impurity, with nonseminal/seminal discharge is an assumption. This is important to notice. Perhaps the alignment works differently. What if, in the mind of the ancient writer, nonseminal discharge represents a distortion of seminal discharge, so that it is not opposed to it but is rather a permutation of it? What if nonseminal discharge, an abnormal flow, is seen by the ancient writer to be something generically

---

84. See Mary Douglas's essay "Couvade and Menstruation," in *Implicit Meanings*, 60–72, esp. pp. 60–62. Douglas notes, "The same holds good for menstruation: in tribal society it is not universally hedged with ritual taboos. Each primitive culture makes its own selection of bodily functions, which it emphasizes as dangerous or good. The problem is to understand the principles of selection" (p. 60).

akin to semen, even though it does not result in life and does not even have the capacity to create life?[85]

Wenham suggests something like this in his explanation of the impurity of nonseminal discharge.[86] He seems to treat it as a protracted case of seminal emission. He writes, "Similarly too we presume that male semen was viewed as a 'life liquid.' Hence its loss whether long-term (15:1–15) or transient (15:16–18) was viewed as polluting."[87]

An examination of the nature of the flows and their relationships is helpful at this point. Nonanomalous male flow has different duration of impurity than anomalous male flow. Cycle is an insignificant factor with respect to the purity or impurity of male flow. Furthermore, the substance of the two flows differs. The first is called שכבת־זרע and the latter is called זוב. On the other hand, the nonanomalous female flow may or may not have the same duration as the anomalous female flow. Furthermore, the two flows are the same substance. Both are called דם. Thus, the *relationship* of anomalous to nonanomalous in the male and female sections is not entirely parallel when duration and substance are examined. Nevertheless, the placement of nonanomalous and anomalous flows in the structure of the text indicates that the writer, in fact, considered them to be typologically similar.

The qualification of "loss of life potential" is the most plausible explanation for this typological similarity. Men's anomalous flow, although not the same substance as semen, like semen, comes from the genitals. It is a sign of illness or infection, which can potentially affect the life-giving capacity of the couple.[88] That the author perceived the potential of the life-giving semen itself to be somehow compromised is at least a possibility. He may have perceived male anomalous flow as effecting "diminished" capacity or as symbolic of it. This may be enough to account for its association with the "death pole" of the polarity.

Thus, a reworking of the alignments associated with the life/death polarity resolves this particular anomaly.

A second anomaly suggested by Eilberg-Schwartz and Hoffman is, Why does the blood of birth pollute if that blood represents creation

---

85. The question may then arise, Why does urine not have the same association? Urination is a normal condition that occurs as a matter of regular practice in humans before ejaculation becomes a matter of regular practice in the average person's life. Thus, urination has a history of nonassociation with creation of life during the lifespan of the average male. Nonseminal discharge does not. It is an abnormal condition. Furthermore, some nonseminal discharge can affect the capacity to produce life.

86. Wenham, "Why," 434. See also Milgrom, *Leviticus*, 933–34; Eilberg-Schwartz, *The Savage*, 183.

87. Wenham, "Why," 434.

88. At the very least, something like gonorrhea, passed to a woman, may cause her sterility.

of new life? But what if the correspondence that matters to the ancient mind is simply the *association with the capacity* to create life? In other words, the blood of birth is part of the blood that created life, even though it has not become that life. It is part of the total process. Thus, the impurity is caused not so much because the blood is wasted as it is because the blood has an *association* and *potential,* a mantic power or capacity for creating life.[89] Whatever blood is seen as part of the process that actually creates life but has not become that life also pollutes, whether residual left from a process completed or whether an essential component of the life to be created. In fact, perhaps such blood pollutes to an even greater degree.[90]

---

89. One might object that blood from a scraped knee is in the same way associated with the blood that sustains life in the injured person, even if, as a small amount, it is not essential to the life of that person. I can only surmise that the same *correspondences* do not hold for blood that is involved in the process of creating new life and blood that is involved in the process of sustaining an existing life. In other words, something about blood involved in the process of *creating* life makes all of it pollute, while this same something is lacking in blood involved in the process of *sustaining* life such that all of it does not necessarily pollute. Perhaps the correspondence that matters is that all blood involved in the process of creating life is perceived as essential to that process, while blood from a scraped knee is not essential to the process of sustaining the life of the injured party. He or she can afford to lose a little.

90. Leviticus 12 distinguishes at least two of the stages of lochial discharge that occur after birth. See David P. Wright and Richard N. Jones, "Discharge," *ABD*, 2:205. The first seven days after the birth of a male the woman is unclean כימי נדת דותה. This is the time during which the *lochia cruenta* flows. This flow consists chiefly of blood. For the next two to three weeks the color of the flow becomes paler until it is a creamy color (*lochia alba*). Finally, the flow disappears. This accounts for the seven days and thirty-three days of purification for a male baby. However, a male baby requires half the time of purification that a female baby requires. If that which has the potential to create life has the power to pollute, then that a baby female, who eventually has the power to create life, would cause greater pollution than the male baby makes sense. Half of the purification period is for that pollution caused by the mother's flow and half is for the baby female's potential to duplicate her mother's pollution. Why this potential pollutes in this way at birth and not continuously throughout her life is another question, the answer to which can only be surmised. Perhaps proximity to the mother's pollution in conjunction with her own potential doubles the pollution of the situation requiring twice the period for cleansing. Archer writes, "Given this widely attested belief in the power of the fortieth day, why did the Hebrews see fit to add a further forty days consequent on the birth of a female child to the mother's period of impurity? The only possible explanation for this revision of the original superstition is that a daughter was regarded in some sense as inflicting 'double impurity' on her mother, first (as with a son) on account of the blood of her birth (the original taboo = forty days impurity) and secondly on account of her being female (additional taboo = extra forty days impurity)" (Archer, *Her Price*, 37–38.). Of course, the difference would be explained by proponents of the controllability/uncontrollability polarity by stating that the female is in some way invested with the quality of uncontrollability and thus requires the double time. Nevertheless, it must be noted that whichever polarity is chosen — life/death or controllability/uncontrollability — the same "stretch" must be made with respect to the female child. As the potential to create life is not yet fully developed in the female child, so also those qualifications (see Archer, "Bound," 51) that invest her

A related question is, If both semen and menstrual blood create new life, why does menstrual blood pollute more?[91] If the life/death polarity is constitutive, then more must be said than simply that "the life is in the blood." The life is also in the semen. Menstrual blood spilled is blood that would have created the life of a child. Semen spilled is semen that would have created the life of a child. However, semen in general manifests life only as potential, whereas blood in general manifests life not only as potential when contributing to the birth of a child, but also as actual life. It is essential to the *actual* life of creatures. Perhaps this double qualification is the source of the difference in severity between menstrual blood and semen.

A third anomaly raised by Eilberg-Schwartz and Hoffman is, Why does semen pollute during intercourse if this is the very act necessary for the creation of new life? The same rationale can explain this anomaly that explained the blood of birth anomaly. Semen has the power to create life. It is this association that constitutes the impurity of intercourse, whether or not life results.

Thus, the blood itself, a gender-neutral factor, rather than the gender of the blood is responsible for the severity of the impurity of woman's genital discharge and the consequent difference in duration of time for purification between the man and woman.[92]

Summary

The two-part structure, conveying the primary concern of the writer for mediation of genital-discharge impurity, exhibits astonishing gender symmetry with respect to that primary concern. This symmetry is remarkable since point of view and language depicting the sex act reveal the unsurprising fact that woman's position is highly circumscribed by man within the worldview of the writer, and that the writer takes such circumscription for granted. It is remarkable since the author has also selected a word — דוה — to signify the menstruant, which negatively qualifies her vis-à-vis the man. Most differences between the male and female sections can be explained as a function of gender-neutral factors, including the blood. The blood, as a gender-neutral factor, does not nullify or qualify the remarkable, deliberate gender equivalence set forth by the structure.

---

with the uncontrollability that the male fears are not yet fully developed. See Hoffman, *Covenant*, 151–54, 164–65; also Eilberg-Schwartz, *The Savage*, 186–89.

91. Eilberg-Schwartz, *The Savage*, 186.

92. See Cohen, "Menstruants," 276. Cohen suggests that the difference in duration of separation on account of impurity between male and female nonanomalous flow is "probably because menstruation lasts longer than ejaculation." See also the explanations for the danger of menstruation among "ancient peoples" as suggested by William Phipps, "The Menstrual Taboo in the Judeo-Christian Tradition," *JRH* 19 (winter 1980) 299.

The structure is the reason that statements similar to the following statement by Thistlethwaite cannot describe Leviticus 15:

> Pollution concepts are essential to understanding women's "otherness" in the biblical worldviews.... The reproductive secretions of women are dirty because this particular cultural system has set off the reproductive capacity of women in a particular way.[93]

To the contrary, her reproductive secretions are dirty because, like the man's secretions, they are genital discharges.

CONCLUSION

In Leviticus 15, two sets of contrasting conceptual associations comprise the author's conceptualization of women. One set suggested by point of view, language depicting the sex act, and vocabulary signifying the menstruant pictures woman as marginalized, objectified, and periodically unhealthy on account of her normal bodily discharge. Her agency is curtailed. Her discharge is "different."

The second set of conceptual associations, suggested by the structure, pictures the woman as equal to the man. She, like he, is responsible for maintaining the purity of the community. She, like he, is protected. Her agency is equal to his. Furthermore, her discharge is typologically equivalent to his discharge. Although the material of her discharge, blood, is more virulent than the material of his discharge, that virulence does not derive from gender. It derives from the inherent nature of blood, which contributes to life.

Thus, although menstruation has association, even in the present text, with illness, the structure demonstrates that the author has made a conscious decision to treat menstruation as if it were a normal phenomenon.

The association of menstruation with illness in the present text, indicated by the use of דוה, may be a function of the implicit and unconscious assumptions of the writer's worldview and the culture from which he comes. The same may be true for the effects of point of view and language depicting the sex act. His conscious decision, therefore, to treat menstruation as if normal is remarkable.

Milgrom underscores the point:

> Against this backdrop of Israel's immediate and remote contemporaries and what was probably the dominant practice within Israel itself..., the Priestly legislation on the menstruant is all the more remarkable. First

---

93. Susan Brooks Thistlethwaite, "'You May Enjoy the Spoil of Your Enemies': Rape as a Biblical Metaphor for War," *Semeia* 61 (1993) 63.

and foremost, she is neither banished from the community nor even isolated within her home. The implicit assumption of the pericope on the
menstruant is that she lives at home, communicating with her family and
performing her household chores.[94]

BIBLIOGRAPHY

Archer, Léonie J. "Bound by Blood: Circumcision and Menstrual Taboo in Post-
Exilic Judaism." In *After Eve: Women, Theology and the Christian Traditions*, ed.
Janet Martin Soskice, pp. 38–61. London: Marshall Pickering, 1990.

Cohen, Shaye J. D. "Menstruants and the Sacred in Judaism and Christianity."
In *Women's History and Ancient History*, ed. Sarah B. Pomeroy, pp. 273–99.
Chapel Hill: University of North Carolina Press, 1991.

Douglas, Mary. *Implicit Meanings*. London and Boston: Routledge & Kegan Paul,
1975.

Eilberg-Schwartz, Howard. *The Savage in Judaism*. Bloomington: Indiana University Press, 1990.

Frymer-Kensky, Tikva. "Sex in the Bible." In *In the Wake of the Goddesses*, pp. 187–
98. New York: Fawcett Columbine, 1992.

Hoffman, Lawrence A. *Covenant of Blood*. Chicago: University of Chicago Press,
1996.

Milgrom, Jacob. *Leviticus 1–16*. AB 3. New York: Doubleday, 1991.

Parunak, H. Van Dyke. "Transitional Techniques in the Bible." *JBL* 102 (1983)
525–48.

Phipps, William. "The Menstrual Taboo in the Judeo-Christian Tradition." *JRH*
19 (winter 1980) 298–303.

Wegner, Judith Romney. *Chattel or Person*. New York: Oxford University Press,
1988.

Wenham, Gordon J. *Leviticus*. NICOT. Grand Rapids: Eerdmans, 1979.

———. "Why Does Sexual Intercourse Defile (Lev 15:18)?" *ZAW* 95 (1983) 432–
35.

Whitekettle, Richard. "Leviticus 15.18 Reconsidered: Chiasm, Spatial Structure
and the Body." *JSOT* 49 (1991) 31–45.

Wright, David P. *Disposal of Impurity*. SBLDS. Atlanta: Scholars Press, 1987.

Wright, David P., and Richard N. Jones. "Discharge." *ABD*, 2:204–7.

---

94. Milgrom, *Leviticus*, 952–53.

7

On the Task of a Text and
Concept Analysis in Psalm 2

Randy G. Haney

INTRODUCTION

Débats et combats concerning purpose and practice as well as concerning substantive research issues are becoming familiar albeit evolving features of the landscape of historical-critical methodology in the interpretation of biblical texts, especially with reference to the category of "royal psalms," of which Psalm 2 is an exemplar. The methodological state of affairs in the interpretation of the royal psalms for almost the past two centuries has been found to be a disconcerting one when it came to interpreting the psalms on their own terms, with reference especially to their own subject matter.[1] Specifically, there was no work that endeavored to answer the guiding question, Within the world projected by literary works such as the royal psalms, what are the *substantive* criteria according to which they themselves are organized? Moreover, it was also observed that the basic exegetical order of the day wound up being the "matching" of the royal psalms by the interpreter with some hypothetically reconstructed "situation," which then somehow automatically circumscribed the text with a particular "meaning" (i.e., psalms for the king's enthronement, psalms for a New Year festival, psalms for a covenant festival, or psalms for a royal Zion festival).

In contrast to this situation, the point of departure for this brief discussion will be the final form of the text of Psalm 2. Such a departure point for exegetical analysis has been presupposed in biblical scholarship as an authentic and justified basis for scientifically controlled investigations precisely because it undertakes its task in a relatively neutral mode without assuming answers to any of the accompanying difficulties.

The following attempt to set out the parameters of a text and concept study of Psalm 2 is gratefully dedicated to my teacher, mentor, and friend, Professor Rolf P. Knierim.

1. For a detailed overview of the history of research see my dissertation, " 'And All Nations Shall Serve Him': Text and Concept Analysis in Royal Psalms" (Ph.D. diss.; Claremont Graduate School, 1999) 8–161.

Furthermore, while a cadre of methodological techniques in the arena of historical-critical exegesis could be employed, there is an explicit mode of inquiry to be utilized in viewing, organizing, and giving shape and significance to the text of Psalm 2. The purpose of this essay is to indicate some of the conceptual aspects in Psalm 2, specifically focusing on structure analysis of the text and the concomitant reconstruction of the infratextual concepts in the text itself that have effectuated function within the final form of the text. Text and concept analysis, to be sure, is a historical-critical method informed by the historicality of the text itself and not dissociated from that reality. And in all fairness it should be stated that all along in the history of research on the royal psalms there were floating assumptions about the issue of "concept"[2] with respect to interpreting the texts. It appeared that most everyone was doing his or her own brand of "concept criticism." It must be said, however, that the manner in which the "concept(s)" of the texts was adjudicated commenced from the larger ancient Near Eastern environment coupled with the extreme subjectivity on the part of some of the interpreters' far-fetched theories and much less, if at all, from the individual texts themselves. At any rate, it is the contrast in method and results that is of concern at the moment, and not the issue of who is more or less right. The difference in the specific text and concept method of analysis (stemming from the ever-developing form-critical scholarship of Rolf P. Knierim) that will be conscripted into service in this essay is that the "concept" presupposed and operative in and controlling the text of Psalm 2 itself will be reconstructed. This is programmatically distinct from what has been witnessed in the history of research in that in Knierim's approach the *text itself* institutes the agenda for its own interpretation. And it must be made abundantly clear that what Knierim

---

2. The adjudication of what "concepts" are possesses a long and checkered history, and is a significant issue but one that goes beyond the confines of the present study. It is well known that "concept" is one of the oldest and most equivocal terms in the philosophical vocabulary. Even though it remains as a perpetual source of controversy, it is functional because of its ambiguity as a sort of passkey through the mazes indicated by the philosophical theories of perception, thinking, and being. The various definitions and descriptions of conceptual use that appear in scholarship are neither exhaustive nor unambiguously clear. No one disavows, though, that we are able to do such things as identify types of a kind or learn the meanings of words. To be sure, internecine conflicts are always possible in this regard. In an effort to head off these conflicts, some have proposed also that "concept" be generally understood as a variable whose meaning is to be determined in a context-specific manner related to a theory. Once this is implemented, it enables the theorist to move systematically from one kind of concept to another. For further discussion, see the collection of essays in P. Henle, ed., *Language, Thought, and Culture* (Ann Arbor: University of Michigan Press, 1958); P. Geach, *Mental Acts: Their Content and Objects* (London: Routledge & Kegan Paul, 1957); from a Thomistic viewpoint, J. F. Peifer, *The Concept in Thomism* (New York: Bookman Associates, 1952); and more recently, J. A. Fodor, *Concepts: Where Cognitive Science Went Wrong* (Oxford: Clarendon, 1998).

means by "concept" is not the same as "theme," or "plot," or "motif," or "notion." Such devices do play a role in the interpretation of texts but they do not either self-evidently or necessarily represent the concepts that comprise the immediate reason for and meaning of an individual text. Now, one may understand Knierim's use of "concept" to refer to that governing focus or concern presupposed and controlled by the surface text itself which is ultimately accountable for all of the surface level features of a text. In other words, crucial to a text's interpretation as a cohesive and coherent structure is the designation and interpretation of the concept of the text's structure. And it is the case that structure analysis of a text commences with the scrutiny of the composition (explicit surface level data) of that text. Knierim's emphasis, at this point on the nature of structure analysis, can be seen as bespeaking an *aesthetic* act referring to artistic creation in how the text came to be; indeed, it is an interest in form and quality, with a central focus on knowledge, a cognitivism of sorts, while at the same time anything that has aesthetic value is not de facto assumed to be more of a symbol of religious truth and/or divine revelation. This is the case despite the fact that artistic creation in how a text comes to be is never totally creative but always involves an element of technique where some given material is utilized for the purposes of artistic imagination. The internal activity of imaginative creation already enmeshes itself in a molding of a specific given medium, namely, the language that must be used to shape meaning. And even though the linguistic formulation provides the centerpiece of artistic creation, there is still the technical requirement concerned with affording these imagined representations a tangible existence for others. Thus, since no one but the artist/writer can render this service, the subjective dimension of artistic creation must involve not merely the generation of aesthetic images in the artist's mind, but also the activity of giving them an external form. This activity remains as a ubiquitous element of artistic creation. To be sure, the text's structure, form, setting, intention, and genre all portend aesthetics as an intrinsic ingredient of the text and concept methodology of Knierim. Thus, what we ask from literature, on Knierim's theory, is *knowledge* that addresses fundamental concerns of humanity and shapes them in an accessible form. The point of writing/creating literature is ultimately to cater to aesthetic interests, to promote this human understanding, for it is in literature that persons and events and situations are *given* a form that enables us to obtain insights into new possibilities of human character and human life, personal and social.[3]

---

3. This disquisition about artistic creation with respect to literature is a signal one, but one that is well beyond the scope of this essay. Since it was H. Gunkel who blazed a

The task of structure analysis is not concluded when the text's composition has been recognized, because no explanation has been offered for it. At this juncture is where it is necessary to identify the inexplicit infratextual data referred to as the *concept* of the composition of the text. The process of reconstructing this infratextual conceptuality begins in recognizing that in Knierim's approach, as was stated earlier, the texts themselves not only trigger the interpretive questions, they (the texts!) actually establish the program for their own exegesis. And the search for answers to these questions triggered by the texts is constitutive of the reconstruction of the infratextual concepts that account for the existence of the texts.

In order to exemplify this methodology, I will discuss some of the conceptual aspects in Psalm 2. An initial task involved in a text and concept study of Psalm 2 is the ascertaining of where its major parts are and how those major parts are related to the whole.

THE STRUCTURE OF PSALM 2:1–12

The following structure represents the surface composition of the text and the signals that show the infratextual conceptuality.

Psalm 2
A Drama of Conflict between Two Factions:
Yahweh and His King Versus the Nations, 2:1–12

I. Narrative by the Writer (re: the vanity of the rebellion of nations)	2:1–9
A. The Rebellion Itself	1–3
1. Introduction of a two-part question	1
a. The question proper	1aα
b. The two parts to the question	1aβ+b
1) First part: expressive of unrest	1aβ+γ
a) Statement of the past continuing action —רגשׁ	1aβ
b) Identity of participants —גוים	1aγ
2) Second part: expressive of audacity	1b
a) Identity of participants —לאמים	1bα
b) Statement of the present action —הגה	1bβ
c) Statement expressing the futility of the action —ריק	1bγ

new path in the province of type classifications in biblical literature, one should begin the discussion there. Then, in terms of antecedent influences on Gunkel, attention should be given to J. G. Herder. On Herder, see esp. R. Critchfield and W. Koepke, eds., *Eighteenth-Century German Authors and Their Aesthetic Theories: Literature and the Other Arts* (Columbia, S.C.: Camden House, 1988); G. G. Iggers, *The German Conception of History: The National Tradition of Historical Thought from Herder to the Present* (rev. ed.; Middletown, Conn.: Wesleyan University, 1983); and R. E. Norton, *Herder's Aesthetics and the European Enlightenment* (Ithaca, N.Y.: Cornell University Press, 1991).

2. A description of the two opposing factions   2

  a. The first faction composed of two members   2a+b

    1) First member   2a

      a) Present action — יצב   2aα

      b) Identity — מלכי־ארץ (re: first identifying feature   2aβγ
        of cosmology)

    2) Second member   2b

      a) Identity — רוזנים   2bα

      b) Past and continuing action — יסד   2bβγ

  b. The second faction composed of two members   2c+d

    1) First member: יהוה   2c

    2) Second member: משיחו   2d

3. Citation of a dual declaration of the intensifying of the   3
  rebellion (expressed in plowing terminology)

  a. First declaration: (expressed as an intensive resolve   3a
    [Piel with cohortative])

    1) Declaration proper   3aα

    2) The act expressed (re: tearing apart of the מוסרות)   3aα+β

  b. Second declaration: (expressed as an intensive resolve   3b
    [*hiph'il* with cohortative])

    1) Declaration proper   3bα

    2) The act expressed (re: casting off of the עבתים "from us")   3bα-γ

B. The Reactions to the Rebellion   4–9

  1. Yahweh's reaction stated in three parts (narrator in background)   4–6

  a. Statement of the first part   4

    1) Framed in reference to his first designation   4a

      a) The designation: יושב בשמים   4aα+β
        (re: second identifying feature of cosmology)

      b) The reaction: ישחק   4aγ

    2) Framed in reference to his second designation   4b

      a) The designation: אדני   4bα

      b) The reaction: ילעג   4bβ+γ

  b. Statement of the second part (expressed climactically: אז)   5

    1) Framed in reference to his third designation   5a

      a) The reaction: ידבר אלימו   5aα-γ

      b) The designation: אפו   5δ

    2) Framed in reference to his fourth designation   5b

      a) The designation: חרונו   5bα

      b) The reaction: יבהלמו   5bβ

  c. Statement of the third part (expressed emphatically: ואני)
    (re: Yahweh's declaration)   6

    1) His installation of his own king   6a

      a) Personal reply of Yahweh: ואני   6aα

      b) Personal activity of Yahweh: נסך   6aβγ

    2) His assignment of his holy hill of Zion as the royal seat   6b
      of his king (re: third identifying feature of cosmology)

2. King's reaction (re: the fact that Yahweh had installed him) (narrator in background)	7–9
a. Announcement (re: the declaring of the divine decree)	7a
b. Quotation	7b–9
1) Adoption formula (expressed as a contrast)	7b–c
a) Sonship by natural selection (re: you are my son)	7b
b) Sonship by adoption (re: I today have begotten you)	7c
2) Divine promise (re: rights of sonship)	8–9
a) Universal dominion	8
(1) re: inheritance of nations	8a
(2) re: possession of the ends of the earth	8b
b) Power to achieve it (expressed figuratively)	9
(1) Break them with a rod of iron	9a
(2) Dash them to pieces like a potter's vessel	9b
II. Speech of the Writer	2:10–12
A. Call to Attention (expressed consequentially: ועתה)	10
1. First consequence	10a
a. Identity of those involved: מלכים	10aβ
b. First imperative: השכילו	10aγ
2. Second consequence	10b
a. Identity of those involved: שפטי ארץ	10bβ+γ
b. Second imperative: הוסרו	10bα
B. Summons to Submit	11–12b
1. With reference to Yahweh	11
a. Serve with fear	11a
b. Rejoice with trembling	11b
2. With reference to the son	12a–b
a. Kiss him (expressive of paying homage)	12aαβ
b. Be warned	12aγ-ζ
1) anger of Yahweh	12aγδ
2) you will perish with regard to the way	12aεζ
c. Result: anger of Yahweh comes quickly	12b
C. Commendation	12c
1. Commendation proper: אשרי	12cα
2. Recipients	12cβ-δ

ANALYSIS

Composition of the Surface

A text and concept analysis of Psalm 2 initially presupposes that the text of the psalm possesses grammatical and syntactical cohesion on the surface (i.e., its composition). In other words, the text is more than a mere list of independent words and chains of unrelated sentences. Thus, as a part of the explanation of the text of Psalm 2 in its entirety, one must distinguish the paraphrasing of the text's surface from the reconstruction of its infratextual concept. The discussion now moves to consider the composition of the surface of the text.

The unit Ps. 2:1–12 is constituted by two major parts that address the concerns of the writer: "Narrative by the Writer" (I. = vv. 1–9) and "Speech of the Writer" (II. = vv. 10–12). Narrative, content, and semantic criteria differentiate these two major parts. Indeed, the psalm opens and concludes with the words of the writer, while the opposing factions are depicted by the writer as speaking for themselves. In this way the writer achieves a dramatic effect, thematically, in communicating the reflections and emotions intimated by what is witnessed. Substantive indicators, such as who is speaking or acting, and how they are doing this, and the relationships between them, play an important role in the overall composition of the psalm; but it should be construed that the writer is always in the background, compositionally speaking.

The first unit, "Narrative by the Writer" (I. = vv. 1–9) commences with the narration in the smaller unit, "The Rebellion Itself" (I.A. = vv. 1–3), which is further composed of the "Introduction of a Two-Part Question" (I.A.1. = v. 1), a "Description of the Two Opposing Factions" (I.A.2. = v. 2), and a "Citation of a Dual Declaration of the Intensifying of the Rebellion" (I.A.3. = v. 3). There is nothing perfunctory or boring about the opening scene, which serves to set the mood for the entire narrative. A central, two-part question is addressed by the writer concerning circumstances that involve the reason for the activities of the rebels (I.A.1. = v. 1). The hurly-burly of insurrection on the part of the nations and their kings combines with the writer's perspective (and definitely not that of the rebels!) that such an insurrection is in vain. The participants in this conflict are composed of two factions: the kings of the earth and the rulers versus Yahweh and his anointed one (I.A.2. = v. 2). To be sure, the rebels do not share the writer's perspective about the futility of the rebellion, as they want to tear apart their bonds and cast off their cords (I.A.3. = v. 3).

The writer is specific about the next scene, contained in "The Reactions to the Rebellion" (I.B. = vv. 4–9), in its assuming cosmic contours. First, the writer narrates the threefold reaction of Yahweh to the rebellion (I.B.1. = vv. 4–6). Yahweh, who is said to be sitting in heaven, initially reacts to the rebellion with "laughter," which bespeaks an attitude of scorn and mockery. The motive for Yahweh's laughter comes in the narration of the second and third parts of Yahweh's reaction to the rebellion (I.B.1.b.+c. = vv. 5–6). In the second part Yahweh is determined to speak to the rebels in his wrath and to terrify them in his fury (I.B.1.b. = v. 5), while in the third part Yahweh announces the installation of a king of his own choice in Zion (I.B.1.c. = v. 6). Yahweh is enthroned in heaven, to be sure, while his king (i.e., his anointed one) is enthroned on earth, specifically in Zion. Secondly, following from the narration of Yahweh's reaction to the rebellion, the writer narrates the reaction of Yahweh's chosen king, especially regarding the fact that Yahweh had installed him (I.B.2.). The installation of Yahweh's king is depicted as a finished transaction, and the announcement of the decree of Yahweh refers to a decree that had already been given in the past (I.B.2.a.). Moreover, this king is said to be Yahweh's "son" by adoption through his being "begotten" (i.e., "elected" and "installed" by Yahweh) (I.B.2.b. = v. 7b–c). As a natural consequence to Yahweh's installation of his king on Zion this king is now told to "ask" Yahweh for special privileges, specified in terms of an "inheritance" and a "possession" (I.B.2.b. = vv. 8–9). What it comes down to is that Yahweh will permit his king to have universal dominion over the nations and the ends of the earth; and Yahweh will grant his king the power to achieve this dominion (expressed figuratively as "breaking" and "pulverizing" them).

In the second major part of the psalm is contained the "Speech of the Writer" (II.A.–C. = vv. 10–12), which is further composed of a "Call to Attention" (II.A.), a "Summons to Submit" (II.B.), and a "Commendation" (II.C.). In essence, the writer is presenting his or her own advice to the foreign kings and judges of the earth. First, the writer admonishes them to act prudently with regard to the implications of what has transpired in Yahweh's enthronement of his own king. The writer summons them, furthermore, to submit to Yahweh in serving him with fear and rejoicing with trembling. And, without a doubt, this scene increases the sense of haste and precipitancy, for if the foreign kings and judges in their submission to Yahweh do not also submit to his "son" (the king) by way of "kissing" the son, it would result in disaster ("his anger is kindled quickly") (II.B.1.+2. = vv. 11–12). The writer concludes the speech by declaring a commendation for all who seek refuge in Yahweh. Happiness would come, in addition to the vassalic relationship engendered in serving him, to those who submit to Yahweh.

Infratextual Concept

Looking beyond the surface level (composition) of the text of Psalm 2, the next task in a text and concept explanation of the psalm is the reconstruction of its inexplicit infratextual conceptuality. This has been aptly referred to as the conceptual coherence of the text in its parts and as a whole.[4] It is helpful to commence with an enumeration of the con-

---

4. See R. Knierim, *Text and Concept in Leviticus 1:1–9: A Case in Exegetical Method* (FAT 2; Tübingen: J. C. B. Mohr [Paul Siebeck], 1992) 3. Knierim claims that it is possible that surface level expressions of a text may point to a text's conceptual coherence but the concepts themselves are fundamentally *infratextual*. See also H. Utzschneider, *Das Heiligtum und das Gesetz: Studien zur Bedeutung der sinaitischen Heiligtumstexte (Ex 25–40; Lev 8–9)*

ceptual indicators/signals in the psalm, which will be articulated in the
form of questions. Seeking answers to these questions is constitutive of
reconstructing the concepts that are responsible for the existence of the
texts and that go on operating in the texts as authenticated by the presence of the questions themselves. Typical questions of the kind we are
interested in are contained in the following list.

List of Conceptual Indicators

(1) What form does the composition of the psalm acquire? (2) What
is the relationship between Yahweh, the king, the other nations, and
the writer of the text? (3) Is Psalm 2 based on actual historical events?
(4) Does the text allow for historicizing? (5) Is it possible that the text
of the psalm points to and/or presupposes a relationship between ideology and history in that the one who is praised as "the king" is
conceptualized as *the* representative of Yahweh in all the earth? (6) If
there is an ideology concept present in the text, does this mean that the
role of ideology is assumed as fully operative? (7) What is the relationship of perfect and imperfect verb forms in the psalm? (8) What are the
conceptual temporal perspectives? (9) Does the fact that something is
declared and/or presupposed by the text to have occurred in the past
possess any significance for a present happening, or for that matter, a
future one? (10) What is the semantic and conceptual range of a particular word in a given context? (11) Why does the text mention that the
activity of the nations and the peoples is "in vain"? (12) What is the hierarchy of the reconstructed conceptual system of this psalm? Since my
present task is to indicate only the general contours of a text and concept explanation of Psalm 2,[5] I will limit my focus to two examples that
exemplify the process of reasoning and exegesis, and then from there
attempt to show how Psalm 2 is to be explained.

Discussion

גוים and לאמים. A careful contemplation of the relationships in the
psalm between its conceptual terminology and its action-oriented lan-

---

(OBO 77; Göttingen: Vandenhoeck & Ruprecht, 1988) 15–16. Utzschneider differentiates
between the *Kohäsion* of a text, which comprises the function and result of components in
the surface of the text uniting the text together, and the *Kohärenz* of a text, referring to the
conceptual integrity of a text as a whole. The components in the *Kohäsion* of a text include
sounds, words, sentences, and sentence groups, each of which can function as indicators
of conjunction, disjunction, subordination, and other principles of organization. To refer
to the *Kohärenz* of a text is to characterize a *Sinnkontinuität* (i.e., a continuity of meaning) fixed by the surface level expressions of the text that signal and bind the concepts
together.
    5. For the details, see Haney, " 'And All Nations Shall Serve Him,' " 172–234, where I
analyze Psalm 2.

guages must be carried out. The conceptual terminology constitutes signals that indicate key persons, places, or objects, while the action-oriented language found in the verbs signals primarily the progression of activities. In terms of conceptual terminology, we immediately en-counter the word pair גוים and לאמים in a two-part question that concerns their activities. Upon closer examination, we must ask what the rela-tionship is between the referents of the word pair. Is there a logical relationship between them that has been presupposed in that each term emphasizes a particular aspect of the whole that is connoted by the cor-relative juxtapositioning of the two terms? A study of the usage of the two terms in the Bible is particularly instructive. For example, גוי, which occurs over five hundred times in the Hebrew Bible, is never utilized in conjunction with Yahweh's name. By this is meant that we never ob-serve the construction גוי־יהוה occurring in the Hebrew Bible. But this is not to say that many גוים do not become לאם for Yahweh's sake, as for ex-ample, in Zech. 2:15. Also, within the concept of גוי there is not the least notion of personal ties. גוי speaks of massive conglomerates bound to-gether from without and not within. In Genesis 10, the so-called Table of Nations exclusively treats of גוים. Moreover, when גוי is employed in the Bible, it is usually used with ממלכה "kingdom." So it is that when the Israelites demanded a king, it was in order that they would become like all the גוים (1 Sam. 8:20). If we also consider on an individualistic plane the referents of גוי, we learn that those referents are comprised of earthlings — a person in a crowd — basically a statistic (cf. Job 34:29).[6] Now, when we study the use of לאם in the Bible, we discover that it usually refers either to "people" as an ethnic community (Gen. 25:23, referring to Jacob and Esau; or Isa. 51:4, referring to Israel) or "people" in general (Prov. 11:26). Besides the reference in Ps. 2:1, לאם is also used with גוי in Isa 34:1; 43:9; Ps. 44:3, 15; 105:44; 149:7. Also, there is the intriguing phenomenon taking place in Isaiah wherein לאם is situated solely as the second coordinate in several instances of poetic word pairs (cf. 17:12–14; 41:1; 43:4; 43:9; 49:1; 51:4; 55:4; 60:2). And, with respect to Gen. 25:23 and 27:27, לאם crops up in the disquisition about the eth-nic hostilities that exist between Israel and Edom. Finally, in Hab. 2:13 and Jer. 51:58 there is a quite similar use of language, with לאם and ריק coming in close linguistic proximity to each other. The putative up-shot of all this is that it becomes clear that when a text such as Psalm

---

6. For a brief but incisive discussion of some of the issues, see N. K. Gottwald, *The Tribes of Yahweh* (Maryknoll, N.Y.: Orbis, 1979) 509–11. See also E. A. Speiser, " 'People' and 'Nation' of Israel," *JBL* 79 (1960) 157–63; L. Rost, "Die Bezeichnungen für Land und Volk im Alten Testament," in A. Alt, ed., *Festschrift Otto Procksch zum sechzigsten Geburtstag am 9. August 1934 überreicht* (Leipzig: A. Deichert'sche Verlagsbuchhandlung, 1934) 125–48. Also highly serviceable is the article by A. R. Hulst, "עם/גוי *'am/gôy*, people," *TLOT*, 2:896–919.

2:1 juxtaposes לְאֹם and גּוֹי, it does so deliberately to signal a conceptual distinction in how to understand the terms. Indeed, the translation and comprehension of these two terms involve more than just mere words — it goes right to the very structure of a highly organized society.[7] The references to גוים and לאמים in Psalm 2 point to the text's understanding of "peoples," not simplistically in the sense of a group, a gang, a crowd, or population, but peoples in the sense of peoples as a comprehensive sociopolitical, and worldwide pluralistic, union of nations who do not wish to stand under the direct guidance of Yahweh and his anointed one. The inevitable result is that conflict is made necessary in that the rebels perceive that an injustice is being foisted upon them by Yahweh. The nature of such injustice appears, at the outset, to be more than just the achieving of the submission of the rebels. It also involves the forced integration of the rebels into a single community of faith (cf. 2:12c in the use of חסה, "to take shelter"). The *Qal* active participle of חסה underscores the community's need of protection (cf. Ps. 31:20; 5:12; 34:23). In order to have asylum the community must "hide itself" (with the secondary sense of "having confidence") in Yahweh.[8] Furthermore, in construing גוים and לאמים together with מלכי־ארץ and רוזנים, we conclude that the text is signaling an all-inclusive perspective, and therefore, the main emphasis is not just on one king of one nation, but it is a worldwide unity of rebellion. Thus, the overriding factor had come to be the political unit and its administrative subunits, regardless of ethnic composition (cf. לאם). Indeed, this was a megastructure comprised of diverse ethnic elements. And to be sure, the גוים and the לאמים are understood as having yielded their places to the מלכים and the רוזנים who are their leaders, and who effect the actual decisions about the rebellion.[9] The writer, as a contemporary of the narrated events, does not mention the names of the nations that were in rebellion.

---

7. See F. Delitzsch, *A Commentary on the Book of Psalms*, vol. 1 (trans. D. Eaton; New York: Funk and Wagnall, 1883) 121. Delitzsch construes גוים and לאמים together with מלכי־ארץ and רוזנים as referring to "a general rebellion of the Gentile world against Yahweh and his anointed, something akin perhaps to a universalistic perspective." But in saying this, Delitzsch still has not interpreted the relationship of גוים and לאמים to each other.

8. E. Gerstenberger, "חסה, *ḥsh*, to take shelter," *TLOT*, 2:464–65. In Ps. 31:20 the psalmist speaks of the abundant goodness that Yahweh has laid up for those who fear him and "made" (פעל) for those who take refuge (חסה) in him. In Ps. 5:12 the text declares that the person who takes "refuge" (חסה) in Yahweh should rejoice forever, while in Ps. 34:23 Yahweh is said to "ransom" (פדה) the life of his servants and not to condemn those who take refuge in him.

9. See B. Gosse, "Le Psaume 2 et l'usage rédactionnel des Oracles contre les Nations à l'époque post-exilique," *BN* 62 (1992) 18–24. Gosse emphasizes what he perceives as the key redactional role played by Isaiah 34 in that Edom serves as the representative of the nations acting against Israel. See also B. Dicou, "Literary Function and Literary History of Isa 34," *BN* 58 (1991) 30ff.

On the Relationship between Ideology and History in Psalm 2. At this juncture in our discussion the connection between language and ideology provides the touchstone for clarifying the relationship between ideology and history in Psalm 2. In speaking of this "clarifying" as "interpretation," there are two primary considerations that must be kept in mind. First, it is inescapable that we are dealing with discourse. Language that has been realized in speech or writing is *already* an interpretation. Events and actions are interpreted by the writer of Psalm 2, who routinely employs interpretative procedures to make sense of them and others. Thus, to begin an analysis of discourse is to produce an interpretation of an interpretation. The second consideration deals with the creative character of the interpretative process. It is a highly questionable assumption that the meaning of the text can be simply "read off" from its syntax. This is not to denigrate the importance of formal methods of analysis, though. The study of ideology can be pursued in evaluating the ways in which the term "ideology" denotes a more or less systematically developed and comprehensive group of ideas comprising cognitive meaning.[10] Understood in this way, ideology's function is to convey a specific connotation representing a neutral value to the reader, and not to express or elicit attitudes of either a positive or negative evaluation of some kind. Ideology, then, is understood as neither good nor bad but simply as a truism — as the study of ideas and/or concepts. But we should also not undercut the importance of social and historical circumstances in the interpretation of the ideology. It seems that the study of the system of ideas has to be considered in its relation to reality, to the society, and to the environment. Whatever the values are that dominate the ideology also set the goals and regulate the conduct. Moreover, history and historical periods come into view in the interdependence between ideology and reality. Every historical period possesses its own explicit set of values, its guiding principles, with a large area of activities being controlled by its (the historical period) normative order. What we study, then, are those external expressions that comprise consequences of the activities of this historical period guided by its world outlook. In this connection of inquiring into social-historical conditions in the interpretation of ideology, Giovanni Garbini well states his point regarding the interpretation of the Hebrew Bible.

---

10. The concept of ideology and its many different definitions are important topics but are beyond the scope of this essay. Recommended reading should include but not be limited to J. B. Thompson, *Studies in the Theory of Ideology* (Berkeley: University of California Press, 1984); T. Eagleton, *Ideology: An Introduction* (New York: Verso, 1991); A. Naess, *Democracy, Ideology and Objectivity: Studies in the Semantics and Cognitive Analysis of Ideological Controversy* (Oxford: Basil Blackwell, 1956).

It is often said that the Bible is a religious book and not a history book. That is true, but it is still rather vague.... [W]hat is not thought about enough is that when the Old Testament was written as a book of religion, the concept of religion was different from ours; that is the case not only because more than two millennia have passed since then but because after the Old Testament, the New Testament has modified the very concept of religion, providing the beginning of that way of looking at things which is still essentially ours today. In some cases to talk of ideology is tantamount to talking of theology, but the two terms are not always interchangeable, because Hebrew religion...included things which today seem to us to be external to religion. Historical conceptions, political reports can only seldom be considered expressions of a "religious" view of life...but when a people becomes "holy," every action in everyday life and every political event becomes a religious phenomenon.[11]

The social phenomenon depicted in Psalm 2 is one that is dominated by a religious-theological ideology, and the cultures discussed therein are affected by values and modes of thought of this outlook. Within the context of this world outlook, the expressions in Psalm 2 gain an understanding. Thus, the discussion of the idea system in Psalm 2, substantively speaking, is provoked by the question at this point, What is the relation between Yahweh and the nations according to the psalm? In order to rebel, the rebels must know (or, are assumed by the text to know) against what they rebel, and also why. Is the rebellion mentioned in this psalm a justified one? It is altogether possible that it is. We have a clue early on in the psalm that the nations are considered as degraded in terms of their relationship to Yahweh (cf. ריק). Hans-Joachim Kraus points out, "In the world of the nations Israel stands in total isolation, belonging only to Yahweh."[12] And the immediacy of the special relationship between Yahweh and his anointed/king, who establish room for Yahweh's people and her history, is disclosed by the fact that Yahweh has delegated his power to his anointed one, his "executive officer," to smash the nations (I.B.2.) if they rebel against him. The fact of Yahweh's involvement itself in this respect is an adequate basis for the understanding of Yahweh as the universal God, who is politically and militarily active in defending his king against the uprising of foreign nations (cf. Ps. 2:8–9; 110:1–2, 5–6; 132:17–18). The momentousness of this understanding "attests not only to the precarious historical conditions under which Israel always existed but also to the tension between the strategies of the historical empires and those of Yahweh

---

11. G. Garbini, *History and Ideology in Ancient Israel* (trans. J. Bowden; New York: Crossroad, 1988) xv.

12. H.-J. Kraus, *Theology of the Psalms* (Minneapolis: Augsburg, 1986) 59. It is unfortunate that Kraus has facilely assumed in his discussion that Zion and Israel are synonymous. The text of Psalm 2 nowhere mentions Israel.

which lie at the heart of the course and meaning of human history."[13] Israel's relationship with the historical God is defined by Israel's ideology of Yahweh's historical involvement on Israel's behalf. But to say this only prompts another question, How do we draw a dividing line between what is perceived as "history" and what is perceived as ancient Israelite "religious ideology"? Again, Garbini's comments are apropos in his bid to delineate the "historical" conception of the Hebrew Bible.

> [T]hat political thought which identifies itself with religious thought... and that religious thought which makes itself historical thought and creates a fictitious but sacral history come together in a circularity which in our all too knowing language is no longer politics or religion or history — but only ideology.[14]

Thus, in terms of the relationship between ideology and history in Psalm 2, the substance-critical issue does not turn on the mere presence of an ideological impetus that is believed to manipulate the exposition of events in the psalm. No historiography can lay claim to ideological neutrality, as a particular worldview is always present. The crucial substance-critical issue at this juncture resides in the actuality that the ideological impetus in the psalm has a regulative *value* that serves to oversee the narrative itself. And, in this respect, it is curiously interesting that, historically, Israel was almost always subordinate/subjected to the kings of the great empires and their gods. In the ideology of Psalm 2, it is the other way around. The king on Zion is the great king of the earth. And what we have in terms of Hebrew "religion," as portrayed in Psalm 2, is the appropriation of a sacral history as the vehicle for a "mythification of thought."[15] This "mythification" of thought ostensibly serves to dehistoricize and fix the events of the cosmos-chaos relationship in terms of what *naturally* happens repeatedly when the plans of the nations violate the plans of Yahweh (cf. the chaos of the turmoil of nations in Ezekiel 38–39). Chaos (in the form of the turmoil of nations) as a threat to the cosmic order is portrayed by the psalmist as that which must be overcome, conquered, and controlled. Psalm 2 speaks of the ideological relations of domination and the religio-ethnic loyalty

---

13. R. Knierim, "The Interpretation of the Old Testament," in *The Task of Old Testament Theology: Substance, Method, and Cases* (Grand Rapids: Eerdmans, 1995) 100.

14. Garbini, *History and Ideology*, xvi.

15. T. Eagleton, *Ideology*, 188. The process of interpreting this "mythification" of thought and the many relationships engendered in that process are crucial topics but are beyond the scope of this essay. A fine place to start, though, is the work by C. Long, *Alpha: the Myths of Creation* (New York: George Braziller, 1963). In reference to the Bible one should consult H. Gunkel, *Schöpfung und Chaos in Urzeit und Endzeit mit Beiträgen von H. Zimmern* (Göttingen: Vandenhoeck & Ruprecht, 1895), and B. Anderson, *Creation Versus Chaos: The Reinterpretation of Mythical Symbolism in the Bible* (New York: Association Press, 1967).

to Yahweh being represented as legitimate. When Yahweh exercises his faithfulness in protecting his king, the destinies of the nations are decisively altered. These nations have been placed to serve Yahweh, but are, as they rebel, forced into submission to the anointed one, who is Yahweh's representative of all nations equally on earth, if they are to be regarded as legitimate. The nations are *in their own right* considered legitimate if they serve Yahweh and submit to his anointed one. Yahweh does not grant the nations their own theological validity for which his anointed one is conceived of simply as a symbol. Yahweh is the universal God of all humankind from the perspective of the writer of Psalm 2. It is no wonder, then, that the nations are rebelling, since Yahweh has established his anointed as ruler over the nations unto the ends of the earth. The understanding of Yahweh's justice is also at stake: we have in Psalm 2 a particularistic theological ideology functioning for the submission of what is held to be universally valid for the legitimation of the nations at the expense of the nations' own right to be considered legitimate as nations in and of themselves.[16]

Furthermore, in regard to the "mythification" of thought, the writer depicts the conceptual center of the "historical" movement in this drama of conflict with Yahweh's act of defending his king against the nations. In this depiction everything is ideologized "and bent to the sole purpose of showing the truth of a particular religious vision — a vision which presents the history of the Hebrew people as a theatre for the work of God, thus creating a new type of mythology."[17] In the same way that the writer represented Yahweh as saving his king from the aggressive *self-defense* of the nations (and thus carrying forward the portrayal of a salvific phenomenon), the same holds true for the depicted "historical" situation of trouble. Once the human situation is appraised and evaluated in terms of potential trouble, there is the prompt perception that Yahweh is involved, since the writer records not only Yahweh's direct reaction to the trouble (I.B.1. = vv. 4–6), but also his indirect reaction to it, given by the writer through the words of Yahweh's anointed one (I.B.2. = vv. 7–9). There is no indication or description of the historical situation(s) precipitating the trouble. That situation is already presupposed. What is crucial at this point to discern is the ideological interpretation of that situation. Once again, the writer's focus falls on Yahweh and his king, especially in the portrayal of their reactions to the trouble, as well as the writer's own concluding speech. And what

---

16. See R. Knierim, "On Gabler," in *Task of Old Testament Theology*, 549. In this regard, note the provocative comments of J. L. McKenzie: "The eternity of Israel is the created reflection of the eternity of Yahweh, who has joined Israel to himself by covenant and promise" (*A Theology of the Old Testament* [New York: Doubleday, 1974] 269).

17. Garbini, *History and Ideology*, 61.

we come away with is an ideologized "interpretation" of a historical episode marked by religio-ethnic connotations. Also, it would appear that the roots of this ideology are essentially mythological.

The Conceptual System of Psalm 2. *Summary Listing.* Psalm 2:1–12 operates and is composed on a number of diverse conceptualities. It is the conceptual aspects that determine the structure of the text. In addition to the list of conceptual signals listed above (see "List of Conceptual Indicators"), there are a number of other conceptual indicators that would have to be studied: (1) the presupposed relationship between the nations and the peoples as opposed to the kings of the earth and the rulers; (2) the presupposed relationship contained in the textual reference "against Yahweh and his anointed"; (3) the presupposed relationship between the concept of rebellion and the words "bonds" and "cords"; (4) the presupposed connection between the text's reference to "he who sits in heaven — the Lord" and the reference to what is happening on the earth; (5) the affiliation between "laughs" and "derision" as opposed to "wrath" and "fury"; (6) the meaning of "Yahweh will terrify them"; (7) the presupposed relationship between "my king," and "his anointed one," and "Zion"; (8) the construal of the "decree of Yahweh" with respect to the statement "I today have begotten you"; (9) the meaning or reason why the text says "ask of me"; (10) the presupposed relationship between "breaking" and "dashing in pieces"; (11) the presupposed relationship between "kings" and "rulers" as opposed to the later reference to "kings" and "judges"; and (12) the presupposed connection between "serving Yahweh" and the writer's use of a string of imperatives in vv. 10–12 (especially concerned with "kissing the son").

Stratification of These Conceptualities. The numerous major conceptual aspects are arranged in a particular sequence in the text. The sequence is neither random nor coincidental. Also, the basis of the sequential ordering of the text is not that Yahweh speaks or the writer speaks. The focus of the text falls on the sequence of events in their occurrence envisioned in the text. This sequence also presupposes a logical and chronological relationship in that the rebellion must occur (or be in the process of occurring) *before* there can be any reaction(s) to it, which in turn must precede the writer's call to attention, summons to submit, and commendation for those that do submit. Thus, it is clear that the sequence cannot be reversed.

In the text of the psalm there is not one iota of description about the historical situation that precipitates the trouble. That situation is apparently presupposed. What does present itself to be understood is the ideological interpretation of that situation by the writer. The conceptual

indicators that point to and/or presuppose rebellion cannot be construed as logically and chronologically presupposing those indicators
that speak about "reactions" to the rebellion. Furthermore, with respect
to the temporal aspects that serve to reinforce the dramatic narrative
movement in the entire text up to the עתה in II.A. (= v. 10), it again becomes clear that such a combinatorial use of both perfect and imperfect
verb forms develops not in simplistic terms of stylistics but as an ideological commentary on the central conceptual aspect in the psalm. And,
it also seems to be unambiguous here in Psalm 2 that ideology stands in
contrast to history. The most important conceptual aspect in Psalm 2 is
centered on the enthronement of Yahweh's king on Zion. The rest of the
psalm is concerned with events happening *after* the enthronement. In
other words, from the standpoint of the hierarchy of the text, all other
conceptual perspectives are subordinate to that of the enthronement of
Yahweh's king. Thus, why are the nations rebelling? Precisely because
they perceive that an injustice is being forced upon them by Yahweh,
having to do with their submission to Yahweh's elected and installed
king, whose dominion extends over the ends of the earth. And it is
at this point that the ideological commentary kicks in, because *nowhere*
in the history of the Hebrew people do we see that the king on Zion
was/is represented as the great king of the earth.[18]

---

18. The construal of this underscores the necessity of further study concerning the
relationship between cosmos and history in ancient Israel's theology as well as the difficult issue of Yahweh's justice and Israel's relationship to the nations. Such studies are
beyond the scope of this essay, but one could begin with R. Knierim's essays "Cosmos
and History in Israel's Theology" and "Israel and the Nations in the Land of Palestine
in the Old Testament," in *The Task of Old Testament Theology*. Correlatively, and quite ap-
propriately, one should also consult Jewish sources, such as R. Goldenberg, *The Nations
That Know Thee Not: Ancient Jewish Attitudes toward Other Religions* (New York: New York
University Press, 1998); J. D. Levenson, *Sinai and Zion: An Entry into the Jewish Bible* (New
York: Winston Press, 1985); J. Neusner, "The Religious Uses of History," *History and Theory*
5 (1966) 153–71; D. Novak, *The Election of Israel: The Idea of the Chosen People* (Cambridge:
Cambridge University Press, 1995).

Selected Bibliography

Critchfield, R., and W. Koepke, eds. *Eighteenth-Century German Authors and Their Aesthetic Theories: Literature and the Other Arts*. Columbia, S.C.: Camden House, 1988.

Eagleton, T. *Ideology: An Introduction*. New York: Verso, 1991.

Fodor, J. A. *Concepts: Where Cognitive Science Went Wrong*. Oxford: Clarendon, 1998.

Garbini, G. *History and Ideology in Ancient Israel*. Translated by J. Bowden. New York: Crossroad, 1988.

Goldenberg, R. *The Nations That Know Thee Not: Ancient Jewish Attitudes toward Other Religions*. New York: New York University Press, 1998.

Gottwald, N. *The Tribes of Yahweh*. Maryknoll, N.Y.: Orbis, 1979.

Haney, Randy G. "'And All Nations Shall Serve Him': Text and Concept Analysis in Royal Psalms." Ph.D. diss. Claremont Graduate School, 1999.

Henle, P., ed. *Language, Thought, and Culture*. Ann Arbor: University of Michigan Press, 1958.

Iggers, G. G. *The German Conception of History: The National Tradition of Historical Thought from Herder to the Present*. Rev. ed. Middletown, Conn.: Wesleyan University, 1983.

Knierim, R. P. *Text and Concept in Leviticus 1:1–9: A Case in Exegetical Method*. FAT 2. Tübingen: J. C. B. Mohr (Paul Siebeck), 1992.

———. "The Interpretation of the Old Testament." In *The Task of Old Testament Theology: Substance, Method, and Cases*. Grand Rapids: Eerdmans, 1995.

Naess, A. *Democracy, Ideology, and Objectivity: Studies in the Semantics and Cognitive Analysis of Ideological Controversy*. Oxford: Basil Blackwell, 1956.

Norton, R. E. *Herder's Aesthetics and the European Enlightenment*. Ithaca, N.Y.: Cornell University Press, 1991.

Novak, D. *The Election of Israel: The Idea of the Chosen People*. Cambridge: Cambridge University Press, 1995.

Peifer, J. F. *The Concept in Thomism*. New York: Bookman Associates, 1952.

Rost, L. "Die Bezeichnungen für Land und Volk im Alten Testament." *Festschrift Otto Procksch zum sechzigsten Geburtstag am 9. August 1934 überreicht*, ed. A. Alt. Leipzig: A. Deichert'sche Verlagsbuchhandlung, 1934, 125–48.

Thompson, J. B. *Studies in the Theory of Ideology*. Berkeley: University of California Press, 1984.

Utzschneider, H. *Das Heiligtum und das Gesetz: Studien zur Bedeutung der sinaitischen Heiligtumstexte (Ex 25–40; Lev 8–9)*. OBO 77. Göttingen: Vandenhoeck & Ruprecht, 1988.

8

Structure and Coherence in Amos 4

John E. Hartley and William Yarchin

Professor Knierim has aptly drawn attention to the analysis of a text's structure in the process of exegesis, demonstrating the significance it can have for interpretation.[1] A thorough description of Knierim's method of structure analysis is presented in Anthony Campbell's instructive article "Structure Analysis and the Art of Exegesis."[2] A key strength of this approach is the emphasis on detecting the influence of underlying concepts — often implicit in the text's features, including its structure — in determining the coherence of a text. Inspired by Knierim's method, our intention is to demonstrate the coherence of the sermon in Amos 4.

STRUCTURE ANALYSIS

Amos 4 is often treated as consisting of four or five independent units, vv. 1–3, 4–5, 6–11, 12, and 13.[3] Contemporary commentators, however, find that several of these units belong together, particularly 4:4–13.[4]

---

1. See crucial works by R. Knierim; for example, *Text and Concept in Leviticus 1:1–9: A Case in Exegetical Method* (FAT 2; Tübingen: J. C. B. Mohr [Paul Siebeck], 1992); "The Book of Numbers," in *Die Hebräische Bibel und ihre zweifache Nachgeschichte* (FS R. Rendtorff; eds. E. Blum, C. Macholz, and W. Stegemann; Neukirchen: Neukirchener, 1991) 155–69; "On the Theology of Psalm 19," in *The Task of Old Testament Theology: Substance, Method, and Cases* (Grand Rapids: Eerdmans, 1995) 322–50.

2. In H. Sun and K. Eades, eds., *Problems in Biblical Theology: Essays in Honor of Rolf Knierim* (Grand Rapids: Eerdmans, 1997) 76–103.

3. E.g., J. L. Mays (*Amos: A Commentary* [OTL; Philadelphia: Westminster, 1969] 71–84) discusses Amos 4 in three blocks, vv. 1–3, 4–5, 6–13, paying little attention to how any of these paragraphs relate to each other, save for a sentence on the interconnectedness of the segments in vv. 6–13 (p. 77). W. Rudolph ("Amos 4,6–13," in J. J. Stamm et al., eds., *Wort-Gebot-Glaube: Beiträge zur Theologie des Alten Testaments, Walter Eichrodt zum 80. Geburtstag* [ATANT 59; Zurich: Zwingli, 1970] 27–28), however, takes the position that 4:6–13 is a self-contained unit that had no connection to 4:4–5.

4. J. Jeremias (*Der Prophet Amos* [ATD 24/2; Göttingen: Vandenhoeck und Ruprecht, 1995] 47), for example, says that 4:4–13 is a seamless unit distinct from the preceding both in style and theme. S. Paul (*Amos* [Hermeneia; Minneapolis: Fortress, 1991] 138, 141–42, 149–50) points out that 4:4–13 are held together by the bold contrast between the satirical invitation to sin by sacrificing (vv. 4–5) and the recounting of the series of punitive catastrophes (vv. 6–11); the exhortation to face Yahweh is the climax to the series of catastrophes (vv. 12–13).

4:1–3 is taken as an independent oracle because it contains both an accusation and a warning of judgment;[5] many scholars, though, place it with 3:9–13 as a member of the utterances against the nobility of Samaria.[6] By contrast, our purpose in this brief article is to give evidence that 4:1–3 indeed belongs with 4:4–13.[7] The discussion of this claim is important, for, as Campbell points out,[8] the richest interpretation of a text requires sensitive discernment of the beginning and ending of that text.[9]

At the outset it is important to note that chapter 4 belongs to the larger unit 3:1–4:13, clearly delineated by the שמעו את הדבר הזה ("hear

---

5. T. H. Robinson (*Die Zwölf kleinen Propheten* [HAT 14; Tübingen: J. C. B. Mohr (Paul Siebeck), 1964] 85) describes it as "ein vollständiges und selbständiges Stück." See also G. Fleischer, *Von Menschenverkäufern, Baschankühen und Rechtsverkehrern: Die Sozialkritik des Amosbuches in historisch-kritischer, sozialgeschictlicher und archäologischer Perspective* (BBB 74; Frankfurt: Athenäum, 1989) 80. H. McKeating (*Amos, Hosea, Micah* [CBC; Cambridge: Cambridge University Press, 1971] 31–38) discusses 4:1–3, 4–12, and 13 as distinct units. H. W. Wolff (*Joel and Amos* [Hermeneia; Philadelphia: Fortress, 1977] 205) discusses 4:1–3 as an independent judgment speech, but he does notice a link with the preceding oracles by means of the oath formula (3:9–15). S. Paul (*Amos*, 128) identifies 4:1–3 as an oracle of judgment in a new section with thematic ties to 3:9–15: the leadership of Samaria and the oppression of the poor.

6. D. Stuart (*Hosea–Jonah* [WBC 31; Waco, Tex.: Word, 1987] 329) identifies 3:9–4:1–3 as part of a compound oracle consisting of four units: 3:9–11, 3:12, 3:13–15, 4:1–3. These four oracles all treat the guilt of the wealthy leaders of Samaria and the coming devastation Israel will experience in war. D. U. Rottzoll (*Studien zur Redaktion und Komposition des Amosbuchs* [BZAW 243; Berlin: de Gruyter, 1996]) argues that the final form of Amos has been laid out in a palestrophic pattern. The layer of 3:9–4:3 contains speeches against Samaria (pp. 125–45). The alignment we suggest here would not necessarily destroy this palestrophic pattern. J. Jeremias (*Amos*, 38–39) locates 4:1–3 in the collection of words against Samaria.

7. A few scholars have come close to this position. A. R. Guenther (*Hosea, Amos* [BCBC; Scottdale, Pa.: Herald, 1998] 280–81) finds Amos 4 to be a unit consisting of four oracles: vv. 1–3, 4–5, 6–11, 12–13. However, he does not go on to interpret these Yahweh utterances as an integral unit.

In a creative discussion, H. M. Barstad (*The Religious Polemics of Amos: Studies in the Preaching of Am 2, 7B–8; 4,1–13; 5,1–27; 6,4–7; 8,14* [VTSup 34; Leiden: E. J. Brill, 1984] 59) finds that Amos 4 is "a coherent speech unit." He divides this speech as follows: the address to the people of Samaria (v. 1), pronouncement of judgment (vv. 2–3), exposure of mistaken cultic activities at Bethel and Gilgal (vv. 4–5), enumeration of disasters throughout Israel for non-Yahwistic worship (vv. 6–11), threat of greater disaster (v. 12), and doxology (v. 13). In his presentation of a new way of reading Amos 4, however, he does not elaborate on the interrelationship of these units in the chapter. F. I. Andersen and D. N. Freedman (*Amos* [AB 24A; New York: Doubleday, 1989] xxix–xxx) place 4:1–3 in the section 3:9–4:3, "Messages for Israel//Samaria." Nevertheless, before discussing in detail 4:1–3, there is a section entitled "Introduction to Chapter 4" (pp. 412–18), containing an outline that treats all segments of ch. 4 as a unit. In the extensive discussion, however, these authors give little attention to the significance of the coherence of the units that make up 4:1–13.

8. Campbell, "Structure Analysis," 78.

9. Barstad (*Religious Polemics*, 59) says, "It follows that no part of the text should be allowed to be treated in isolation, but that each unit of the text must be viewed in light of the whole of the prophet's preaching."

this word") formula standing at 3:1 and 5:1. This larger unit (3:1–4:13) opens with a second person plural address (3:1–2) that makes a general announcement, which, until one reaches 3:2b, sounds like a standard cult-prophetic call for the assembly to receive words of blessing. In a cultic setting 3:2b strikes with a powerful surprise by tying עֲוֹנוֹת ("iniquities") directly to the people. That jolting announcement of condemnation is defended by a reflection on the prophetic compulsion to proclaim (לְהִנָּבֵא) such negative divine words (3:3–8). This defense is distinguished amid the surrounding oracles, for it lacks any direct address to Israel. Next, some "other peoples" are addressed as they are called to see for themselves the oppression in Samaria and to hear that its strongholds will be destroyed (3:9–11). Samaria is referred to in the third person here. The gathered peoples are then called to bear witness to the fact that Yahweh's judgment will be upon the cultic structures and wealthy residences of Israel, still referred to in the third person (3:13–15).

At 4:1 there is a return to the direct second person address form. Disaster is announced to Israel as an impending expulsion into exile (4:2–3) and as a catastrophic, unmistakable encounter with Yahweh (4:12–13). All of ch. 4 is distinguished by the second person plural direct address form, including the satirical call to worship and the review of evidence for failure to repent (4:4–5, 6–11). This style marks 4:1–13 as a discrete section within the larger unit.

Having noted the general parameters of chapter 4 as a section, we proceed with a structure analysis of the chapter.

Announcement of Disaster upon Israel — Amos 4:1–13

A. Expressed in brief to the women of Samaria: for indulgent oppression 4:1–3
   1. Call to hear a Yahweh utterance 4:1
     a. Call proper 4:1aα
     b. Characterization of addressees 4:1aβ–b
       1) In general terms (metaphor, location) 4:1aβ^1
       2) In specific terms 4:1aβ^2–b
         a) Actions of addressees cited: oppression of poor 4:1aβ^2
         b) Attitudes of addressees cited (by quotation): 4:1b
           careless indulgence
   2. Utterance proper 4:2–3
     a. Announcement of disaster 4:2–3bα
       1) Qualifications of disaster: Yahweh oath 4:2a
         a) Disaster is certain (oath formula) 4:2aα
         b) Disaster is imminent (יָמִים בָּאִים formula) 4:2aβ
       2) Disaster proper: exile 4:2b–3bα
     b. Yahweh utterance formula 4:3bβ

B. Expressed in detail to the people of Israel: for failure to repent 4:4–13
  1. Cause of failure: cultic unfaithfulness 4:4–5
    a. Yahweh utterance 4:4–5
      1) Call to worship 4:4–5a
        a) Call to transgress at worship centers 4:4a
        b) Call to participate in various cultic activities 4:4b–5a
          (1) In scheduled offerings 4:4b
            (a) Morning sacrifices 4:4bα
            (b) Third-day tithes 4:4bβ
          (2) In presentation of offerings of well-being 4:5a
            (a) Thanksgiving offerings 4:5aα
            (b) Freewill offerings 4:5aβ
      2) Affirmation of Israel's zeal for such worship 4:5bα
    b. Yahweh utterance formula 4:5bβ
  2. Evidence of failure: record of Israel's historical disasters 4:6–11
    a. Yahweh-utterance 4:6
      1) Utterance proper, on first disaster (famine) 4:6a–bα
        a) Sending of famine by Yahweh 4:6a
        b) Israel's failure to repent 4:6bα
      2) Yahweh utterance formula 4:6bβ
    b. Yahweh utterance 4:7–8
      1) Utterance proper, on second disaster (drought) 4:7–8bα
        a) Sporadic withholding of rain by Yahweh 4:7–8a
        b) Israel's failure to repent 4:8bα
      2) Yahweh utterance formula 4:8bβ
    c. Yahweh utterance 4:9
      1) Utterance proper, on third disaster (blight and locust) 4:9a–bα
        a) Sending of plague by Yahweh 4:9a
        b) Israel's failure to repent 4:9bα
      2) Yahweh utterance formula 4:9bβ
    d. Yahweh utterance 4:10
      1) Utterance proper, on fourth disaster 4:10a–bβ¹
      (pestilence and war casualties)
        a) Sending of pestilence and war by Yahweh 4:10a–bα
        b) Israel's failure to repent 4:10bβ¹
      2) Yahweh utterance formula 4:10bβ²
    e. Yahweh utterance 4:11
      1) Utterance proper, on fifth disaster (earthquake) 4:11a–bα
        a) Sending of earthquake by Yahweh 4:11a
        b) Israel's failure to repent 4:11bα
      2) Yahweh utterance formula 4:11bβ
  3. Consequences of failure: impending divine encounter 4:12–13
    a. Judgment impending 4:12
      1) Summary of past disciplines as divine actions 4:12a
      2) Summons for Israel to prepare for a theophany 4:12b

b. Hymnic support	4:13
1) Description of theophany	4:13a
a) Call to attention	4:13aα
b) Descriptions of God	4:13aβ–αε
(1) Creator	4:13aβ
(2) Revealer of thoughts	4:13aγ
(3) Transformer of nature	4:13aδ
(4) Controller of the earth	4:13aε
2) Proclamation of God's name	4:13b

According to our structure analysis, 4:1–13 is an announcement of an impending catastrophic disaster upon Israel: an unnamed enemy, presumably Assyria, will devastate Samaria, taking the leadership captive. While several historical disasters that Yahweh brought on Israel have failed to evoke repentance from Israel, Yahweh is now going to cause a catastrophe whose effect will be unmistakable. Indeed, Israel will experience it as a disastrous theophanic encounter.

This announcement has two major components. The first one (vv. 1–3) announces Samaria's coming defeat, calling the audience to hear (v. 1) and then describing the audience's fate (vv. 2–3). The "call to hear" has several distinguishing features. After the initial call, which stands in the second masculine plural, Amos directs the address to the noblewomen of Samaria. The mixture of genders has the effect of addressing all of Israel's leadership, even though the focus centers on the noblewomen. The reference to their husbands as "their lords" supports this interpretation. Amos continues his unconventional ways by addressing the noblewomen (see Isa. 3:16–4:1 for another rare example of a prophetic address to women), and then he characterizes them with descriptive participles that serve to condemn them for the pressure they put on "their lords" in order that they might hold frequent, elaborate feasts (cf. 6:4–7). Then Amos vividly paints the humiliation these proud women will be submitted to when Samaria is demolished (vv. 2–3ba). This announcement of disaster is sealed into certainty by Yahweh's own oath (v. 2a).

The second component (vv. 4–13) announces that this impending disaster will be an encounter with Yahweh. Israel's destiny of disaster is based on their rebellion against Yahweh, compounded by their consistent failure to repent. Consequently, they must prepare for an appearance by Yahweh. This component has three segments that, altogether, illuminate Israel's failure vis-à-vis Yahweh: their transgression-laden cultic zeal (vv. 4–5), their failure to repent despite God's repeated disciplines (vv. 6–11), and the unmistakable judgment that will attend God's appearing (vv. 12–13).

The first segment (vv. 4–5) is a satirical call to worship presented as a Yahweh utterance.[10] By twisting a call to go to a local shrine to celebrate their relationship with Yahweh, Amos ironically calls the people to rebel in their zealous manner of presenting numerous sacrifices and offerings (v. 4a). Thus the Israelites gladly traveled to the cult centers to keep the festivals. That Amos exhorts them to make sacrifices, either daily or on the first day of the feast, and to present the tithes, every third day, or on the third day of the feast, bespeaks that these Israelites evidenced a zeal in worship that went far beyond the demands of the law, the very demands designed to maintain their covenant relationship with God despite the inclination of humans to transgress. But the Israelites had turned these occasions into self-indulgent feasting. Furthermore, since the sacrifices that these people are called to present are voluntary offerings of well-being,[11] we can surmise that the call is directed to the rich nobility, for only they had the financial resources

---

10. If the two commands for rebelling, פִּשְׁעוּ ("rebel") and הַרְבּוּ לִפְשֹׁעַ ("multiply rebelling"), are removed from this call to worship, it becomes a splendid encouragement to go to a shrine and participate in the cultic activities. Even if כִּן (v. 5b) is translated "indeed," it would not in itself be accusatory, but rather affirming that Israel is zealous in worship; and with those three words bracketed that is just what v. 5b does: it states in a positive sense the enthusiasm of Israel in their various cultic activities. The inclusion of the פֶּשַׁע phrases, however, changes everything, especially with reference to v. 5b. Normally כֵן ("thus") would refer to the various imperatives: בֹּאוּ, הָבִיאוּ, קַטֵּר, קִרְאוּ, הַשְׁמִיעוּ ("come, bring, make smoke, announce, proclaim"); but the פֶּשַׁע imperatives create a certain ambiguity that poetically makes the point of the utterance.

The ambiguity concerns how the כֵן of v. 5b is to be taken: does it refer to the listed cultic activities, which would be expected in this genre (call to worship), or does it refer to the פֶּשַׁע imperatives? The latter choice would have the utterance say that Israel has been enthusiastic in פֶּשַׁע. The former option would have the utterance say that Israel has been enthusiastic in genuine cultic observance. Both options are involved in what the text is saying. The poetic and rhetorical force of this utterance derives from the "both/and" nature of the פֶּשַׁע reference. It is precisely in the avidly observed cultic practices that Israel has multiplied פְּשָׁעִים ("rebellions" or "transgressions"); since Israel has "loved" to observe them, they have "multiplied transgressions." This utterance reveals that Israel's acts of Yahweh worship are acts of פֶּשַׁע, a breaking faith with Yahweh, who is supposed to be honored in the cult. Israel is worshiping Yahweh by their פְּשָׁעִים ("rebellions"); that is, it is פְּשָׁעִים that they are offering to Yahweh. The more avidly Israel observes cultic practices, the more thoroughly Israel commits transgressions against the very God Israel think themselves to honor.

11. The Israelites make pilgrimages to the important shrines in order to present numerous offerings of well-being or peace offerings (שְׁלָמִים; cf. Leviticus 3), specifically praise offerings (תוֹדָה) and freewill offerings (נְדָבוֹת; cf. Lev. 7:11–18). According to the law, such sacrifices could be freely offered at any time as a means of expressing gratitude to God. The majority of the meat provided by animals belonging to this class of offerings was returned to the presenter in order that a family might have a joyful feast. Only with this kind of offering was it possible to present leavened bread. Thus, the people have engineered the practices of the cult in order that it might be the basis of great, joyful festivals.

Conversely there is no reference to these Israelites' presenting whole burnt offerings or sin (purification) offerings. This omission suggests that in traveling to the shrines the

to present so many offerings so frequently. This social fact establishes a link between the audience in the first Yahweh utterance (vv. 1–3) and the audience of the second Yahweh utterance (vv. 4–5). The first audience is the nobility living in Samaria, and the second audience is the rich upper class living throughout northern Israel. The concluding line to the call recognizes Israel's love of making so many offerings. In short, two points are scored in this utterance: (1) Israel's cultic acts are actually acts of פֶּשַׁע ("rebellion"), and (2) Israel's zeal in worship is actually zeal against Yahweh.

The second segment (vv. 6–11) contains a series of Yahweh utterances that rehearse for Israel a sequence of disasters that have befallen the land. These disasters are presented in five units. Each speech unit, identified by the Yahweh utterance formula, has two major elements: (1) a description of the disaster, and (2) an assertion of Israel's failure to repent before God's disciplines. The disasters recounted are famine (v. 6), sporadic drought (vv. 7–8), blight and locust (v. 9), pestilence and casualties in war (v. 10), and an earthquake or a fiery conflagration (v. 11). We will argue that the conceptual assumption underlying this text is the covenant between Yahweh and Israel. Within such a context Yahweh would have been bringing these disasters upon Israel in order to prompt them back to a restored covenant relationship through repentance.

The climax of this oracle is reached in the third segment (vv. 12–13).[12] It warns Israel of the culminating consequence of their failure to heed the disciplines. This pronouncement has two parts: (1) a warning to the people to prepare themselves for God's appearing (v. 12), and (2) a recitation of God's power as displayed in a theophanic appearance (v. 13). Because Israel has failed to become aware of their rebellions against Yahweh and because they have refused to change their ways, they must now prepare themselves to meet God. The language "prepare to meet your God" definitely adverts to a theophany. God is about to enter the scene in an appearance that will lead to Israel's total defeat in war. Although the term הכון ("prepare," niph'al) is not often used for the people's preparing themselves for a theophany (note the hiph'il forms in 1 Sam. 7:3; Zeph. 1:7; Ps. 10:17; 78:8; 2 Chron. 35:6, 14), "meet your God" may connote a theophanic encounter. Indeed, the quintessential Israelite text of theophanic encounter at Sinai (Exodus 19) features precisely the terms found in Amos 4, as Yahweh commands Moses to have the people "prepare" (נכנים, niph'al participle, vv. 11, 15) "to meet God"

---

people went to celebrate their abundance, their wealth, rather than with a contrite attitude seeking to find expiation for their wrongdoing along with Yahweh's forgiveness.

12. Verse 12 is introduced by לכן, "therefore." S. Paul (Amos, 149 n. 101) notes that in Amos this particle introduces "a dramatic climax" (cf. 5:11, 13; 6:7), while Stuart (Hosea–Jonah, 337) adds that it is used to introduce judgment sentences.

(הָאֱלֹהִים לִקְרַאת, v. 17) at the mount. הָכוֹן is also used for alerting people to prepare for war.[13] This warning is, then, that the Israelites are about to meet God during a hard battle with frightful consequences. That is, their defeat will be so spectacular that God himself will be visible as active in what takes place. The Israelites, particularly those from the nobility, will be deported; such a terrible fate is the severest curse mentioned in the covenant curses (e.g., Lev. 26:27–33). Thus, the Israelites must prepare themselves for the manifestation of God's presence, the very God proclaimed in the following hymnic lines. This proclamation of God's identity also substantiates for Israel that the divine suzerain is indeed capable of bringing upon them this ultimate malediction.[14]

CONCEPTUAL ASSUMPTIONS UNDERLYING AMOS 4[15]

Clearly, Amos builds his sermon here on the fact that God and Israel are in covenant. That covenant is central to Amos's preaching is evident in the well-known verse that opens the larger unit of which ch. 4 is a part: "Only you have I known among the families of the earth; therefore, I will punish you for all your iniquities" (3:2).[16]

An integral component of covenants in the ancient Near East are blessings and curses. Lists of blessings and curses for the Sinaitic covenant are found in Leviticus 26 and Deuteronomy 27–28.[17] When the

---

13. Ezek. 38:7 (S. Paul, *Amos*, 151–52); also in the *hiph'il* Jer. 46:14; Nah. 2:3.

14. The hymnic language of 4:13 that lauds God's power to create and to destroy reflects the theophanic tradition of the cult (cf. Psalms 46; 97; also Mic. 1:2–5).

15. R. Knierim (*Text and Concept*, 23–28) has stressed the importance of identifying the conceptual assumptions that lie behind the text itself and that can account for its various features.

16. Around the middle of the twentieth century, several scholars came to recognize that the covenant served as the background for understanding Amos's message. M. O. Boyle ("The Covenant Lawsuit of the Prophet Amos III 1–IV 13," *VT* 21 [1971] 338–39) reviews the history of this development. One may mention in particular R. E. Clements's *Prophecy and Covenant* (SBT 43; London: SCM, 1965); he argues that Amos's attitude to the covenant for understanding God's dealings with Israel and the threats of judgment was the reason his book became a part of the canon (pp. 35–44). H. G. Reventlow (*Das Amt des Propheten bei Amos* [FRLANT 80; Göttingen: Vandenhoeck und Ruprecht, 1962] 75, 89–90) posits that Amos filled the role of covenant mediator; in Am 4:6–11 Amos then was performing a cursing ritual. G. Fohrer (*Introduction to the Old Testament* [with E. Selling; trans. D. Green; Nashville: Abingdon, 1968] 432–33) discounts Reventlow's view on the basis that these conclusions are a result of using form criticism beyond its capability of discovering information; that is, the determining of a text's life setting is not the same as discovering an institution.

17. These curses are drawn from a model similar to that found in Lev. 26:14–33. Reventlow (*Amt*, 83–87), too, argues for a relationship between these curses and Leviticus 26. Others, however, view this text to be closer to Deuteronomy 28 (so Boyle, "The Covenant Lawsuit," 352). There are three major reasons: (1) there is a reference to Egyptian pestilence in Deut. 28:27, 60, but none in Leviticus 26; (2) the "futility curse" in 4:8 is

subordinate party to a suzerainty covenant is faithful, the suzerain or the gods bless that party. However, should the party persist in violating the terms of the covenant, the suzerain or the gods may punish the other party by activating any of the covenant curses.

Having accused Israel, particularly the leadership, of violations of covenant obligations, Amos enumerates various disasters that God has brought against Israel as punishments. This list assumes a hierarchy of punishments, just as is unfolded in Leviticus 26, which warns that Yahweh would increase the disciplining punishments for two reasons: (1) the people's stubborn refusal to repent, and (2) God's determination to break down Israel's stubborn resistance. Amos is assuming that persistent disobedience leads the suzerain to inflict a series of distresses that increase in severity by reviewing seven calamities that Israel experienced in five stages. Since any curse against a people is terrible, some scholars do not find any progression in this list. But a comparison of the first distress, famine (v. 6), with the last, earthquake causing such devastation that it was likened to the destruction of Sodom and Gomorrah (v. 11), supports a progression in the severity of the disasters. Amos also assumes that God brought on Israel the various calamities in order that the people might become aware of their wrongdoing and repent. These two dimensions of covenant curses are clearly found in Leviticus 26: (1) the sequence of maledictions in that text are designed to produce repentance, and (2) the maledictions are viewed as increasing by the repetitive phrase "if in spite of these punishments you have not turned back to me...I will continue to plague you" (Lev. 26:21, 23–24, 27–28). Another point of contact between Amos and Lev. 26 is the stress on God's role in implementing the curses: אני גם; (אנכי vv. 6, 7) and אף אני (Lev. 26:16, 24, 28, 41).

Further support is found in the reference to God's taking an oath, for this has its background in covenant; as Stuart points out, to swear an oath is the "determination to enforce a covenant."[18]

INTERPRETIVE IMPLICATIONS

The inclusion of vv. 1–3 with vv. 4–13 allows for a more nuanced interpretation of vv. 4–13 by giving a fuller setting to account for

---

found in Deut. 28:30–31, 38–41, but not Leviticus 26; (3) Sodom and Gomorrah occur in Deut. 29:22–23 but not in Leviticus. It is hard to decide which of these two chapters influenced Amos 4, especially since curses were stylized throughout the ancient Near East. However, the two distinguishing features of these curses — that their design was to lead Israel to repentance and that when Israel fails to repent God increases the intensity of the curses — are distinctive to Leviticus 26. Wolff (*Joel and Amos*, 213–14) provides a chart comparing these passages; he points out that 4:6–11 has close affinity with Leviticus 26.

18. Stuart, *Hosea–Jonah*, 352.

God's resolve to judge Israel. Here are the arguments for our structure analysis that locates 4:1–3 with 4:4–13.

Several features signal that the first two Yahweh utterances (4:1–3, 4–5) belong to the same larger speech unit. In them, Amos gives the reasons that God will appear to execute the severest judgment against Israel. Both begin with an imperative, "hear"[19] and "come" respectively. Both are characterized by biting irony. In the first, Amos addresses the noblewomen of Samaria as "cows of Bashan," that is, elegant, affluent nobility. Those women might have relished this metaphor, just as some stylish American women in the latter part of the twentieth century liked being called "foxes." Amos then mocks the aristocrats by calling them "lords" rather than "husbands," and yet picturing them as puppets to their wives' demands.[20] This wording would be especially derisive in a patriarchal society, in which men assumed that they held all the power. These women are condemned for pressuring their husbands to employ oppressive tactics to increase their income so that they might buy their wives drink. "Drink" is a metonym for partying in particular and for luxurious living in general; that is, it represents all the fineries that accompany wealth. Amos then goes on to exploit the irony by picturing these plump, elegant women as being either carried out of the city in fish baskets or drawn through breaches in the wall by some type of hooks.[21] Either way, the manner of their departure from the capital will be most humiliating for these proud women. In the second utterance, Amos caustically condemns the Israelites for their distorted religious zeal by facetiously calling them to rebel against Yahweh in offering up an abundance of sacrifices at Bethel and Gilgal, the very sacrifices that

---

19. It occurs four times in Amos 3–5 (3:1, 13; 4:1; 5:1).

20. The reason that Amos uses the rare term for "husband" in Scripture, אדן, "lord" (e.g., Gen. 18:12; Judg. 19:26–27), instead of one of the usual terms, either איש or בעל, is not certain. Beside interpreting it as ironic S. Paul (*Amos*, 129) suggests (similar to Andersen and Freedman, *Amos*, 421) that this term establishes a contrast between "their lords" and "the Lord," who swears against their activities (v. 2). This usage is certainly to be numbered among Amos's uses of surprise and reversals in this speech.

21. The meaning of ענוה and סירות דונה, translated in NRSV "hooks" and "fishhooks," is far from certain. Are the women to be dragged through the breaches being tied together with ropes attached to hooks dug into their bodies or are they to be carried out as corpses in fish baskets? S. Paul (*Amos*, 130–35) presents a thorough analysis of these words and arrives at this translation: "you shall be transported in baskets, and the very last one of you, in fishermen's pots" (p. 128). However, T. Kleven ("The Cows of Bashan: A Single Metaphor at Amos 4:1–3," *CBQ* 58 [1996] 215–27) argues forcefully that the women are being driven out in single file, like cattle being driven from one place to another. This reading has the advantage of Amos's continuing the imagery of the women as cows. The verb יצא ("go out") also supports the understanding that these people are being taken into captivity. In further support, Kleven cites iconographic evidence from both Egypt and Assyria that shows captives being led about by ropes. The multiple arguments favor Kleven's reading over Paul's; nevertheless, the question is not yet conclusively resolved.

provided them large quantities of meat as the basis for their elaborate feasting. Another feature is the inclusive placement of the term שִׁמְעוּ ("hear"). It opens the Yahweh utterance in vv. 1–3, and in the *hiph'il* ("proclaim") it is the final imperative of the satirical call to worship (vv. 4–5). Whereas Amos was trying to get the leaders' attention, they were so busy announcing their numerous sacrifices that they could not hear the prophet's call. The composite of these shared characteristics indicates a rhetorical resonance between the first two Yahweh utterances in this sermon.

The bond between these two Yahweh utterances, furthermore, implies that the nobles' abuse of the poor produced the wealth not only to satisfy the demands of their wives for drink, but also for them to purchase animals for making such frequent sacrifices. That is, their unjust treatment of the poor sponsored Israel's cultic festivities. This interpretation is confirmed by the fact that Amos elsewhere accuses Israel of oppressing the poor in the same context as he attacks distortions in their worship that are particularly appalling to God. Blatant mistreatment of the poor is closely linked with abuses at the sanctuary in 2:6–8. In ch. 5 there are many words against injustices done to the poor (vv. 7, 11–12), as well as reference to how God hates their feasts and manner of worship (vv. 21–23). In 3:13–15 God announces that the altars and the luxuriant houses of the Israelites alike would be devastated; this judgment is presumably because Israel committed transgressions both in erecting splendid altars and in building luxurious houses with funds gained from oppressive economic practices. The repetition of these terms reveals that Israel's rebellion against Yahweh is rooted in a faithlessness that expresses itself in both economic and religious practices.

There are also strong ties between the first two Yahweh utterances (vv. 1–5) and the series of afflictions Israel has experienced (vv. 6–11). The strongest tie is cause and result: God brought these hardships on the people of the covenant as consequences for their faithlessness. In light of the covenant, these disasters were "disciplines" brought on Israel so that they would become aware that their practices were appalling to God and repent. That God's intent in bringing on Israel this sequence of calamities was disciplinary is clearly conveyed by the refrain "yet you [Israel] did not return to me." The refrain has the added affect of turning this section into a third accusation against Israel: their guilt in failing to repent.

A bond between vv. 4–5 and vv. 6–11 is Amos's use of poignant irony in sequencing these two segments with the formulations וְגַם אֲנִי and וְגַם אֹכִי (vv. 6–7), bearing the sense of "while I, on my part...." The formulation highlights the unexpected reciprocal dynamics of Israel's worship and Yahweh's patronage: while Israel has been busily sacrificing and making offerings and pilgrimages, Yahweh has not been reciprocating with regular rain and harvest cycles, or even providing them with protection from their enemies. Israel's continuation in faithlessness via abundant, but transgressive, sacrifices parallels God's continuing to discipline them with a sequence of disasters. Consequently, their refusal to repent despite God's repeated efforts to alert them to their precarious position in the covenant meant that they were provoking God to bring against them the heaviest punishment under the terms of the covenant. This sets the stage for the climactic call for the Israelites to prepare themselves to meet God (vv. 12–13).

The integration of vv. 1–5 with vv. 6–11 is substantiated further by the presence of several themes in the rehearsal of disasters that have ties with either or both of the preceding divine utterances. Lack of food (v. 6) makes a stark contrast both with the metaphor of the well-fed cows of Bashan (v. 1) and with the worshipers' feasting on an abundance of meat at the local shrines (v. 5). Sporadic occasions of drought in the land caused inhabitants of the struck village to wander about from city to city in desperate search for water (v. 7). Their haphazard wandering contrasts both with the direct march of exuberant pilgrims to the shrines at Bethel and Gilgal in anticipation of joyous feasting and with the straight paths through which the noblewomen will be led out of the decimated city. Whereas the distressed wanderers never found enough to satisfy their thirst, the pilgrims gorged themselves with the meat from their sacrifices. And while distressed peasants were traveling about in search of water to drink, the noblewomen of Samaria were encouraging their husbands into abusive financial practices in order to gain sufficient wealth to buy them drink, presumably expensive liquors. Furthermore, the stench rising from the corpses of slain young men and horses strewn on the battlefield (v. 10) makes a morbid poetic connection with the sweet smell ascending from the multitude of sacrifices offered at the shrines (vv. 4–5). In reality, the smoke from Israel's sacrifices was so putrid in God's nostrils that it was comparable to the stench rising from the decaying corpses on a forsaken battlefield. Finally, the image of a remnant connoted in the metaphor of "a brand plucked from the fire" (v. 11) echoes the theme of the nobility escaping the devastation of Samaria (v. 3).

There is also a powerful conceptual dynamic in juxtaposing these series of calamities (vv. 6–11) to the satirical call to worship. The people's expectation of divine blessing as a result of their zealous worship deviated drastically from their actual experience of disaster after disaster. In other words, because of their properly, frequently, and enthusiastically observed cultic activities, the Israelites likely expected — in terms

of the implied covenant background — sufficient rain in season leading to bumper harvests, and protection from pestilence and from defeat
by their enemies. Their high expectations set the stage for the surprise in this sermon's asserting that these many calamities had actually
come from Yahweh. But Israel did not perceive in these disasters the
need to return (שׁוב) to Yahweh any more than they recognized that
their energetic performance of cultic acts was actually transgression
against Yahweh. That is, the Israelites' devotion to self-indulgent cultic
observances blinded them to their need for "turning to Yahweh."

Thus, these three sections present three different levels of transgressions by which Israel has jeopardized their covenant relationship with
God: (1) oppression of the poor, (2) rebellion against Yahweh by the
manner of their presenting so many offerings, and (3) their refusal to
repent in light of Yahweh's warnings. The interweaving of these motifs
among the three sections is strong evidence that the first utterance to
Samaria is an integral part of the lines that follow in vv. 4–13.

The characteristics of the climactic summons to prepare for God's appearing also requires this broader context, especially since the opening
words — "thus I will do to you" — are most elliptical. The audi-
ence/reader must fill in what it is that God will do. In fact, leaving this
to the audience gives this summons a more terrifying force than if the
prophet had spelled out the punishment, since human imagination is
generally more fertile than a written description. We have in this sermon, then, a strong rhetorical ploy. The context of all of ch. 4, cohering
as a unit, is crucial for the listeners to supply the right kind of specific
meaning to this general announcement.

Israel's lack of response to the enumerated sequence of disasters implies that God was about to bring on Israel an even greater catastrophe.
In light of the covenant curses, it was to be the most severe malediction: defeat in war leading to exile. In the sequence of disciplines for
Israel's violations of the covenant in Leviticus 26, exile was the ultimate
discipline. The mention of Sodom and Gomorrah in the preceding malediction functions as a clear signal that Israel was about to experience the
worst calamity, especially since these two cities were totally destroyed
by God's hand. The reference to these cities certainly adds gravity to
the warning. That this indeed was the judgment Israel was about to experience is confirmed by the judgment vividly described in the initial
Yahweh utterance (vv. 1–3); there God swore that the noblewomen were
going to be being led through the breaches in the wall, presumably as
captives. Thus, the first Yahweh utterance helps direct the audience's
attention to the specific design behind the general term "do" in v. 12.

In interpreting these components together, the phrase "the coming days" in v. 3 refers to the coming theophany in v. 12 as Israel's

ultimate and inescapable defeat in war. The juxtaposing of these sections produces reciprocity of interpretation. That this indeed is Amos's proclamation is confirmed by his use of ironic surprise in redefining the Day of Yahweh (5:18–20). Whereas Israel took the Day of Yahweh as a day of their ultimate triumph above all the mighty nations, Amos was telling them that it would be a day of distress, devastation, and judgment.

CONCLUSION

Amos 4, then, is a textual unit constructed out of several themes common to the Amos collection. They have been brought into coherence by the underlying concept of covenant expectations and consequences. This sermon announces Israel's complete national defeat, leading to exile for the nobility, a climactic consequence to chronic unfaithfulness. Thus, it contributes to the major theme found throughout the book of Amos (e.g., 2:13–16; 3:11, 14–15; 5:2, 3, 5, 18–20; 6:7, 11; 7:8–9; 8:2–3, 9–12; 9:1, 9–10). Employing the rhetoric of surprise, Amos takes the very things that his audience would point to as evidence of their privileged relationship with God — the increasing wealth of the upper class and the zealous worship practices at the major cult centers — and turns this evidence into an indictment of their faithlessness that will lead to certain defeat and exile.[22] Such ironic reversal has its conceptual foundation in the covenant between Yahweh and Israel. This dramatic reversal in Amos's proclamation is conveyed by a variety of structural, poetic, and thematic devices, as described in these pages.

---

22. The element of surprise in accusations and judgments being announced contrary to apparent expectations resonates throughout these verses as elsewhere in Amos. For example, the prophet suddenly turns the force of rhetoric against the Israelite audience in 2:6–16; in 3:1–2 the assuring reference to election is jarringly juxtaposed with a threat of judgment for iniquities; in 5:18–20 Amos turns traditionally hopeful expectations for the Day of Yahweh into dread.

Bibliography

Andersen, F. I., and D. N. Freedman. *Amos: A New Translation with Introduction and Commentary.* AB 24A. New York: Doubleday, 1989.

Barstad, H. M. *The Religious Polemics of Amos: Studies in the Preaching of Am 2, 7B–8; 4,1–13; 5,1–27; 6,4–7; 8,14.* VTSup 34. Leiden: E. J. Brill, 1984.

Boyle, M. O. "The Covenant Lawsuit of the Prophet Amos III 1–IV 13." *VT* 21 (1971) 338–62.

Campbell, A. "Structure Analysis and the Art of Exegesis." In *Problems in Biblical Theology: Essays in Honor of Rolf Knierim,* ed. H. Sun and K. Eades, 76–103. Grand Rapids: Eerdmans, 1997.

Fleischer, G. *Von Menschenverkäufern, Baschankühen und Rechtsverkehrern: Die Sozialkritik des Amosbuches in historisch-kritischer, sozialgeschictlicher und archäologischer Perspektive.* BBB 74. Frankfurt am Main: Athenäum, 1989.

Jeremias, J. *Der Prophet Amos.* ATD 24/2. Göttingen: Vandenhoeck & Ruprecht, 1995. Also *The Book of Amos,* trans. D. Stott. OTL. Louisville: Westminster John Knox, 1998.

Kleven, T. "The Cows of Bashan: A Single Metaphor at Amos 4:1–3." *CBQ* 58 (1996) 215–27.

Knierim, R. *Text and Concept in Leviticus 1:1–9: A Case in Exegetical Method.* FAT 2. Tübingen: J. C. B. Mohr [Paul Siebeck], 1992.

———. "On the Theology of Psalm 19." In *The Task of Old Testament Theology: Substance, Method, and Cases,* 322–350. Grand Rapids: Eerdmans, 1995.

Mays, J. L. *Amos: A Commentary.* OTL. Philadelphia: Westminster, 1969.

Paul, S. *Amos.* Hermeneia. Minneapolis: Fortress Press, 1991.

Reventlow, H. G. *Das Amt des Propheten bei Amos.* FRLANT 80. Göttingen: Vandenhoeck & Ruprecht, 1962.

Rottzoll, D. U. *Studien zur Redaktion und Komposition des Amosbuchs.* BZAW 243. Berlin: de Gruyter, 1996.

Rudolph W. "Amos 4,6–13." In *Wort-Gebot-Glaube: Beiträge zur Theologie des Alten Testaments, Walter Eichrodt zum 80. Geburtstag,* ed. J. J. Stamm et al., 27–31. ATANT 59. Zurich: Zwingli, 1970.

Stuart, D. *Hosea-Jonah.* WBC 31. Waco, Tex.: Word Books, 1987.

Wolff, H. W. *Joel and Amos.* Hermeneia. Philadelphia: Fortress Press, 1977.

9

The Organizational Concept
of Leviticus 1–3

Rodney R. Hutton

In his study of the opening rubric of Leviticus 1, Rolf Knierim called attention to a serious problem that affects the meaning of this legislation, namely, the tension that exists between the opening case specified in 1:2 on the one hand and the subcases outlined in 1:3–17 on the other.[1] The governing case in v. 2 suggests that the following legislation will address itself to the *types of animals* that are available for sacrifice, the qualifications that govern the acceptability of the "cattle" and "sheep" that are ritually suitable for presentation. As noted by Knierim, there is a tension that jars the reader when arriving at v. 3 and finding that, instead of the rubric dealing with the type of animal permitted for presentation, the rubric is now governed by the concept of the *types of sacrifice* to be offered. So the governing structural principle is found in the statement of the main cases in 1:3 (עלה), 2:1 (מנחה), and 3:1 (זבח שלמים). Knierim notes that the situation could have been smoothed over had an editor changed the text of 1:2 to read, "If anyone from among you brings a *qorban* for Yahweh, you shall bring either an *'olah* or a *minchah* or a *zebach shelamim.*" But the tension within the existing text suggests to Knierim that a process of "resistance" has been at work. There was a battle between major alternative organizational principles (types of animals versus types of sacrifices), and one alternative was "resisted" when the text chose another principle for its organization.[2]

Knierim has indeed identified an important rhetorical clue to the compositional strategy of Leviticus 1, and I am in full agreement that the tension here is significant for understanding the structure of the legislation. One aspect of Knierim's meticulous study with which I wish to enter into conversation, however, is the limits imposed upon it by focusing exclusively upon Lev. 1:1–9 rather than seeking to understand

---

1. Rolf Knierim, *Text and Concept in Leviticus 1:1–9: A Case in Exegetical Method* (FAT 2; Tübingen: J. C. B. Mohr [Paul Siebeck], 1992). Karl Elliger had also noted the tension, asking how the subject of the עלה could possibly appear so fully unprepared. Characteristically, Elliger chose to ascribe such tensions to complicated redactional activity (*Leviticus* [HAT 1/4; Tübingen: J. C. B. Mohr, 1966] 10–11, 27–28).

2. Knierim, *Text and Concept,* 11–12.

the text within the context of its larger framework. Indeed, Knierim himself is aware of this dilemma, and the reader senses a significant hesitancy over the question of the adequacy of beginning with the specific pericope prior to dealing first with the larger context.[3] Nevertheless, Knierim suggests that both avenues are "equally legitimate," and so begins by isolating the first pericope, Lev. 1:1–9, for his careful and detailed study. I wish to suggest, however, that, if the question of the tension between Lev. 1:2 and 1:3ff. is placed within the context of the structure of the larger unit, what Knierim understood to be a struggle of "resistance" taking place within the text when it chose one organizational principle over another is simply a logical and coherent rhetorical device that evidences not "resistance" and "rejection," but rather, skillful compositional technique.

LEVITICUS 1–7 AS A UNIT

The implicit danger of isolating a pericope from its larger context surfaces with Knierim's reflections on the absence of a compliance report at the end of Lev. 3:17, where he feels one ought properly to exist. Such lack of a compliance report or other concluding formula at the end of the legislation governing the three types of sacrifice in chs. 1–3 is heightened, argues Knierim, by the fact that the legislation in 4:1 continues with a new introductory report formula, וידבר יהוה אל־משה לאמר ("And YHWH said to Moses"). Knierim suggests that a compliance report was not needed to conclude the legal prescriptions at 3:17, because "the emphasis on their origin was so decisive that their content . . . was sufficient evidence for their mediation through Moses, so that this mediation did not have to be explicitly mentioned."[4] If, however, one considers the macrostructure of Leviticus 1–7, it is clear that the lack of a summary formula at 3:17 is an intentional rhetorical signal of the material's structure and not, as Knierim suggests, an *e silencio* omission based upon the stature of Moses' persona.

The entirety of chs. 1–7 is governed by one single summary report formula at 7:37–38: זאת התורה . . . אשר צוה יהוה את־משה בהר סיני ("This is the instruction . . . which YHWH commanded Moses at Mount Sinai"). By referring specifically to the full range of legislation covered in chs. 1–7 (לעלה למנחה ולחטאת ולאשם ולמלואים ולזבח השלמים, 7:37), the legal editor signals that the preceding unit in chs. 1–7, unbroken by further compliance reports or concluding formulae, is a coherent and self-contained collection. Though the "syntax" of this collection is signaled by the

---

3. Knierim, *Text and Concept*, 3–4.
4. Knierim, *Text and Concept*, 5–6.

repeated use of the introductory formula וידבר יהוה אל־משה לאמר at several places (4:1; 5:14, 20; 6:1, 12, 17; 7:22, 28), any concluding formula is intentionally withheld until the end of ch. 7 so that the coherence of this unit is stressed and can be clearly set off from the following section, the ordination of Aaron and his sons in chs. 8–10.

Leviticus 1–7 and the Qorban

What the legislative items in chs. 1–7 have in common is that they concern the presentation of the קרבן (*qorban*). However, the term *qorban* is itself problematic and requires further analysis to determine its relation to the legislation of Leviticus 1–7. The term קרבן is derived from the root קרב, meaning "be or draw near," and the specifically cultic term הקריב, "present [an offering]." In a general sense it refers to anything that is presented as an offering, and in some cases refers to items that were only tangentially related to the sacrificial cult, such as gold/silver vessels and ox carts (see below). The question is, however, what the term means in Lev. 7:38. Do the items listed in v. 37 exhaust the various types of *qorban* presentations? Or are there other forms of *qorban* not included in v. 37? If v. 37 presents the full listing of offerings that could rightly be designated *qorban*, then this group consists strictly of those sacrifices (parts of) which were burned by priestly action on the sacrificial altar. Such are precisely the sacrifices we have sketched out in chs. 1–7. Is it possible, however, that there are other "presentations" than those indicated in v. 37, including those that were *not* burned in a sacrificial ritual?

Of the forty-seven occurrences of the term קרבן, forty-three clearly refer to such presentations that are to be burned. There are only four occurrences, actually clustered into three texts, in which the *qorban* may not have been burned, but precisely here the texts are ambiguous or problematic.

In Num. 31:50, the *qorban* that is brought by the military officers to Moses includes "articles of gold, armlets and bracelets, signet rings, earrings, and pendants," items that could obviously not be directly intended for sacrificial use, but instead were brought into the sanctuary as a "memorial for the Israelites" (זכרון לבני־ישראל). Nevertheless, the items in question were presented by the commanders "in order to make atonement" (לכפר) on their own behalf before YHWH. Assuming that the term לכפר here maintains something of its technical sense, in which the application of sacrificial blood upon the altar is required for such atonement, how is it that such items could serve their purpose unless they were converted into the appropriate livestock to be presented for the appropriate atonement sacrifice? As such, the items here presented as *qorban* have precisely the function served by those sacrifices that in whole or part were burned upon the sacrificial altar.

A more problematic text is that of Numbers 7, which lists the tribal gifts presented to the sanctuary. The second — and larger — section, 7:10–88, includes such items as silver plates, silver basins, and golden dishes among the items presented as *qorban* by the tribal leaders — again, items that could not be intended for sacrificial presentation. Three factors, however, directly link these vessels with the sacrificial cult, and specifically with the burning of sacrificial offerings. First, all of the vessels contain items that are exclusively intended for such a burning ritual: flour mixed with oil "for a grain offering" and incense. Second, these offerings are accompanied by animals obviously intended for sacrificial usage, especially burnt offerings, sin offerings, and sacrifices of well-being. Third, the governing rubric indicates that these presentations were brought "to the altar" upon the "dedication of the altar" (7:10). It seems evident, then, that the items mentioned — including the vessels themselves in which some of them are presented — are intended for the burning ritual that takes place on the altar. The entire list stands under the defining rubric of items intended for the altar — that is, for the fire rituals.

The first part of this text, Num. 7:1–9, provides a list of items presented by the tribal leaders to the Levitical families engaged in the sanctuary "service" (עבדה). That this *qorban* was not intended for consumption on the altar is suggested by two facts. First, as objects intended for use by the Levitical families it could have no sacrificial function since the Levites were precluded from the altar ceremonies according to P legislation. Second, that the potentially ambiguous term עגלת in this passage means not simply "heifers" — which indeed might have indicated animals intended for sacrifice, along with "cattle" (בקר) and "bulls" (שור) — but rather "carts" intended to haul the temple furniture is indicated by v. 9, which contrasts the use of such "carts" with the work of "carrying on the shoulder" (בכתף ישאו). Here, then, the term *qorban* is used of items "presented" (הקריב) for sanctuary use, quite apart from any specific sacrificial function. Nevertheless, it is possible that the use of the term *qorban* was suggested precisely because of its connection with animals that were regularly associated with altar sacrifice, particularly since the note regarding the *qorban* is immediately preceded by the remark that Moses had finished anointing and consecrating the altar (7:1).

Finally, Lev. 2:12 itself preserves a use of the term קרבן in a context that is quite removed from altar sacrifice. The rubric here concerns the presentation of a *qorban* that has either leaven or honey in it, in either case disqualifying it for consumption by fire upon the altar. Although

such an offering is prohibited to the altar ritual, it nevertheless is referred to as a *qorban*, even if it is given the further designation of קָרְבַּן
רֵאשִׁית, an "offering of choice products."

In several cases, then, the term *qorban* is ambiguous. While it nearly
always relates to sacrificial items subject to (partial) consumption on the
altar, precisely those sacrifices that form the subject of chs. 1–7, there
are a few cases in which the term *qorban* refers to noncombustible items
intended for general cultic "presentation." In all but one case, however,
even these instances link the *qorban* to the altar or to the altar sacrifices.[5]

The Syntax of Leviticus 1:2

Given this ambiguity implicit in the term *qorban*, the syntax of Lev. 1:2
becomes particularly troublesome. According to the Masoretic accentuation (the placement of the *athnach* under the word לַיהוה), all the cases
that follow are concerned with the presentation of the *qorban*, as stated
in the protasis (אָדָם כִּי־יַקְרִיב מִכֶּם קָרְבָּן לַיהוה), and they specify three different groups from which the *qorban* might be offered: from domestic
animals in general (מִן־הַבְּהֵמָה), from cattle (מִן־הַבָּקָר), and from the flock
(מִן־הַצֹּאן). This Masoretic accentuation follows the narrower definition of
the term *qorban*, according to which it is related exclusively to sacrifices
presented for consumption upon the altar. According to this reading,
there is no other type of *qorban*. Every *qorban* must be an animal suitable for sacrifice. The difficulty with this reading, however, is its lack of
coherence with the following prescriptions, which concern themselves
simply with cattle (בָּקָר, 1:3–9; 3:1–5) and flock (צֹאן, 1:10–13; 3:6–16). The
term בְּהֵמָה is anomalous within the prescriptions themselves, though
some take the inclusion of this term in the apodosis to be a later ac-
commodation intended to include the offerings of fowl (מִן־הָעוֹף) that
follow in vv. 14–17.[6] The term בְּהֵמָה can hardly serve to indicate birds,
however, since elsewhere the terms בְּהֵמָה and עוֹף are used precisely as
groups exclusive of one another (Gen. 6:7; 7:23; 8:17), and the term בְּהֵמָה
relates solely to quadrupeds, indeed even to impure ones that would be
excluded from altar sacrifice.[7]

The Masoretic accentuation is most likely an incorrect interpretation
of the text, and the main case presented in Lev. 1:2 is almost certainly
concerned with a specific type of *qorban*, namely, a *qorban* of domes-

---

5. Ina Willi-Plein's intimation that the term *qorban* relates in some unique way
to the עֹלה because it represents the "'Annäherung' an den göttlichen Bereich" obviously overlooks the fact that the term is not reserved for the עֹלה alone (*Opfer und
Kult im alttestamentlichen Israel: Textbefragungen und Zwischenergebnisse* [SBS 153; Stuttgart:
Katholisches Bibelwerk, 1993] 89.

6. Jacob Milgrom, *Leviticus 1–16* (AB 3; New York: Doubleday, 1991) 166.

7. Milgrom, *Leviticus 1–16*, 145–46.

ticated animals (as opposed to other types of *qorbanim*). According to
this view, the protasis concludes with the term מן־הבהמה.[8] What follows
then is a listing of the specific types of domesticated animals that are
available for this type of *qorban*. This interpretation of the syntax follows the broader definition of the term *qorban*, in which it includes not
only the offering of animals for combustible sacrifice but also other
types of "presentations" in general. It is because of this broad understanding of what constitutes a *qorban* that the text must specify more
precisely which type of *qorban* is under consideration, namely, a *qorban*
of domesticated animals presented for combustible sacrifice.

The legislation introduced in Lev 1:2 is directed toward the presentation of the "*qorban* of domestic animals," a specific type of *qorban* among
other possible *qorbanim*. The protasis of this main case governs all the legislation inclusive of Lev. 7:28–36, and the unit is given its final shaping by
the concluding remark in 7:38 that God commanded the people of Israel
"to bring their offerings to the Lord" (להקריב את־קרבניהם ליהוה). The main
case in Lev. 1:2 serves, therefore, not to introduce only the legislation that
follows in 1:1–9, nor even the legislation in chs. 1–3, but rather, to introduce the entire scope of *qorban* legislation found in chs. 1–7. To suggest
as Knierim does that it would have been more appropriate had the case
in 1:2 read "if anyone from among you brings a *qorban* for Yahweh, you
shall bring either an 'olah or a minchah or a zebach shelamim" overlooks
the syntactical relationship between 1:2 and 7:28 and fails to recognize
the main case for what it is: an introduction to the *qorban* legislation of
the entire first unit, chs. 1–7. That this legislation concerns a specific type
of *qorban*, namely, the "livestock" *qorban*, accounts for the fact that the
focus of the protasis lies precisely upon the designation of the types of
animals that are available for presentation. Whereas Knierim took this
focus upon the type of animal to have been intentionally "resisted" by a
jarring shift to the type of sacrifice in 1:3, I understand it to be a perfectly
coherent syntactical signal that properly sets the stage for the entire unit.

The Substructure of Leviticus 1–7

The principal unit, Leviticus 1–7, is subdivided into three major subsections:

1. Instructions directed to the people (1:2–5:27)

2. Instructions directed to the priests (6:1–7:21)

3. Further instructions directed to the people (7:22–36)

---

8. Cf. the impossible construction of John Hartley: "When anyone among you
presents an offering to Yahweh, you are to present as your offering an animal from either
the herd or the flock" (*Leviticus* [WBC 4; Dallas: Word, 1992] 7).

The first two units are parallel in that they both review the listing of sacrifices that are under consideration in this *qorban* legislation. They are ordered as follows:

1:2–5:27	6:1–7:21
'olah (burnt offering)	*'olah* (burnt offering)
minchah (grain offering)	*minchah* (grain offering)
	minchah (grain offering) of anointing
zebach shelamim (sacrifice of well-being)	*chattat* (sin offering)
chattat (sin offering)	*'asham* (guilt offering)
'asham (guilt offering)	*zebach shelamim* (sacrifice of well-being)

Several patterns are evident in these two lists. The foundational sacrifices, the *'olah, minchah,* and *zebach shelamim,* consistently appear in that order, as do similarly the two expiatory sacrifices, the *chattat* and the *'asham.* There are, however, several significant differences between the two lists. The "instructions to the priests" include a sacrifice not included within the "instructions to the people," the "*minchah* of anointing" (מֹשָׁחה), which is inserted into the middle of the list. This sacrifice, however, concerns only the priests and so is logically absent from the first list and is added at this point in the instruction for two reasons. First, the term *minchah,* used of the people's *minchah* in 6:7–11, attracts to itself the instruction concerning the priests' *minchah,* which then immediately follows in 6:12–16. Second, this instruction concerning the priests' *minchah* is added at this point prior to the instruction concerning the expiatory sacrifices in 6:17–7:10 because the latter two, especially the blood rituals, necessarily presuppose the "anointing" of the priest, who must be ordained prior to performing the expiatory rituals described.[9]

One question relates to the original setting of the "*minchah* of the priest's anointing" in 6:12–23. This instruction originally concerned the selection and "anointing" of the chief priest, high priest, or the priestly "chief officer" (פָּקִיד נָגִיד)[10] in the temple establishment, the one selected "from among his colleagues' (וְהכֹהֵן הַמָּשִׁיחַ תַּחְתָּיו מִבָּנָיו, 6:15).[11] As such, it likely had nothing to do with the ordination of priests in general, and therefore represents a secondary insertion into this list. Nevertheless, its placement here is quite logical given the fact that the editor of this instruction, according to his own concluding formula in 7:37, took the

---

9. Thus the order of the material in Lev. 8:1–9:24. It is Moses rather than Aaron or the priests who performs the blood rites of the sin offering and burnt offering in 8:14–30. Aaron and his sons do not perform any such rites until after their "ordination" (9:1–24).

10. E.g., Jer. 20:1, the title used of Pashhur.

11. So the clear reference to הכֹהֵן הַמָּשִׁיחַ in Lev. 4:3.

instruction of the *"minchah* of anointing" to be nothing other than an offering of "ordination" (מלואים). Since the instruction concerning the "ordination" (מלואים) of Aaron and the priests in Lev. 8:1–36 involves conspicuous references to their being "anointed" (משח, 8:12, 30), the original setting of the instruction in 6:12–23 is co-opted by the present context and is put to the use of referring no longer to the "anointing" of the singular priestly leader but rather to the "ordination" of the entire corps of priests.

The two lists, therefore, are both internally and externally coherent and logically arranged. One further question, however, is why the legal editor transposed the types of sacrifices in 7:37, placing the "offering of ordination" *after* the two expiatory sacrifices rather than prior to them, as one would have expected given their ordering in the "instructions to the priests." One might only surmise that, by so doing, the editor was providing a transition to the following instructions concerning the ordination of Aaron and his sons in chs. 8–10. In this latter instruction, the sacrifices appear in the following order: sin offering (8:14–17), burnt offering (8:18–21), and in the last position the sacrifice of ordination (מלואים, 8:22–29). It was perhaps its *concluding* role in the ordination rituals that were to follow that prompted the editor to place the מלואים in final position in 7:37, thus preparing the reader for the coming instruction.

The remaining question concerning the structure of chs. 1–7 relates to the sudden shift *back* to instruction to the people in Lev. 7:22–36. This instruction falls where it does because it relates to the theme of eating the flesh of the sacrifice of well-being, which is discussed from the priestly perspective in 7:11–21. The question is why this instruction relating to the people's consumption of the sacrifice of well-being was not dealt with in conjunction with the prohibition against eating the fat or blood of the sacrifice of well-being in Lev. 3:17. The rationale for postponing this instruction until the end of the unit must lie in its emphasis upon the priestly portion that is reserved for consumption by the officiating priest, a topic that is completely lacking in Leviticus 3, where the focus is strictly limited to the fact that "all fat is YHWH's" (3:17), thereby precluding the eating of any of the fat (or blood) of the animal. The topic of the priestly consumption of the *zebach shelamim* is first introduced in the "instructions to the priests" in 7:11–21. It is never specified in this section, however, which portion belongs to the priest. The function of the concluding legislation in 7:28–36 is therefore to provide the necessary information required for the implementation of the priestly ritual. As such, this third section within the unit is less a third independent section than it is a concluding paragraph to the instructions to the priests, dealing with the matter of the priestly consumption of the sacrifice of well-being. In this sense, the thematic connectedness of 7:22–36 with what precedes is in dramatic tension with the disjunctive rhetorical signal given in the introductory formula in 7:22, and is perhaps intended to be so strong that the disjunction is overcome in favor of its conjunction.[12]

LEVITICUS 1–3 AS A UNIT

Leviticus 1–3 thus stands as a unit within the larger complex of *qorban* instruction in chs. 1–7 and within the more immediate collection of instruction to the people in 1:2–5:26. As already indicated, it is rhetorically marked as a unit by the formula in 4:1 that introduces the next section concerning the sin offering. The unit 1–3 is itself subdivided into three distinct sections:

1. Instructions concerning the burnt offering (1:3–17)

2. Instructions concerning the grain offering (2:1–16)

3. Instructions concerning the sacrifice of well-being (3:1–17)

Within this unit, however, there are significant difficulties with the legal syntax, which complicates how Lev. 1:2 relates to the whole. The syntax of this legal paragraph is as follows:

Statement of the main case:

(1:2aβ+bα1)[13] אדם כי־יקריב מכם קרבן ליהוה מן־הבהמה

    Statements of the subcases:

    (1:3aα) אם־עלה קרבנו מן־הבקר

    (1:10a) ואם־מן־הצאן קרבנו...לעלה

    (1:14a) ואם מן־העוף עלה קרבנו ליהוה

Statement of the main case:

(2:1aα) ונפש כי־תקריב קרבן מנחה ליהוה

    Statements of the subcases:

    (2:4a) וכי תקרב קרבן מנחה מאפה תנור

    (2:5a) ואם־מנחה על־המחבת קרבנך

    (2:7a) ואם־מנחת מרחשת קרבנך

Statement of the main case:

(3:1a) ואם־זבח שלמים קרבנו

---

12. The existing tension is given a redactional explanation by Israel Knohl, who reads into it the editorial activity of HS (Knohl's "Holiness School"), which updated the earlier PT (Knohl's "Priestly Torah") to accommodate it to the innovative injunction barring profane slaughter (*The Sanctuary of Silence: The Priestly Torah and the Holiness School* [Minneapolis: Fortress, 1995] 50–51).

13. On the problem of the placement of the *athnach*, see above, p. 189, under "The Syntax of Leviticus 1:2."

Statements of the subcases:

אם מן־הבקר הוא מקריב (3:1bα)

ואם־מן־הצאן קרבנו לזבח שלמים ליהוה (3:6a)

Statement of the sub-subcases:

אם־כשב הוא־מקריב את־קרבנו (3:7aα)

ואם־עז קרבנו (12:a)

Because this legal paragraph relates to the offering of cattle (בקר) and flock (צאן), 1:2, and because both the first case (the burnt offering) and the third case (the sacrifice of well-being) refer respectively to these two groups whereas the second case (the cereal offering) obviously does not, it is often argued that the rubric concerning the cereal offering in ch. 2 was a latter interpolation into the unit comprised originally of instructions regarding the two mentioned animal sacrifices.[14] The legal syntax also suggests a coherence between the first and third paragraphs: following the initial statement of the concern of the unit — the presentation of the livestock *qorban* — the two main cases that relate to the livestock *qorban* have identical syntactical markers:

Case one: אם־עלה קרבנו (1:3aα1)

Case three: ואם־זבח שלמים קרבנו (3:1a)

The marker אם immediately defines these two main cases as parallel subcases under the overarching rubric of "livestock *qorban*." In syntactical tension with this is the syntax of the second case (the *minchah*), which uses a formula — ונפש כי־תקריב — that characteristically introduces not a subcase but a main case. The second case thus presents a syntactical disruption of what would otherwise be a smooth flow from the first to the third case.[15]

Supporting this contention is the fact that the instruction in chs. 1 and 3 is consistently cast in a traditional third person address (m.sg.), with the exception of a few glaring divergences in the introductory and concluding clauses, which are attributable to the reworking of the material in the final editorial process.[16]

---

14. E.g., Rolf Rendtorff, *Studien zur Geschichte des Opfers im Alten Israel* (WMANT 24; Neukirchen-Vluyn: Neukirchener, 1967) 8–9.

15. The comment by Milgrom (*Leviticus 1–16*, 178) that the term כי here represents the voluntary nature of the offering, as with the burnt offering (so 1:2), misses the fact that the protasis of 1:2, in which the כי is found, does not initiate the instruction on the burnt offering. The term כי does not mark voluntary as opposed to involuntary acts, but rather, is a fixed style of legal syntax marking main cases as opposed to subcases.

16. So the sudden shift to 2m.pl. in 1:2 (מכם and תקריבו את־קרבנכם), likely under the influence of the direct address to the people as a whole. Cf. the shift to 2m.pl. once again in 3:17, likely representing the editorial hand at work. By concluding with 3m.pl., the editor forms an inclusio around the section by recalling the opening 3m.pl. phrase in v. 1. Otherwise the language is consistently 2m.sg.

In opposition to the consistency of usage in the first and third paragraphs, the paragraph concerning the grain offering exhibits a mixed style that suggests an interpolation by a different hand.[17] The opening ונפש כי־תקריב maintains the voice of the third person, carried over from ch. 1, but introduces ambiguity in the use of the feminine term נפש. When the identical term תקרב appears again in v. 4, it is not at all clear whether it is still pursuing the third person or has shifted to the second person. It is only with the introduction of the second subcase in 2:5, and the use of the term קרבנך, that the reader knows for certain that a fundamental shift to second person singular has indeed been made. More confusion is created in v. 8, however,[18] and the paragraph continues in v. 11 with another anomalous shift — this time to 2m.pl. — in the instruction concerning the prohibition against offering that which is leavened or sweetened with honey as a combustible sacrifice. Finally, the dominant voice of 2m.sg. is resumed with the instruction concerning the inclusion of salt in the sacrifice (v. 13) and is maintained through the closing rubric concerning the grain offering of firstfruits (מנחת בכורים, vv. 14–16). Such a composite style can be adduced as evidence for the editorial reworking of this material as it was interpolated into a preexisting unit of instruction relating to the presentation of "livestock" qorban, comprised of chs. 1 and 3.

If, as is often suspected, the unit in chs. 1–3 has indeed resulted from such a secondary interpolation of a rubric concerning the grain offering into the context of the primary animal sacrifices — the burnt offering and the sacrifice of well-being — the question before us is how the text is to be read in its present form. If the syntax of the legal protases betrays the discontinuity of their earlier form, then the continuity of their present form is marked by the editor's use of declaratory formulae to punctuate for the reader how the syntax of the final form is to be understood and read.

1. The primary formula is אשה ריח ניחח ליהוה ("an offering by fire, a pleasing odor to YHWH").[19] This formula concludes each subcase in the first paragraph (1:9bβ, 13bβ, 17b), the main case and its resumption in the second paragraph (2:2bβ, 9b), the first subcase in the third paragraph (3:5b),

---

17. Hartley, *Leviticus*, 4. On the stylistic unevenness of ch. 2, see Rolf Rendtorff, *Leviticus* (BKAT III/2; Neukirchen-Vluyn: Neukirchener, 1990) 82–83.

18. The use of 3m.sg. והקריבה in v. 8b again breaks this pattern, but the term might as well be read as a *hiph'il* imperative. The LXX, however, also takes והבאה in v. 8a as 3m.s. (προσοισει), thus reading the entire verse in 3m.sg.

19. Cf. the alternative forms אשה ליהוה (2:16b); לחם אשה ליהוה (3:11b); לחם אשה לריח ניחח (3:16b). That the term אשה relates to the notion of "fire" is not at all clear, and since the study by J. Hoftijzer ("Das Sogenannte Feueropfer," VTSup 16 [1967] 114–34) has been taken by many to be cognate to the Akk. *eššesu* ("offerings") or Ugaritic *itt* ("gift"), which may have been an older term for sacrificial offerings. Cf. Willi-Plein, *Opfer und Kult*, 91–92.

and each of its sub-subcases (3:11b, 16b).[20] Its use is therefore pronounced and strikingly consistent throughout the section, giving it its principal theme, and setting chs. 1–3 off from those that follow as those sacrifices that provide a "soothing aroma" for YHWH.[21]

2. The second paragraph is also punctuated with the declaratory formula relating to the priestly portion: קֹדֶשׁ קָדָשִׁים מֵאִשֵּׁי יהוה. This formula follows the statement concerning the "remainder of the grain offering" (וְהַנּוֹתֶרֶת מִן־הַמִּנְחָה) in 2:3b and 10b.

What we see, therefore, is that the legal editor has taken disparate material and fused it together into a congruous whole, overcoming the tension explicit in the syntax of the legal protases by the use of declaratory formulae that themselves serve further to define the legal syntax and give the unit its present coherence.

If, indeed, the three paragraphs are intended to be read as a coherent unit, we must return to the question of how the opening legal case in Lev 1:2 is to be understood, asking once again whether the shift in focus from "type of animal" to "type of sacrifice" is one that marks a discordant "process of resistance" in establishing an organizational principle (so Knierim) or whether it reflects a coherent editorial method of arranging a composite text.

As suggested above, although it is true that the opening rubrics in Leviticus 1–3 contain information concerning the type of sacrifice to be offered (burnt offering, grain offering, and sacrifice of well-being), the opening statement in Lev. 1:2 does not serve merely to introduce chs. 1–3, but rather, to introduce the entire breadth of *qorban* legislation contained in chs. 1–7. This is why the statement of the central case in 1:2, listing material that is to be dealt with in chs. 1–7, does *not* specify the type of sacrifice, but leaves it more generally related to the *qorban*, specifically the *qorban* of domestic animals. Because of this purposeful and coherent syntactical marker, the legal editor is faced with a dilemma: does he continue the legislation relating to the burnt offering (1:3–17) with a syntactical marker indicating that it is a new main case (...אָדָם כִּי יַקְרִיב or its equivalent)? To do so would be awkward and redundant. He chooses instead to introduce it with the marker indicating that it is a subcase of the *qorban* legislation (...אִם). By so doing, however, he needs to identify two features of the subcase at the same time, namely, the type of sacrifice and the type of animal. It is this "double duty" served by the protasis of the first subcase that provides the tension noted by Knierim, suggesting a "resistance" and a shifting of focus

---

20. The formula is always found immediately following the note that the priest shall immolate the sacrifice (וְהִקְטִיר הַכֹּהֵן, 1:9b, 13b, 17a; 2:2b, 9a, 16a; 3:5a, 11a, 16a).

21. Hartley, *Leviticus*, 3.

at an awkward time. However, the legal editor, realizing the potential confusion, signals to the reader how to understand the matter by carefully crafting the syntax of the legal protases. He does so by varying the syntax of the subcases before him. First, each of the main subcases in chs. 1 and 3 are marked by the following syntax:

... (animal) מן־ (אם) קרבנו (sacrifice) אם־.[22]

By placing the sacrifice in first position, he signals to the reader that a *double* shift has been made, and that the primary shift is to the type of sacrifice, followed secondarily by the shift to the type of animal. On the contrary, the editor marks each of the sub-subcases of this *qorban* instruction with a different syntax:

... (sacrifice)(ל) ... (animal) ואם־מן־.[23]

By inverting the order, placing the *animal* first and relocating the sacrifice to last position, the editor signals to the reader that the shift initiated in the first instance (primary stress on type of sacrifice) has already been made, and so no longer needs to be stressed. What comes before the reader now is a shift in the type of animal, while the type of sacrifice stays unchanged.

When understood according to their structural components, we see how orderly, intentional, and consistent the editor is in providing the necessary syntactical signals allowing the reader to understand the logic of the instruction's organization. Rather than betraying confusion due to a "process of resistance" taking place, it does, I think, quite the contrary.[24]

A central issue in the conversation has been the disruptive placement of the instruction concerning the grain offering into the middle of instruction concerning the sacrifice of domestic animals. What would have prompted such an interruption of the thematic listing? In interpolating the instruction concerning the grain offering into this material, placing it squarely between instructions concerning the burnt offering and the sacrifice of well-being, the editor was merely following — or was even perhaps constrained by — traditional associations. First, the grain offering (מנחה) served principally as an accompanying sacrifice to the burnt offering (עלה). Copious texts refer to the grain offering as being — to use a culinary metaphor — the bread side dish to the main

---

22. 1:3aα; 3:1a+bα.

23. 1:10a, 14a; 3:6a. Note how the sub-sub-subcases in 3:7a and 12a are marked with yet a different syntax, clearly marking their tertiary order: קרבנו ... (animal) אם־.

24. I also disagree with Milgrom's creative but unnecessary suggestion that the syntax outlined here has less to do with intentionality than with a "not notably successful" conflation of various formulae used elsewhere (*Leviticus 1–16*, 168).

course, speaking of the sacrifice of "a burnt offering with its grain offering."[25] Though on rare occasion the grain offering might also serve as an accompaniment to other sacrifices,[26] it is clear that it principally followed the presentation of the burnt offering. In Lev. 9:2–21, for example, though the grain offering is listed consistently after the burnt offering that it accompanies, the grain offering is omitted from the summary list in v. 22, likely because its identity was wholly linked to the burnt offering. The grain offering was such an integral part of the burnt offering that it therefore did not require separate mention.[27]

Furthermore, the lists of sacrifices recorded throughout the OT indicate two fundamental and fixed associations:

1. When the עלה and (שלמים) זבח are listed together, never does the latter precede the former.[28]

2. In such lists, the עלה is nearly always listed first, followed by the מנחה, and, always in last position, the (שלמים) זבח. The זבח stays in last position even when the expiatory sacrifices, the חטאת and the אשם, are included in the list.[29]

---

25. E.g., Exod. 29:38–46; Lev. 14:19–20, 31; 23:12–13, 18, and often elsewhere in Numbers and Ezekiel. That such an association transcends the strict confines of priestly instruction is indicated by Judg. 13:15–19, 21.

26. Accompanying either an עלה or a זבח (Num. 15:8–10), an ambiguous reference to "their grain offerings" in Num. 6:15 may relate the grain offering to the sin offering as well. It should be noted, however, that in Ezek. 45:23–25 the grain offering accompanies only the burnt offering (the bulls and rams) and not the sin offering (the goat). Otherwise, there is no evidence that the sin offering was ever "accompanied" by a grain offering.

27. It seems unlikely to me that the instruction concerning the grain offering was placed here because, like the material in chs. 1–5, it presents "ritual" (so Rolf Rendtorff, *Die Gesetze in der Priesterschrift: Eine gattungsgeschichtliche Untersuchung* [FRLANT 62; Göttingen: Vandenhoeck & Ruprecht, 1954] 19–20). Even less satisfying is the suggestion that the two are connected because the grain offering is a "cheaper form of the burnt offering" (so Frank H. Gorman Jr., *Leviticus* [ITC; Grand Rapids: Eerdmans, 1997] 26), though this tradition goes back to talmudic times. See Rendtorff, *Leviticus*, 84; Nehama Leibowitz, *New Studies in Vayikra (Leviticus)*, vol. 1 (Jerusalem: Eliner Library, 1993) 42–43.

28. Not only in priestly instruction and narrative (Lev. 9:2–22; 23:37; Num. 6:13–17; 7:1–88; 15:8–10; Ezek. 45:15, 17b), but also in DtrH (Josh. 22:23, 29; 1 Kings 8:64; 2 Kings 16:13) and the prophetic literature (Isa. 43:23; Jer. 17:26; 33:18; Amos 5:22). On the association of the two sacrifices, cf. Leonhard Rost, *Studien zum Opfer im Alten Israel* (BWANT 6/13; Stuttgart: Kohlhammer, 1981) 83–84.

29. Though the lists in Numbers 7 place the grain offering before the burnt offering, the summary list in 7:87–88 gives the standard listing: burnt offering, grain offering, sin offering, *zebach*. Exceptions to this are very rare: Isa. 43:23 and Jer. 17:26 (burnt offering, *zebach*, grain offering); Ezek. 45:15 (grain offering, burnt offering, *zebach*). The order burnt offering, grain offering, sin offering, *zebach* presents what is likely an administrative ordering reflecting the practice of bookkeeping. In actual practice (procedural ordering), the sin offering preceded the burnt offering in order to prepare for the ritual by means of purification. On this, see A. F. Rainey, "The Order of Sacrifices in Old Testament Ritual Texts," *Bib* 51 (1970) 485–98; Gary A. Anderson, "Sacrifice and Sacrificial Offering (OT)," *ABD*, 5:876–77. That the sacrifice of well-being (זבח שלמים) consistently comes in last po-

The order of burnt offering, grain offering, sacrifice of well-being therefore represents a traditional ordering that constrained the editor to place the instruction concerning the מנחה in its present location between the instruction concerning the עלה and זבח שלמים. Because the interpolated instruction did not relate to the matter specified in 1:2, namely, the presentation of the domestic animal *qorban*, the editor let stand the syntax that marked it in its earlier form (ונפש כי־תקריב...) rather than introduce it as a parallel subcase with a hypothetical form (ואם מנחה קרבנו...).

CONCLUSION

What I have hoped to demonstrate with this analysis of the legal syntax of Leviticus 1–3 is the careful, intentional, and conventional nature of its language and ordering. While the syntax of Lev. 1:2 does indeed seem to betray a tension within the immediate text of Lev. 1:1–9, the point of this study is to demonstrate that, when considered within the larger framework of chs. 1–7, the legal editor could not have ordered it any differently, nor could he have more clearly indicated via the syntax of the section how the reader was to conceive of the relationship of the parts to the whole. Whereas Knierim, in his analysis of the material, suggested that there is an unnecessary tension that exists between 1:2b and 1:3ff. demonstrating redactional influence and a purposeful editorial process of resistance,[30] I hope to have suggested that there is no tension, whether necessary or not. The syntax is precisely what one would have expected from a skilled legal editor who produced a coherent and smooth reading. One can only surmise that the same careful attention to the syntax of such priestly instruction throughout the rest of the book of Leviticus will generally demonstrate a similar consistency of skillful editorial technique.

---

sition is perhaps due to its character as a "concluding sacrifice" in which it "completes" or "brings into wholeness" (שלם) the ritual ceremony (Rendtorff, *Studien zur Geschichte des Opfers*, 133).

30. Knierim, *Text and Concept*, 11–12.

Bibliography

Anderson, Gary A. "Sacrifice and Sacrificial Offering (OT)." *ABD*, 5:870–86.

Gerstenberger, Erhard. *Leviticus: A Commentary.* OTL. Louisville: Westminster John Knox, 1996.

Gorman, Frank H., Jr. *Leviticus.* ITC. Grand Rapids: Eerdmans, 1997.

Hartley, John. *Leviticus.* WBC 4. Dallas: Word, 1992.

Hoftijzer, J. "Das Sogenannte Feueropfer." In *Hebräische Wortforschung. Festschrift zum 80. Geburtstag von Walter Baumgartner,* 114–34. VTSup 16. Leiden: E. J. Brill, 1967.

Knierim, Rolf. *Text and Concept in Leviticus 1:1–9: A Case in Exegetical Method.* FAT 2. Tübingen: J. C. B. Mohr, 1992.

Knohl, Israel. *The Sanctuary of Silence: The Priestly Torah and the Holiness School.* Minneapolis: Fortress, 1995.

Leibowitz, Nehama. *New Studies in Vayikra (Leviticus),* vol. 1. Jerusalem: Eliner Library, 1993.

Milgrom, Jacob. *Leviticus 1–16.* AB 3. New York: Doubleday, 1991.

Rainey, A. F. "The Order of Sacrifices in Old Testament Ritual Texts." *Bib* 51 (1970) 485–98.

Rendtorff, Rolf. *Die Gesetze in der Priesterschrift: Eine gattungsgeschichtliche Untersuchung.* FRLANT 62. Göttingen: Vandenhoeck & Ruprecht, 1954.

———. *Leviticus.* BKAT III/2. Neukirchen-Vluyn: Neukirchener, 1990.

———. *Studien zur Geschichte des Opfers im Alten Israel.* WMANT 24. Neukirchen-Vluyn: Neukirchener, 1967.

Rost, Leonhard. *Studien zum Opfer im Alten Israel.* BWANT 6/13. Stuttgart: Kohlhammer, 1981.

Willi-Plein, Ina. *Opfer und Kult im alttestamentlichen Israel: Textbefragungen und Zwischenergebnisse.* SBS 153. Stuttgart: Katholisches Bibelwerk, 1993.

10

The Transition from
the Old Generation to the New Generation
in the Book of Numbers:
A Response to Dennis Olson

Won W. Lee

In a revision of his Yale dissertation, *The Death of the Old and the Birth of the New: The Framework of the Book of Numbers and the Pentateuch,* Dennis Olson initiates a noteworthy shift from previous scholarship on the structure of Numbers.[1] As the title indicates, his contribution lies in treating the structural analysis of Numbers as "the central problem" in the interpretation of the book and in discussing systematically a proposal that the superstructure of Numbers is based on the death of the old generation and the birth of the new generation.[2] Olson's thesis can be summarized: the book of Numbers has a "convincing and meaningful" structure; it is based on the compositional signal formed by the two census reports in chs. 1 and 26; these reports mark a clear transition from the old generation who came out of the land of Egypt to the new generation about to enter the land of Canaan; this compositional signal illuminates the governing concept, the death of the old generation (because of their disobedience of Yahweh they must die off in forty years wandering in the wilderness) and the birth of the new generation (in contrast, because of their obedience of Yahweh they possess the possibility to enter the promised land).[3]

This essay would not exist in its present form without Dr. Simon De Vries's careful reading and numerous editorial suggestions. The author greatly appreciates his suggestions in writing style and his encouragement for pursuing excellence in scholarship.

1. D. T. Olson, *The Death of the Old and the Birth of the New: The Framework of the Book of Numbers and the Pentateuch* (BJS 71; Chico, Calif.: Scholars Press, 1985).

2. R. P. Knierim acknowledges the contribution of Olson's work and encourages future exegetes "to be more critically conscious when addressing this subject [the structural question in Numbers] than has been characteristic of past attempts" ("The Book of Numbers," in *The Task of the Old Testament Theology: Substance, Method, and Cases* [Grand Rapids: Eerdmans, 1995] 381).

3. Olson's thesis has been adopted and modified by many commentators. For example, one of three structures that Jacob Milgrom proposes is based on the two generations:

The kernel of Olson's thesis is the generational succession of the Israelites during the wilderness period. According to him, this generational succession occurs at the second census list in Numbers 26. Since there is no clear statement made regarding this succession in Numbers, proposing it as the constitutive criterion for the structure of Numbers in the highest level is purely hypothetical.[4] Important questions emerge. In

(1) the generation of the Exodus, which has two subparts, (a) the organization of the wilderness camp (1:1–10:10) and (b) the march from Sinai to Transjordan (10:11–25:19); (2) the generation of the conquest (26:1–36:13). The other two are based on topographical-chronological data and on his reconstruction of the theological-literary structure of the Hexateuch. See Milgrom, *Numbers* (JPS Torah Commentary; Philadelphia: Jewish Publication Society, 1990] xiii–xvii; idem, "Numbers, Book of," *ABD*, 4:1146–48. Milgrom reiterates major points of Olson's content and thematic analysis without critical evaluation of Olson's thesis as a whole. Milgrom, however, follows the accepted delimitation of the Sinai pericope as ending in 10:10 and presupposes a more specific concept for "the new generation," that is, the generation of the conquest, one of the five major themes of the Pentateuch developed by Martin Noth. In his analysis, Milgrom borrows the two-generation scheme from Olson, yet abandons Olson's conceptuality in embracing the traditional duality of the Israelites' activities after Sinai revelation and preparations for entering the promised land. See also, K. D. Sakenfeld, *Numbers: Journeying with God* (ITC; Grand Rapids: Eerdmans, 1995) 4–11.

4. A few passages in Numbers are related to the concept of the generational succession of the Israelites (14:26–35; 26:63–65; 32:6–15). 14:26–35 provides the basis and reason for this concept, whereas 26:63–65 and 32:6–15 mention it without a clear statement of the actual transition from the old to the new generation. This point is to be discussed in detail later. Scholars have proposed various criteria for the structure of Numbers: chronological markers, geographical references, source-critical grounds, tradition-historical themes, and conceptual factors. Numbers contains numerous chronological markers, most of them imprecise, and yet there are a few precise dates in 1:1; 9:1, 5; 10:1; and 33:3, 38, which show approximately thirty-eight years and eleven months as the duration of Israel's wilderness experience, according to Numbers (cf. Deut. 1:3). Numbers also includes various place names through which Israel journeys (e.g., 33:5–49). The distinction between geographical and topographical indicators is imperative for designating the former as the constitutive criterion for the structure of Numbers. By definition, the former includes the latter; thus, these two cannot be equally significant (see G. B. Gray, *A Critical and Exegetical Commentary on Numbers* [ICC; Edinburgh: T. & T. Clark, 1903] xxii–xxix; G. J. Wenham, *Numbers* [TOTC; Downers Grove, Ill.: Inter-Varsity, 1981] 14–18). Due to the existence of at least three major documentary sources (J, E, P), Numbers may be divided according to their interrelations (see D. Kellermann, *Die Priesterschrift von Numeri 1,1 bis 10,10: Literarkrit. u. Traditionsgeschichtl. Untersucht* [BZAW 120; Berlin: W. de Gruyter, 1970] 2–3). Martin Noth uses the combination of the tradition-historical themes ("revelation at Sinai," "guidance through the wilderness," and "guidance into the land") as the criterion (Noth, *Numbers: A Commentary* [trans. J. D. Martin; OTL; Philadelphia: Westminster, 1968] 1–2; idem, *A History of Pentateuchal Traditions* [trans. B. W. Anderson; Atlanta: Scholars Press, 1981]). Some examples of the conceptual factors are generational transition (Olson, *Death of the Old*, passim. B. A. Levine, *Numbers 1–20* [AB 4A; New York: Doubleday, 1993] 57–62), a spiritual journey (T. W. Mann, *The Book of the Torah: The Narrative Integrity of the Pentateuch* [Atlanta: John Knox, 1988] 127), and preparation and execution of Israel's migratory-sanctuary campaign (Knierim, "Book of Numbers," 380–88). The comparison of suggested criteria and evaluation of the methods for reconstructing them should be included in determining the constitutive criterion for the superstructure of Numbers. This task demands a thorough discussion, which lies outside the purview of the present essay.

view of the wide variety of material found in Numbers, how is Olson's claim that this transition happens at the second census list in Numbers 26 to be defended? Does his discussion reflect an empirically controlled investigation for verifying the legitimacy of his proposed concept? If his discussion turns out to be an impressionistic surface reading of the text, can his concept be qualified as the generative conceptuality responsible for the structure of Numbers at the highest level? Can his claim that the census lists in chs. 1 and 26 function as the macrostructural signals in Numbers be substantiated? These questions are related intrinsically. To address them demands analysis of textual evidence from Numbers 1 and 26, the location and arrangement of the texts in the extant book, and of the function of the texts for signaling the conceptuality of the entire book. Without this conceptuality the extant book cannot be understood intelligently.

Olson's discussion of Numbers 1 and 26 seems unaware of the distinctiveness and connectedness of these questions; hence his argument must remain misdirected and circular. Accordingly, the present essay begins with a critical review of Olson's proposal as a whole, to be followed by his evidence that the census lists in chs. 1 and 26 constitute the central macrostructural signal. It then focuses on the main question concerning the point at which the transition from the old to the new generation occurs in Numbers. The essay goes on to argue that Num. 21:1–3 is the turning point between the end of the exodus generation and the call of the succeeding generation to be the new carrier of Yahweh's land promise. Since this is related to Olson's claim that the generational succession is the constitutive criterion for the macrostructure of Numbers, the essay also briefly addresses the claim that the generational succession is operative only in Num. 15:1–36:13 and not in the entire book of Numbers.

A REVIEW OF OLSON'S THESIS

At the outset, the title of Olson's book, *The Death of the Old and the Birth of the New*, is problematic or at least ambiguous. This title assumes the existence of two generations of the Israelites during the wilderness period and a decisive transition between them. Not the existence of two separate generations but the formulation of the transition between them is the problem. The succession of generations is marked by the *death* of the previous generation and the *birth* of the new generation. Olson identifies the chronological and geographical evidence for this transition. He takes the phrase "after the plague" in 26:1 to mean "after the death of the rest of the first generation." He also takes the geographical notice "in the plains of Moab by the Jordan at Jericho" in 26:3 as an indication that this new generation does not begin in the wilderness as the first generation did, but as they now stand at the edge of the promised land.[5] This transition assumes that the new generation *replaces* the old generation only *after* the old generation has died off. Thus, Olson's title suggests that the total of Israel's wilderness period is eighty years, calculated according to the wilderness period in which the two separate generations spent time. A period of forty years has to elapse in order that the exodus generation may die off, and then due to the faithlessness of the exodus generation the new generation must wander another forty years. But an eighty-year total based on the temporal succession of two consecutive generations is clearly in conflict with the well-known forty-year scheme of Israel's wilderness experience.[6] Exod. 7:7 states that Moses was eighty years old when he spoke to Pharaoh, and Deut. 34:7 (cf. 31:2) states that he was 120 years old when he died. The forty-year span of Moses' prophetic life alone corresponds to the duration of Israel's wandering in the wilderness. Olson seems to reflect chronological dissonance with this textual data.

The solution rests on how the biblical term "generation" (דור) must be understood. The employment of this term as the period between the birth of parents and that of their children (or the death of one generation and the birth of another) is neither prominent in the OT nor normative.[7] Instead of generation B replacing generation A after the death of generation A, the life span of these two generations must have overlapped. They are not contemporaneous, but do live simultaneously sharing a portion of the time. Since any two, or even three, generations have to be coexistent, the overlapping of generations is in principle presupposed in the concept of דור.

This overlapping of generations is assumed in Yahweh's punishment to Israel's failure: "But your little ones ... I will bring in, and they shall know the land that you [the exodus generation] have despised" (14:31). This text suggests that the new generation about whom Olson talks had already been born in Egypt, but may include the newborn of the wilderness. Thus, the text assumes that the death of the exodus generation does not, and cannot, mean that the new generation has just been born. Rather, the new generation gradually takes over and is called upon to be the new carrier of the divine land promise at the end of the forty-year

---

5. See Olson, *Death of the Old*, 84–85.

6. The forty years as the duration of Israel's journey from its liberation out of Egypt to its entrance into the land of Canaan has been firmly established throughout the Bible (Exod. 16:35; Num. 14:33, 34; 32:13; Deut. 2:7; 8:2, 4; 29:5; Josh. 5:6; Neh. 9:21; Ps. 95:10; Ezek. 4:6; Amos 2:10; 5:25).

7. See D. N. Freedman, J. Lundbom, and G. J. Botterweck, "דור," *TDOT*, 3:168–91; cf. G. Gerleman, "דור," *TLOT*, 1:333–35.

wandering. They must continue to suffer the common forty-year hardship in the wilderness because of their forebears' faithlessness (14:33). Thus, Yahweh's response to Israel's failure does not consider the possibility of successive generation in the chronological sense. Two separate generations are coexistent and overlap each other within the forty-year wilderness period; as the exodus generation is dying off, the new generation suffers the same forty years. Whereas the suffering for the former generation is to be death, that of the latter is to be "shepherds in the wilderness." At the end of the forty years the latter will stand alone as the new carrier of Yahweh's land promise.

Substantively, Olson presents three kinds of evidence for his argument that the census lists in Numbers 1 and 26 are the macrostructural signals for the entire book of Numbers, two of them being formal and content indicators from the book itself and the third a redactional device.[8] Methodologically, these items of evidence are indicative of a purely surface reading on Olson's part and do not reflect thorough exegesis. In this way, a theological hermeneutic in which the death of the old generation is caused by their disobedience of Yahweh and in which the birth of a new, obedient generation gives them hope of entering the promised land is imposed on the text. This construct inevitably leads Olson to suppress or ignore much contrary textual evidence.

A categorical evaluation of Olson's three kinds of evidence is in order. First, with regard to the formal indicators, Olson takes the phrase "after the plagues" in 26:1 as a chronological signal with a theological meaning, "after the death of the rest of the first generation." The phrase in and of itself, however, introduces only a temporal shift from the previous event, 25:1–18, to the following, 25:19–26:65, and functions to delimit the latter as a distinct literary unit. But why does this phrase among numerous imprecise chronological markers in Numbers carry this specific meaning? The subjective use of a phrase is one thing, but whether the proposed meaning of that phrase can be verified by concrete textual evidence is another. The phrase has a specific theological meaning for Olson, but only because he assumes this from what he takes to be the structural significance of Numbers 26.[9] The same logic

---

8. Olson, *Death of the Old*, 83–118. Olson spends fourteen pages (84–97) on the first two evidences while the rest of the discussion (97–118) deals with the overall Priestly editorial intention for the larger context of Genesis to Numbers as a whole. On the surface, this statistic reveals that what he does is not what he claims to do (Numbers as it stands is the beginning point for the structural inquiry). For a brief analysis of Olson's thesis as a whole, see R. P. Knierim's "Prolegomena," in *The Book of Numbers* (FOTL; Grand Rapids: Eerdmans, forthcoming) 10–13.

9. For an example of how to draw significant meaning from an imprecise chronological marker by a close reading of the text, see Simon J. De Vries, "The Time Word *maḥar* as a Key to Tradition Development," *ZAW* 87 (1975) 65–79.

applies to Olson's use of "in the plains of Moab by the Jordan at Jericho" in 26:3. For Olson, this is a geographical notation pertaining to the
new generation, in contrast with the beginning of the old generation in
the wilderness. One should note that the same locality has already been
mentioned in 22:1. If this particular locality communicates the meaning
Olson suggests, then 22:1, not 26:3, should be the point of the beginning for the new generation. In addition, he interprets the locality in
22:1 and 26:3 to be "the boundary of the promised land," and accordingly interprets 22:1 as suggesting that the old generation was given a
"privilege of again coming to the brink of the promised land."[10] What
Olson has done is assign two different meanings to the same locality:
22:1 is for the old generation and 26:3 is for the new generation. Such
procedures prejudice evidence gained from the independent analysis of
these two passages.

Olson goes on to argue that in the two census lists, linguistic similarities and a similar sequence of censuses (the twelve-tribe census list
first and the Levites' census list second) provide a symmetrical pattern
for the entire book of Numbers. But symmetry should involve correspondence in size, in shape, and in the relative positions of parts on
each side of the dividing line, not necessarily an even distinction of elements. Olson also misuses the term "parallel" in his argument that
Numbers has parallels between the two halves of the book that are demarcated by ch. 26. But having a number of corresponding materials
does not mean that the two halves are actually parallels. They certainly
do not have identical syntactic elements in corresponding positions, nor
do these extend in the same direction or at an equal distance apart at
every point. Olson's misemployment of such terms enhances his tendency to read the text superficially. Even the cohesiveness within each
half of the book that he claims to recognize is strictly based on an empirical survey of the content of each rather than on the accumulation of
exegetical results from independent studies of the component parts of
the whole.

Second, Olson's argument on thematic or content indicators is based
on his interpretation of three key passages. He argues that the phrase
"and of all your number, numbered from twenty years old and upward"
in 14:29 pertains to the same category of the people mentioned in 1:3;
also that the theme of the tribes of Reuben's and Gad's unwillingness
to help the other tribes in Numbers 32 is related to the theme of the
death of the old and the birth of the new in Numbers 13–14; and further that 26:63–65 connects the theme of Numbers 13–14 to the second

---

10. Olson, *Death of the Old*, 96; idem, *Numbers* (IBC; Louisville: John Knox, 1996) 139.

census of the Israelites.[11] The dependence of Numbers 32 on Numbers 13–14 is clear: Moses' speech to the tribes of Reuben and Gad in 32:6–15 is less understandable without the spy story. By connecting these two passages, Olson makes two conclusions: (1) that generational transition is the dominant concept in Numbers 13–14, and (2) that that transition occurs prior to Numbers 32. While his second point is self-evident, it makes no special contribution, but the validity of his first point needs to be discussed further.

Olson's tendency toward superficial readings of the text is once again demonstrated. If his way of relating Numbers 13–14 to Numbers 1 by the phrase "and of all your number, numbered from twenty years old and upward" is sustainable, Yahweh's punishment would affect only those who were numbered in Num. 1:3. What, then, about the Levites who have been numbered separately from the rest of the twelve tribes? Are the Levites part of Yahweh's death sentence on the Israelites? What about Moses, Aaron, and Miriam; are they not to share the same fatal destiny of the entire exodus generation? Since only Caleb and Joshua among the exodus generation are to be exempted from Yahweh's punishment and will inherit the promised land (14:24, 30), the Levites, Miriam, Aaron, and Moses cannot expect to escape from Yahweh's punishment on the Israelites. No matter how implicitly suggested, they are part of the exodus generation and surely share the same fate. Numbers 13–14 as a whole determines their fate and foreshadows the meaning of their rebellions in Num. 16:1–17:15 (Korah's rebellions [Eng. 16:1–50]) and in 20:1–13 (Moses and Aaron's rebellion).[12] Thus, Numbers 13–14 reveals much more of the scope of Yahweh's punishment than what Olson would draw from the corresponding phrase of Num. 1:3.

Moreover, Olson would understand Num. 26:63–65 as determining the meaning of 26:4, and regarding it as "a programmatic summary" of the structure of Numbers.[13] It is difficult to verify this characterization one way or another. The question to be answered is how, and on what basis, Olson comes to this understanding. Despite Olson's stress on the function of the text within its extant literary context, he does not seek out its meaning and function within the larger unit, 25:19–26:65 (Eng. 26:1–65). Instead, he attempts to determine its meaning by comparing

---

11. Olson, *Death of the Old*, 90–98. Olson's understanding of the spy story in Numbers 13–14 will be discussed below.

12. The ever narrowing progression of parties responsible for rebellions, from the whole community (esp. 14:1–4) through the Levites to Moses and Aaron, suggests that the fate of all the exodus generation is determined already in Numbers 13–14, and that both Num. 16:1–17:15 and 20:1–13 provide a necessary rationale for the inclusion of the leaders in the irreversible fate of the exodus generation.

13. Olson, *Death of the Old*, 92, 217, n. 6, respectively.

the various traditions involved in the twelve-tribe lists and the census numbers. Accordingly, for him the text serves as "the last word" regarding the purpose of the census list in Numbers 26, which is to mark the beginning of the new generation whose high numbers express the gracious extent of Yahweh's blessing on Israel, just as with the old generation mentioned in Numbers 1, at the same time indicating a partial fulfillment of the patriarchal promise.[14] For him the text is meaningful because of its contribution to the overarching theme that he develops from other texts and not in its own right. He ignores the text's function within its present literary context. The text offers the concluding statement concerning Yahweh's command for a census of the Israelites. Its purpose is to prepare the Israelites for the allotment of the land, not to organize them for an upcoming journey, as in Numbers 1. This purpose is clearly evident in Numbers 26. The content of Yahweh's command to Moses and Eleazar (26:2) shows less interest in the military aspect of the census than in 1:2–3. Moses and Eleazar's command to the Israelites fails to mention a military purpose for this census (26:4). 26:52–56 states that the population to be numbered in this census provides the basis of the division of the land of Canaan. The Levites are to be numbered separately from the other tribes because they are not to have any inheritance in the land of Canaan (v. 62b), not because they are set apart for special service related to the tabernacle, as in 1:48–54 and 3:5–10. Thus, Numbers 1 and Numbers 26 do not have the same purpose.[15] Regarding the purpose of this second census, 26:63–65 fails to provide any new information. This means that the text is not essential to the concept of Number 26 as a whole. Its function is to lead the reader back to v. 3 and thus clarify any possible misunderstanding that may be caused by v. 4b. In the present literary context, v. 63 restates the content of v. 3 while vv. 64–65 clarify the identity of those who are enrolled by Moses and Eleazar in vv. 5–51 that they are not the ones who were enrolled by Moses and Aaron in the wilderness of Sinai.[16] Thus, vv. 63–65 are meaningful only in that sense that they conclude the census report, not because they contribute to the purpose of the census, to the preparation for the allotment of the land, or to the purpose that Olson proposes.

Third, regarding the third type of evidence, Olson argues that the *toledot* formulae and the wilderness itineraries are marks of conscious

---

14. Olson, *Death of the Old*, 55–81.

15. Knierim argues convincingly that these two chapters do not even have the same function in the extant book. He concludes that "the relationship of the second census to the first is referential in nature, but it does not indicate two structurally equal narrative parts, neither on genealogical nor on theological grounds" ("Prolegomena," 12).

16. See Levine, *Numbers 1–20*, 60.

editorial shaping not only in Numbers but in the entire Pentateuch.[17] Olson's contribution lies in his persistent inquiry of the role and function of these indicators in the canonical form of the text. However, he employs the *toledot* formulae in Genesis to define the meaning, function, and location of Num. 3:1 within the book of Numbers. The framework of the overall Priestly narrative, which is based on the occurrences of the *toledot* formulae in Genesis, becomes the criterion for the structure of Numbers, with Num. 3:1 occupying the focal point. However, the interrelationships among the *toledot* formulae, the genealogies, and the tribal lists in Genesis, as well as in Numbers 1–4 and Numbers 26, are not entirely clear. Which occurrences are determinative? Structurally, the *toledot* formula in Num. 3:1 should serve as the determinative macrostructural signal in Numbers if it actually does share a meaning and function identical with those in Genesis. This would require that the structure of the Pentateuch would have to be constructed. According to Olson's treatment, two examples can be listed:

Structure One (based on Olson's claim on the *toledot* of Jacob) as "the most important one")

I. Generations up to the *toledot* of Jacob	Gen. 1–Exod. 1:7
II. Generations after the *toledot* of Jacob	Exod. 1:8–Deut. 34
A. Events up to the *toledot* of Aaron and Moses	Exod. 1:8–Num. 2
B. Events after the *toledot* of Aaron and Moses	Num. 3:1–Deut. 34
1. Old generation	Num. 3:1–Num. 25:18
2. New generation	Num. 25:19–Deut. 34

Structure Two (based on the new generation as "the final goal of the *toledot* series within the Pentateuch")

I. Preparation: generations up to the end of "the exodus generation"	Gen. 1–Num. 25
II. Goal: the new generation	Num. 26–Deut. 34

These two proposed structures are based on the concept of succeeding generations, as signaled by *toledot* series in the Pentateuch. Olson's claim is that this grand framework of the Priestly tradition is "consistent with the definitive structure of the book of Numbers in its present form."[18] But his proposal for a bipartite structure involving the death of the old generation in Num. 1:1–25:18 and the birth of the new generation in Num. 25:19–36:13 offers an entirely different structure, one that presupposes the two census reports, rather than the *toledot* formula as the criterion upon which this structure is based. The clear discrepancy

---

17. Olson, *Death of the Old*, 97–125.
18. Olson, *Death of the Old*, 114.

between his analysis and what he proposes as a result of that analysis is apparent.

In short, Olson is to be commended for his analysis of the differences between the two generations, but he seeks to prove this idea with unclarified perspectives and criteria, and by disturbing the evidence to conform to his preconceived idea. His exegesis does not allow the textual evidence freedom to support, undercut, or reconceptualize his own idea. Ideas should not be idealized as his have been. The end result is that his structure of Numbers is an imposition on the biblical text incapable of being substantiated or accounting for the signals that Numbers does provide.

NUMBERS 21:1–3 AS THE TURNING POINT
FROM THE EXODUS GENERATION TO THE NEW GENERATION

Numbers itself does not clearly mention the point at which the transition from the exodus generation to the new generation occurs. Nevertheless, it presupposes that the transition must have occurred at some point between Yahweh's pronouncement of death of all the Israelites in 14:26–35 and an editorial statement within the census report at 26:64–65. If the new generation does not begin to emerge until Numbers 26, as Olson argues, it is difficult to understand the futuristic orientation of the laws in Numbers 15 and 19, the narrative of the Israelites' defeat of Kings Sihon and Og in 21:21–35, and of their utter destruction of the Canaanites in 21:1–3 whom they could not defeat in the narrative of 14:39–45. These cannot belong to the old generation destined to be exterminated in the wilderness. Also, how is one to account for the strategic location of the story of Balaam immediately after the Israelites' encampment at the boundary of the promised land ("in the plains of Moab beyond the Jordan at Jericho," 22:1), along with its message that Yahweh's universal power is being displayed on behalf of the Israelites? Why have the texts that report the death of Miriam and Aaron and the transgression of Moses and Aaron against Yahweh been clustered together in ch. 20? By the same token, why have so many direct military accounts been gathered in Num. 21:1–3, 21–31, and 32–35?[19] On the other hand, why are there two rebellion narratives immediately following the narratives of the events that supposedly boast about Israel's confidence in Yahweh? These are about the serpent scourge in 21:4–9 (following the account of Israel's victory over the Canaanites

---

19. The other three direct military accounts in Numbers are 14:39–45; 20:14–21; 31:1–54. There are six more indirect accounts of Israel's military campaign: 10:11–36 (vv. 35–36); 21:10–20 (vv. 14–15); 22:1–24:25; 25:19–26:65 (vv. 1–4a); 32:1–42; 33:50–56.

in 21:1–3) and about Israel's apostasy to Baal of Peor through their sexual behavior in 25:1–18 (following Yahweh's blessing on Israel through
the foreign prophet Balaam in 21:1–24:25). Are the two rebellion narratives actually indicative of the exodus generation's rebellious attitude,
as Olson argues? Unsatisfied with Olson's proposal, this essay identifies 21:1–3 as a decisive mark of generational transition. It regards this
passage's content, present location, relation to other units within chs.
15 through 26, and governing conceptuality as a turning point in the
fulfillment of Yahweh's land promise. The text represents a call for the
new generation of the Israelites to carry out the conquest of the land of
Canaan that the exodus generation has forfeited.

Yahweh's death sentence upon the Israelites over forty years is recorded at 14:26–35 and carried out completely at 20:1–29. All three of
the distinct units within ch. 20 (vv. 1–13, vv. 14–21, and vv. 22–29) signal the end of the exodus generation and they pave the path for the
new generation. Formal evidence for this is that topographical markers
and chronological references within ch. 20 point to the completion of
Yahweh's punishment of the exodus generation. All agree that Israel's
encounter with Edom (vv. 14–21) and the death of Aaron (vv. 22–29)
occur in the fortieth year at Kadesh or in its vicinity (Mount Hor). It
is also clear that Yahweh's denial of further leadership for Moses and
Aaron (vv. 2–13) occurs at Kadesh. In contrast, it is not altogether clear
whether this event occurs in the fortieth year, since an incomplete date
is given for Israel's arrival at Kadesh. In 20:1 Israel arrived at Kadesh,
which is said to be located in the wilderness of Zin (cf. 20:14, 16,
22; 27:14; 34:36, 37), in "the first month" without specifying the year,
whereas in 13:26 the spies are said to return after surveying the land
of Canaan and they come to Kadesh, which is said to be located in
the wilderness of Paran, where Israel arrived immediately after leaving
the wilderness of Sinai (10:12; 12:16; 13:3). Thus, there is geographical
incongruity together with chronological incongruity.

Baruch Levine argues that these incongruities result from the inter-
play of the two sources, the Yahwist-Elohist (JE) and the Priestly (P).
Numbers 13:26 reflects the historiography of the JE narrative, which
has the Israelites arrive at Kadesh very soon after they leave the wilderness of Sinai (cf. 32:8). They stay a short time in Kadesh after failing to
penetrate Canaan, and spend most of the remaining thirty-eight years
wandering in the wilderness east of Edom and south of Moab.[20] On
the other hand, Num. 20:1 reflects the historiography of the P tradi-

---

20. Levine, *Numbers 1–20*, 55. His reconstruction of JE's version of the Israelites'
itinerary is based on Dtr historiography (cf. Deut. 1:19, 46; 2:14; Josh. 14:6–12; Judg.
11:6–7).

tions, which have the Israelites arrive at Kadesh in the fortieth year; they spend most of the thirty-eight years in northern Sinai, the locale of the wilderness of Paran.[21] Regardless of the origin of these incongruities, their purpose and function in the extant text remain unanswered. Why did the Priestly authors revise the JE version of Israel's itinerary, thereby reconstructing their own record keeping the Israelites in Sinai for thirty-eight years of further migration, and narrating their arrival at Kadesh only in the fortieth year? The answer should be clear in light of Yahweh's punishment of the exodus generation. By mentioning Kadesh, the Priestly authors have located the rebellion of Moses and Aaron at the same place where the Israelites' unprecedented rebellion previously occurred, thus rationalizing the inclusion of Moses and Aaron in the doomed fate of all the exodus generation. By placing Kadesh in the wilderness of Paran, northern Sinai, they also show that Yahweh's threat to punish the exodus generation by having them die out in *this* wilderness, that is, the wilderness of Paran (14:29, 32–33, 35), is carried out. By offering an incomplete date, the Priestly authors have attempted to loosen the tension created by the JE version of Israel's arrival at Kadesh at the beginning of the schematic forty-year wilderness period. More importantly, they have dated the rebellion of Moses and Aaron in the fortieth year (cf. 33:36–39). By doing this, the Priestly writers have stressed the continuous rebelliousness of the exodus generation during the entire forty years and have characterized the leaders' rebellion as the climax of a series of rebellions. Thus, for them the forty-year wilderness period begins with the whole community's rebellion but ends with the leaders' rebellion. The mention of Kadesh and "the first month" in the extant text of Num. 20:1 reflects this intention.[22]

The contents of ch. 20 reinforce the claim that this chapter marks the end of the exodus generation. The first unit (vv. 1–13) begins by reporting the death of Miriam, one of the three high-ranking leaders within the hierarchical organization of the Israelites' sanctuary camp (v. 1), and goes on to recount Yahweh's denial of prophetic leadership to Moses and Aaron (vv. 2–13). Yahweh's characterization of the sin of

---

21. Levine, *Numbers 1–20*, 57. For Levine, the Priestly authors created "an impractical itinerary, leading first to the Red Sea, then to Kadesh, and then back to the Red Sea and Edom by virtually the same route!" T. B. Dozeman goes one step farther than Levine. Presupposing two layers of the Priestly accounts, he argues that the Priestly writers are responsible for making this itinerary impractical by changing the sequence of travel of the pre-Priestly account (Dozeman, "The Wilderness and Salvation History in the Hagar Story," *JBL* 117, no. 1 [1998] 37–40).

22. Milgrom (*Numbers*, 464) asserts that the reason for the insertion of Kadesh and of the incomplete date in 20:1 is to locate the rebellion of Moses and Aaron at Kadesh and to date it in the fortieth year. His assertion is correct, but he does not provide any explanation for it.

Moses and Aaron as a sign of a distrust causing them not to sanctify Yahweh in the eyes of the Israelites (v. 12a) is connected with Israel's distrust of Yahweh's plan for them in chs. 13–14.[23] As punishment for their sin, Yahweh denies them responsibility for leading the people into the promised land (v. 12b). Since this denial of Moses and Aaron's leadership implies their exclusion from inheriting the land and their death in the wilderness, Yahweh's punishment of them is in essence the same as Yahweh's punishment of the exodus generation. This punishment has already been foreshadowed in their response to the people's rebellion in the spies incident (14:5).[24] In effect, vv. 2–13 rationalizes the inclusion of Moses and Aaron in the doomed fate of the exodus generation.

Moreover, Yahweh's punishment of Moses and Aaron comes to the foreground in the rest of ch. 20. The second unit of this chapter (vv. 14–21) features Edom's refusal of Israel's petition for a peaceful passage and Israel's wish to avoid a military confrontation as Edom comes out with the sword. This is the Israelites' first encounter with other peoples since dealing with the Amalekites and the Canaanites. It assumes that Moses' role as the leader of Israel has already been significantly reduced. Moses recedes into the background after v. 4, where he sends messengers,[25] Yahweh not being present to support Moses. The myste-

---

23. According to M. Margaliot, the *hiph'il* of the *niph'al* נאמן must be translated as "to trust My faithfulness (as my messengers to you and as to the people)." By relating this word to the concept of covenant, Margaliot expands the idea that leaders are supposed to impress on the people Yahweh's faithfulness to them as the God of their covenant (Margaliot, "The Transgression of Moses and Aaron — Num 20:1–13," *JQR* 76, no. 2 [1983] 222–23). Locating נאמן ב in covenantal relationship, however, is uncertain due to a lack of sufficient references. On the other hand, in Num. 14:11 Yahweh complains that the people "have not trusted in me" (לא־יאמינו בי). Since this reference is understood as Yahweh's anger toward the people because they have not trusted the divine plan to bring them into the promised land and its fulfillment, 20:12 can be understood in a similar way. Moses and Aaron fail to trust Yahweh's commitment and faithfulness for the people's needs, causing serious consequences. This interpretation is consistent with the usage of "sanctify" in Yahweh's characterization of the leaders' behavior. Within the verses concerning Moses and Aaron's sin, the verb קדש appears once in the *niph'al* (Num. 20:13), once in the *pi'el* (Deut. 32:51), and twice in the *hiph'il* (Num. 20:12; 27:14). The dominant conceptual aspect of these forms can be seen from other passages (*niph'al*: Lev. 10:3; 22:32; Isa. 5:16; Ezek. 20:41; 28:22, 25; 36:23; 38:16; 39:27; *pi'el*: Ezek. 36:23; *hiph'il*: Isa. 8:13; 29:23), which suggest that the essence of the sin of the leaders is their misrepresentation to the people of Yahweh's fidelity to the divine promise to help them.

24. T. R. Ashley, *The Book of Numbers* (Grand Rapids: Eerdmans, 1993) 247–48. Ashley discusses in detail how Moses and Aaron prostrated themselves in front of the rebellious people. The sharp contrast between Moses and Aaron's initial response to the people and Caleb and Joshua's persistent responses to them (13:30; 14:6–9) suggests that Moses and Aaron are passive or defensive. Although Moses does intercede with Yahweh on behalf of the people, his initial response, prior to Yahweh's appearance, shows cowardice, foreshadowing his distrust in the Meribah incident.

25. The gradual decreasing of Moses' involvement in the events that follow supports this point. Moses is totally absent in both 21:1–3, where Israel defeats the Canaanites, and

rious absence of Yahweh in this unit implies two things: (1) that Moses and Israel's request for passage is not directed by Yahweh, and (2) that Moses' leadership will not be easily restored in the face of the Israelites' interference with his negotiations and Edom's refusal.

Furthermore, Num. 20:14–21 as a whole reveals more than a reduced leadership role for Moses. These verses strengthen the function of 20:2–13, which provides a reason for Moses being included in Yahweh's punishment with the entire exodus generation. First, by sending messengers to the king of Edom for passage through his territory, Moses disobeys Yahweh's command to him regarding Israel's migration from Kadesh: "Turn tomorrow and set out for the wilderness by the way to the Red Sea" (14:25b). Second, in light of the fact that the shortest way to enter Canaan from Kadesh-barnea (other than to take the southern route where Israel failed) is to travel straight east through Edom's territory,[26] Moses' request for safe passage through Edom means he is taking the initiative to search for another approach to Canaan after the Israelites' disastrous attempt to penetrate the land from the south. In regard to the precise route for entering the promised land, both the Israelites and Moses become guilty of going their own ways rather than Yahweh's. In Num. 13–14 it is the Israelites who had rejected Yahweh's plan and took the initiative to enter Canaan; now in 20:14 it is Moses who takes the initiative to seek the easiest way to Canaan, disregarding Yahweh's explicit directive. Third, both Israel's attempt and Moses' attempt fail. If the Israelites' defeat by the Amalekites and the Canaanites may be interpreted as an initial and partial fulfillment of Yahweh's punishment on the entire exodus generation, Moses and Israel's retreat from Edom can be understood as the continuing (or even climactic) fulfillment of Yahweh's punishment. Fourth, it is not coincidental that Israel's encounter with Edom is placed immediately after Yahweh has denied Moses and Aaron's leadership. The unit, 20:14–21, serves to make sure that Yahweh's punishment on Moses and Aaron is neither extreme nor unfair, but "measure for measure" and fully justifiable, as compared with their crime. While 20:1–13 shows Moses' failure to remain the chief representative of Yahweh to the people by misrepresenting Yahweh's in-

---

in 21:21–31, where the Israelites not only defeat, but also dispossess and occupy the entire land of, the Amorites. In 21:32–35 Moses is portrayed as being afraid of Og and his troops, revealed in Yahweh's admonition, and as lacking confidence in the military logistics, presupposed by Yahweh's instruction. Although Moses sends the spies, it is the Israelites who actually capture the villages of Jazer (v. 32) and kill all of the Bashanites (v. 35). Moreover, 31:1–54 in its entirety stresses Moses' cultic role by suggesting that he is more concerned with purity matters than with victory in battle. Thus, Moses' involvement, especially in its military aspect, has diminished significantly after the denial of his prophetic leadership.

26. Cf. Ashley, *The Book of Numbers*, 388.

tention for them, 20:14–21 reveals his failure to remain the chief leader of the people by guiding them to a route other than Yahweh's. Moses, like the rest of exodus generation, fails to trust Yahweh's ability to bring Yahweh's people into the promised land. As a result, Moses shares the same destiny as that generation. He must die in the wilderness and will not enter the promised land.[27]

The third unit (vv. 22–29) ends the chapter with three points: (1) Israel's march to Mount Hor (v. 22) might be seen as another attempt to penetrate Canaan from the south. After refusing to take the easiest way to Canaan from Kadesh, Moses and Israel skirt Edom by journeying across Edom's northern border. This is the last of Moses and Israel's attempts to enter Canaan by their own routes in disobedience to Yahweh's command. (2) Aaron's death suggests the imminence of Moses' own death in the immediate textual context, that of Yahweh's punishment on Moses and Aaron, as well as the end of the exodus generation. It marks as well the completion of Yahweh's punishment of them within the larger context of Yahweh's punishment on the entire exodus generation. (3) The transference of Aaron's high priesthood to his son Eleazar is parallel to the transition from the exodus generation to the next generation. Eleazar's new priesthood signals the dawn of Yahweh's calling of the next generation to carry out the divine land promise. The first two preceding points demonstrate the final scene of the activities of the exodus generation, while the third point provides a hint of the second generation's entrance upon the scene.

As implied by the transference of the high priesthood from Aaron to his son, Eleazar in 20:22–29, 21:1–3 heralds the advent of the next generation of the Israelites.[28] Four arguments, based on (1) the text's unique content, (2) the chronological setting, (3) a comparison with other direct military accounts, and (4) its placement within the present literary context, support this claim. First, note that 21:1 reports Israel's initial defeat by the king of Arad, possibly reflecting their total failure as reported in 14:39–45; that Hormah in v. 3b is the very place to which the exodus

---

27. Milgrom (*Numbers*, 464) understands 20:14–21 as "a personal blow to Moses who now knows that he cannot enter the land but must die en route." This understanding psychologizes and lacks textual support.

28. The claim that 21:1–3 shows the generational succession for the Israelites could be a logical step from the assertion that ch. 20 marks the end of the exodus generation. However, the former claim can also be established on its own terms based on the structural significance of 21:1–3. Hence, there is no circularity between these two claims; rather, the former is complementary to the latter. See Levine, *Numbers 1–20*, 57–62. Levine concludes that the Priestly writers interpolate 21:1–3 into its present location in order to signal "the entrance of the second generation." His argument is based on a source-critical analysis that chooses the Priestly chronology over against the Yahwist-Elohist chronology. The present essay arrives at the same conclusion but on different grounds.

generation was pursued by the Canaanites and the Amalekites, according to 14:45b; that their opponents were inhabitants of the promised land, rather than any other ethnic group in the Transjordan regions; and finally, that the result is Israel's complete victory (vv. 2–3a), the very opposite of their total defeat in 14:45. These facts suggest that the victory over the Canaanites in 21:1–3 is to be attributed to the new generation rather than to the exodus generation. Otherwise, there is little meaning both for the divine decree that sentences the exodus generation to death in the wilderness[29] and to the divine endorsement of חרם war against the Canaanites. Additionally, 21:1–3 is also unique in portraying Israel as a single and united political entity.[30] This may be coincidental, but it may also be indicative of a new attitude on the part of the new generation regarding the conquest of the promised land: campaigning for the promised land as a single body with a unanimous intent. Compared to the exodus generation, who presumed that their expedition would be successful even though Yahweh and Moses would be absent from their midst (14:41–43), Israel's determination to be victorious over the Canaanites, demonstrated in their making of a vow to Yahweh to utterly destroy them, shows the new attitude of the new generation. Yahweh's acceptance of Israel's vow enhances this point because it shows an extension of divine forgiveness to the exodus generation as this new generation carries out the fulfillment of the divine land promise made to their ancestors. Furthermore, 21:1–3 entirely excludes Moses. Israel's victory is achieved without Moses' presence or involvement. Why does the text leave Moses out of this epochal victory over the Canaanites? The answer is clear: Moses is excluded simply because he belongs to the exodus generation. The operative concept of the text does not require Moses and prevents him from sharing the new generation's victory over the Canaanites.[31]

---

29. Yahweh swears with an oath by his own person to punish the Israelites. The fact that this divine oath form occurs only twice (14:21, 28) in the entire Pentateuch indicates the severity of Yahweh's punishment as well as the certainty that Yahweh's punishment is nonnegotiable and irreversible.

30. See T. L. Fearer, "Wars in the Wilderness: Textual Cohesion and Conceptual Coherence in Pentateuch Battle Traditions" (Ph.D. diss., Claremont Graduate School, 1993).

31. Milgrom, *Numbers*, 458. In light of a larger redactional purpose, Milgrom understands that the event of 21:1–3 is Moses' desperate attempt to enter the promised land directly from the south after the rebuff by Edom and the death of Aaron. This understanding presupposes two things: 21:1–3 is Moses' activity, and his attempt is a failure because "he was forced to retreat" (21:4a). The text, however, is not about Moses' activity, but Israel's activity without Moses, and the text is clear that Israel as a single entity destroys the Canaanites completely. Milgrom fails to deal with this rather obvious evidence. For 21:4a, it can be viewed as Israel's "retreat," but it may point to something else in the present context (this point will be discussed below).

Second, 21:1–3 is placed after Aaron's death, which occurs in the fifth month of the fortieth year. This suggests that the period implied by the text is the latter part of the forty-year wandering in the wilderness. Since the exodus generation must die out during the forty years, Israel's victory over the Canaanites at the end of the fortieth year must be a signal for the new beginning of the next generation.

Third, 21:1–3 reports the first of Israel's four military victories. It introduces a series of narratives about continual successes (the other three are in 21:21–31; 21:32–35; 31:1–12), and it deals with the Canaanites, the present inhabitants of the promised land. No further defeat or retreat from enemies is reported following this text. Could it be the exodus generation who is responsible for these continual victories, starting from the overpowering of the Canaanites and growing to that of the Transjordan peoples, the Amorites, the Bashanites, and the Midianites? Could this old generation "merit the praise of Balaam, who not only extols their impressive military might, but even eulogizes their favored relationship to YHWH?"[32] It can only be the second generation who, at the end of the forty years of wandering, now successfully executes an ongoing military campaign against the Canaanites and against enemies in the Transjordanian territories.

Fourth, the placement of 21:1–3 within the extant text reinforces the claim that this passage heralds the new generation as the carrier of the divine land promise. It is placed between the report of the event that occurred at Mount Hor (20:22–29) and that of Israel's setting out from Mount Hor (21:4a). In other words, its placement interrupts the literary continuity of 20:1–21:10, implying an itinerary from Kadesh to Oboth via Mount Hor. Verse 21:4a provides an explanation for this interruption: "From Mount Hor they [the Israelites] set out by the way to the Red Sea, to go around the land of Edom." By mentioning Mount Hor as the place of departure, v. 4a presupposes the event of 20:22–29. By noting that they "go around the land of Edom," v. 4a clarifies the ambiguous direction in 20:21b. By stating that Israel sets out "by the way to the Red Sea," v. 4a speaks of Israel's implementation of Yahweh's command in 14:25b. While the first two items point to the writer's attempt to minimize the tension caused by the placement of 21:1–3, the third item implies a reason for this placement. Israel's following of Yahweh's direction is reported immediately after the report of its victory over the Canaanites, directly opposite to what the exodus generation had done in its abortive attempt to penetrate Canaan from the south, in Moses' seeking the easiest way to get to Canaan from Kadesh, and in Israel's move across the northern border of Edom. Thus, Yahweh's command

---

32. Levine, *Numbers 1–20*, 58.

in 14:25b is finally fulfilled in 21:4a. The decision to approach Canaan
via the Transjordan clearly shows Israel's faithfulness to Yahweh's command, and this faithfulness must be attributed to the second generation.
Moreover, the second generation's implementation of Yahweh's command is the reason why, after the total destruction of Canaanite towns,
they did not continue directly northward to conquer all of Canaan, the
ultimate goal of their campaign. Their suffering in the wilderness for
forty years due to their forebears' faithlessness (14:33) may be another
reason for their turning away from Canaan and toward the Transjordan
regions. Thus, 21:4a functions to reduce the tension created by 21:1–3
and at the same time to upstage the second generation's implementation
of Yahweh's command in 14:25b.

Thus far, the discussion on the three units of Num 20 and 21:1–3 justifies the claim that 21:1–3 marks the decisive transition from the end of
the Exodus generation to the call of the new generation to be the new
carrier of the divine land promise. Olson's choice of the second census
list in Numbers 26 as the crucial point has been proven to be insufficient. Even the title of his book implies the eighty years for Israel's
wilderness period, which is in clear conflict with the well-established
forty-year scheme. Finally, but by far not unimportantly, the concept
of the generational transition cannot be the generative conceptuality
responsible for the superstructure of Numbers, let alone that of the Pentateuch, contrary to Olson's claim. Although the concept is present in
Numbers, its operation is limited in scope. This is not what explains the
location and arrangement of the disparate materials within the book. It
is subordinate to other conceptual factors, in particular, the preparation and execution of the Israelites' sanctuary campaign, the failure and
success of the campaign, Yahweh's land promise to their ancestors, and
Yahweh's election of Israel.[33]

In the final analysis, Olson's generational transition is structurally
subordinate to Israel's failure to conquer the promised land from the
south. Numbers 13–14 reports that the Israelites are located at the edge
of the promised land, have an opportunity to conquer the land for
the first time since being liberated from the bondage of Egypt, then
forfeit this chance by their failure to trust Yahweh, thus failing to ac-
complish the purpose of this campaign, the conquest of the promised
land, and at the same time receiving from Yahweh a death sentence
upon all the old generation, except Caleb and Joshua, along with the
promise of the fulfillment of the divine land promise on behalf of the

---

33. See Knierim, "Book of Numbers," 380–88. Cf. idem, "On the Subject of War in Old
Testament Theology," *HBT* 16 (1994) 1–19.

next generation.[34] Up until Num. 14:26–35, there is no indication that Yahweh intends to delay Israel's conquest of the promised land. Israel's forty years of wilderness experience is neither part of Yahweh's original plan nor a testing of their faith in Yahweh. It is the punishment for Israel's unprecedented rebellion. But from now on, the places to which the Israelites march, the events that happen during their forty years of wandering in the wilderness, and the peoples they encounter are all to be understood as the direct consequence of this failure. Thus, the generational transition is not the generative conceptuality underlying Numbers 13–14, but originates out of the text while pointing to a simple aspect of Yahweh's response to the Israelites' failure. The definitive condemnation of the exodus generation is one of Yahweh's punishments and can only be an inevitable byproduct in the delayed fulfillment of Yahweh's land promise. The central aspect of Yahweh's punishment is not the killing of the exodus generation but the delay of the promise's fulfillment. The divine land promise will be accomplished only by the next generation, after forty years of wandering in the wilderness, and through a different route than from the south. The delayed fulfillment of Yahweh's promise of the land is therefore the governing conceptuality beneath all of Israel's activities as narrated after the spy story. In other words, this concept is in principle presupposed throughout the rest of Numbers, as well as in materials from the book of Deuteronomy and in Joshua up to chapter 12, along with Judg. 2:10.

---

34. Olson recognizes the significance of the content of Numbers 13–14 (*Numbers*, 86; see also Levine, *Numbers 1–20*, 372): those chapters play "a crucial role" within the structure of Numbers and have the "central place" in the theme and structure of Numbers. However, he does not see the structural significance of Numbers 13–14. Since the two census lists constitute the decisive break within the structure of Numbers, what is their relationship to the spy story? Olson's answers would be that Numbers 13–14 plays a pivotal role with its specific age formula (twenty years old and upward), used in both census reports, through its general story line, as used in the warning of 32:6–15, and by means of its specific contents (the death of the exodus generation and the delineation of the land's borders). All of these are associated with one another in 26:63–65 and 34:1–12. What his answers show is that Numbers 13–14 is significant for the rest of Numbers only insofar as it shares some literary features and content with them. Certainly, Numbers 13–14 provides the theme of the death of the old generation and the birth of the new, but in and of itself this does not play the central or pivotal role for the structure of Numbers.

Selected Bibliography

Ashley, T. R. *The Book of Numbers*. Grand Rapids: Eerdmans, 1993.

Dozeman, T. B. "The Book of Numbers: Introduction, Commentary, and Reflections." In *The New Interpreter's Bible*, 2:1–268. Nashville: Abingdon, 1998.

Fearer, T. L. "Wars in the Wilderness: Textual Cohesion and Conceptual Coherence in Pentateuch Battle Traditions." Ph.D. diss. Claremont Graduate School, 1993.

Gray, G. B. *A Critical and Exegetical Commentary on Numbers*. ICC. Edinburgh: T. & T. Clark, 1903.

Knierim, R. P. "The Composition of the Pentateuch." In *The Task of Old Testament Theology: Substance, Method, and Cases*, by R. P. Knierim, 355–79. Grand Rapids: Eerdmans, 1995.

———. "The Book of Numbers." In *The Task of Old Testament Theology: Substance, Method, and Cases*, by R. P. Knierim, 380–88. Grand Rapids: Eerdmans, 1995.

———. "Prolegomena." In *The Book of Numbers*: The Forms of the Old Testament Literature, by R. P. Knierim. Grand Rapids: Eerdmans, forthcoming.

Levine, B. A. *Numbers 1–20: A New Translation with Introduction and Commentary*. AB 4A. New York: Doubleday, 1993.

Margaliot, M. "The Transgression of Moses and Aaron — Num 20:1–13." *JQR* 76, no. 2 (1983) 196–228.

Milgrom, J. *Numbers*. JPS Torah Commentary. Philadelphia: Jewish Publication Society, 1990.

Noth, M. *Numbers: A Commentary*. OTL. Trans. J. D. Martin. Philadelphia: Westminster, 1968.

Olson, D. T. *The Death of the Old and the Birth of the New: The Framework of the Book of Numbers and the Pentateuch*. Brown Judaic Studies 71. Chico, Calif.: Scholars Press, 1985.

———. *Numbers*. Interpretation: A Biblical Commentary for Teaching and Preaching. Louisville: John Knox, 1996.

11

Moses and Israel in Exodus 1:1–2:25: A Conceptual Examination

David B. Palmer

INTRODUCTION

As an important introductory section in the pentateuchal narrative, Exod. 1:1–2:25 presents a case for exegesis where the underlying conceptuality of the text is not the focus of its surface narrative.[1] For this reason, Exod. 1:1–2:25 presents an excellent opportunity for the exemplification of a methodological focus on the underlying conceptual aspects of texts in their exegesis. Basic to exegesis is the distinction between the surface text and the underlying inexplicit concepts that control that surface text.[2] It is the task of exegesis to reconstruct a text's underlying thought system from the explicit signals in its surface text.

A major exegetical question with respect to Exod. 1:1–2:25 in the final form of the Pentateuch concerns the conceptual relationship of the ma-

---

1. Although there is general agreement on the introductory nature of the material in Exodus 1 and (vv. in the history of interpretation, there is no agreement on the exact delineation of units and subunits, or the relationship of these elements within the macrostructure. Several different interpretations have been offered by various interpreters. For example, see *Überlieferung und Geschichte des Exodus: Eine Analyse von Ex 1–15* (BZAW 91; Berlin: Töpelmann, 1964), where G. Fohrer identifies Exod. 1:1–15:21 as a macrostructural unit in which the initial subunits are 1:1–2:10, denoted "Die Bedrückung der Israeliten und die Geburt Moses," and 2:11–4:31, 6:2–7:7, denoted "Die Erscheinung Jahwes und die Berufung Moses." In "A Structural Transition in Exodus" (VT 22 [1972] 129–42) G. Coats presents a different understanding, arguing that the introductory unit at the beginning of Exodus is 1:1–14. For yet another view see *Exodus* (BKAT 2; Neukirchen: Neukirchener, 1988), where W. H. Schmidt's macrostructure for Exodus as a whole has an intermediate unit comprising 1:1–15:21 and subunits that include 1:1–2:25 as a unit followed by chs. 3–6 as a unit. In this delineation of the text units, Schmidt sees a major break between the end of ch.(vv. and 3:1ff. The present essay understands Exod. 1:1–2:25 to be an introduction to the story of Moses and Israel within the larger macrostructure of the final form of the Pentateuch.

2. The distinction between a text's explicit statements and its underlying thought system is basic for the approach of R. P. Knierim and has played an increasingly important role in his publications and Ph.D. seminars from the late 1970s onward. For Knierim's most recent expressions, see *Text and Concept in Leviticus 1:1–9: A Case in Exegetical Method* (FAT 2; Tübingen: J. C. B. Mohr [Paul Siebeck] 1992) iii, 1–4; and in *The Task of Old Testament Theology: Substance, Method, and Cases* (Grand Rapids: Eerdmans, 1995): "A Posteriori Explorations" (pp. 477–79), "Conceptual Aspects in Exodus 25:1–9" (pp. 389–90), and "On the Contours of Old Testament and Biblical Hamartiology" (pp. 24–42).

terials focusing on Moses in Exod. 2:1–22, and those focusing on the בְּנֵי יִשְׂרָאֵל (Israelites) in Exod. 1:1–22 and 2:23–25. This essay presents an exegetical treatment of Exod. 1:1–2:25 that employs infratextual conceptual analysis to examine these aspects.

STRUCTURE

The determination of a text's inherent structure is an essential exegetical step in reconstructing its underlying thought system. A close examination of the final form of Exod. 1:1–2:25 shows that it is comprised of eight individual text-units as follows:

1. Introductory unit 1:1–7
2. The rise of oppression against the בְּנֵי יִשְׂרָאֵל 1:8–14
3. The encounter between the king of Egypt/Pharaoh and the midwives 1:15–21
4. Pharaoh's command to his people 1:22
5. Moses' birth/adoption story 2:1–10
6. Events culminating in Moses' flight to Midian 2:11–15
7. Moses' sojourn in Midian 2:16–22
8. Cry of the בְּנֵי יִשְׂרָאֵל and God's reaction 2:23–25

A focused analysis of the generic and literary features of the text reveals the structural relationships of these text units. Based on such an analysis, the main members of the macrostructure for Exod. 1:1–2:25 may be presented as follows:

Introduction to the story of Moses and the בְּנֵי יִשְׂרָאֵל	1:1–2:25
I. Introductory unit: arrival of the בְּנֵי יִשְׂרָאֵל in Egypt and their proliferation	1:1–7
II. Oppression of the בְּנֵי יִשְׂרָאֵל in Egypt	1:8–22
A. Rise of oppression against the בְּנֵי יִשְׂרָאֵל: first set of measures and their ineffectiveness	1:8–14
B. Encounter between Pharaoh and the midwives: second set of measures and their ineffectiveness	1:15–21
C. Command of Pharaoh to his people: third set of measures	1:22
III. Moses' early life (implicitly related to the בְּנֵי יִשְׂרָאֵל)	2:1–22
A. Moses birth/adoption story: ineffectiveness of measures	2:1–10
B. Story of Moses' flight and sojourn	2:11–22
1. Events culminating in Moses' flight to Midian	2:11–15
2. Moses' sojourn in Midian	2:16–22
IV. Conclusion: cry of the בְּנֵי יִשְׂרָאֵל and God's reaction	2:23–25

Analysis of the text's structure shows major components that focus on the story of the בְּנֵי יִשְׂרָאֵל in Egypt (I, II, and IV) and the story of Moses' early life (III).

INFRATEXTUAL CONCEPTUAL ANALYSIS[3]

Examination of a text's structure leads to the identification and reconstruction of the underlying concepts that control that structure. The examination of the generic and literary elements of Exod. 1:1–2:25 and the description of its structure indicate the operation of a number of subtextual concepts or notions. These notions are as follows:

1. The notion of *God/Yahweh*
2. The notion of *Israel* or *the* בְּנֵי יִשְׂרָאֵל
3. The notion of *the forefathers*
4. The notion of *increased progeny* or *proliferation*
5. The notion of *the land*
6. The notion of *the relationship between God/Yahweh and the* בְּנֵי יִשְׂרָאֵל
7. The notion of *the oppression of the Israelites*
8. The notion of *Moses*

While there are other concepts or notions in the text of Exod. 1:1–2:25, focused analysis indicates that these have a foundational role in forming the text's controlling infratextual conceptuality. The following analysis examines these conceptual aspects of Exod. 1:1–2:25 in greater detail.

The Notion of God/Yahweh

The term אֱלֹהִים as a conceptual indicator in Exod. 1:1–2:25 occurs in 1:17, 20, 21 relating to the midwives, and in 2:23–25 relating to the Israelites. Overall, the term אֱלֹהִים appears eight times in the pericope, and it is in text unit 2:23–25 that אֱלֹהִים is portrayed explicitly as reacting to the plight of the בְּנֵי יִשְׂרָאֵל. Although explicit references to the deity are not abundant in Exod. 1:1–2:25, the concept of the deity or God is presupposed in a determining way and is present throughout the pericope. Without the notion signaled by אֱלֹהִים and implied throughout the narrative, these explicit elements would not be what they are within the narrative. This is indicated by the way in which the narrative of Exod. 1:1–2:25 leads to the culmination involving the description of the divine reaction in 2:23–25.

The term יהוה is not mentioned in Exod. 1:1–2:25, but occurs later in Exodus 3. The conceptual question is whether the text of Exod. 1:1–2:25 is "aware" in its underlying thought of the concept that יהוה expresses. When the question is framed in this way it becomes clear that the text is not unaware but in fact leads toward the explicit mention of the term in

---

3. The term "infratextual" refers to a text's controlling but inexplicit subtextual thought system, which is distinguished from the explicit statements and signals in the text's surface expression. For a discussion of the vocabulary employed in infratextual conceptual analysis, see Knierim, *Text and Concept*, 1–3.

Exodus 3. In this sense, the identification between אֱלֹהִים and יהוה is already implicit in Exod. 1:1–2:25. The conceptual relationship in the text between the terms אֱלֹהִים and יהוה that will become explicit in Exodus 3 is already presupposed.

The notion of God is signaled as operative within the eight subunits of Exod. 1:1–2:25 as follows. In 1:7 God is conceived implicitly as being behind the wondrous proliferation of the בְּנֵי יִשְׂרָאֵל after their arrival in Egypt. This proliferation is expressed with terms that hearken back to the divine decrees in the creation narrative in Gen. 1:20–22, 28 (מלא, שרץ, פרה, רבה), with the one exception being the verb וַיַּעַצְמוּ in Exod. 1:7 (also found in Exod. 1:20). The proliferation of the בְּנֵי יִשְׂרָאֵל implies the hidden activity of God, who gives this proliferation to the בְּנֵי יִשְׂרָאֵל. Further, the notion of God is implied in the development of the narrative beyond Exod. 1:1–7 as the בְּנֵי יִשְׂרָאֵל continue to proliferate despite oppressive measures taken against this proliferation. That God's implicit agency is behind the marvelous growth of the בְּנֵי יִשְׂרָאֵל is also implied in the king of Egypt's statements that acknowledge this growth.

In 1:9–10 the notion of God is implied indirectly by Pharaoh's hypothetical fear that the עַם בְּנֵי יִשְׂרָאֵל will go up from the land. Pharaoh is depicted in the text as an obstacle not only to the proliferation of the בְּנֵי יִשְׂרָאֵל but also to their going up from Egypt and therefore as an antagonist against the God who is presupposed as the source of such developments. Exodus 1:10 hearkens back to 1:1, when the בְּנֵי יִשְׂרָאֵל, then fewer in number, entered Egypt. Pharaoh is portrayed conceptually in his role as an obstacle to בְּנֵי יִשְׂרָאֵל going back, now as a numerous and mighty people.

In text unit 1:15–21 God (אֱלֹהִים) appears explicitly. The notion of God is operative in the text's explicit statement that the midwives feared God and therefore did not do as they were instructed by Pharaoh. The question is what concept of the deity is implied in their fear of him. Did they fear God as a matter of conscience and so did not do what they regarded as being obviously immoral regardless of the fact that it was the בְּנֵי יִשְׂרָאֵל who were the object of the strategy? Or, does the narrative conceptualize them as having feared God (אֱלֹהִים) not only as God but also implicitly as the God of Israel (of the בְּנֵי יִשְׂרָאֵל) and so did not follow Pharaoh's instructions, but in fact did the opposite? These reconstructions represent two distinct concepts. The notion of God is operative in the explicit statement that God treated the midwives well for their actions. God's treating the midwives well and giving them households (בָּתִּים) is closely associated in the narrative with God's implicit action in the continuing proliferation of the בְּנֵי יִשְׂרָאֵל.

The notion of God also stands implicitly behind the ineffectiveness of the three sets of measures taken up against the בְּנֵי יִשְׂרָאֵל that were identified in the macrostructure. In the concept of the text, the ineffectiveness of measures is due implicitly to the hidden activity of God.

In 2:1–10 God is implicitly active in the events of Moses' birth, rescue, and adoption. Just as God was implicitly behind the ineffectiveness of the first two sets of measures, so he is implicitly behind the birth, rescue, and adoption of Moses as that which renders the third set of measures ineffective. God implicitly initiates his own set of measures in the raising up of Moses and is behind the marvelous coordination of events concerning the hiding, exposure, discovery, rescue, and adoption of Moses. In 2:11–15 the notion of God is implied in Moses' successful escape from Pharaoh and also in the fortuitous events leading Moses to Reuel's household in 2:16–22.

Finally, in 2:23–25 God is implied in the timeliness of the death of the king of Egypt and its coordinated occurrence with the cry of the בְּנֵי יִשְׂרָאֵל that ascends to God. In 2:23–25 God is portrayed explicitly as acting in the surface text. The concept or notion of God operative in this text is connected with the covenant that he remembers. Upon hearing the cry of the בְּנֵי יִשְׂרָאֵל that has ascended, God remembers his covenant with the patriarchs. At this point in the narrative, the notions of the promises for proliferation of progeny and the land are signaled more explicitly and directly by the reference to the covenant. The concept of God implied here is that of the God who is particularly related to the בְּנֵי יִשְׂרָאֵל by his covenant with Abraham, Isaac, and Jacob.

The conceptual indicators in the text units referring to the deity prompt the question concerning what notion of the deity is implied in this text, since a specific notion of God is presupposed throughout the text. To what or whom does this deity relate and why? What is the nature of God's relationship to the other actants narrated in this text (Israelites, Egyptians, midwives, shepherds, Reuel and his daughters)? Further, how are these relationships affected by God's relationship to the Israelites? Therefore, a set of conceptual questions regarding the notion of אֱלֹהִים in Exod. 1:1–2:25 has to do with the narrative portrayal of אֱלֹהִים as an actant, even if this is only implicit in the narrative. How the deity implicitly acts and reacts, for whom and against whom he acts and reacts, and why he does so are factors that are also conceptually determinative for the notion of the deity itself that is operative in the text.

What is implied in the text is a relationship between אֱלֹהִים and the בְּנֵי יִשְׂרָאֵל that is a given. The midwives are related to אֱלֹהִים conceptually in the text and explicitly by their fear of God and their treatment of the בְּנֵי יִשְׂרָאֵל. Their treatment of the בְּנֵי יִשְׂרָאֵל was the sphere in which their narrated fear of אֱלֹהִים was specifically actualized. The Egyptians are related to אֱלֹהִים, the God of the text's concept, in a negative way. Both the Egyptians' and the midwives' narrated relationships to God in the text's concept are based implicitly on their relationships to and treatment of the בְּנֵי יִשְׂרָאֵל. This is the case implicitly, although explicitly the reaction of God to the midwives is stated to be due to their fear of God. In contrast, Israel is focused on particularly for beneficial and primary relationship with אֱלֹהִים as a given. This is implied throughout the narrative development of Exod. 1:1–2:25 and comes to explicit expression in Exod. 2:24–25. At the presuppositional level there is already in Exod. 1:1–2:25 a specifically defined relationship between אֱלֹהִים and the בְּנֵי יִשְׂרָאֵל that undergirds the narrative.

The Notion of Israel or the בְּנֵי יִשְׂרָאֵל

The term בְּנֵי יִשְׂרָאֵל, which is a conceptual signal in the text, occurs seven times throughout Exod. 1:1–2:25. Its first appearance is in 1:1 in the introduction to the family name list, where it refers to the sons of Jacob, the tribal heads of the Israelites. In later references the term refers to the multiplied people who have increased in number while in Egypt. It therefore refers to the sons of Jacob, the ongoing descendants of Jacob, and most broadly to the people or nation of Israel.

The term עַם referring to the בְּנֵי יִשְׂרָאֵל occurs in 1:9 and 1:20. In addition, the term עַם is used in reference to the Egyptians in 1:9 and 1:22. The term עַם is used to reference the בְּנֵי יִשְׂרָאֵל as a people over against the Egyptians as a people. The referencing of one people vis-à-vis the other is clearly evident in 1:9, 1:20, and 1:22. Exodus 1:9 begins the report of the speech of the new king of Egypt to his people concerning a different people, the בְּנֵי יִשְׂרָאֵל. The two peoples are narrated in mutual reference vis-à-vis each other in the text. In 1:20 and 1:22 the same phenomenon occurs. Exodus 1:20b contains the report of the continued proliferation of the עַם as a part of the narrative conclusion of the encounter of the king of Egypt/Pharaoh with the midwives. In the following text unit, which narrates the third set of measures, Pharaoh commands כָּל־עַמּוֹ. That is, he commands his people as those who are set narratively in mutual reference over against the עַם, whose proliferation continues unchecked, as narrated in 1:20b. This עַם is the בְּנֵי יִשְׂרָאֵל. In addition to the reference to growth into a numerous people, עַם is used of the בְּנֵי יִשְׂרָאֵל when the relationship of the Israelites to the Egyptians is a narrative focus.

While the בְּנֵי יִשְׂרָאֵל are described as an עַם, the term עַם is dependent upon and subordinate to the concept of the בְּנֵי יִשְׂרָאֵל in the thought system of the narrative. This is the case not only when עַם refers to the בְּנֵי יִשְׂרָאֵל, but also indirectly when עַם is used in reference to the Egyptians as the people of Pharaoh. The Egyptians are an עַם whose

primary significance in the narrative's concept is that they are not the
עַם of the בְּנֵי יִשְׂרָאֵל and therefore function as a foil vis-à-vis the בְּנֵי יִשְׂרָאֵל.
Moreover, as an עַם they oppress the בְּנֵי יִשְׂרָאֵל. Implicitly in the text the
Egyptians receive their conceptual definition and valuation by means of
the term עַם vis-à-vis the בְּנֵי יִשְׂרָאֵל. In the overarching macrostructure,
the occurrences of the term עַם referring to the בְּנֵי יִשְׂרָאֵל over against the
Egyptians in Exod. 1:1–2:25 anticipate the use of עַם in Exod. 3:7, where
יהוה/אֱלֹהִים speaks of the בְּנֵי יִשְׂרָאֵל as עַמִּי, "my people."

Forms of the Gentilic term עִבְרִי[4] occur seven times in Exod. 1:1–2:25.
The occurrence of these terms denoting Hebrews must be compared
with the Gentilic terms הַמִּצְרִֹית in 1:19 and מִצְרִי in 2:11, 2:12, and 2:14.
In the narrative composition of the pericope, הָעִבְרִֹית are set over against
הַמִּצְרִֹית in 1:19, and an אִישׁ מִצְרִי is set over against an אִישׁ עִבְרִי in 2:11.
Moreover, the reference to עִבְרִים in 2:13 still has in view the distinction
between the אִישׁ מִצְרִי and the אִישׁ עִבְרִי that occurred in 2:11. Generally, forms of the Gentilic term עִבְרִי are found in Hebrew narrative in
speeches by or to non-Hebrews, or are used when Hebrews are distinguished from non-Hebrews. The juxtaposition of עִבְרִי/עִבְרִים/עִבְרִֹית
with מִצְרִי/מִצְרִֹית in 1:19 and 2:11–14 supports this Gentilic sense for the
term עִבְרִי in Exod. 1:1–2:25. In the concept of this narrative, the distinction between the עִבְרִים and the מִצְרִים functions in the service of the
concept expressed by the term בְּנֵי יִשְׂרָאֵל. The narrative's distinction between the Hebrews and the Egyptians serves to advance the narrative's
underlying ideological interest in the benefit of the בְּנֵי יִשְׂרָאֵל.[5]

The conceptually related term אָח occurs twice in Exod. 1:1–2:25. The
first occurrence is in the death notice in 1:6, where it refers to the fa-
milial brothers of Joseph who were referenced previously in the family
name list in 1:2–4. The second occurrence is in 2:11, where Moses goes

---

4. M. Greenberg argues that עִבְרִי is used in the Hebrew Bible as a Gentilic term and
not as a class designation (*Understanding Exodus* [New York: Behrman House, 1969] 27),
and N. M. Sarna argues that the term עִבְרִי has an ethnic rather than a geographic de-
notation (*Exodus* [JPS Torah Commentary; Philadelphia: Jewish Publication Society, 1991]
265–66). An ethnic sense for the term עִבְרִי in the Hebrew Bible would be the case even
though what constitutes ethnicity as such is not altogether clear. The point concerning
the use of the term עִבְרִי in Exod. 1:1–2:25 in juxtaposition with the term מִצְרִי is that the
narrative conceives of the Hebrews vis-à-vis the Egyptians ethnically.

5. The narrative of Exod. 1:1–2:25 does not address the question concerning whether
there are עִבְרִים who are not בְּנֵי יִשְׂרָאֵל or vice versa. M. Greenberg notes as significant the
reference to יהוה as הָעִבְרִים אֱלֹהֵי in Exod. 5:3 and considers it to be equivalent to the reference to יהוה as אֱלֹהֵי יִשְׂרָאֵל in Exod. 5:1 (*Understanding Exodus*, 27–28). In Exod. 5:1–3 the
term עִבְרִי occurs in the narration of a speech to a non-Israelite, Pharaoh. The construction (הָעִבְרִיִּם) הָעִבְרִים אֱלֹהֵי יהוה occurs in Exod. 3:18; 7:16; 9:1; 9:13; 10:3, either in narrated
speeches to Pharaoh or in narrated instructions for such speeches. In addition, הָעִבְרִים by
implication are equated with Yahweh's people by the use of the term עַמִּי in Exod. 7:16; 9:1;
9:13; 10:3.

out to see אֶחָיו, "his brothers." In this case the proliferated people of the בְּנֵי יִשְׂרָאֵל are referred to as אַחִים, and they are related as brothers. The reference in 2:11 hearkens back to the previous reference in 1:6. This term is also under the conceptual umbrella provided by the conceptually controlling term בְּנֵי יִשְׂרָאֵל.

The notion of Israel or the בְּנֵי יִשְׂרָאֵל is signaled as operative within the eight subunits of Exod. 1:1–2:25 as follows. In 1:1–6 the term בְּנֵי יִשְׂרָאֵל refers initially to the sons of Jacob, as the first generation of the בְּנֵי יִשְׂרָאֵל. Subsequently, in 1:7 בְּנֵי יִשְׂרָאֵל refers to the numerous descendants. The generations in which the proliferation took place are not narrated. The simple fact of the marvelous proliferation is the conceptually controlling element, and the concept focuses on the proliferation or marvelous numerical increase itself since this sets the stage for the return to the land by means of the exodus events due to the oppression.

In 1:8–14 the term בְּנֵי יִשְׂרָאֵל occurs in 1:9, 12, and 13. The first occurrence of the term in this section is in 1:9, and it appears in the report of the king of Egypt's speech to his people. The issue concerning the בְּנֵי יִשְׂרָאֵל that has presented a problem for the Egyptians is their proliferation. The בְּנֵי יִשְׂרָאֵל are now so numerous as to be an entire עַם. In 1:12 and 1:13 the Egyptians recoil in dread from the בְּנֵי יִשְׂרָאֵל and afflict them more intensively. The notion signalized by the term בְּנֵי יִשְׂרָאֵל and the character of the בְּנֵי יִשְׂרָאֵל as numerous and mighty are conceptually controlling elements for the infratextuality of 1:8–14. The ironic ineffectiveness of the measures adopted by the Egyptians to thwart the proliferation of the בְּנֵי יִשְׂרָאֵל serves conceptually to reinforce this character of the בְּנֵי יִשְׂרָאֵל.

In the text unit 1:15–21 the term בְּנֵי יִשְׂרָאֵל does not occur but the equivalent term עַם does, which hearkens back to the occurrence of עַם in 1:9. Nevertheless, the concept signaled by בְּנֵי יִשְׂרָאֵל is presupposed in the text unit. The focus has shifted from the בְּנֵי יִשְׂרָאֵל as a whole to one segment within it, the male infants of the בְּנֵי יִשְׂרָאֵל. In addition, the concept of the בְּנֵי יִשְׂרָאֵל is implicitly operative in 1:22, though not specifically mentioned. The overt command of the king of Egypt/Pharaoh to his people has the male infants of the בְּנֵי יִשְׂרָאֵל in view explicitly, but implicitly this still has to do with the בְּנֵי יִשְׂרָאֵל.

The situation is more complex in Exod. 2:1–10 in that the term בְּנֵי יִשְׂרָאֵל does not occur in the Moses birth/adoption story. However, 2:1 refers back to the name list of the בְּנֵי יִשְׂרָאֵל in 1:2 when it mentions the name לֵוִי. The marriage and birth notices in 2:1–2a form a particular instance that is undergirded conceptually by the overall proliferation reported in 1:7. This indicates that while the narrative in 2:1–10 has focused on the case of one family unit and an infant, the concept of the בְּנֵי יִשְׂרָאֵל who are in Egypt still forms its background and conceptual frame of reference. Therefore, the birth/adoption story of Moses is still undergirded by the notion or concept signaled by the term בְּנֵי יִשְׂרָאֵל and its associated notions, though the narrative has turned to focus specifically upon Moses.

The notion of the בְּנֵי יִשְׂרָאֵל undergirds the narrative sequence of text unit 2:11–15, in which Moses goes out to his אַחִים to see their affliction. The term אָח is a clear, direct signal of this, and it hearkens back to the term אָח that occurs in the death notice of Joseph and his brothers found in 1:6. The concept of the בְּנֵי יִשְׂרָאֵל undergirds this aspect in the narrative. Although Moses has been adopted by Pharaoh's daughter, the use of the term אָח in 2:11 serves conceptually to associate Moses with the בְּנֵי יִשְׂרָאֵל as his brethren. The succeeding narrative concerning the Egyptian whom Moses strikes down reinforces this association. The text's presupposed notion of the distinction between the עִבְרִי or בְּנֵי יִשְׂרָאֵל and the Egyptians undergirds this, just as does the notion of the oppression of the בְּנֵי יִשְׂרָאֵל by the Egyptians. The notion of the בְּנֵי יִשְׂרָאֵל is also implied in Moses' attempted mediation between the two Hebrew men narrated in 2:13–14a. These conceptual indicators hearken back to the conceptual indicators found previously in 1:1–7 and 2:11.

The conclusion of section 2:16–22 places Moses in Midian, in Reuel's household, with a family and a new son, Gershom. However, the significance of Gershom's name is that Moses still understands himself to be an alien in a foreign land. This notion of being an alien raises the question concerning the concept of homeland or patronage that is the conceptual reflex of Moses' sense of being an alien. More simply, if Moses is an alien in Midian, where or in what is Moses' home or patronage in the text's concept? Is Moses' "home" Egypt and his patronage his identity as the son of Pharaoh's daughter? The surface text would indicate this. Moses fled and now he is an alien. However, in an implicit and more fundamental sense in the text's concept Moses is an alien because he is not currently with his brethren, the בְּנֵי יִשְׂרָאֵל. The implicit concept of the בְּנֵי יִשְׂרָאֵל is at work here, just as more subtly the concept of the land is behind the notion of Moses' sojourn as an alien and its allusion to the continued existence of the בְּנֵי יִשְׂרָאֵל as aliens in Egypt since they are outside the land.

In text unit 2:23–25 the notion or concept of the בְּנֵי יִשְׂרָאֵל is explicitly present in 2:23–25, since at this point the narrative turns its focus explicitly to the plight of the בְּנֵי יִשְׂרָאֵל in Egypt. The implicit question for the implied reader/hearer concerns the relationship that has arisen between Moses' situation in Midian and the Israelites' situation in Egypt now that the king of Egypt has died and the cry of the בְּנֵי יִשְׂרָאֵל has ascended to God.

In sum, the concept expressed semantically in the terms בְּנֵי יִשְׂרָאֵל, עַם בְּנֵי יִשְׂרָאֵל ,עִבְרִיּוֹת ,עִבְרִים, and אָחִים is the concept of a people who have a particular relationship to God and who also have a particular relationship to each other as members of this entity. This is expressed in the conceptually controlling term בְּנֵי יִשְׂרָאֵל, to which the other terms are related in conceptually subordinate relationships. This subordination extends also to the relationship with Jacob and the twelve family heads as descendants that is also implied in the term בְּנֵי יִשְׂרָאֵל.

The Notion of the Forefathers

Exodus 1:1–7 opens the introduction section of 1:1–2:25 with a family name list of the בְּנֵי יִשְׂרָאֵל that gives the individual names of the family tribal heads, that is, Jacob's sons. In 2:24 it is stated that God remembered his covenant with Abraham, with Isaac, and with Jacob. The בְּנֵי יִשְׂרָאֵל are conceptualized as a people that has a specific connection with the past. This specific connection is its relationship to the forefathers. First it is the relationship to Abraham, Isaac, and Jacob and then the relationship that is tied to Jacob's individual sons, who are named in 1:2–4. This notion of the forefathers of the בְּנֵי יִשְׂרָאֵל includes, among other things, the idea of continuity with a specific past. It is a past that belongs particularly to the בְּנֵי יִשְׂרָאֵל and that is integrally related to the promises of increased progeny and the land.

The story of the בְּנֵי יִשְׂרָאֵל in Egypt narrated in Exod. 1:1–2:25 presupposes the patriarchal story narrated in Genesis 12–50 as well as the notion of the patriarchs/forefathers. The notions of progeny/proliferation and the land appear to be the fundamental aspects of the notion of the patriarchs/forefathers in the text of 1:1–2:25. The promises given to the forefathers concerning these are implicit, driving conceptual elements in the narrative of 1:1–2:25, which focuses on the plight of the בְּנֵי יִשְׂרָאֵל in Egypt and upon Moses' early life. An important signal indicating this is the reference to the בְּרִית אֱלֹהִים with the patriarchs in 2:24b. Other notions regarding the forefathers that might have been expected do not appear. For instance, a notion of the forefathers as pedagogical examples for piety does not appear at all in 1:1–2:25. The patriarch's lives under the promises are in no wise invoked as examples to sustain or encourage the בְּנֵי יִשְׂרָאֵל as they wait in Egypt for the promises and for Moses. The notion of progeny/proliferation appears explicitly, while the notion of the land is implicit. Increased progeny and the land are the goal of the promises to the patriarchs and are the significant aspects of Israel's continuity with its specific past.

Conceptually, therefore, the notion or concept of the patriarchs/forefathers is subordinated to the concepts of the proliferation of the בְּנֵי יִשְׂרָאֵל and the land. The specific connection to the forefathers is by means of the promise of progeny and the land. The conceptual reason for the previous narration of the lives of the patriarchs/forefathers is the promise of progeny/proliferation and the land as the land of the בְּנֵי יִשְׂרָאֵל. This reason was the conceptually generating reason that operated in the setting of the narrators of the final form of the Pentateuch, who considered themselves also to be the בְּנֵי יִשְׂרָאֵל. Without the notions of progeny and the land, the narration of the patriarchal traditions would have been of a different kind than it is, and would have been transmitted for very different reasons.

The Notion of Increased Progeny or Proliferation

The notion of increased progeny or proliferation of the בְּנֵי יִשְׂרָאֵל is present explicitly in Exod. 1:1–2:25. Conceptually, it is presupposed for all of 1:1–2:25, and further, it is prominent and signaled explicitly in a number of places in the component text units of 1:1–2:25. This notion appears explicitly in 1:7, 9–10, 12a, and 20b. Although this notion does not appear explicitly after 1:20 in 1:1–2:25, it is operative implicitly as an aspect of the conceptuality underlying 1:1–2:25. It is implicitly present in text units 1:22, 2:1–10, 2:11–15, 2:16–22, and 2:23–25.

The notion of increased progeny or proliferation in Exod. 1:1–2:25 has reference contextually to the same notion within the larger pentateuchal narrative. The language of 1:7 involves an allusion to Gen. 1:20–22, 28a. The point of the allusion is the assertion that the בְּנֵי יִשְׂרָאֵל in Egypt have proliferated in a way that is in fulfillment of the creation mandate to humankind. In addition, the notion of proliferation of the בְּנֵי יִשְׂרָאֵל looks back to the promise of increase given to the patriarchs narrated in Genesis 12:2aα; 15:4–5; 17:5–8; 18:17–18; 22:16–17; 26:2–4, 24; 28:3–4, 13–15. Moreover, this contextual reference is one aspect signaled by the explicit mention in Exod. 2:24b of the covenant with Abraham, Isaac, and Jacob. The final form of Exod. 1:1–2:25, which includes 1:7 as a part of the larger pentateuchal narrative, is most likely due to P or a P layer that has taken up major elements of the Yahwistic narratives. If this is the case, the promise to the patriarchs has been linked to the creation blessing, and the common conceptual aspect is the notion of increased progeny or proliferation.

Examination of this conceptual aspect of Exod. 1:1–2:25 raises the question of the relationship of the king of Egypt's/Pharaoh's actions to the proliferation of the בְּנֵי יִשְׂרָאֵל. Clearly, the narrative develops in such a way as to advance this notion of proliferation. In a sense, the king of Egypt/Pharaoh figure is a foil over which the proliferation triumphs in the text's concept. The narrated actions of the king of Egypt/Pharaoh actually serve to advance the notion of Israel's proliferation. The marvelous proliferation of the בְּנֵי יִשְׂרָאֵל is narrated at the conclusion of the introductory unit comprised by 1:1–7. This proliferation constitutes the driving reasons for the events narrated in text units 1:8–14 and 1:15–21. The concluding elements of each of these sections relate the ineffectiveness of the measures taken against the proliferation, and the continuance of the proliferation of the בְּנֵי יִשְׂרָאֵל. In addition, the problem for the Egyptians of the proliferation and the failure of the previous measures is the reason for Pharaoh's command in 1:22. The narrator's implicit purpose regarding Israel's election as involving multiplication is discerned shaping the narrative determining who and what the king of Egypt/Pharaoh is.

What is not explicit is the relationship of the notion of increase to the elements of the story of Moses' early life found in Exod. 2:1–22. However, when it is considered that the Moses birth/adoption story is first a particular case of proliferation within the broader בְּנֵי יִשְׂרָאֵל, and second a further instance of the ineffectiveness of the measures taken by the Egyptians against this proliferation, the implicit role of the concept of the proliferation for the Moses story becomes evident. Conceptually, Moses functions in the service of the בְּנֵי יִשְׂרָאֵל, and the aspect of proliferation undergirds the בְּנֵי יִשְׂרָאֵל in the sense that the proliferated people now need to be delivered. Hence, the need for and function of the deliverer, Moses. In text unit 2:23–25 the narrative focus shifts back to the בְּנֵי יִשְׂרָאֵל and the implicit relationship of the notion of the proliferation of the בְּנֵי יִשְׂרָאֵל to the other notions becomes more clear.

The Notion of the Land

The notion of the land of promise, which is forward-looking and oriented toward the land of Canaan, is not explicitly present in the surface text of Exod. 1:1–2:25, in contrast with the notion of the proliferation of the בְּנֵי יִשְׂרָאֵל. Nevertheless, it is presupposed, and functions in a conceptually controlling way. This appears when the intratextual signals in Exod. 1:1–2:25 are carefully analyzed in conjunction with its contextual relationships within the pentateuchal narrative as a whole.

This presupposition appears when the question is raised concerning why it was necessary in the concept of the text to list specifically the names of the tribal heads who came into Egypt in 1:1, at the opening of the introduction found in 1:1–2:25. Those listed are the first-generation sons of Jacob and also the tribal heads in the concept of the twelvefold tribal components of Israel. The answer conceptually in terms of the contextual relationships is that it was necessary to list specifically those who left the land to enter Egypt with Jacob, since it would be those who would leave Egypt subsequently in the exodus to enter the land once again and inherit it. The בְּנֵי יִשְׂרָאֵל were to inherit the land in a manner by which it was distributed to them according to their tribal allotments. Without some such conceptually generating reason, the specific list of names would not have appeared in the simple notice that Jacob and family entered Egypt. This indicates a setting in which the family tribal heads and tribal system relative to the possessed land were important to the narrators. One possible setting for the conceptualization of the final form of the narrative would be one in which the people were already in the land, which is understood to be heritable according to the tribal components. Another possible setting would be one in which the standpoint of residence in the land was presupposed by the narrators in view of the prospect of regaining such residence. In this case, the exilic or postexilic community would be the setting for a renarration and resignification of the beginning of the story of the return of בְּנֵי יִשְׂרָאֵל to the land from Egypt for the purpose of its inheritance. Although the family name list in Exod. 1:2–5 does not present a genealogy, it provides a point of genealogical reference for the exilic and postexilic communities, which had a genealogical interest.

The underlying notion of the land and Israel's need to leave Egypt in order to go to the land is implied in the statement expressing the hypothetical fear of the king of Egypt/Pharaoh in 1:10. Contextually, the land is also the inexplicit goal for the larger narrative extending through the Exodus, Sinai, Wilderness, and Plains of Moab narratives. With respect to 1:10, the culminating fear of Pharaoh's speech is that the Israelites may "go up from the land" (וְעָלָה מִן־הָאָרֶץ).[6] In a sense, this culminating fear is not coherently related to the conjectures articulated

---

6. The following may be consulted further concerning issues in the scholarly discussion of Exod. 1:10. See K. Rupprecht, "עלה מן הארץ (Ex 1:10, Hos 2:2): 'sich des Landes bemächtigen'?" ZAW 82 (1970) 442–47. Rupprecht responds to the exegetical problem of Exod. 1:10 raised in an exegetical note by M. Lambert. The issue is whether עלה מן הארץ should be translated "sich des Landes bemächtigen." The issue reflects the difficulty in finding a logical reason for Pharaoh's fear that Israel would "go up from the land," that is, leave the land. According to Rupprecht, some have suggested the translation "seize or take control of the land." In this case, the Pharaoh's fear would be a numerically substantial Israel taking control of the land of Egypt, which would seem to fit more logically with the fears of Pharaoh. Rupprecht compares Exod. 1:10 with Hos. 2:2 and also Gen. 2:6. He concludes that the expression in Exod. 1:10 is to be translated "and they will go up from the land." Exod. 1:10 cannot be used to support a special sense for עלה מן הארץ in Hos. 2:2.

See also J. Wijngaards, "הוציא and העלה: A Twofold Approach to the Exodus," VT 15 (1965) 91–102. Wijngaards argues for two distinct conceptualizations of the exodus as expressed in these two prominent terms. He then traces the occurrence of these terms in various literary strands understood generally according to classical source-critical theory. According to Wijngaards, the formula with הוציא has three basic elements: the verb הוציא, the object (Israel or its equivalents), and the determination "from Egypt" (or its equivalents). This formula occurs particularly in the legislative parts of the OT. He holds that legal traditions such as Dtr law, P, and HG employ it to an almost complete exclusion of the העלה formula. It is also absent from the early prophets, Isaiah, Hosea, Amos. He concludes that the הוציא formula expresses a strict liberation from slavery. It addition, he claims that this formula was originally understood to refer directly to the deliverance at

in the surface text by the Pharaoh that precede it. He fears that a numerically substantial Israel may join with enemies in time of war. The
expected culminating fear would more logically be that these numerous
Israelites would stay in Egypt and seize control over the Egyptians. In
such a scenario, the departure of the Israelites would actually be a relief. The fact that later in the narrative surface the Pharaoh will decide
to use the Israelites as a source for corvée labor is insufficient to explain
the previously enunciated fear in the terms in which Pharaoh expresses
it. It can be seen that proceeding from the underlying conceptuality, the
king of Egypt/Pharaoh and the Egyptians are portrayed in the narrative
implicitly as an obstacle to the land promise just as they are portrayed
explicitly as an obstacle to the multiplication promise. This reflects the
notion of the exodus, whose final goal is the land. It might be argued
that the expression presupposes only the exodus and not the land of
Canaan or the conquest of it. However, in the light of 1:1–7, which describes the entrance of the בְּנֵי יִשְׂרָאֵל into Egypt with the implication of
the need to return to Canaan, and the broader context of the pentateuchal narrative, the goal of the exodus is implicitly the land and not
simply the removal of oppression. That the בְּנֵי יִשְׂרָאֵל left the land and
entered Egypt (1:1) implies that they need to go back (narration of exodus events, events at Sinai, events in the wilderness, and arrival in the
plains of Moab as staging area for launch of the campaign for the land).
The events of the oppression leading to the complex of exodus events
function in the service of this need conceptually. In this sense, the goal
of the land generates the narration of the oppression events for the sake
of the exodus, which will ultimately lead to the land.

   Contextual aspects of the larger pentateuchal narrative that indicate
the land of Canaan broadly as the goal of the exodus are extensive. The complex of exodus events themselves, narrated in Exod.
3:1–15:21, are followed by the journey to Sinai. The Sinai pericope

---

the sea. The הוציא formula was introduced into the Exodus-Landgiving scheme only at a
later stage. This formula holds a key position in the Dtr scheme.
   The העלה formula, which is different, also has three elements: the verb העלה, the object
(Israel or its equivalents), and the determination "from Egypt" (or its equivalents). This
formula is well attested in the pre-Dtr and early prophetic texts (contrary to הוציא). This
formula is frequently enunciated in immediate connection with the coming into the land.
Wijngaards concludes that this formula must have been at home in the northern kingdom,
particularly at the sanctuaries of Bethel and Dan. According to Wijngaards, the העלה formula seems to have functioned in the Exodus-Landgiving scheme from the beginning.
The formula itself is apt to imply the terminus ad quem, the land (cf. Exod. 3:8, 17; 33:1).
Although it is an exodus formula, is has the potential of including the giving of the land.
Further, the הוציא formula recalls the miraculous liberation at the Sea of Reeds, while the
העלה formula that visualizes the exodus as culminating in the landgiving can only have
arisen after the conquest. Subsequently, the הוציא formula was worked into the landgiving
scheme.

(Exod. 19:1–Num. 10:10) itself is a preparation for the campaign march toward the land (Num. 10:11–21:35), which culminates in Israel's stay in the plains of Moab (Num. 22:1–Deut. 34:12), the narrative setting for Moses' testament (Deut. 1:1–34:12).[7] Moses' testament in Deuteronomy is forward-looking toward the campaign of conquest and Israel's life in the land. When the intratextual aspects and the contextual relationships of Exod. 1:1–2:25 are examined, the implicit concept of the land that is operative in the context of the larger narrative also is implicitly operative in Exod. 1:1–2:25 as a subunit of that larger narrative. In addition, the notion of the land as the goal of the exodus events is expressed explicitly in the immediate context in Exod. 3:7–10.

The Notion of the Relationship between God/Yahweh and the בְּנֵי יִשְׂרָאֵל

This notion involves a conceptual relationship between two previously considered notions. These are the notion of God/Yahweh and the notion of the בְּנֵי יִשְׂרָאֵל. It is clear from all the signals of the text and the development of its narrative that there is presupposed in this narrative conceptually the notion of a unique relationship between Israel and God/Yahweh and that the story is narrated from this standpoint. God/Yahweh relates to Israel in a way that is distinct from all others, and he deals specifically with Israel for Israel's sake and benefit. This can be seen by examining the relationship presupposed in the text between God/Yahweh and Israel, and between God/Yahweh and Egyptians or Midianites. In this sense, the notion of the relationship between Israel and non-Israelites is conceptually derivative from the notion of the unique relationship between God/Yahweh and Israel, which is in fact constitutive for Israel.

The notion of the relationship between the בְּנֵי יִשְׂרָאֵל and the non-בְּנֵי יִשְׂרָאֵל is actually a reflex of the unique relationship of the בְּנֵי יִשְׂרָאֵל with God/Yahweh. The conceptual evaluation of the non-Israelites in the text is determined by their treatment of the Israelites. The relationship of the non-Israelites to יהוה/אֱלֹהִים, who has uniquely related himself to Israel, is also determined by their treatment of Israel. Whether the midwives are Hebrew or non-Hebrew in the narrative is an important interpretive question but it is not material to this

---

7. For a detailed examination of the relationship of these major blocks of material within the pentateuchal narrative, see R. P. Knierim, "The Composition of the Pentateuch," in K. H. Richards, ed., *SBL Seminar Papers*, 1985 (SBLSP 24; Atlanta: Scholars Press, 1985) 393–415 (published subsequently in Knierim, *Task of Old Testament Theology*, 351–79). For Knierim's discussion on the nature of Israel's migration following the narrated events at Sinai as a migratory campaign, see "The Book of Numbers," in *Task of Old Testament Theology*, 380–88. In seminars Knierim has also referred to this as the campaign march to the land, since more is presupposed in it than simply the notion of migration.

issue. Clearly, the midwives of the Hebrew women and the king of
Egypt/Pharaoh are portrayed as taking different stances toward the
בְּנֵי יִשְׂרָאֵל and their proliferation. Just as clearly, the midwives and the
king of Egypt/Pharaoh are assigned different values within the concept
of the text for this reason. This aspect is part of the infratextual conceptuality of Exod. 1:1–2:25 and an aspect of its underlying ideological
stance.

The establishing of בָּתִּים ("households") for the midwives and the
mention of their names is significant. The king of Egypt/Pharaoh figure
is a primary actant in the narrative but is unnamed and anonymous. In
contrast, the midwives are named specifically on analogy to the first-
generation sons of Jacob in 1:1–4, where each of them and his house
(וּבֵיתוֹ) is said to have entered Egypt. There are two possible explanations
for the fact that the midwives are named specifically in connection with
their households. On the one hand, if they are narrated as Hebrews, the
midwives, though women, come to have their own family houses within
the family groups of the בְּנֵי יִשְׂרָאֵל. On the other hand, if the midwives
are narrated as non-Israelite women who served as midwives for the Hebrew women, then it is suggested that they were foreigners who came
to be included in the blessing of the בְּנֵי יִשְׂרָאֵל.[8]

The Notion of the Oppression of the Israelites

The rise of the oppression against the Israelites and the measures employed by the Egyptians in that oppression are narrated in text units
1:8–14, 1:15–21, and 1:22. The conceptual questions concern how this
oppression is conceived in the text's thought system and what its relationship is to the other notions. Specifically, the question is which of
the text's notions are determined by and subordinated to which. Significantly, the oppression is narrated as the oppression of the בְּנֵי יִשְׂרָאֵל,
not simply as an oppression by the Egyptians in general. Oppression
of other peoples is not mentioned. Also, the oppression itself is presupposed to be unjust. If it were not presupposed to be unjust, it would
not be oppression. Also, the oppression is narrated explicitly as rising
in reaction to the proliferation of the בְּנֵי יִשְׂרָאֵל and the prospect that
the בְּנֵי יִשְׂרָאֵל might go up from the land of Egypt. In the history of interpretation, the narrative concerning the Egyptian oppression in Exod.

---

8. Among others, M. Greenberg has discussed the ethnic identity of the midwives as
portrayed in Exod. 1:15–21 (*Understanding Exodus*, 26–29). He states that "tradition does
not speak with one voice concerning the ethnic affiliation of the midwives." He notes
further that the view that they were Hebrews is not the oldest view and that there are
weighty arguments against it. In this regard, the command of Pharaoh to *all* his people in
1:22 suggests that the previous instruction went to some of them, that is, the midwives.
In addition, the Semitic sounding names of the midwives does not imply that they were
Hebrews. A similar situation is seen in Genesis in the Egyptian maidservant Hagar.

1:1–2:25 has frequently been read as if this narrated oppression was the primary moving cause for God/Yahweh's action in exodus deliverance, with the journey to the land being added as a subsequent independent aspect. This reading misjudges the implicit concept underlying the narrative.

Conceptually, the oppression is narrated from the standpoint of the proliferation of the בְּנֵי יִשְׂרָאֵל as its occasion, and from the standpoint of the land as its final goal by means of the exodus. In the concept of the broader pentateuchal narrative, it is necessary for the בְּנֵי יִשְׂרָאֵל to go to the land. Moreover, this would be the case conceptually irrespective of their oppression or lack of oppression. In this sense, the narration of the oppression in Exod. 1:8–22 that has arisen as a reaction to the proliferation of the בְּנֵי יִשְׂרָאֵל, including its presupposed quality of injustice, conceptually is in the service of the exodus, whose goal is the land.[9] In the text's implicit concept, what creates the need for the exodus is not primarily the oppression. Instead, it is primarily the implicit need for Israel to go the land that is the generating conceptual reason. The oppression is conceptually subsidiary though narratively prominent and functions subordinately to this implicit but primary reason. Conceptually, deliverance from oppression without exodus would have been insufficient.

The Notion of Moses

The notion of Moses in Exod. 1:1–2:25 is complex, involving the contextually presupposed notions of his call, commission, and vocation as deliverer, judge, mediator between Yahweh and the people, and giver of the Torah. The episodes of Moses' delivering activity and attempt at mediation between the disputing Hebrews in text unit 2:11–15, as well as his delivering activity for the daughters of Reuel in text unit 2:16–22, should be seen as inchoate movements that have a forward-looking reference to aspects of Moses' vocation. These aspects are established in, and only become effective due to, his call and commission. The

---

9. On different concepts of justice in the Pentateuch and their relationships to other concepts, see R. P. Knierim ("Justice in Old Testament Theology," in *Task of Old Testament Theology*, 96–97) as follows: "This theology of justice is found especially in Exodus–Joshua, and in analogous texts in the Old Testament. Included in it are the traditions in Exodus and Numbers about the defeat of those nations who resist Israel's campaign march into the promised land. This concept states that Israel's oppression of the Canaanite nations and Israel's liberation from Egyptian oppression are equally just. It justifies, and this in the name of Yahweh, both liberation of and oppression by the same people. The obvious problem of two mutually exclusive concepts of justice is assumed in the Old Testament to be resolved by reference to the concept of Israel's election as Yahweh's people. On this basis, justice is what serves Israel's election by and covenant with Yahweh, rather than and regardless of a principle of justice that is the same for all nations."

principal conceptual question regarding Moses in 1:1–2:25 concerns the
relationship between the Moses concept and the concept of the בְּנֵי יִשְׂרָאֵל
and its complex of notions in 1:1–2:25. Specifically, is the concept of the
בְּנֵי יִשְׂרָאֵל in the service of the concept of Moses or vice versa, and which
is the presupposition for which?

An important indicator provided by the structure analysis of Exod.
1:1–2:25 given above is the enframing of the story of Moses' early life
in 2:1–22 within the story of the בְּנֵי יִשְׂרָאֵל in Egypt found in 1:1–22
and 2:22–25.[10] Exodus 1:1–22 includes the narrative of the rise of their
oppression. Exodus 2:22–25 narrates their cry for help and the divine
reaction to this cry, which hearken back to text unit 1:8–14. Another
signal is found in text unit 1:22. The Moses elements are linked with
the preceding narrative by 1:22, in part by the schema of the narration
of a command followed by the narration of the compliance or lack of
compliance with that command. Ironically, it is the daughter of Pharaoh
who does not comply with Pharaoh's command in Moses' case. In addition, the Moses elements are linked with the immediately subsequent
elements in 2:23–25 by the timely coordination of the death of the king
of Egypt with the report of the cry of the בְּנֵי יִשְׂרָאֵל that ascends to God.
The death is timely in that Moses' return to his brothers is thereby fa-
cilitated. The circumstance that led to the flight to Midian in the first
place has been removed. Nevertheless, the emphasis in text unit 2:23–
25 is upon the בְּנֵי יִשְׂרָאֵל and their cry that has ascended, and on God,
who thereupon reacts explicitly.

The signals in Exod. 1:1–2:25 as a whole indicate that the Moses elements in 2:1–22 are subordinated conceptually to the concerns of the
בְּנֵי יִשְׂרָאֵל in 1:1–2:25 even though the material in 2:1–22 focuses upon
Moses. While Moses is the primary focus, and of supreme importance
subsequently in the narrative after 3:1ff. to the relationship of יהוה/אֱלֹהִים
to the בְּנֵי יִשְׂרָאֵל, the concept of Moses presupposes the concept of the
בְּנֵי יִשְׂרָאֵל. In this sense, the Moses concept depends on the concept of
the בְּנֵי יִשְׂרָאֵל with its complex of notions and not vice versa. The concept
of Moses and its narration could not have been generated in a vacuum.
That is to say it would not have been generated and narrated in the absence of the concept of the בְּנֵי יִשְׂרָאֵל and their relationship to יהוה/אֱלֹהִים.
In sum, the surface text in 2:1–22 focuses on Moses but the inexplicit
concept that has generated the structure of Exod. 1:1–2:25 is that Moses

---

10. The relationship of elements of the Moses birth/adoption story in Exod. 2:1–10 to
ancient Near Eastern parallels has been discussed by, among others, H. Gressmann (*Moses
und seine Zeit: Ein Kommentar zu den Mose-Sagen* [FRLANT 18; Göttingen: Vandenhoeck &
Ruprecht, 1913]) and B. S. Childs (*The Book of Exodus: A Critical, Theological Commentary*
[OTL; Philadelphia: Westminster, 1974]; "The Birth of Moses," *JBL* 84 [1965] 109–22).

is in the service of the בְּנֵי יִשְׂרָאֵל who are related to Abraham, Isaac, and Jacob with whom יהוה/אֱלֹהִים has related himself by בְּרִית (Exod. 2:24b).

The story of the בְּנֵי יִשְׂרָאֵל in Egypt in Exod. 1:1–2:25 that includes the early events of Moses' life prior to his call and commission is implicitly the introduction to the larger story of Moses proper that follows in 3:1ff. This story of Moses proper is in the service, conceptually, of the בְּנֵי יִשְׂרָאֵל and their presupposed relationship to יהוה/אֱלֹהִים and the aspects of that relationship. Therefore, already in the introduction in 1:1–2:25 we have signals that indicate that the Moses story involving the Moses vocation account with its call, commission, and execution — the *Vita Mosis* — cannot be understood apart from the בְּנֵי יִשְׂרָאֵל and their relationship to יהוה/אֱלֹהִים.[11] Without the concept of the people of Israel there would have been no reason to narrate anything concerning Moses or to remember it as tradition. Therefore, Exod. 1:1–2:25 should be termed the introduction to the story of Moses *and* the בְּנֵי יִשְׂרָאֵל. Remove the concept of the בְּנֵי יִשְׂרָאֵל, their proliferation, and the goal of their land, and the set of concepts closely related to these, and there would be no generative reason to narrate Moses himself.

Nevertheless, while this is the case, it is also true that conceptually the בְּנֵי יִשְׂרָאֵל cannot become what they are to be apart from Moses' central role. The pentateuchal narrative itself also could not exist if the concept of Moses were removed from it. The discussion above should not be understood as diminishing the importance of Moses. On the contrary, Moses is central to and constitutive for the narrative. There is only one other actant who conceptually is more important than Moses. This actant is יהוה/אֱלֹהִים. Otherwise, Moses is of central importance to the subsequent narrative for the particular relationship of the בְּנֵי יִשְׂרָאֵל to יהוה/אֱלֹהִים.

CONCLUSION

The discussion of the infratextual concepts operative in Exod. 1:1–2:25 has shown the importance of the conceptual function of each for the underlying conceptuality of that text. In addition, the discussion of each notion at times brought about a discussion of its relationship to other distinct concepts. In the course of the discussion it became increasingly clear that one notion in the text could not be understood adequately apart from its relationship to other notions in the text's underlying

---

11. R. P. Knierim has identified the genre of the Pentateuch as the *Vita Mosis*, or Biography of Moses, which has its introduction in Genesis 1–50. According to Knierim, the Pentateuch has a bipartite structure reflecting the main elements of the introduction in Genesis and the biography proper, which extends from Exodus though Deuteronomy. See Knierim, "Composition of the Pentateuch," 393–415.

thought. In turn, this phenomenon indicated that these other distinct notions or concepts were not incidentally related to the individually discussed concept but integrally related to it. It also became clear that some notions were subordinated or subsidiary to other notions conceptually. For example, the notion of the forefathers functioned in the service of the concept of the land. Therefore, it has become clear that we are not dealing with a group of more or less independent concepts in Exod. 1:1–2:25. The concepts discussed above as signaled in the text of Exod. 1:1–2:25 are more than simply a collection of themes related to the text. Instead, the concepts together form a conceptuality by virtue of their systemic relationships given the text of Exod. 1:1–2:25 and its context.

The conceptuality underlying Exod. 1:1–2:25 and its contextual relationships includes a specific relationship between the notions of יהוה/אֱלֹהִים; the בְּנֵי יִשְׂרָאֵל; their proliferation; their relationship to the non-בְּנֵי יִשְׂרָאֵל, to the land, to their forefathers, to their oppression, and to Moses. These component concepts define and reinforce one another. The term that best describes the conceptual complex involving all these components and their systemic relationships in the underlying thought system of the text is "election."[12] This is the case even though the characteristic philological terms expressing election in the Hebrew Bible do not appear in Exod. 1:1–2:25. The idea of the unique and particular relationship of the בְּנֵי יִשְׂרָאֵל to יהוה/אֱלֹהִים that is presupposed in Exod. 1:1–2:25 is elective or selective in nature. The non-בְּנֵי יִשְׂרָאֵל do not have this relationship with יהוה/אֱלֹהִים. Rather, the non-בְּנֵי יִשְׂרָאֵל are viewed and implicitly valued by virtue of the relationship they sustain to the בְּנֵי יִשְׂרָאֵל. When God is narrated as implicitly ready to act at the end of Exod. 2:23–25, implicitly he is ready to act for the בְּנֵי יִשְׂרָאֵל, not for all the oppressed within the creation horizon provided by Genesis 1–

---

12. For discussions of the idea of election more broadly in the Hebrew Bible, see the following: P. Altmann, *Erwählungstheologie und Universalismus im Alten Testament* (BZAW 92; Berlin: Töpelmann, 1964); O. Eissfeldt, "Partikularismus und Universalismus in der Israelitisch-Judischen Religionsgeschichte," *TLZ* 79 (1954) 283–84; K. Galling, *Die Erwählungstraditionen Israels* (BZAW 48; Giessen: Töpelmann, 1928); K. Koch, "Zur Geschichte der Erwählungsvorstellung in Israel," *ZAW* 67 (1955) 205–26; W. J. Phythian-Adams, *The Call of Israel: An Introduction to the Study of Divine Election* (London: Oxford University Press, 1934); G. Quell, "ἐκλέγομαι B. Election in the Old Testament," *TDNT*, 4:145–68; H. H. Rowley, *The Biblical Doctrine of Election* (London: Lutterworth, 1950); B. E. Schafer, "The Root Bhr and Pre-Exilic Concepts of Chosenness in the Hebrew Bible," *ZAW* 89 (1977) 20–42; J. Scharbert, "'Erwählung' im Alten Testament im Licht von Gen 12,1–3," in E. Zenger, J. Gnilka, et al., *Dynamik im Wort: Lehre von der Bibel, Leben aus der Bibel* (Stuttgart: Katholisches Bibelwerk, 1983) 13–33; C. Schedel, "Bund und Erwählung," *ZTK* 80 (1958) 493–515; H. Seebass, "בחר," *TDOT*, 2:74–87; S.-T. Sohn, *The Divine Election of Israel* (Grand Rapids: Eerdmans, 1991); T. C. Vriezen, *Die Erwählung Israels nach dem Alten Testament* (ATANT 24; Zurich: Zwingli, 1953); H. Wildberger, *Jahwes Eigentumsvolk* (ATANT 37; Zurich: Zwingli, 1960); H.-J. Zobel, "Ursprung und Verwurzelung des Erwählungsglaubens Israels," *TLZ* 93 (1968) 1–12.

11 as a contextual element. The conceptuality underlying Exod. 1:1–2:25 and Exod. 3:1ff. may be reconstructed and paraphrased as follows. Israel (= בְּנֵי יִשְׂרָאֵל) is elected by Yahweh/God for exclusive relationship, and for proliferation, and for possession of the land. The central mediator through whom this elective purpose for Israel will be realized is Moses.[13] Through Moses' call, commission, and resultant vocation as deliverer and giver of the Torah, the Yahweh/Torah-of-Moses ethos and cult is bestowed that is to be actualized by Israel in its land. Joshua realizes the legacy deriving from Moses' mediatorship initially in the conquest of the land. Though Moses himself does not lead the conquest, it is nevertheless implicitly predicated upon the Mosaic ethos. Though Joshua actualizes the possession of the land initially, implicitly the land will be held by the people only through the Mosaic traditions and ethos. As a result, it may be said that Exod. 1:1–2:25 is the introductory element within the story of the outworking of this elective purpose in which Moses and the *Vita Mosis* are in the service of Israel's election by יהוה/אֱלֹהִים for the land. When read with an awareness of its underlying conceptual aspects, Exod. 1:1–2:25 is not simply the story of the rise of oppression leading to the emergence of the needed deliverer, though these themes are prominent. Conceptually, the narrative is about the unfolding history of Israel's election by Yahweh/God, the outworking of which is to be realized through the central mediatorial role of Moses.

---

13. The role of Moses in the Pentateuch has been a focus in scholarship, as exemplified in the following publications: E. F. Campbell, "Moses and the Foundations of Israel," *Int* 29 (1975) 141–54; G. W. Coats, *Moses: Heroic Man, Man of God* (JSOTSup 57; Sheffield: JSOT Press, 1988); idem, *The Moses Tradition* (JSOTSup 161; Sheffield: JSOT Press, 1993); Gressmann, *Mose und seine Zeit*; Knierim, "Composition of the Pentateuch"; E. Osswald, *Das Bild des Mose in der kritischen alttestamentlichen Wissenschaft seit Julius Wellhausen* (TA 18; Berlin: Evangelische Verlagsanstalt, 1962); H. Schmid, *Mose: Überlieferung und Geschichte* (BZAW 110; Berlin: Töpelmann, 1968); W. H. Schmidt, *Exodus, Sinai, und Mose* (EdF 191; Darmstadt: Wissenschaftliche Buchgesellschaft, 1983); H. Seebass, *Mose und Aaron, Sinai und Gottesberg* (AET 2; Bonn: H. Bouvier, 1962); R. Smend, *Das Mosebild von Heinrich Ewald bis Martin Noth* (BGBE 3; Tübingen: J. C. B. Mohr, 1959); J. Van Seters, *The Life of Moses: The Yahwist as Historian in Exodus-Numbers* (Louisville: Westminster John Knox, 1994); P. Weimar, *Die Berufung des Moses: Literarwissenschaftliche Analyse von Exodus 2, 23–5, 5* (OBO 32; Göttingen: Vandenhoeck & Ruprecht, 1980).

Selected Bibliography

Altmann, P. *Erwählungstheologie und Universalismus im Alten Testament.* Berlin: A. Töpelmann, 1964.

Coats, G. W. *Moses: Heroic Man, Man of God.* JSOTSup 57. Sheffield: JSOT Press, 1988.

——. *Exodus 1–18.* The Forms of Old Testament Literature 2A. Grand Rapids: Eerdmans, 1999.

Fohrer, G. *Überlieferung und Geschichte des Exodus: Eine Analyse von Ex 1–15.* BZAW 91. Berlin, 1964.

Galling, K. *Die Erwählungstraditionen Israels.* BZAW 48. Giessen: Töpelmann, 1928.

Greenberg, M. *Understanding Exodus.* New York: Behrman House, 1969.

Gressmann, H. *Mose und Seine Zeit: Ein Kommentar zu den Mose-Sagen.* FRLANT 18. Göttingen: Vandenhoeck & Ruprecht, 1913.

Knierim, Rolf P. "The Composition of the Pentateuch." In *Society of Biblical Literature Seminar Papers* 24, ed. K. H. Richards, pp. 393–415. Atlanta: Scholars Press, 1985.

——. *Text and Concept in Leviticus 1:1–9: A Case in Exegetical Method.* FAT 2. Tübingen: J. C. B. Mohr, 1992.

——. *The Task of Old Testament Theology: Substance, Method, and Cases.* Grand Rapids: Eerdmans, 1995.

Propp, W. H. C. *Exodus 1–18: A New Translation with Introduction and Commentary.* AB 2. New York: Doubleday, 1999.

Rupprecht, K. "עלה מן הארץ: (Ex. 1:10, Hos 2:2): 'sich des Landes bemächtigen'?" *ZAW* 82 (1970) 442–47.

Schmidt, W. H. *Exodus.* BKAT 2/3. Neukirchen: Neukirchener, 1988.

Van Seters, J. *The Life of Moses: The Yahwist as Historian in Exodus-Numbers.* Louisville: Westminster/John Knox, 1994.

Wijngaards, J. "הוציא and העלה: A Twofold Approach to the Exodus." *VT* 15 (1965) 91–102.

12

Psalm 82

Tércio M. Siqueira

The main intention of an exegesis is to reconstruct the assumptions that are embedded in the explicit declarations of the text. Each biblical text is a living body. That is why when one speaks of embedded assumptions in the text, it means that the exegesis seeks to analyze the underground aspects that are operative in Psalm 82 generating and controlling its form and content. In other words, the exegetical work goes well beyond the paraphrase. Each text carries an intention imagined by the author, in the context of socioeconomic and religious circumstances, among others. Therefore, it would be naïve and superficial to take this psalm without trying to capture the socioeconomic problems embedded in the text, which are the generators of the conflicts reflected in its words.

To study Psalm 82, it is necessary primarily to analyze its literary genre and its setting. A point of departure can be established from these two aspects in order to attempt to know the intention of the Psalmist. The form and language in which it is presented work together for the clarification of the sociological setting.

FORM AND LANGUAGE

Structure

Among the psalms entitled "to Asaph," Psalm 82 is characterized by its literary prophetic genre. Its literary structure points to this characteristic.

I. Report of Elohim/Yahweh proclamation	vv. 1–7
A. Circumstance (words of the psalmist)	v. 1
B. Citation of Elohim/Yahweh word	vv. 2–7
1. Accusation	v. 2
2. Evidence	vv. 3–4
3. Verdict	v. 5
4. Sentence	vv. 6–7
II. Appeal of the psalmist	v. 8

I dedicate this essay to Rolf Knierim, whom I have had the privilege to know as professor and dear friend, in gratitude for all that he has represented to his students and to the study of the Old Testament.

Observations about the Structure

Psalm 82 is delimited by vv. 1 and 8, with v. 5 as the core. Verses 2–6 show the argumentation of the psalmist about the conflict between the people of Yahweh and the Canaanite religion. The causes of this conflict are the reason for Yahweh's intervention at the heavenly council. The question *'ad mātay*, "Until when?" (v. 2), is answered through the imperatives of vv. 3–4 and the continuity of the tribunal's decision (vv. 5–7). The expression *'ad mātay* suggests a situation of danger and emergency verified by Elohim/Yahweh. The world's stability was in jeopardy (cf. Exod. 10:3; Ps. 89:47; 74:9; Num. 24:22).

Observations about the Text's Language

Psalm 82 shows, in this structure, a dynamic well suited to the prophetic language, both in content and in the sequence of ideas. The axis of the psalm is in vv. 2–4, wherein is established the principal motivation for the composition. Starting at the question *'ad mātay*, "until when?" the psalmist goes on to show his and Elohim's indignation, and to accuse and condemn the practice of injustice done by the perverse *rěšā'îm* against the weak (*dal*), the orphan (*yātôm*), the miserable (*'ānî*), and the needy (*'ebyôn*). It is interesting to notice that vv. 3 and 4, in the imperative, have a double purpose: to make evident the incompetence of the gods toward the human beings, and to constrain them to do the function they apparently were commissioned to do. As in a legal forum, the evidences of the crime are presented in all phases of the judgment, but v. 5 concentrates three more: "do not know" (*yāda'*), "do not understand" (*bîn*), and "walk in the darkness" (*hālak*). As a formal act, the proclamation of the sentence against the accused must happen at the ending of a judgment in the tribunal (vv. 6–7). In a demonstration that the psalmist knew the tradition, he appeals to Elohim to judge all the perverse on earth (cf. Deut. 1:17; 19:17; Ps. 58:2–12).[1]

The way of communicating and the language of the psalmist belong to the realm of the prophets. There is no repetition of other prophetic literary formulas in the construction of the psalm, but it is noticeable that the pattern, the language, and the theme occur frequently with the prophets. As an example, take the pronouncement of Isa. 1:4–9. Here, the prophet begins by accusing the people from the interior of Judah and from Jerusalem (v. 4) and ends by acting out a dispute in the tribunal or the justice forum (vv. 5–9). In this dispute, the accuser raises up an accusatory question (v. 5a) and the evidence (justification) for that

---

1. Latin American exegesis has read this Hebrew text in a particular manner, seeking to understand the socioeconomic environment in which its author and the community lived.

accusation (vv. 5b–9). The idea of taking people to court for a *rîb* ("judgment") is especially clear in Hosea (2:4; 4:4) and in Jeremiah (2:9, 29), where the judicial dispute language is present. In fact, it is not necessary that the term *rîb* be present in order to characterize a pericope as one of dispute in the court of justice. This is the case with Psalm 82: it is an authentic example of the internal procedure of a judgment, at the gates of cities and villages, or, later, at the court of Jerusalem.

The language of Psalm 82 has a poetic disposition. It is difficult to define its poetic form. We cannot affirm that the entire psalm is in the form of parallelism of members, although vv. 3 and 4, for example, take that disposition. The other verses are an example of the affirmation that the Hebrew poetry does not have a defined form. We cannot apply a scheme in order to understand it. Psalm 82 is an example of Hebrew poetry. It is more a thought structure than a stereotyped literary form. It is presented in the form of repetitions and variations; this flow of ideas is not only for stylistic reasons, but also, above all, for didactic purposes. Psalm 82 is a rich example of this form of literary expression.

Therefore, Psalm 82 leads the reader to widen his or her comprehension about the people of Israel: first, they were familiar with judiciary language, because it is present not only among judges; second, this language was popular, even in the liturgy; and third, it appears that the judges' environment was open to people not only from Jerusalem's upper class.

TEXT SETTING

Psalm 82, especially for its reference to the historic place (v. 1), represents an important document for research on religious diversity in Israel. It points to an important and clarifying detail: the Israelite resistance toward other religions was not at the level of doctrine, but above all in the practice of justice. This detail is important, especially in the context of the worship service, where it is supposed that this psalm was collected.

The Text in Its Historical Context

This poetry begins by describing the circumstance where it was born (created) and bears meaning: in the meeting (*'ēdāh*) of the gods. The reference is quite strange for the OT, but is possibly predictable, given the close familiarity of the Israelites with the Canaanites in Palestine.

The Old Testament uses the term *'ēdāh* to indicate (1) company, band (Ps. 68:31; Hos. 7:12); (2) troop, congregation (Ps. 1:5; 22:17; 86:14); (3) congregation of Israel (1 Kings 8:5; 12:20; Ps. 111:1; Prov. 5:14) and

congregation of El (Ps. 82:1). As Ps. 82:1[2] describes the presence of the
God of Israel in a universal meeting of gods from all nations (v. 8) to
judge them for their administrative performance, it is possible to think
that it was a general conference of El, congregating all deities of the
world. Having the root *yā'ad* ("meet, congregate"), the expression *'ădat
'ēl* suggests that Elohim, God of Israel, was at a meeting whose president was El (v. 1). The fact that Elohim stood up to talk indicates that
he was sitting down, and with the gesture of standing up to talk was
showing respect to the god who presided over the council.[3]

The expression *'ădat 'ēl*, "council of El," needs a more careful analysis. In the ancient Middle East, the polytheist mythologies of different
people shared a common element. It is the concept that every nation
was guided by a pantheon of gods led by one of them, called "highest god." Among the Sumerians this god was called, according to the
place, Anu or Enlil, and in Babylon, Marduk; among the Canaanites he
was called El; for the Egyptians his name was Re and Atum. The Hit-
tites called their highest god Taru. The reason why each one of these
gods was considered by their worshipers as "highest god" can be found
with their titles: "father of the gods," "creator of the created beings,"
"lord of all living creatures," "king of heaven and earth." From these
titles it is possible to realize that all these peoples saw the highest god
as a superior being, based especially on the notion of creator, supreme
governor, and sustainer of the world.[4]

The information gathered at the opening of Psalm 82 (v. 1) seems to
touch directly upon the theme of El's pantheon, exactly at a time of one
of his councils. In the case of the Canaanite pantheon, Yahweh partici-
pated in one of these assemblies, probably with Baal and Astarte, among
others. The highest god El was the president of the divine council, the
one who delegated authority to the gods to implement order and justice
at the different parts of the cosmos. Baal had the responsibility to implement justice at the most important area of production of the world:
the fertility of creation.

In Israel, the *'ădat 'ēl* was seen as something strange. Nevertheless,
condemnation is not directed against the presidency of El, but against
the gods responsible for the implementation of justice in the different realms of the cosmos. In vv. 2–8 the psalmist demeans the gods
responsible for implementing justice to mortal beings. The *'ădat 'ēl* is
not directly involved in this condemnatory plot. This apparent confor-

2. See R. P. Knierim, *The Task of Old Testament Theology: Substance, Method, and Cases*
(Grand Rapids: Eerdmans, 1995) 171–224.

3. L. Koehler and W. Baumgartner, *Lexicon in Veteris Testamenti Libros* (2d ed.; Leiden:
Brill, 1958) 682.

4. See M. H. Pope, "El in the Ugaritic Texts" (VTSup 2; Leiden: Brill, 1955) 25–32.

mity of the psalmist with the "divine council" concept may help in the understanding of a statement such as "let us make humankind in our image" (Gen. 1:26) and of an unusual statement by the prophet Jeremiah, "if they were present at my council" (Jer. 23:22), although in this passage he uses a synonym for *ʿēdāh*, which is *sôd*. It is possible that some traditions in Israel transferred the concept of council of El to council of Yahweh.

The Old Testament has a form of seeing the action of Yahweh, God of Israel: first, the creation and the sustenance of the world represent the execution and the continuous implementation of justice; second, Yahweh delegates authority for the implementation of justice not to the gods, but to the real administration, the sages, the legislature, and the prophets, among others. His guiding principle to delegate authority to the implementers is varied, and is concerned with the calling (Exod. 3:1–12; Judg. 6:7–24; Isa. 6:1–10; Jer. 1:4–10), the anointing (2 Sam. 16:1–23), and the gift of wisdom (1 Kings 3:4–15). The criteria for this administration was *ṣedeq* ("justice") and its implementation happened through *ṣĕdāqāh* ("righteousness, salvation acts"), *mišpāṭ* ("justice"), *ʾĕmet* ("faith"), *ʾĕmûnāh* ("fidelity"), *ḥesed* ("kindness"), and *šālôm* ("plentiful life").

According to the psalmist's report (v. 1), it is necessary to understand that Israel was an assimilator of the Canaanite culture. In this particular problem, this information gives the understanding that Elohim/Yahweh adapted the notions of El and supplanted him as the highest god, commanding an authentic revolution in the established theology of the ancient Middle East. What once was a duty of the gods of the pantheon was now delegated to those called and anointed by Yahweh.

Thus, this old understanding of the ancient Middle East serves as a background to the theological traditions of the OT. Israel emerged in its midst, adapting it, and, naturally, constructing its own version in a highly creative manner.

Date and Place

It is a hard task to establish a date and a place for Psalm 82. If the researcher starts with the information of the superscription, "to Asaph," the situation becomes complicated because this psalm is not like the other compositions attributed to Asaph, especially in size and literary genre (see Psalms 50; 73–83).[5]

The question of the psalm's date has been analyzed intensively. There are several reasons to place this psalm in the monarchic period.

---

5. See M. D. Goulder, *The Psalms of Asaph and the Pentateuch*, Studies in the Psalter 3 (JSOTSup 233; Sheffield: Sheffield Academic Press, 1996).

The theme of conflict with the Canaanites, the archaic language, the distressing problem of the orphan (*yātôm*), the preaching in defense of the poor, and the indoctrination of the monotheist theology are typical of the preexilic period. On the other hand, Psalm 82 has signs of the presence of the articulation of the sage, through the binary style of the poetry (see Proverbs 10–15; Job). And it is also possible to perceive that the "until when?" questioning, the repetitive use of synonyms for "poor" (*dal, 'ebyôn, 'ānî, rāš*), the universalistic tone of v. 8, and some similarity with Ezek. 28:1–10 have characteristics of the beginning of the postexilic period.

It is difficult to establish the place for the psalm. It is not hard to establish, though, that the setting where this composition was developed was a prophetic one. From there, it is possible to locate three main settings in biblical prophecy: Jerusalem, the region of Shephelah and of the mountains of Judah, and among the land workers of the northern kingdom. The signals connecting this psalm to Jerusalem are scarce. The main indication resides in the conflict between Yahweh and Baal, a conflict without a fixed location, either in the kingdom of Judah or in the kingdom of Israel.

It is known, however, that before the establishment of the Israelites, the Canaanites occupied a wide stretch of land west of the Jordan, from the south of Beersheba as far as Syria, ending approximately at Phoenicia. From information given by the prophets Amos and Hosea and by the Dtr history (1 Kings 18:20–46) it is possible to gather some light on the location of the great political and religious conflicts with the Canaanites. The region north, most certainly, was the setting that created and propagated Psalm 82. The language of this psalm is quite similar to the preaching of Amos and Hosea.

Interpreting Psalm 82 in the same scenario as that of the eighth-century prophets solves many difficulties. The literary genre used by the author — visionary, exhortative, and imperative in the appeal to change life — speaks in the prophetic style. The next step in this study will demonstrate that the literary typology of Psalm 82 has close connections with prophetic activity.

THE CHARACTERS OF THE PSALM

Throughout the oral tradition, poetry, narratives, and laws, among other literary productions, were submitted to varied interpretations according to the specific need. It appears, though, that Psalm 82 does not have parallels in the Bible. Hence, the best approach to its study is to take its literary form and look for the approximate intention of the author.

The axis of Psalm 82 is neither apologetic nor didactic. It is a little of both but primarily it evolves around the administration of justice in the world, not only in Israel.

First, it is necessary to observe that the psalm exposes a conflict. On one side are the gods responsible for the administration of the cosmos, and on the other side are some inhabitants of earth. The psalmist is preoccupied with the situation of the people of the earth who suffer the rigors of the bad administration by the gods of the Canaanite pantheon. The psalmist's denunciation is clear: the ones responsible for justice allow the *'āwel* ("bad") and the *rĕšā'îm* ("wicked") (v. 2) to be in charge of the administrative politics of the world, denying the opportunities for wholesome and abundant life for the needy worker (*dal*), the miserable (*'ānî*), the poor (*rāš*), the exploited (*'ebyôn*), and the orphan (*yātôm*) (vv. 3–4).[6]

Those Who Cause Instability in the World

The text says that two types of members of the world community are acting and controlling the politics (v. 2) and putting at risk life in the entire universe. Translating the two agents as "bad" and "wicked" is risky, since it may fall into a generic definition. Both meanings recall an objective category.

The *rĕšā'îm* ("wicked") are the first ones cited in this accusation. They were seen in the OT as a constant threat to the lives of the people around them (Jer. 5:26; Ps. 119:95, 110; 140:5, 9), and as those who do not hesitate in killing people, even innocent ones, to achieve their wicked goals. That is why they are always in opposition to the just ones (Psalm 1). The complaint of the believers of Yahweh alludes to the aggression of these wicked ones (Ps. 10:2; 11:2).

Concerning the *'āwel*, this term bears the meaning of corrupter of the wholesome community life. Such persons twist the truth and create injustice for their own gain. This is why all is *'āwel* ("perverted"), and humankind is abominable to Yahweh (Deut. 25:16; Prov. 29:27). The use of this term is associated with the context of social law (Lev. 19:15, 35; Ps. 7:4; 37:1; Ezek. 3:20; 18:24). The words, among others, that describe their actions are the verbs *'ānāh* ("oppress," 2 Sam. 7:10) and *ḥāmas* ("rape," Ps. 72:14), the adjective *rāšā'* ("guilty," Isa. 26:10), and the nouns *pešaʿ* ("offense," Ezek. 33:12), *ḥāmās* ("violence," Ezek. 28:16), *dām* ("crime," Mic. 3:10), and *mirmāh* ("wrong," Ps. 43:1).

Both terms indicate opposition to the *ṣaddîq* ("just"). That is why the wicked and false persons are mentioned in open confrontation with *sedeq/sĕdāqāh* ("justice, righteousness," Isa. 26:10; 59:4) and all attitudes concerning community *šālôm*: loyalty, kindness, trust, fidelity.

---

6. For these meanings in the Hebrew Bible, consult *TLOT*, vols. 1 and 2.

The "Clients" of Elohim

Verses 3–4 mention five "clients" whom the God of Israel rises to defend in the midst of the ordinary council of the gods. All of them belong to the category of socially abandoned people. Nevertheless, each one of the mentioned terms has its own peculiarity.

First, the Hebrew term *dal* is mentioned twice. This is a term that has many occurrences outside the OT, and it has the meaning of poverty that causes anguish (Old Akkadian meaning), many times by the forced labor (Assyrian and Babylonian meaning), or of being poor in relation the possession of cattle (Phoenician meaning). The cult laws in Lev. 14:21 allow for exemption of offering for the *dal* based on the fact that he does not own any possessions.[7]

Second, Psalm 82 mentions *'ebyôn*, a word that indicates a socially weak person, but that carries a characteristic that gives the person a prominent place among all poor: an *'ebyôn* is a person who possesses a special relationship with the divinity, an idea present throughout the ancient Middle East. It seems that this content passed on to the Hebrew, because in the songs both of complaint and of thanksgiving the believers present themselves as poor and needy, claiming their right to receive justice (Deut. 14:28–29; Isa. 58:7; Ps. 72:2, 4, 12–13; 112:9). It is not perceptible in the biblical texts in the idea of humility, but in the idea of material misery in opposition to riches (Ps. 49:3; 112:9; Prov. 31:20).

Third, Elohim, God of Israel, refers to the *'ānî* ("afflicted") as one of the groups devastated by the insensibility of the gods of the Canaanite pantheon. Analyzing the meaning of *'ānî* in the context of the ancient Middle East and the OT, it is possible to realize that the term has a strong concrete and sociological meaning, contrary to the spiritualized one — humble and pious — found in the postexilic period. Psalm 82 maintains the original meaning of *'ānî* as referring to someone in a state of economic weakness, and therefore with little value as a human being.

Fourth, Psalm 82 uses *rāš* for another group of "clients" in Elohim's denunciation of the gods. Last-cited in the text, *rāš* ("poor") is the more neutral designation of a person's social condition. *Rāš* is frequently used as the opposite of *'āšîr* ("rich," 2 Sam. 12:1–4; Prov. 14:20; 18:23; 22:2, 7; 28:6). Of the twenty-one occurrences of this term, fourteen are in the book of Proverbs. The defense of the poor social stratum by the psalmist suggests that the context of this psalm is near to a time and place where the rich and landowners mingled with the people. This manner of speaking by the psalmist puts him close to the social conflicts of the end of the eighth century.

---

7. H.-J. Fabry, *"dal,"* TDOT, 3:208–30.

The fifth character in this process cited by the prosecutor and judge, Elohim, is the *yātôm* ("orphan"). Throughout the OT, the orphan and the widow form a group of people who deserve protection. In the legal domain, the orphan has the benefit of levirate law (Deut. 25:5–10; cf. Exod. 22:21), which the prophets and the sages used in defense of the well-being of the community (Isa. 1:17; Jer. 5:28; 22:3; 49:7–22; Ezek. 22:7; Zech. 7:9–10; Prov. 15:25; 19:17). It is interesting to note that Elijah, in his task of rescuing the values of the Yahwist spirituality during the government of the Omride dynasty, gives priority to the reestablishment of the dignity of the widow and the orphan (1 Kings 17:7–24). The defense of the orphan may be a telling sign of the war to defend the territory. The conflicts with the Assyrians before the fall of Samaria (721 B.C.E.) had serious effects upon the integrity of the family.

The pronounced use of these five terms close together in the prophetic literature, in the instructions to the sages, and in the codes of law reinforces the idea that poverty, regardless of its origin, was abominable in the eyes of God.

PSALM 82: AN OVERVIEW

Psalm 82 can be called a prophetic hymn. It has all the characteristics of a pronouncement made by the prophets, especially those of the eighth-century B.C.E. Elohim acts as a prosecutor assisting five groups of needy people of the society, and assumes the judge's position for the gods in the council, he tries to protect the needy against the permissive government of the world and promulgates an ultimatum (vv. 2–4). He shows himself to be just and compassionate to the defenseless poor, and to the careless administrator gods he shows the rigor of the codes of law.

Psalm 82 must be seen as a historic document of the OT theology. The author was a faithful Yahwist. He was confronted by the acute problem between the monotheistic ideal intended by the Israelites and the popular and dominant Canaanite theology. While the Canaanites tried to manipulate Baal through religion in order to achieve their goals, many times unethical ones, the faithful Yahwists saw in their God acts of justice in search for the community's *šālôm*. It was with this intention that he intervened in the council of El.

Many biblical texts describe Yahweh's governance of the universe. He is the one who sustains the created world. Not only the "Zion" theology[8] affirms this (Ps. 103:19), but also the prophetic Psalm 82 reaffirms

---

8. See M. Schwantes, "Esperanças Messiânicas e Daviditas," *Estudos Bíblicos* 23 (1989) 18–29; T. M. Siqueira, "The People of the Land in the Monarchic Period" (Ph.D. diss., Methodist University of São Paulo, 1997).

the same sovereignty, although in a different way. Basically, the formation of theology outside Jerusalem included sensitivity toward the socially needy and the earth. Yahweh, God of Israel, did not agree with the gods and their politics of government for the world. The accusation against them was not related to jealousy or doctrine, but particularly to ethics in government (v. 2). After reciting to the gods their code of duties (vv. 3–4) as the basis for his accusation, Elohim gives his conclusive verdict: the gods did not know their own professional duties (v. 5a). And it is this incompetence and the lack of acts of justice that would bring a worldwide catastrophe: "all the foundations of the earth are shaken" (v. 5b).

This psalm contains the report of a revolutionary act of God. The reason for this divine act was linked with the complete absence of justice in the administration of the world. Elohim then assumed the responsibility of guardian of the justice code for the world. When the psalmist calls to Elohim, "judge the earth" (v. 8), he wants to say that from now on, justice will be the greater concern of our only God.

It is possible to conclude that Elohim will protect the rights of the poor — dal, 'ebyôn, 'ānî, rāš, and yātôm — whose cries and claims he hears. The quality of his justice is well explained, especially in the book of Psalms. Here, the concept of ṣedeq/ṣĕdāqāh ("justice") is intensively treated because it is the only criterion for sustenance and rectification of the order in the world created by God. Contrary to the other gods of the pantheon, Elohim's governmental criterion is founded not in the decisions of a dîn ("tribunal") of human beings (cf. v. 7) that confers the justice possible. Psalm 89:14 affirms that ṣedeq ûmišpāṭ ("justice and law") are the basis of Yahweh's government, and that ḥesed wĕ'ĕmet ("kindness and fidelity") are before him (cf. Ps. 97:2). In other words, the criterion for administering and sustaining the creation is based on justice, peace, kindness, love, compassion, faith, and fidelity.

Selected Bibliography

Alonso Schökel, Luis, and Cecilia Carniti. Salmos II (Salmos 73–150). São Paulo: Paulus, 1998.

González, A. El Libro de los Salmos. Barcelona: Editorial Herder, 1984.

Goulder, Michael D. The Psalms of Asaph and the Pentateuch. Studies in the Psalter 3. JSOTSup 233. Sheffield: Sheffield Academic Press, 1996.

Knierim, Rolf P. The Task of Old Testament Theology: Substance, Method, and Cases. Grand Rapids: Eerdmans, 1995.

Kraus, Hans-Joachim. Psalms 60–150: A Commentary. Minneapolis: Augsburg Fortress, 1989.

Nasuti, Harry. Tradition History and the Psalms of Asaph. SBLDS 88. Atlanta: Scholars Press, 1988.

13

On Yahweh's Court in Hosea 4:1–3

Yoshihide Suzuki

TRANSLATION OF THE TEXT: ISSUE AND PROBLEM

Hear the word of Yahweh,
  O sons of Israel;
For Yahweh has a lawsuit
  against the inhabitants of the land;
because there is no faithfulness, no loyalty,
  and no knowledge of God in the land.
Cursing, lying, murdering,
  stealing, and committing adultery break out;
  bloodshed follows bloodshed.
Therefore the land mourns,
  and all who live in it languish;
together with the wild animals
  and the birds of the sky,
  even the fish of the sea perish. (Hos. 4:1–3)

The small unit of Hos. 4:1–3 is filled with legal terms such as "lawsuit,"[1] "cursing,"[2] "lying,"[3] "murdering" "stealing,"[4] "committing adultery,"

---

1. Regarding the translation of Hebrew word ריב, see "a contention" (W. R. Harper, *A Critical and Exegetical Commentary on Amos and Hosea* [ICC; Edinburgh: T. & T. Clark, 1905]); "einen Hader" (K. Marti, *Das Dodekapropheton* [KHC 13; Tübingen: J. C. B. Mohr, 1904]); "Gericht" (H. W. Wolff, *Dodekapropheton 1 Hosea* [BKAT 14/1; Neukirchen-Vluyn: Neukirchener, 1963]; ET, "a lawsuit," *Hosea* [trans. G. Stansell; Hermeneia; Philadelphia: Fortress, 1974]); "a complaint" (J. L. Mays, *Hosea* [OTL; Philadelphia: Westminster, 1969]); "a controversy" (M. J. Buss, *The Prophetic Word of Hosea* [BZAW 111; Berlin: Töpelmann, 1969]); "an indictment" (NRSV); "a dispute" (F. I. Andersen and D. N. Freedman, *Hosea* [AB 24; Garden City, N.Y.: Doubleday, 1980); "a case" (NJPS).

2. Since the testimony by the witness in court is always verified by an oath in the name of God, which in ancient times took the form of conditional self-imprecation, we are inclined to translate the Hebrew אלה as "cursing." Needless to say, an allusion of its basic meaning ("to swear, to take oath") is "to bear false witness in the name of Yahweh" according to the context of this unit. Hosea seems to indicate ironically that bearing false witness is rampant among the people at that time. Regarding oaths at trial, see, H. J. Boecker, *Recht und Gesetz im Alten Testament und im Alten Orient* (Neukirchen-Vluyn: Neukirchener, 1984) 27–28.; ET, *Law and the Administration of Justice in the Old Testament and Ancient East* (trans. J. Moiser; Minneapolis: Augsburg, 1980) 35ff.

3. Cf. "lying" (NRSV), "dishonesty" (NJPS). The term is not used in the general sense here, but as a specific legal term with a criminal sense like "perjury." See Wolff, *Hosea*, 83ff. (ET, 65ff.).

4. The general meaning of the Hebrew word is "stealing" (NRSV, NJPS). According

and "bloodshed."[5] Naturally, the reader has no difficulty seeing that Yahweh the God of Israel is ready to indict the people of Israel. The oracle itself is formulated in the idiom of speech in the court, and our unit is constituted as a court speech.[6] According to the announcement concerning the lawsuit, the judge of this case is Yahweh.[7]

In addition to the legal character of our unit, it must be noted that many biblical scholars have already indicated the nature of lawsuit in the prophetic oracle and also the so-called rîb-pattern, which is presupposed in this unit too. Obviously, the rîb-pattern is used in various contexts for expressing the legal relationship between Yahweh and Israel and not just for disputes between the groups and peoples in the Old Testament.[8] In fact, the Hebrew word רִיב (rîb) must be suitable for Hosea to conceptualize his oracle that the divine judgment is imminent against the defendant.[9]

Furthermore, what we have here is not only the proclamation of an indictment but also the sentence of a death penalty to Israel (4:3).[10] The total destruction of the creatures of the land is clearly stated in the context. Therefore, no one will miss the core of Hosea's message: Yahweh's judgment will inevitably come to the defendant.

However obvious the core message of the prophet may be, some basic questions are left for us. Even if knowing that the indictment is

---

to A. Alt, it may be "kidnapping" (see "Das Verbot des Diebstahls im Dekalog" (1949), in *Kleine Schriften zur Geschichte des Volkes Israel* [3 vols.; Munich: C. H. Beck'sche, 1959] 1:333–40).

5. We do not treat the legal background relating to the Decalogue in this essay.

6. See C. Westermann, *Grundformen prophetischer Rede* (BEvT 31; Munich: Kaiser, 1971) 143–47.

7. See Hos. 12:3.

8. For instance, Hosea 12 is one of the typical cases, where the rîb-pattern functions to clarify the cause and effect of the divine judgment. Accordingly, Hosea is able to demonstrate that the death penalty would be inevitable for the defendant, Ephraim. See also Gen. 31:26ff.; Jer. 26:7ff.

9. The Hebrew term רִיב ("lawsuit") is used in, for example, Hos. 12:3; Mic. 6:2; Isa. 1:23; 34:8; 58:4; Jer. 15:10; 25:31; Ezek. 44:24. In the book of Hosea, the rîb-pattern is found in 12:1–15 as well as in 4:1–3. Regarding the prophetic idea of lawsuit, see H. B. Huffmon, "The Covenant Lawsuit in the Prophets," *JBL* 78 (1959) 285–95; G. W. Wright, "The Lawsuit of God: A Form-Critical Study of Deuteronomy 32," in B. W. Anderson and W. Harrelson, eds., *Israel's Prophetic Heritage: Essays in Honor of James Muilenburg* (New York: Harper, 1962) 26–67.

10. See B. Gemser, "The Rîb- or Controversy-Pattern in Hebrew Mentality," in M. Noth and D. W. Thomas, eds., *Wisdom in Israel and in the Ancient Near East* (VTSup 3; Leiden: Brill, 1955) 120–37; Huffmon, "The Covenant Lawsuit in the Prophets"; H. Harvey, "Le 'Rîb-Pattern,' réquisitoire prophétique sur la rupture de l'alliance," *Bib* 43 (1962) 172–96; E. von Waldow, *Die Traditionsgeschichtliche Hintergrund der Prophetischen Gerichtsreden* (BZAW 85; Berlin: Töpelmann, 1963; J. Limburg, "The Root RYB and the Prophetic Lawsuit Speeches," *JBL* 88 (1969) 291–304; K. Nielsen, *Yahweh as Prosecutor and Judge* (JSOTSup 9; Sheffield: Sheffield University Press, 1978); G. Liedke, "רִיב streiten," *THAT*, 2:771–77.

proclaimed with definitive court speech, readers of the text may raise questions. Where would the trial be opened? How could the defendant represent the entire "inhabitants of the land" or "sons of Israel"?[11] How could the defendant appeal his arraignment before the judge? Who would be the witnesses of the indictment? Who would be the court members other than the judge and the defendant, specifically, who would be the plaintiff? Why must the animals on the land, the birds of the sky, and the fish of the sea perish together with the human beings on the land because of their death penalty? Is the indictment only a warning for the people of Israel? These are some of the questions that could be raised by the notion of divine lawsuit, רִיב (rîb), in the prophecy of Hosea.

In this essay, we start our interpretation with the structural elements of the unit, so that we may ascertain how Hosea understood the religious reality of Yahweh worship among the people of Israel. Also, we must analyze an allusion that Hosea has suggested: the absence of the defendant from the divine court. Then we have to verify the purpose of Hosea in conceptualizing the fictional divine court against the people of Israel in his prophecy. Hopefully, these issues will focus on the vocation and the task of authentic Yahweh prophets like Hosea.

LAWSUIT OF YAHWEH: THE JUDGE AND THE DEFENDANT

The Hebrew term *rîb* functions to indicate the situation of the judge, the plaintiff, and the defendant. It also suggests the reason why the trial would be necessary, for the indictment is always defined with the charge. In my opinion, these legal settings by Hosea in our unit are related to the contemporary religious circumstances of the Israelite people. The setting of the trial of Yahweh works well to transmit the legal statement to the reader with definite terminology. Therefore, Hosea seems to express successfully Yahweh's will of judgment by addressing the criminal charge to the defendant.

Our interpretation starts by analyzing the composition of the unit in view of its legal constituents. According to our analysis, the unit is composed of four factors of legal proceedings: (1) the summoning of the defendant to the lawsuit, (2) the cause of the indictment against the defendant, (3) the prosecution of the defendant with a criminal charge, and (4) the sentence of the death penalty upon the defendant. Because of these components, one does not fail to understand that the divine judgment is inevitable for the defendant.

---

11. Cf. an argument by Andersen and Freedman, *Hosea*, 331n. and 336.

On the other hand, it is noteworthy that certain constituents are missing from this unit, for example, reference to the witnesses,[12] and the defendant pleading unfair to the criminal charge.[13] These are essential to legal proceedings in general.[14]

It is interesting that no space is given for the defendant to plead innocence.[15] Since no reference is made to a not-guilty plea to the criminal charge, the unit suggests that the trial seems to end without the defendant appearing in court. In fact, the sentence is proclaimed immediately after the criminal charge.

Reading the context of our unit from a legal perspective, one may doubt whether the defendant is present at the trial. Indeed, one might be inclined to admit that Hosea intentionally expresses the behavior of the defendant as not being present before the judge. This is our analysis of the unit, that the defendant is absent from the court in this divine trial.

Here is the crucial point for our interpretation: Hosea has made a conscious effort to drop the reference to the plea by the defendant against the charge. In other words, Hosea alludes to the reality of the defendant being absent from the court; namely, the inhabitants of the land would ignore the divine trial. Based on our interpretation that the defendant is absent from the court, one might be able to assume to know the religious attitude of the defendant behind the text: the inhabitants of the land may no longer appear in the court even though the messenger of Yahweh declared the divine court opened against them. This is mainly because they had no consciousness of their guilt before Yahweh.

According to our assumption, that must be the contemporary circumstances of the inhabitants of the land to whom Hosea had to address his message as a prophet. There must exist some sort of barrier between the people of Israel and Hosea the prophet of Yahweh.[16] It is a communication gap.

It seems that the cause Hosea has adopted in the trial could be related to a religious reality surrounding the inhabitants of Israel, as Hosea implies in our unit, for they are thought to be indifferent to

---

12. See Gen. 31:37; Jer. 26:11; 42:5.

13. Cf. Hos. 12:8. The speech by Ephraim functions as a plea of not guilty to the charge in the total structure based on the *rîb*-pattern in Hosea 12.

14. See H. J. Boecker, *Redeformen des Rechtslebens im Alten Testament* (WMANT 14; Neukirchen-Vluyn: Neukirchener, 1970) 152–53; 160–68.

15. The typical case of pleading innocence of the crime is found, for example, in Jer. 26:12–15; Hos. 12:8; Job 31:5ff.

16. See Wolff, *Hosea*, xxv (ET, xxx). Wolff indicates that some kerygmatic units were written down soon after Hosea had delivered his message.

the divine charge (4:2). They seem to have no consciousness of committing the crimes charged by Yahweh. The words of Hosea allude to how the inhabitants do not fear God. The indifference to committing such crimes is explained by Hosea as there being "no knowledge of God." It is supposed that the inhabitants may not appear in the divine court even if the summons was sent to them. This crisis in the court is represented by the composition of the unit,[17] alluding to the defendant being absent from the trial.

Hosea has deliberately composed the unit with particular intention. His aim is to allude to the religious and moral circumstances among the people of Israel. The unit is somehow short in view of adopting the *rîb*-pattern. According to our assumption, Hosea urges the reader to see the tragic reality of his contemporaries who dare to commit deadly crimes with disregard for the divine eyes.

Thus, Hosea utilizes a rhetorical device by conceptualizing what the serious situation of the people of Israel is. It is mainly because Hosea could no longer expect logical communication between the prophet and the addressee of the divine message as well as between Yahweh and the people of Israel.[18] He must find it quite difficult to make the people understand that they are the defendant in the divine court. Nevertheless he has utilized a genre with logical cause-and-effect explanations. There seems to be ambivalence in Hosea when he conceptualizes the message that the divine judgment would come upon his contemporaries. In other words, according to their sense of legal justice, the people of Israel would not admit any guilt, even if the divine judgment would be sentenced on them.[19] They seem to take it for granted that they are innocent of any divine charges because of their lack of self-consciousness.[20] No matter how difficult it might be, Hosea has to conceptualize the imminent divine judgment on his contemporaries, even though no one would listen to his message,[21] except a few of his disciples.[22]

Our next question is concerning the issue of how Hosea conceptualizes the divine judgment against the people of Israel, and why it should be the court before Yahweh.

---

17. Cf. Andersen and Freedman, *Hosea*, 333.
18. Cf. Hos. 6:5.
19. See Hos. 2:7b–15.
20. Hos. 7:2a; 12:9.
21. Hos. 6:4–6; 9:7
22. See Wolff, *Hosea*, xiv, xxv (ET, xvii, xxx).

YAHWEH'S WILL OF JUDGMENT: FICTION AND REALITY

We have started our consideration with a recognition that there must be a particular reason for the way in which Hosea has conceptualized the divine court. What Hosea has adopted in his message in our unit is not an ordinary prophetic warning.[23] Supposing Hosea has a motivation to condemn the inhabitants of the land because of their unconsciousness of the criminal charge, we had to ask why the absence of the defendant in the divine court must be the crucial signal for Hosea. It must be noted that the judge and the plaintiff in this court are no one but Yahweh the God of Israel. But how could it be a realistic oration to the contemporaries of Hosea?

Although the trial settled by Hosea manifests the legal and the religious relationship between Israel and Yahweh, we must admit that the trial itself is a fiction. Since the contemporary situation for the prophet is a tragic one in that the inhabitants of the land could no longer recognize their guilt before Yahweh their God, one could say that Hosea needed to define them as the defendant of a criminal charge and force them to stand in front of the judge. According to Hosea, the court would be opened regardless of whether they refuse the trial itself. In other words, Hosea managed to conceptualize the circumstances of his contemporaries by means of setting the fictional court where the people of Israel should be summoned.

It was not an easy choice for Hosea. The fiction of the trial would be effective only if the reader or the addressee of the oracle might be ready to understand its real meaning regarding the divine judgment. The tragic situation is that there is a communication gap between the sender of the message and the recipients of it. For Hosea, the recipients of the oracle are not able to realize the divine will insofar as they refuse to appear in the divine court. They refuse to appear because of their stiff-necked religious attitude toward their God, which Hosea has suggested several times in his prophecy.[24] According to the common understanding of the inhabitants of the land, their God is always merciful in granting them fullness of blessing.[25] They are not, so to speak, ready to meet their God in any tragic circumstances.[26]

As one of the causes of the divine indictment, Hosea takes into account "no knowledge of God" (4:1b). If there is no knowledge of God

---

23. For instance, see, among others, C. Westermann, *Grundformen prophetischer Rede*, 143–45.; W. E. March, "Prophecy," in J. H. Hayes, ed., *Old Testament Form Criticism* (San Antonio, Tex.: Trinity University Press, 1974) 141–77.
24. See, for example, Hos. 4:4–19; 6:1–3, 4–6; 7:11; 8:11ff.; 10:1ff.
25. See Hos. 6:1–3.
26. Hos. 8:2.

among the people of Israel, the indictment should become meaningless, even though Hosea has declared that Yahweh has a lawsuit. Without knowledge of God, the people of Israel could never understand that Yahweh is angry with them. "No knowledge of God" suggests that they are unconscious of their own behavior when they profane the name of God. In addition, "no faithfulness, no loyalty"[27] means no fear of God. Thus, "no knowledge of God" symbolizes how the accused, who should be the defendant in the divine trial, knows nothing about the trial or the indictment against him.

However the plaintiff may indict the defendant with the charge of "cursing, lying, murdering, stealing, and committing adultery" (4:2a), the indictment itself is in vain because the defendant is absent from court and ignores the charge. That means that they ignore Yahweh the God of Israel, who meets them as judge. The result of ignoring the criminal charge is that "bloodshed follows bloodshed" (4:2b).

This manifests the religious and the legal reality of the times when Hosea lived as Yahweh's prophet. In fact, what seems to be a most serious matter in the eyes of our prophet is the senselessness of the people, the lack of religious faithfulness or loyalty to Yahweh the God of Israel.

Supposing such a social and religious crisis as we have noted, one may ask how a prophet like Hosea could have made the divine will of judgment known to the inhabitants of the land. In my opinion, this crisis is the reason why Hosea has utilized the legal genre in addressing the people of Israel. In short, Hosea must make the people of Israel be a defendant standing before the judge, at least in a fictional setting of a trial.

Once again we must remember that the lawsuit proclamation could not reach its recipients due to their lack of consciousness of the criminal charge. The result of the setting in fiction is obvious: the defendant will not appear before the court, nor take the legal opportunity to plead innocent of the criminal charge to the judge.

Based on this point of view, the situation is clear as to the death penalty to the defendant, the people of Israel. Because they live quite indifferently to the divine will, the judgment will come upon them by calamity. They will not understand the divine meaning behind the disaster. If the divine meaning is lost, then "the land mourns and all who live in it languish" — it is a tragedy. We assume that Hosea's aim is found in this logical consequence expressed by the legal language.

---

27. See H. W. Wolff, " 'Wissen um Gott' bei Hosea als Urform von Theologie," in *Gesammelte Studien zum Alten Testament* (TB 22; Neukirchen-Vluyn: Neukirchener, 1964) 182–205. In regard to "no loyalty," cf. his translation "Bundestreue" (182).

ENCOUNTER WITH YAHWEH THROUGH JUDGMENT:
SENTENCE OF GUILTY AND JOINT RESPONSIBILITY

Based on our observations on the composition of Hos. 4:1–3, we summarize that Hosea conceptualizes the divine court in the framework of
a fiction. The legal setting gives him an opportunity to define what the
serious crime before Yahweh is all about. He has adopted the fiction of
the trial in his message in a rhetorical way so that he could make the
defendant stand before Yahweh regardless of what the people of Israel
would respond to.

On the other hand, our question now comes to whether the fiction of
the divine court would fit with the sentence of the death penalty in Hos.
4:3. Our consideration is focused on the joint responsibility.[28] The issue
is whether the sentence of the death penalty itself makes sense in the
event that the defendant is absent from court, whether the fiction of the
divine court really functions to let the inhabitants of the land realize
the divine will in the midst of the historical catastrophe, whether they
could understand it as a penalty from Yahweh, and so on.

Presupposing with Hosea that there is no room for the inhabitants of
the land to meet their God despite the fact that the cult was prosperous
at that time,[29] it can be said that the people refuse to stand before their
furious God not only in the fictional setting of the trial but also in the
historical destruction itself. The inhabitants of the land are definitely
not ready to meet their God in tragic circumstances.[30]

Surprisingly, Hosea claims the death penalty to be the total destruction of the inhabitants of the land together with the animals of the
land, the birds of the sky, and even the fish of the sea. As a matter
of logical consequence, it is not possible to determine why the animals,
the birds, and the fish should perish together with the defendant on
account of his criminal acts. This joint responsibility could never be attributed to the so-called "corporate personality."[31] Here we claim that
this joint responsibility for the death penalty also is a fiction by Hosea.

Hosea conceptualizes the tragedy in the form of fiction because of the
communication gap between his contemporaries and him. The inhabitants of the land could acknowledge the divine will, and they could be

---

28. According to J. L. Mays, "the announcement of punishment (V. 3) states the
sentence of the divine court" (*Hosea*, 61).

29. See Hos. 4:8, 12; 8:11; 13:2.

30. Hos. 6:1–3 must represent how the people responded deceptively. See also Hos.
7:14; 11:7.

31. Cf. H. W. Robinson, *Corporate Personality in Ancient Israel* (rev. ed.; Philadelphia:
Fortress, 1964). The concept of "corporate" does not include the creatures in general.
According to Hosea, it may be symbolized as the togetherness in 2:20; however, it is a
fiction.

the only representatives in the land who are eligible to know the God of Israel. When the inhabitants of the land, i.e., the people of Israel, refuse the divine judgement, other creatures such as "the wild animals," "the birds of the sky," and "the fish of the sea" would have no way to recognize the cause and effect of divine punishment and destruction. Their destruction would be totally meaningless.[32] This situation is presented by Hosea in the form of fiction. Fiction has the function of revealing the meaningless death of the people of Israel. In fact, Hosea states it as self-destruction in his prophecy.[33]

On the contrary, if they should meet their God in the midst of catastrophe, their death would become meaningful in view of a divine encounter through judgment. However, in that case the fiction of the trial becomes nonsense after all. In addition to that, an affirmative perspective of encounter with God is impossible, since there is no way for them to recognize their fate as the death penalty without knowing the trial. The communication gap will end in tragedy in the historical catastrophe as well as in the divine trial according to Hosea.[34]

Thus, they will never encounter Yahweh in such a catastrophe as in the fall of Samaria,[35] and then they will die for nothing. Ironically, their destruction has nothing to do with the divine character in the historical reality, however their meaningless fate reveals the divine judgment to the contrary. In short, their fate must be characterized as self-destruction in the eyes of Hosea.

We indicate here that Hosea states the death penalty of joint responsibility through the natural disaster,[36] caused by the crimes as well as the related religious and moral unconsciousness of his contemporaries. The death penalty will come to the inhabitants of the land and reveal the meaningless destruction. It symbolizes the chaos.

It could be the only way for Hosea to conceptualize the death penalty to which the defendant was sentenced regardless of whether he followed or refused to follow the court procedure in front of the judge, and whether or not he ignored the divine interventions in the real world. Only by the fiction could Hosea successfully symbolize the major responsibility of the defendant.

---

32. Hos. 5:14f. If Yahweh returns to the divine abode, in other words, God withdraws from the realm of history, then the historical destruction would lose its divine character and become totally meaningless.

33. Hos. 4:14. Regarding the built-in consequences, see K. Koch, "Is There a Doctrine of Retribution in the Old Testament?" in J. L. Crenshaw, ed., *Theodicy in the Old Testament* (Philadelphia: Fortress, 1983) 57–87; see especially 64–69.

34. For instance, see Hos. 5:8ff.; 6:1–6; 7:8ff.; 8:7f.; 9:3; 9:16; 10:5ff., 11ff.; 14:1.

35. Hos. 14:1; 2 Kings 17:1–6.

36. Wolff indicates it as a great drought (*Hosea*, 85 [ET, 68]).

FICTION AS THOUGHT: VOCATION AND ROLE OF THE PROPHET

The result of our consideration concerning the reality that Hosea has managed to conceptualize with the fiction of a divine trial leads us to reexamine the role of a prophet like Hosea. The prophets in ancient Israel are not defined only as those who delivered oracles in public.[37] The role of the prophet must be distinguished from that of the medium in general. Hosea is not the type of prophet whose vocation is to vocalize the divine speech as what he had heard.

If our interpretation of the unit of Hos. 4:1–3 is correct, we must assume that a role of Hosea as a prophet is recognized in his conceptualizing of divine will by means of his own concept of logic. Hosea has adopted fiction as a tool of expressing thought. It works well when he draws an eschatological scenario of the divine judgment.

If the scenario of the judgment in the form of destruction (4:3) could be illustrated only by a fiction, as the divine court set by Hosea (4:1), the view of the historical catastrophe of Samaria (14:1) would be a fiction too. According to our interpretation, the reference to the fall of Samaria has nothing to do with Hosea's motivation to verify the historicity of the destruction with pictorial accuracy. He also reminds the reader, or the addressee, of its historical meaning, i.e., Yahweh's will.

Interestingly, Hosea describes the destruction of Israel also in Hos. 5:14–15 as well as in 4:3. A similarity in both cases is undeniable. The fiction is a part of metaphor for Hosea. His reference to the Syria-Ephraimite war in 5:14–15 is full of rhetorical expressions:

> For I am like a lion to Ephraim,
>   like a young lion to the house of Judah.
> I, even I, will rend and go away;
>   I will carry off, so that none shall rescue.
> I will withdraw to my abode
>   until they realize their guilt
>   and seek my face.
> When they are in distress, they will ask for me.

The nature of the metaphor is obvious. According to Hosea, Yahweh will attack the army of Israel almost like an Assyrian army itself, and suddenly return to the divine place. This is a fiction in that Yahweh will act in the middle of the battlefield to beat the Israelite soldiers to the

---

37. Cf. Max Weber, *Das antike Judentum* (Gesammelte Aufsätze zur Religionssoziologie 3; Tübingen: J. C. B. Mohr) 281–82; ET, *Ancient Judaism* (trans. H. H. Gerth and D. Martindale; New York: Free Press, 1952) 267–68; idem, *Wirtschaft und Gesellschaft: Grundriß der verstehenden Soziologie* (Tübingen: J. C. B. Mohr [Paul Siebeck], 1922) 268ff.; ET, *The Sociology of Religion* (trans. E. Fischoff; Boston: Beacon, 1956) 46–59. In regard to recent examination on the role of prophets, see D. L. Petersen, *The Roles of Israel's Prophets* (JSOTSup 17; Sheffield: JSOT Press, 1981) 9–15.

ground. Then Hosea expresses that Yahweh will return to the divine place from the battlefield, that is, withdraw from the historical plane. This action of going into and out of the historical plane is a fiction by nature. This example leads us to affirm that Hosea uses a fiction in his rhetoric to conceptualize how the judgment will come upon the people of Israel.

If our interpretation is correct, Hosea utilizes a fiction to proclaim that the divine judgment will come into the historical plane regardless of whether any human perspective is conscious or unconscious of the divine judgment. That does not mean that Hosea's prophecy of the judgment is unrealistic. On the contrary, Hosea's sense of reality is observed in his image of judgment.

For Hosea, fiction is his major tool of conceptualization of the divine will. Only by means of fiction could Hosea conceptualize the catastrophe as the death penalty. He must be conscious of his vocation as a prophet of Yahweh in his role as the witness in the trial.

Selected Bibliography

Boecker, H. J. *Recht und Gesetz im Alten Testament und im Alten Orient.* Neukirchen-Vluyn: Neukirchener, 1984. ET: *Law and the Administration of Justice in the Old Testament and Ancient East.* Trans. J. Moiser. Minneapolis: Augsburg, 1980.

———. *Redeformen des Rechtslebens im Alten Testament.* WMANT 14. Neukirchen-Vluyn: Neukirchener, 1970.

Huffmon, H. B. "The Covenant Lawsuit in the Prophets." *JBL* 78 (1959) 285–95.

Gemser, B. "The *Rîb-* or Controversy-Pattern in Hebrew Mentality." VTSup 3 (1955) 120–37.

Harvey, H. "Le 'Rîb-Pattern,' réquisitoire prophétique sur la rupture de l'alliance." *Bib* 43 (1962) 172–96.

Koch, K. "Is There a Doctrine of Retribution in the Old Testament?" In *Theodicy in the Old Testament,* ed. J. L. Crenshaw, pp. 57–87. Philadelphia: Fortress, 1983.

Liedke, G. "ריב streiten," *THAT.* Band 2, ed. E. Jenni and C. Westermann, pp. 771–77. Munich: Kaiser, 1984.

Limburg, J. "The Root RYB and the Prophetic Lawsuit Speeches." *JBL* 88 (1969) 291–304.

Nielsen, K. *Yahweh as Prosecutor and Judge.* JSOTSup 9. Sheffield: Sheffield University Press, 1978.

von Waldow, E. *Die Traditionsgeschichtliche Hintergrund der Prophetischen Gerichtsreden.* BZAW 85. Berlin: Alfred Töpelmann, 1963.

Westermann, C. *Grundformen prophetischer Rede.* BEvT 31. Munich: Kaiser, 1971.

Wolff, H. W. " 'Wissen um Gott' bei Hosea als Urform von Theologie." In *Gesammelte Studien zum Alten Testament,* 182–205. TB 22. Neukirchen-Vluyn: Neukirchener, 1964.

Wright, G. W. "The Lawsuit of God: A Form-Critical Study of Deuteronomy 32." In *Israel's Prophetic Heritage: Essays in Honor of James Muilenburg,* ed. B. W. Andersen and W. Harrelson, pp. 26–67. New York: Harper, 1962.

14

Absence of G-d and Human Responsibility in the Book of Esther

Marvin A. Sweeney

INTRODUCTION

In his recent study of the Jewish Bible after the Holocaust, Emil Facken-heim argues that, in the aftermath of the Shoah, the existence of both Jews and Christians and their reading of the Bible can never again be what it once was.[1] As a result of the Shoah, Jews became the children of Job, for whom choice was destroyed. Christians, on the other hand, have been given a new choice, to acquiesce in the destruction of Jews and Judaism or not to acquiesce and to identify with Jews unto death. Such a scenario calls for a radical rethinking of theology, both Jewish and Christian, and a rethinking of the paradigms by which biblical books are read. This essay explores such a rereading of the book of Esther, clearly one of the most difficult theological books of the Hebrew Bible, in the aftermath of the Shoah.[2] Esther presents tremendous challenges to both Christian and Jewish scholars in their attempts to incorporate an assessment of the book within the framework of a comprehensive theological interpretation of the Hebrew Bible, such as that called for by Rolf Knierim.[3] The book presents the story of the origins of the Jew-ish holiday of Purim, in which Esther, the Jewish queen of the Persian

---

The author dedicates this essay to the memory of Charles V. Dorothy, Ph.D.

1. Emil Fackenheim, *The Jewish Bible After the Holocaust: A Rereading* (Bloomington: Indiana University Press, 1990) 19.
2. For discussion of theological issues posed by the Shoah, see especially Steven T. Katz, "Jewish Faith after the Holocaust: Four Approaches," in *Post-Holocaust Dialogues: Critical Studies in Modern Jewish Thought* (New York: New York University Press, 1985) 141–73, and Clark M. Williamson, *A Guest in the House of Israel: Post-Holocaust Church Theology* (Louisville: Westminster John Knox, 1993). For discussion of the implications of the Shoah for biblical theology in particular, see my essay, "Reconceiving the Paradigms of Old Testament Theology in the Post-*Shoah* Period," *BibInt* 6 (1998) 142–61. See also Edward L. Greenstein, "A Jewish Reading of Esther," in Jacob Neusner, Baruch A. Levine, and Ernest S. Frerichs, eds., *Judaic Perspectives on Ancient Israel* (Philadelphia: Fortress, 1987) 225–43, which presents a survey of issues relevant to a Jewish reading of the book of Esther.
3. See Rolf P. Knierim, "The Task of Old Testament Theology," in *The Task of Old Testament Theology: Substance, Method, and Cases* (Grand Rapids: Eerdmans, 1995) 1–20, esp. 1–7. Knierim's study does not take up Esther, but it conveys one of the plurality of theologies

monarch Ahasuerus, and her uncle Mordecai save the Jewish population of the Persian Empire from extermination at the hands of the evil
royal minister Haman. The root of the theological difficulty lies in the
complete absence of any mention of G-d in the Hebrew version of the
book, generally conceded to be the oldest version of Esther, which functions as sacred Scripture in both Protestant Christianity and Judaism.
Although chance and coincidence play important roles in the plot of
the narrative, the book portrays the deliverance of the Jewish community not as an act of G-d, but as the result of actions by the human
protagonists of the story.

In addition to the focus on human rather than divine action, other
factors present problems to Christian theologians in particular, such
as the alleged focus on Jewish "nationalism" or "particularism" rather
than upon "universal" values, and the slaughter of the enemies of
the Jews throughout the Persian Empire following the discovery of
Haman's plot.[4] As a result, Christian biblical theologians frequently express perplexity or hostility in their attempts to interpret Esther, and
some have even questioned the role of Esther as a book of Christian
Scripture.

Nevertheless, Esther constitutes one of the books of both the Christian and Jewish Bibles, and it must be taken seriously as such, particularly in the aftermath of the Shoah.[5] The book addresses the potential
extermination of the Jewish people by a Gentile nation, and it does
so in a context in which G-d fails to act in any clearly demonstrable
manner. This has especially important implications for Christian bibli-

---

in the Hebrew Bible that must be accounted for. For summaries of discussion concerning
the book of Esther, see Carey A. Moore, "Esther, Book of," *ABD*, 2:633–43; Gillis Gerleman, *Esther* (BKAT 21; Neukirchen-Vluyn: Neukirchener, 1973), esp. 1–7; Lewis B. Paton,
The Book of Esther (ICC; Edinburgh: T. & T. Clark, 1908), esp. 97–118.

4. For a critique of those who charge that "nationalism" permeates the book of Esther, see Jon D. Levenson, "The Scroll of Esther in Ecumenical Perspective," *Journal of
Ecumenical Studies* 13 (1976) 440–52.

5. For discussion of the use of the Hebrew term *Shoah*, rather than "Holocaust," to label the attempted genocide against the Jewish people during World War II, see Zev Garber
and Bruce Zuckerman, "Why Do We Call the Holocaust 'The Holocaust'? An Inquiry into
the Psychology of Labels," *Modern Judaism* 9 (1989) 197–211; repr. in Zev Garber, *Shoah:
The Paradigmatic Genocide: Essays in Exegesis and Eisegesis* (Studies in the Shoah 8; Lanham,
Md.: University Press of America, 1994) 51–66. As Garber and Zuckerman note, the term
"holocaust" is a translation of the Hebrew term, *ōlâ*, or "whole burnt offering," which was
offered daily in the ancient Jerusalem temple (see Leviticus 1). Its function was in part to
honor G-d and to aid in maintaining the stability of the created world (see Jon D. Levenson, "The Temple and the World," *JR* 64 [1984] 275–98). The use of the term "Holocaust"
thereby implies that the attempted murder of European Jews was somehow sanctioned by
G-d and that it was intended to serve the divinely created world order. By contrast, the
Hebrew word *šō'â* simply means "destruction" and implies no theological legitimization
of the attempted genocide or moral evaluation of its victims.

cal interpretation, which relies primarily on a theological paradigm by which to read the Bible. It demonstrates that theology alone may not provide a fully adequate framework for the interpretation of the Bible in Christianity.[6] G-d is sometimes absent or fails to act in the Bible or in the world at large, and human beings are therefore left to assume responsibility for overcoming evil in the world.

In keeping with these concerns, the balance of this essay treats three topics: (1) problems posed by the absence of G-d and violence in Esther to interpreters of the Hebrew Bible; (2) the generic literary character of Esther and the presentation of its primary protagonists; and (3) evaluation of the themes absence of G-d and human action in a post-Shoah reading of the book.

THE ABSENCE OF GOD AND VIOLENCE IN ESTHER

The absence of G-d in Esther clearly constitutes the basis for difficulties with the book in both Judaism and in Christianity. G-d is never mentioned in any direct manner, although many take the references to "relief and deliverance...from another quarter" in 4:14 or to the efficacy of fasting in 4:16 as veiled references to the Deity.[7] Others point to the role that coincidence or chance plays in seeing to the deliverance of Jews from Haman's plot as signs of divine intervention or control of events:[8] Mordecai, while sitting at the gate, by chance overhears a plot to assassinate Ahasuerus and warns the king through Esther (2:19–23); Haman just happens to approach Ahasuerus at a time when the king wishes to honor Mordecai for saving him from the assassination attempt (6:1–11); Haman accidentally falls on Esther's couch just as Ahasuerus reenters the banquet hall, convincing the king that Haman meant to assault her sexually (7:7–8). Nevertheless, such contentions appear to be rationalizations for the absence of G-d in the text; chance does indeed play a role, but Esther, Mordecai, Ahasuerus, and others make decisions and undertake actions that ultimately see to the deliverance of the Jewish people.

Others argue that G-d must have appeared in the book in some form, but that a later reworking of Esther removed any reference to the Deity.[9] There is absolutely no objective evidence for such a conclusion, as

---

6. See my essay, "Why Jews Should Be Interested in Biblical Theology," *CCAR Journal* 44, no. 1 (winter 1997) 67–75, esp. 71–72, which questions whether theology offers an adequate basis for a comprehensive interpretation of the Hebrew Bible.

7. For example, Sandra Beth Berg, *The Book of Esther: Motifs, Themes and Structure* (SBLDS 44; Missoula, Mont.: Scholars Press, 1979) 177–79.

8. For example, David J. A. Clines, *The Esther Scroll: The Story of the Story* (JSOTSup 30; Sheffield: JSOT Press, 1984) 153–58.

9. Moore, "Esther," 2:636.

no pre-Masoretic manuscript or version of the book is extant. No copy of Esther has been found among the scrolls from the Judean wilderness, which, with only a few exceptions, are generally regarded as the earliest extant Hebrew manuscripts of the Bible. The early Greek versions of Esther contain various texts that do not appear in the Hebrew version of the book and that refer explicitly to G-d. Nevertheless, the references to G-d in the Greek versions of Esther appear in texts that are generally regarded as secondary additions to or reworkings of the earlier Hebrew form of the book.[10] The Greek versions of Esther constitute some of the earliest attempts to interpret the book. In part, the additions to Esther likely reflect the discomfort felt by the translators or composers of the Greek texts of Esther, who sought to overcome the problems posed by the absence of G-d in the text by adding material that refers specifically to the Deity and to prayer by the major protagonists. Nevertheless, interpreters must recognize that G-d simply does not appear in the earliest form of the book of Esther, and its major Jewish characters demonstrate no clear interest in G-d or in Jewish religious practice.

The second major problem in the interpretation of Esther is the portrayal of the massacre of Haman, his family, and his supporters. Following the revelation of Haman's plot to exterminate the Jews of the Persian Empire, Ahasuerus grants Jews the right "to gather and defend their lives, to destroy, to slay, and to annihilate any armed force of any people or province that might attack them, with their children and women, and to plunder their goods" (8:11). Haman was hanged, and on the day that Haman's decree was to take place, Jews in the capital of Susa attacked and killed the ten sons of Haman and eight hundred of Haman's supporters. On the next day, Jews throughout the empire killed seventy-five thousand of those who hated them. The result of the massacre was two days of feasting and rejoicing and the institution of the festival of Purim. Many have seen in these actions a vengeful, bloodthirsty, and chauvinistic spirit that can hardly serve as an inspiring model for forgiveness, mercy, and kindness. To be fair, however, such interpretations generally fail to note that the killing was limited to those who sought to kill Jews, and the narrative states repeatedly that Jews refused to take plunder from their victims. The celebration was for the deliverance of the Jewish people from destruction, not for the opportunity to destroy others.[11]

---

10. For a full discussion of the literary character of the Hebrew and the two Greek versions of the book of Esther, see Charles V. Dorothy, *The Books of Esther: Structure, Genre, and Textual Integrity* (JSOTSup 187; Sheffield: Sheffield Academic Press, 1996).

11. See Greenstein, "A Jewish Reading of Esther," 226.

Both the so-called secular nature of the book and its portrayal of violence have clearly caused a great deal of discomfort to its later interpreters, both Jewish and Christian. Rabbinic authorities raised questions concerning Esther's canonical status, insofar as the book might provoke animosity against Jews among the Gentiles, and because Purim was not explicitly authorized by Moses in the Torah.[12] Medieval Jewish commentators went to great lengths to demonstrate that G-d was indeed active behind the scenes in Esther and that the descendants of Haman survived the massacre to study Torah in Bene Berak, the location where Rabbi Akiva, one of the leading sages of talmudic tradition, established his yeshiva, or rabbinical academy, in the aftermath of the Roman destruction of the second temple.[13] Modern Jewish commentators are sometimes ambivalent about Esther. Schalom Ben-Chorin argues that "both festival and book are unworthy of a people which is disposed to bring about its national and moral regeneration under prodigious sacrifice." Elias Bickerman considers Esther to be one of four "strange books" of the Bible because it fails to mention G-d.[14]

Christian interpreters have been even more vociferous in their criticism and frequent rejection of the book. Many early church fathers, including Melito of Sardis (fl. ca. 167), Athanasius (295–373), Gregory of Nazianzus (329–390), Theodore of Mopsuestia (350?–428), and others, denied the canonical status of the book.[15] Martin Luther, the founder of the Protestant Reformation, declared in his *Tischreden*, "I am so hostile to the book (2 Maccabees) and to Esther that I wish they did not exist at all; for they Judaize too much and have much heathen perverseness."[16]

---

12. *b. Megillah* 7a; *y. Megillah* 70d.

13. Barry Dov Walfish, *Esther in Medieval Garb: Jewish Interpretation of the Book of Esther in the Middle Ages* (Albany: State University of New York Press, 1993). For discussion of Rabbi Akiva, see "Akiva," *EncJud*, 2, cols. 488–92. Note well that the yeshivot established by Rabbis Yohanan ben Zakkai in Yavneh and Akiva ben Joseph in Bene Berak are credited with the survival and continuing development of Judaism in the period following the destruction of the second temple by the Romans. For discussion, see Robert Seltzer, *Jewish People, Jewish Thought* (New York: Macmillan, 1980) 245–56; Emil Schürer, *The History of the Jewish People in the Age of Jesus Christ (175 B.C.–A.D. 135)* (4 vols.; rev. and ed. Geza Vermes and Fergus Millar; Edinburgh: T. & T. Clark, 1973) 1:514–28; Isaiah M. Gafni, "The Historical Background," in Shmuel Safrai, ed., *The Literature of the Sages* (CRINT 2 [3.1]; Maastricht: Van Gorcum; Philadelphia: Fortress, 1987) 14–20; Shaye J. D. Cohen, *From the Maccabees to the Mishnah* (Philadelphia: Westminster, 1987) 214–31.

14. Schalom Ben-Chorin, *Kritik des Estherbuches. Eine theologisches Streitschrift* (Jerusalem: Salingré, 1938) 5 (unavailable to me; the translation of his comment is from Bernhard W. Anderson, "The Place of the Book of Esther in the Christian Bible," *JR* 30 [1950] 32–43, 34); Elias Bickerman, *Four Strange Books of the Bible* (New York: Schocken, 1967).

15. Moore, "Esther," 635.

16. Cited in Anderson, "The Place of the Book of Esther," 33. See also Hans Bardtke, *Luther und das Buch Esther* (Tübingen: J. C. B. Mohr [Paul Siebeck], 1964) 72–73. Bardtke

More recently, Wilhelm Vischer states that "the book of Esther presents the Jewish question in full sharpness [das Estherbuch stellt die Juden-frage in voller Schärfe]," and argues that the answer to the question of who should hang on the gallows is to be found in the crucifixion of Jesus, "through whom he grants peace in place of mortal enmity, between Jew and non-Jew [dadurch stiftet er den Frieden für Todfeind-schaft zwischen den Juden und den Nichtjuden]."[17] Robert Pfeiffer states in a diatribe against modern Zionism that "such a secular book hardly deserves a place in the canon of Sacred Scriptures";[18] Bernhard Anderson decries the "fierce nationalism and unblushing vindictiveness which stand in glaring contradiction to the Sermon on the Mount";[19] and Gerhard von Rad omits the book entirely from his acclaimed *Old Testament Theology*, which emphasizes the "Salvation History" that in his view permeates the entire Hebrew Bible,[20] except perhaps for Esther.

Altogether, both Jewish and Christian scholars seem to recoil from Esther because it does not conform to fixed ideas about what should constitute a biblical book. It does not mention G-d, it does not promote religious observance, it does not testify to divine mercy or peace, and it advocates death for enemies. And yet, this is precisely the point. The absence of G-d must be recognized as a fundamental premise of the book; attempts to read G-d into the book violate the integrity of its message and must be rejected categorically. At times in human experience, G-d does not always act in the face of evil, and the book of Esther presents the reader with that reality. Furthermore, the book of Esther is a part of both the Jewish and Christian canons of the Bible. It is sacred Scripture in both traditions, and as such, it demands a hearing on its own terms.

THE LITERARY CHARACTER OF ESTHER AND HUMAN RESPONSIBILITY

In order to assess the significance of Esther's message concerning the absence of G-d in the face of evil, it is necessary to come to some under-standing of the book's generic literary character. On the surface, it is presented as a historical narrative set in the court of the Achaemenid king Xerxes I of Persia (reigned 486–465 B.C.E.), rendered as Ahasuerus in Hebrew. Various features of the book correspond to what is known of

---

provides a comprehensive analysis of Luther's views on Esther, both positive and negative.

17. Wilhelm Vischer, *Esther* (TEH 48; Munich: Kaiser, 1937) 14, 21–22.

18. Robert H. Pfeiffer, *Introduction to the Old Testament* (New York: Harper & Bros., 1948) 743.

19. Anderson, "The Place of the Book of Esther," 32.

20. Gerhard von Rad, *Old Testament Theology* (2 vols.; trans. D. M. G. Stalker; New York: Harper and Row, 1962–65).

the historical monarch Xerxes I. He ruled an empire that extended from India to Ethiopia, had a winter palace at Susa, had a reputation for his lavish banquets and copious drinking, suffered harem intrigues as a result of his sexual appetites, and was known for extravagant promises or gifts as well as for a nasty temper.[21] Various scholars have attempted to establish some element of historicity to the narrative by pointing to these features and by identifying Mordecai with a Persian official named Mardukâ, whose name appears in a text from the late reign of Darius or the early reign of Xerxes.[22]

Nevertheless, there is clearly very little basis for such attempts. Xerxes was never known to have a queen named Vashti or Esther; his queen between the seventh and twelfth years of his reign (cf. Esther 2:16; 3:7) was named Amestris, who was known for her vengeance against Xerxes' paramours. Furthermore, Persian queens were required to come from one of seven noble Persian families, which would have rendered Xerxes' marriage to a Jewish woman such as Esther impossible. Various elements of the narrative do seem to correlate to historical realities of Xerxes and his reign, but they also show a great deal of divergence from the facts. The name of his mother was Atossa, the daughter of Cyrus and wife of Darius, which may well underlie Esther's Hebrew name of Hadassah. The Persian Empire was indeed divided into satrapies, but they numbered twenty and not 127 (cf. Esther 1:1). Xerxes was the target of conspiracy, but it was successful in that he was assassinated in his bedroom by his uncle Artabanus and his grandson Megabyzys.

Overall, the book presupposes the historical figure of the Persian monarch Xerxes, but it is clearly a highly fictionalized account of events in his reign. Elements of reversal and exaggeration, bordering on the comedic, play especially major roles in the development of the plot.[23] Ahasuerus is presented not as the great Xerxes I, king of Persia, who mounted invasions against Greece and built the royal city of Persepolis, but as a weak, fickle, and usually drunken fool who is unable to make any but the most trivial or petty decisions. Ahasuerus deposes Queen Vashti for her refusal to obey his command to "show her beauty" before his drunken (male) guests during a banquet that lasted for 180 days. As a result, he sends a decree throughout the empire that commands women to honor their husbands and that every man be lord in

21. In addition to Moore, "Esther," see Carey A. Moore, *Esther* (AB 7B; Garden City, N.Y.: Doubleday, 1971), esp. xxxiv–xli.

22. See Moore, *Esther*, l, and the literature cited there, esp. A. Ungnad, "Keilinschriftliche Beiträge zum Buch Esra und Ester," *ZAW* 58 (1940–41) 240–44.

23. For an attempt to read Esther along these lines, see Kenneth Craig, *Reading Esther: A Case for the Literary Carnivalesque* (LCBI; Louisville: Westminster John Knox, 1995).

his own house. He selects Esther as his queen as the result of an empire-wide beauty contest in which beautiful young women were prepared for twelve months for the one night they would spend in the royal harem to see if the king would be pleased. Esther's marriage to Ahasuerus is not only improbable because of Persian custom concerning the queenship, but it takes the unlikely motif of the intermarriage of a Jewish woman to a Gentile man to extremes by identifying the Gentile man as the ruler of the greatest empire of the day. Haman's plot to kill all the Jews of the empire was caused by the refusal of Mordecai, the uncle and stepfather of Esther, to bow down before him because he was a Jew. Ahasuerus's command that Haman honor Mordecai for saving the king from an assassination attempt clearly reverses Haman's plan, as he is the one who is to parade Mordecai through the streets of Susa announcing, "So shall it be done to the man whom the king delights to honor." When Haman is identified by Esther at a banquet with the king as the man who desires to kill her and her people, Haman conveniently stumbles onto Esther's couch, just as the king reenters the room, and appears to assault the queen. Haman and his ten sons are hanged on the gallows prepared for the Jews; Mordecai is made prime minister in the place of Haman; and the king issues a decree that allows the Jews of the empire to defend themselves and kill all of their enemies who attempt to attack them. Throughout the narrative, Ahasuerus stands idly by and allows others — Haman, Esther, Mordecai, and his servants — to make decisions for him and to control the course of action.

Clearly, Esther highlights the potential danger to the Jewish people living in diaspora under the control of a foreign monarch, who on the slightest pretext allows his court ministers to enact a program of genocide against them. Just as Ahasuerus deposes Vashti for her refusal to show her beauty, so he authorizes Haman to destroy the Jewish people because it does not profit the king to tolerate him. The arbitrariness of the decision is highlighted by the notice that Haman did not bring his charges to the king until the daily casting of the Pur, or lot, indicated that it was a propitious day to do so. After Haman's plot is exposed, Ahasuerus just as easily decrees that the Jewish people would be able to annihilate any people or province, including women and children, that might attack them (8:11). The book of Esther cannot be taken seriously as historical narrative; it is a parody that presents the problem of threats faced by Jews when living in a Gentile world.[24]

It is in the context of such literary exaggeration and reversal that

---

24. See Lawrence M. Wills, *The Jew in the Court of the Foreign King: Ancient Jewish Court Legends* (HDR 26; Minneapolis: Fortress, 1990), esp. 153–91. Wills considers Esther to be an example of the "Jewish Court Legend" genre.

the identities of the primary protagonists become especially important. Mordecai, Esther, and Haman are identified with figures from past
tradition that speak to the failure of Jews to destroy an enemy that
threatens their existence.[25] Mordecai is identified in 2:5 as the son of Jair,
son of Shimei, son of Kish, a Benjaminite. His pedigree is particularly
important in that it has been long recognized as a means to identify
both Mordecai and his niece Esther as descendants of Saul son of Kish,
the first king of Israel. Haman likewise is named in 3:1 as the Agagite,
the son of Hammedatha, which identifies him as a descendant of the
Amalekite king Agag.

The significance of this identification is essential for understanding
the purposes of the Esther narrative. According to 1 Samuel 15, Saul
lost his kingship for his failure to destroy the Amalekite king Agag
and his retinue in accordance with the command of G-d. It was only
when the prophet Samuel appeared on the scene that Agag was hewn
down, and the prophet declared that Saul had thereby lost his kingship for his failure to obey the command of G-d. The reasons for such a
command appear both in the narrative of 1 Samuel 15 and in the narratives concerning Israel's experience in the wilderness of Sinai. Amalek
is identified in Exod. 17:8–15 and Deut. 25:17–19 as the people who attacked Israel in the wilderness "when you were faint and weary, and
cut off at your rear all who were faint and weary." Because tradition
presents the Amalekites as a people who sought the total destruction of
Israel, a special curse is directed against Amalek to "blot out the remem-
brance of Amalek from under heaven." In essence, Amalek symbolizes,
both in biblical and subsequent rabbinical tradition, the enemy of Israel par excellence who seeks the total annihilation of the Jews.[26] As a
result of his failure to destroy the Amalekites, Saul's kingship quickly
declines. Saul is unable to protect Israel from its enemies, and focuses
instead on his attempts to kill David and even his own son Jonathan.
Consequently, Israel is subjugated to the Philistines and is nearly destroyed. Israel was delivered from destruction only when David was
able to take action to defeat Israel's enemies.

The analogies between Mordecai/Esther and Saul on the one hand
and Haman and Agag on the other hand are central to the purposes of
the narrative, insofar as they point to the issue of attempted genocide
against the Jewish people. Whereas Saul failed to confront the threat
to Israel's survival, and nearly saw the destruction of his people as a
result, Mordecai and Esther indeed take matters into their own hands,

---

25. See Greenstein, "A Jewish Reading of Esther," 230.

26. See "Amalekites," *EncJud*, 2, cols. 787–91. For discussion of moral issues pertaining to the Amalekites in Jewish tradition, see Zev Garber, "Deconstructing Theodicy and
Amalekut: A Personal Apologia," in *Shoah*, 119–36.

and see to the deliverance of Jews from Haman's plot. The narrative takes care to signal that those attacked and killed by the Jews were enemies who sought to destroy them, and it emphasizes this theme by pointing to the refusal of the Jews to take booty from their dead enemies. The identities of those killed as the sons of Haman and those who sought to attack the Jews (9:7–10; and 8:11, 13; 9:1, 5, 16) are entirely in keeping with the Bible's various expressions of corporate punishment and salvation as expressed in the Dtr history (e.g., Joshua 7–8; 2 Kings 17), the Prophetic literature (e.g., Isaiah 6; Hosea 14), and indeed in the New Testament's view of universal human sin and the possibility of redemption (e.g., Romans), in contrast to the greater focus on individual moral accountability regnant in modern Western and, particularly, North American society. The issue is not vengeance, nor is it genocide against the Persians; it is a matter of justice, that is, the fundamental responsibility and universal right of self-protection against those who would murder — in this case, those who would annihilate the Jewish people. The absence of G-d in this scenario is crucial. As in the narrative concerning Saul and Agag, it is the responsibility of the human protagonists of the narrative to confront and destroy the evil. They cannot wait for G-d to carry out this responsibility for them. Mordechai's statement to Esther in 4:14 expresses this concern admirably: "Who knows? Perhaps you have come to royal dignity for just such a time as this." Ironically, despite her status as a woman, and an intermarried one at that, she is the only person who has the power to make a difference. Everything depends upon her.

CONCLUDING EVALUATION

The absence of G-d and human responsibility for the confrontation and eradication of evil are clearly fundamental themes in the book of Esther. In this respect, these themes point to the reality of human experience in that the presence of G-d is not always evident in times of crisis, and human beings are thereby obligated to step forward to act when G-d fails to do so.[27] It is perhaps for this reason that the talmudic sage Rabbi Simeon ben Lakish considers Esther to have been revealed together with the Torah at Sinai, and Jon Levenson states that Esther presents

---

27. For discussion of the human responsibility to act at a time when G-d hides the divine face and to continue to witness to G-d, see Eliezer Berkovitz, *Faith after the Holocaust* (New York: KTAV, 1973), esp. 128–43. Cf. Emil Fackenheim, *G-d's Presence in History: Jewish Affirmations and Philosophical Reflections* (New York: Harper Torchbooks, 1972), esp. 84–92. Fackenheim argues that Auschwitz must be viewed as a command by G-d not to hand Hitler a posthumous victory, that is, to affirm Jewish existence and to continue to wrestle with G-d.

"a profounder and more realistic stance of faith than that of most of biblical tradition."[28]

These themes also point to the role of Esther as sacred Scripture, especially insofar as Esther constitutes a critique of a premise found in most of the biblical literature: G-d will act to punish the wicked and to protect the righteous in a time of danger. Many argue that Esther was not written for this role, as the author of Esther could not possibly have been aware that the work would be incorporated into a much later generic entity known as the Bible,[29] but the use of the Saul and Agag tradition points to the fact that Esther is written with specific intent to interact with an element of scriptural tradition. The author may not have been conscious of the Bible per se, but the author was certainly aware of this particular tradition and employed it in formulating the Esther narrative and its message.

Finally, this reading of the book of Esther has special significance for Christian theology and the interpretation of the Bible in the aftermath of the Shoah. It demonstrates that Christian biblical theology must come to terms with the Jewish character of the Christian Old or First Testament, particularly in relation to the theological reality and legitimacy of the Jewish people in Christian thought.[30] Jews are not fodder for Gentile extermination, either by death or by conversion and theological subordination. Esther calls for human responsibility to confront such evil. Within the context of Christian Scripture, the book of Esther demonstrates that it is a Christian responsibility to recognize this reality and to act upon it by recognizing the continuing legitimacy of Jews and Judaism as a fundamental axiom of Christian theology. G-d cannot perform this task for Christians; rather, much like Esther, Christians must do it themselves.[31]

---

28. *y. Megillah* 70d; Jon D. Levenson, *Esther: A Commentary* (OTL; Louisville: Westminster John Knox, 1997) 21.

29. For example, Michael V. Fox, *Character and Ideology in the Book of Esther* (Columbia: University of South Carolina Press, 1991) 238.

30. Although the Christian Old Testament and the Jewish Tanak are each considered as the "Hebrew Bible," they are not one and the same, as indicated by the very different presentation of the constituent books in each tradition. For a full discussion, see my "Tanak versus Old Testament: Concerning the Foundation for a Jewish Theology of the Bible," in Henry T. C. Sun, Keith L. Eades, et al., eds., *Problems in Biblical Theology: Essays in Honor of Rolf Knierim* (Grand Rapids: Eerdmans, 1997) 353–72.

31. An earlier version of this essay was presented at the Twenty-Seventh Annual Scholars' Conference on the Holocaust and the Churches, 2–4 March 1997, in Tampa, Florida. The earlier version was published on CD-ROM in the proceedings of the conference. The present revised version appears here with the permission of the conference organizers.

Selected Bibliography

Anderson, Bernhard W. "The Place of the Book of Esther in the Christian Bible." *JR* (1950) 32-43.

Berg, Sandra Beth. *The Book of Esther: Motifs, Themes and Structure.* SBLDS 44. Missoula, Mont.: Scholars Press, 1979.

Clines, David J. A. *The Esther Scroll.* JSOTSup 30. Sheffield: JSOT Press, 1984.

Craig, Kenneth. *Reading Esther: A Case for the Literary Carnivalesque.* LCBI. Louisville: Westminster John Knox, 1995.

Dorothy, Charles V. *The Books of Esther: Structure, Genre, and Textual Integrity.* JSOTSup 187. Sheffield: Sheffield Academic Press, 1996.

Fackenheim, Emil. *The Jewish Bible after the Holocaust.* Bloomington: Indiana University Press, 1990.

Fox, Michael V. *Character and Ideology in the Book of Esther.* Columbia: University of South Carolina Press, 1991.

Greenstein, Edward L. "A Jewish Reading of Esther." In *Judaic Perspectives on Ancient Israel,* ed. Jacob Neusner, Baruch A. Levine, and Ernest S. Frerichs. Philadelphia: Fortress, 1987.

Knierim, Rolf P. *The Task of Old Testament Theology.* Grand Rapids, Eerdmans, 1995.

Levenson, Jon D. *Esther: A Commentary.* OTL. Louisville: Westminster John Knox, 1997.

Moore, Carey A. *Esther.* AB 7B. Garden City, N.Y.: Doubleday, 1971.

Pfeiffer, Robert H. *Introduction to the Old Testament.* New York: Harper & Bros., 1948.

Vischer, Wilhem. *Esther.* THE 48. Munich: Kaiser, 1937.

Von Rad, Gerhard. *Old Testament Theology.* 2 vols. ET. New York: Harper & Row, 1962-65.

Walfish, Barry Dov. *Esther in Medieval Garb.* Albany: State University of New York Press, 1993.

Wills, Lawrence M. *The Jew in the Court of the Foreign King.* HDR 26. Minneapolis: Fortress, 1990.

15

On the Theology of the Pentateuch
Tai-il Wang

THE ISSUES

In the years since Gerhard von Rad's *The Form-Critical Problem of the Hexateuch* (1938) appeared,[1] numerous excellent critical works on the formation of the Pentateuch have been published. Traditional historical scholarship has rendered great discussions about the well-known thesis that the Hexateuch was built up on the basis of the "short historical creed" (e.g., Deut. 26:5–9) according to which the primary concept of Israel's history began with the deliverance from Egypt and the settlement in the promised land. Many debates have been underway, especially soon after G. von Rad's two-volume *Old Testament Theology* (1957, 1960) came out,[2] over the questions of Israel's testimony to the saving act of God drawn in the traditions of the book of Exodus.[3] God's acting in history, reflected in the traditions of Israel's own explicit assertions about Yahweh, has been received for decades as an overarching category in OT belief.

This is a revised version of the essay presented at the Biblical Studies Working Group of the Tenth Oxford Institute on 15 August 1997. This is an empirical study. It draws on the work of Rolf P. Knierim, who in his 1984 SBL Seminar paper enables us to parse the literary structure of the Pentateuch, and who in his 1995 book *The Task of Old Testament Theology* applies this understanding to a formal definition of the theology of the Pentateuch. This essay assesses or adjudicates the exegeted message and/or the theology in the Pentateuch in light of the semantic structure of the variant voices present in the Bible.

1. G. von Rad, *Das formgeschichtliche Problem des Hexateuchs* (BWANT 4/26; Stuttgart: Kohlhammer, 1938); ET, *The Problem of the Hexateuch and Other Essays* (trans. E. W. Trueman Dicken; Edinburgh: Oliver and Boyd, 1966) 1–78.

2. G. von Rad, *Theologie des Alten Testaments* (2 vols.; Munich: Kaiser, 1957–60); ET, *Old Testament Theology* (2 vols.; Edinburgh: Oliver and Boyd; New York: Harper and Row, 1962–65).

3. For example, H. G. Reventlow, *Problems of Old Testament Theology in the Twentieth Century* (trans. J. Bowden; Philadelphia: Fortress, 1985) 59–124; G. W. Coats, "Theology of the Hebrew Bible," in D. A. Knight, G. M. Tucker, eds., *The Hebrew Bible and Its Modern Interpreters* (Philadelphia: Fortress; Chico, Calif.: Scholars Press, 1985) 239–62, esp. 246–49; L. G. Perdue, *The Collapse of History: Reconstructing Old Testament Theology* (OBT; Minneapolis: Fortress, 1994) 17–110; R. Rendtorff, "Approaches to Old Testament Theology," in H. T. C. Sun et al., eds., *Problems in Biblical Theology: Essays in Honor of Rolf Knierim* (Grand Rapids: Eerdmans, 1997) 13–26, esp. 14–16.

This understanding contrasted with that of Walther Eichrodt, an OT theologian previous to von Rad, expressed in his three-volume *Old Testament Theology* (1933–1939),[4] in that the exodus story was dealt with only casually. In a "thought-world" of "covenant" according to which Eichrodt arranged OT materials, the testimonies to belief in Yahweh within the context of tradition history were missing.[5] Here we can see two classic examples of how the Pentateuch is understood. In spite of their differences, both were much the same in playing down the final form of the Pentateuch, which needed to be heard as normative in its own terms. Pentateuchal materials were dispersed into the program of providing a systematic framework for any detailed account of OT theology, or Genesis–Deuteronomy was expanded to the following historical book when the former had to be understood as having a distinct character, that is, as Torah.

The recent volume *The Flowering of Old Testament Theology* (1992),[6] edited by Ben C. Ollenburger, Elmer A. Martens, and Gerhard F. Hasel, fosters another scholarly discussion on both method and content of OT theologies. This book gives us, first of all, a feel not only for variations in style, but, more important, for varieties of perspectives in the discipline of OT theology. It then offers five "models" by H. Gese, W. Brueggemann, J. Levenson, P. Trible, and R. Knierim of what the future of OT theology in the twenty-first century ought to be. We do not mean here to deny the utility of the various models of OT theology that have been proposed in *The Flowering of Old Testament Theology*. These approaches are stimulating in themselves, and they illuminate many biblical insights into God and reality, but most of them (except Knierim's) fail to capture a compelling understanding of the multifaceted witnesses of the OT. Their reflections on the method of OT theology have made proposals that are attractive in their own prospect, but have given no answer about how to deal with the plurality of voices of the OT. Indeed, there is reason to believe that only Knierim deals with the recognition of the plurality of the OT with its various theologies.

Pertinent to the discussion is the substantial clarification between exegesis, theology, and hermeneutics. G. Hasel suggested in his monograph a heuristic method of doing OT theology: biblical theology must be concerned with both "what the text meant" and "what it means."[7]

---

4. W. Eichrodt, *Theologie des Alten Testaments* (3 vols.; Leipzig: Hinrichs, 1933–39); ET, *Theology of the Old Testament* (2 vols.; OTL; Philadelphia: Westminster, 1961–67).

5. For this perspective, see Rendtorff, "Approaches to Old Testament Theology," 16–17.

6. B. C. Ollenburger, E. A. Martens, and G. F. Hasel, eds., *The Flowering of Old Testament Theology: A Reader in Twentieth-Century Old Testament Theology, 1930–1990* (SBTS 1; Winona Lake, Ind.: Eisenbrauns, 1992).

7. G. Hasel, *Old Testament Theology: Basic Issues in the Current Debate* (3d ed.; Grand Rapids: Eerdmans, 1972) 81–83, 89.

This view was again stated, with some variations, by many scholars: for example, OT theology combines both "descriptive (to historic Israel's faith) and constructive (to the modern interpreter)" tasks.[8] Such views clearly have spoken their theologies in their own rights. They are preliminary and helpful to build up biblical theology. However, such studies have confused or ignored the distinction between exegesis (describing what is said in the text), theology (adjudicating the messages of the text analyzed by exegesis), and hermeneutics (applying the result of theology for us today, namely, what ought to be confessed). What they proposed is related only to the exegetical and hermeneutical aspects. For them, theology keeps silence.

Recent works on the theology of the Pentateuch, such as written by Norbert Lohfink (1988, 1990 [ET, 1994])[9] and Frank Crüsemann (1992),[10] pose other issues. They lay out a comprehensive appraisal of pentateuchal materials. Lonfink seeks to elucidate the theological concepts in the various layers of the Pentateuch, while Crüsemann explores, by concentrating on the circles, institutions that generated legal statements and their compilations into the layers of the Pentateuch, how the three successive codes of the Pentateuch — for example, the Book of Covenant, Deuteronomy, and the Priestly Code — are combined in an internally contradictory unity.

Of course, such analyses display essentials to the study of biblical theology insofar as they deal with the message of the component part of the Pentateuch; yet, they do not confront the question of what constitutes the Pentateuch as a whole. We have to ask, How are the component messages of the Pentateuch organized in the final form of the Pentateuch? What do we mean by the Pentateuch? The issue here is that recourse is to be made only to the question of the meaning of the whole, which selects, organizes, and presents the component parts, but not to the question of the meaning of its component parts.[11] As Knierim points out clearly, larger corpora that comprise different sources, diverse traditions, disparate genres, and various contents are composed under "the dictate of unifying guiding ideas."[12] The Pentateuch can be seen

---

8. For example, B. S. Childs, *Old Testament Theology in a Canonical Context* (Philadelphia: Fortress, 1985) 12; Coats, "Theology of the Hebrew Bible," 241–50; Perdue, *Collapse of History*, 304–7.

9. N. Lohfink, *Studien zum Pentateuch* (SBAB 4; Stuttgart: Katholisches Bibelwerk, 1988); *Studien zum Deuteronomium und zur deuteronomistischen Literatur I* (SBAB 8; Stuttgart: Katholisches Bibelwerk, 1990); ET, *Theology of the Pentateuch: Themes of the Priestly Narrative and Deuteronomy* (Edinburgh: T. & T. Clark, 1994).

10. F. Crüsemann, *Die Tora: Theologie und Sozialgeschichte des alttestamentlichen Gesetzes* (Munich: Kaiser, 1992).

11. On this perspective, see M. A. Sweeney, "Tanak versus Old Testament: Concerning the Foundation for a Jewish Theology of the Bible," in Sun et al., eds., *Problems in Biblical Theology*, 356.

12. R. Knierim, *The Task of Old Testament Theology: Substance, Method, and Cases* (Grand

as a coherent composition, even though it is undeniably a composite of sources, forms, and traditions reflecting different periods and concerns. Here we must direct the basic form-critical question to the Pentateuch in its final shape: What does the Pentateuch as a whole say about its structure, genre, setting, and intention?

The Pentateuch in its present form is the result of a long and complex history of traditions and editorial activities. Texts and traditions within the Pentateuch are juxtaposed in many ways and on many levels, leading eventually to the final form. The discussions on the formation of the Pentateuch, which have been concerned primarily with an attempt to discover the layers and earlier texts lying behind the final form of the Pentateuch, have made valid contributions to our understanding of OT theology. Yet, they have behaved as if "the final composition, the only fact which is available to us, was not worth discussing."[13] The layers, earlier texts, stages of composition that predate the latest form of the text have been excessively postulated.

In recent years, scholars from widely different perspectives have argued that biblical research ought to move toward looking at the present form of the text as an integral unit.[14] Some recent literary critics, such as Clines (1978), Plaut (1981), Mann (1988), Blum (1990), Boorer (1992), and Whybray (1995), underscore the need for such a movement in their own ways.[15] They emphasize the Pentateuch as a whole rather than its individual components. Their interests do not lie in seeking when, why, and through whom the Pentateuch reached its present form. Their interests lie in asking about the concept governing the composition of the Pentateuch. Nevertheless, we can point out that the overall form of the Pentateuch and the distinctive nature of its components are still generally overlooked.

Rapids: Eerdmans, 1995) 17–20, 52. The term "unifying" is interchanged by Knierim with "systematizing," "(co)relating," "prioritizing," and "hierarchizing." What he neither sees nor proposes is "harmonizing, at least not in the sense that plurality of theological notions is replaced by one another."

13. R. Knierim, "The Composition of the Pentateuch," in idem, *Task of Old Testament Theology*, 352.

14. See R. Knierim, "Old Testament Form Criticism Reconsidered," *Int* 27 (1973) 435–68; idem, "Criticism of Literary Features, Form, Tradition, and Redaction," in Knight and Tucker, eds., *The Hebrew Bible and Its Modern Interpreters*, 123–66; both are included in this volume.

15. D. J. A. Clines, *The Theme of the Pentateuch* (JSOTSup 10; Sheffield: JSOT Press, 1978); G. Plaut, ed., *The Torah: A Modern Commentary* (New York: Union of American Hebrew Congregations, 1981); T. W. Mann, *The Book of the Torah: The Narrative Integrity of the Pentateuch* (Atlanta: John Knox, 1988); E. Blum, *Studien zur Komposition des Pentateuch* (BZAW 189; Berlin: de Gruyter, 1990); Suzanne Boorer, *The Promise of the Land as Oath* (BZAW 205; Berlin: de Gruyter, 1992); R. N. Whybray, *Introduction to the Pentateuch* (Grand Rapids: Eerdmans, 1995).

The question of the messages and theologies of the composition of the Pentateuch in its final form has remained largely unexamined.

KNIERIM'S "THE COMPOSITION OF THE PENTATEUCH"

In 1984 Rolf P. Knierim produced his seminal study "The Composition of the Pentateuch."[16] It was a thorough work on analyzing from the perspective of what he calls the "structure analysis"[17] of the final composition of the Pentateuch, with a view to discovering its compositional strategy, its generic nature, its conceptual coherence, and its theological legitimacy. According to Knierim, the criteria for discerning theologically legitimate priorities for the interpretation of the Pentateuch must obviously be found primarily in the exegetical, namely, the description of the composition of the text at the levels of the final redaction. For heuristic process, we ask, How many parts or literary blocks are juxtaposed in the Pentateuch to which all other parts are subordinate? How shall we define and delimit the different levels of the text in which different signals come to work together? What are the criteria according to which the Pentateuch is organized?

Knierim explores, first of all, what the Pentateuch is. "The Five Books of Moses," the traditional title of the Pentateuch, although unacceptable as a statement about authorship, represents the story that spans in a systematized order of events from the creation of the world to the death of Moses. The story it relates leads us to recognize how the people called Israel came into being as a nation. However, the canonical fivefold division of the Pentateuch cannot claim to reflect its literary structure. Clearly enough, the books of Exodus through Deuteronomy are held together by the narrative of Moses, whose birth is narrated at the beginning of those books (Exod. 2:2) and his death at their very end (Deut. 34:5). Thus, the Pentateuch is seen to be mosaic, although not Mosaic.[18] This observation is important because the text itself forces us to read Exodus–Deuteronomy as a unity. The Pentateuch is thus seen to be inherently bipartite: Genesis and Exodus–Deuteronomy. Put differently, the Pentateuch as a whole is conceptually cast into a systematized structure in that "Genesis, the

---

16. R. Knierim, "The Composition of the Pentateuch," in K. H. Richards, ed., *Society of Biblical Literature Seminar Papers, 1985* (SBLSP 24; Atlanta: Scholars Press, 1985) 393–415. This work is published in Knierim, *The Task of Old Testament Theology*, 351–79, the version cited hereafter.

17. For a descriptive analysis of Knierim's "structure analysis," see Antony F. Campbell, "Structure Analysis and the Art of Exegesis (I Sam 16:14–18:30)," in Sun et al., eds., *Problems in Biblical Theology*, 76–103.

18. Knierim, "The Composition of the Pentateuch," 371. Knierim quotes from Otto Kaiser, *Introduction to the Old Testament* (trans. J. Sturdy; Minneapolis: Augsburg, 1975) 44.

time before Moses, functions as the introduction to, or preparation for Exodus-Deuteronomy, the time of Moses."[19] All other divisions within the Pentateuch are subservient to this bipartite arrangement.

Knierim's focus, while unavoidably interested in the biographical genre of the Pentateuch,[20] restricts analysis to issues of defining the dominant blocks of Exodus–Deuteronomy and its interpretation. Methodologically speaking, Knierim's investigation widens our attention from the short, individual units, each of which appears to have its own literary integrity, up to the larger literary blocks available in which all other short, individual units are subordinate to convey their literary truths. It is this nature that becomes the focus of our discussion: How, then, does the macrostructure of Exodus–Deuteronomy appear to be? What are the criteria according to which such literary blocks are organized?

Knierim argues that Exodus–Deuteronomy is conceptualized as a migration story of the Israelites from Egypt to Moab.[21] He describes the context of discussions about how Exodus–Deuteronomy is organized for the macrostructural level, paying particular attention to the literary strata, chronological frame, topographical data, philological issues, and so forth. In light of this, Knierim focuses attention on the two primary locations by which the whole migratory process is arranged: Sinai and the plains of Moab. According to him, the migration story is governed by the arrival and events at these two locations above all others. A characteristic feature of this redaction leads us to find convincing devices for organizing Exodus–Deuteronomy into the four distinct literary parts: the migration to Sinai (Exodus 1–18), the event at Sinai (Exod. 19:1–Num. 10:10), the migration to Moab (Num. 10:11–36:13), and the event in the plains of Moab (Deut. 1–34).[22]

The structure of the Moses story, displayed by Knierim, reveals the text's overall perspectives and conceptualizations in that the sequence of literary blocks within the final form of the book points to the narrator's message that the final redactor wishes to emphasize. Three important aspects will be highlighted. First, Exodus–Deuteronomy must be identified as a narrative about the migration from Egypt to Moab, which is divided in terms of location into two main parts: "From Egypt to Sinai" (Exodus 1–Num. 10:10), and "From Sinai to Moab" (Num. 10:11–Deuteronomy 34). Second, the conceptual aspect reflected in the structure of Exodus–Deuteronomy shows that the instructions at each location, which seem to be inserted into narrative context (Exod. 19:1–

---

19. Knierim, "The Composition of the Pentateuch," 354–55; cf. R. N. Whybray, *Introduction to the Pentateuch,* 63–84.

20. Knierim, "The Composition of the Pentateuch," 369–79.

21. Knierim, "The Composition of the Pentateuch," 355–69.

22. Knierim, "The Composition of the Pentateuch," 356.

Num. 10:10; Deuteronomy 1–34), reveal the meaning of every previous migration (Exodus 1–18; Num. 10:11–36:13). Third, within the narrative framework and the conceptual implications in it, the Sinai pericope (Exod. 19:1–Num. 10:10), which is reaffirmed by Deuteronomy, Moses' testament, specifically reviews the meaning of Exodus.

Knierim's study differs from many critical studies in that he treats the Sinai pericope as the central part of the Pentateuch. Knierim shows that the Pentateuch devotes its attention more to the Sinai story than to the story of the exodus. On its face, the Sinai pericope seems incoherent enough. Closer analysis of this pericope may reflect overwhelming evidence that the text has been reworked by a long editorial process. No single designation adequately describes the diversity of types, genres, settings, and intentions found there. Yet, Knierim provides textual warrant for understanding the Sinai pericope as a coherent literary unit. Along similar lines, though working from quite different assumptions, some scholars suggest that pentateuchal narrative and legal materials are skillfully woven together in a more integrated manner.[23]

There is room for doubt, however, whether our description of the Sinai pericope as an integral part of the Moses story is entirely adequate. Yet, the collection of laws in the Sinai pericope, which makes up a major part of the extant Pentateuch, represents in its final form a coherent, symmetrical arrangement of materials that fills out the institutional formation of Israel at Sinai. We can present the structure of the Sinai pericope as follows:

The Sinai Pericope (Exod. 19:1–Num. 10:10)

I. The Revelation from the Mountain	Exod. 19:1–40:38
A. Preparation: the covenant-making	Exod. 19:1–24:8
B. Goal: the sanctuary-making	Exod. 24:9–40:38
II. The Revelation from the Tent of Meeting	Lev. 1:1–Num. 10:10
A. Instruction of communal life	Lev. 1:1–27:34
B. Preparation for migration	Num. 1:1–10:10

We have to know that in narrative progress of Exodus 19–40 the two localities set the stage for the basic structural organization of the entire Sinai pericope — that is, "the mountain" and "the camp."[24] These

---

23. For discussion of literary analysis of the Pentateuch, see R. Alter, *The Art of Biblical Narrative* (New York: Basic Books, 1981); Mann, *The Book of Torah*, 1–178; S. Bar-Efrat, *Narrative Art in the Bible* (JSOTSup 70; Sheffield: Almond, 1989 [Heb. original, 1979]); J. P. Fokkelman, *Narrative Art in Genesis: Specimens of Stylistic and Structural Analysis* (Assen: Van Gorcum, 1975); T. C. Eskenazi, "Torah as Narrative and Narrative as Torah," in J. L. Mays, D. L. Petersen, and K. H. Richards, eds., *Old Testament Interpretation: Past, Present, and Future. Essays in Honor of Gene M. Tucker* (Nashville: Abingdon, 1995) 13–30.

24. Knierim, *The Task of Old Testament Theology*, 360.

two mentioned localities, as the fundamental signal for the organization of Exodus 19–40, provide legitimation for "the ascent-descent pattern": "whenever Moses is on the mountain he receives an instruction from Yahweh" (Exod. 19:3, 8b, 20; 20:21; 24:9; 32:31; 34:4), and "whenever he is in the camp he conveys it to the people" (Exod. 19:7, 14, 25; 24:3; 32:15; 33:4; 34:29). Moses goes up to the mountain seven times, and seven times he comes down into the camp.[25] This pattern reflects that the text consists of seven major cycles, each of which has two components: the report of Yahweh instruction on the mountain (19:3–6, 8b–13, 20–24; 20:21–24:2; 24:9–32:14; 32:31–33:3; 34:4–28), and the compliance report of Moses and/or Israel in the camp (19:7–8a, 14–19; 19:25–20:20; 24:3–8; 32:15–30; 33:4–34:3; 34:29–39:43).

It appears that in the final form of the Pentateuch these cycles represent the complexity of concerns that are governed by different aspects from one another, and reflect the progress of what happens at Sinai. These cycles are first connected by "the covenant-making process" between Yahweh and Israel (Exod. 19:1–24:8), and then move on to deal with "the process of making the sanctuary" (Exod. 24:9–39:43; 40:1–38).[26] This state of progress explains the question of why the collections of instructions are placed in the midst of the story of Moses. The Sinai pericope within the Pentateuch is intended to read the total narrative of Exodus as governed by the conceptual aspect of building the sanctuary. This perspective informs that the covenant narrative (Exod. 19:1–24:8) in the Sinai story functions as the condition/preparation for the establishment of the sanctuary in the midst of Israel (Exod. 24:9–39:43; 40:1–38).

How, then, does Exodus 19–40 relate itself to the rest of the Sinai pericope from Leviticus 1 on? It is enough to say that the building of the sanctuary represents the place to which Yahweh's revelation moved from the mountain. Leviticus 1:1 signals that the text moves its places of revelation from the mountain to the tabernacle. As we see with Knierim, who in magnificent fashion pursues profound concepts underlying the OT, the entire Sinai pericope speaks of two stages of revelation in which the first, the revelation from the mountain, was "preparatory and preliminary and provided the condition for the second stage," the

---

25. Cf. Knierim, "The Composition of the Pentateuch," 360–61. There are indications in Knierim's study that the notion of the seventh cycle (34:29–39:43) is put in the Pentateuch. Knierim argues, however, that "the regularity of this ascent-descent pattern is blurred within the block Exod 32:15–34:4." Thus, he does not count Exod. 32:31 and 33:4 in the number of the ongoing encounters between Yahweh and Moses. So he says, "Six times Moses goes up to the mountain, and six times he comes down into the camp."

26. Knierim, *The Task of Old Testament Theology*, 361–62.

revelation from the tabernacle, that is, "the ultimate goal of Yahweh's revelation."[27]

RECONCEPTUALIZING THE "COMPOSITION OF THE PENTATEUCH"

The structure analysis and insights shown above reveal not only considerable artistry in the composition of the text, but also display a highly presupposed conceptuality on the part of the narrator. All the subjects we discuss for theology of the Pentateuch come from this exegetical artistry and conceptuality. We have been discussing that the Pentateuch as it stands emphasizes the biography of Moses in Exodus–Deuteronomy. Although the book of Genesis adds the perspective of "all of human history" to Exodus–Deuteronomy, the extant Pentateuch stands in its own right as a testimony to the biography of Moses. In other words, the final form of the Pentateuch reveals a distinct emphasis on the generic nature of Exodus–Deuteronomy. Thus, we will bypass interpreting the theological aspects of the book of Genesis and will bring Exodus–Deuteronomy into focus in our discussion.

The problem of the theology of Exodus–Deuteronomy lies in the combination of its twofold structure with two subdivisions in each of the two main parts: "the migration of the people from Egypt to Sinai" (Exodus 1–18) and "Yahweh instructions at Sinai" (Exod. 19:1–Num. 10:10); "the migration of the Israelites from Sinai to Moab" (Num. 10:11–36:13) and "the testament of Moses at Moab" (Deuteronomy 1–34). This combination is particularly difficult to interpret because the reasons for it are not explicit in the extant text. Exegetical scholarship in OT studies has examined in various ways these four parts.[28] But such investigations hardly ever involve a claim that the order of combination of these parts within the final form of the Pentateuch points to the overall perspective of the textual meaning that the final redactor wishes to emphasize.[29]

Biblical interpretation can no longer consider these parts to be substantially independent of one another. We would have to address the

---

27. Knierim, "The Composition of the Pentateuch," 367.

28. For example, M. Noth, *A History of Pentateuchal Traditions* (trans. B. W. Anderson; Englewood Cliffs, N.J.: Prentice-Hall, 1972); G. von Rad, "The Form-Critical Problem of the Hexateuch," in *The Problem of the Hexateuch*, 1–78; R. Rendtorff, *The Problem of the Process of Transmission in the Pentateuch* (JSOTSup 89; Sheffield: JSOT Press, 1990); R. Whybray, *The Making of the Pentateuch: A Methodological Study* (JSOTSup 53; Sheffield: JSOT Press, 1987); E. Blum, *Studien zur Komposition des Pentateuch*, 1ff.

29. For a thorough review of this discussion, see D. A. Knight, "The Pentateuch," in Knight and G. Tucker, eds., *The Hebrew Bible and Its Modern Interpreters*, 263–98; D. L. Petersen, "The Formation of the Pentateuch," in Mays, Petersen, Richards, eds., *Old Testament Interpretation*, 31–46.

concepts or concerns of each part in relation to the other within the final form of the book.

The fourfold structure of the Moses story provides important understanding of the perspectives, programs, and concerns of the final redactor of the Pentateuch. Knierim shows that the order of these four parts and their combination cannot be considered accidental. According to Knierim, the instruction at each destination, first at Sinai and then at Moab, actualizes deliberately the meaning of the previous migration. Of course, this combination is to be interpreted in many different ways. Yet, we must interpret reasons for this combination in light of the conceptual presuppositions that are exegetically discernible. Within the Moses story the most important part lies in what takes place at Sinai, the mountain of God. What is important here is that the Sinai pericope, the massive literary block in the extant Pentateuch, is surrounded by two relatively brief narratives reporting what happens in the wilderness before and after Israel's encampment at Sinai: Exodus 1–18 and Num. 10:11–36:13. We can figure out in this combination an essential theological agenda for reconstructing pentateuchal belief. The Pentateuch we discuss is seen to be composed from a perspective antithetical to the traditional assumption that the original core of the pentateuchal theme is the exodus.[30] As we have argued, the theme of liberation or salvation employed in the migration to Sinai is not an end in itself, even if it is certainly perceived in the text as constitutive.[31]

If there is a common conceptual denominator for the combination of two different migration stories — the migration to Sinai (Exodus 1–18) and the migration after Sinai (Num. 10:11–36:13) — it is, besides the fact of migration, the aspect of what happens to Israel during their encampment at Sinai. Just as the first journey story, the story of liberation from Egypt, looks ahead to the constitution of the covenant and sacral community at Sinai, so the second journey story, the forty-year murmurings in the wilderness, looks back upon that formal constitution at Sinai. The ways to and after Sinai are not simply geographical journeys; they are, rather, programmatic migrations. Sinai appears, at first, to be the place to provide "a formal constitution" of a sacral community for "the relationship that found its primary expression in Israel's liberation."[32] Sinai is, then, to be seen as the condition according to which the liberated community is organized as a cultic-theocratic community. It is no wonder, therefore, that the departure from Sinai is seized with a sense of

---

30. See N. K. Gottwald, *The Tribes of Yahweh* (Maryknoll, N.Y.: Orbis, 1979); idem, *The Hebrew Bible: A Socio-Literary Introduction* (Philadelphia: Fortress, 1985).

31. Knierim, "The Composition of the Pentateuch," 357.

32. Mann, *The Book of the Torah,* 99; see also J. D. Levenson, *Sinai and Zion: An Entry into the Jewish Bible* (San Francisco: HarperCollins, 1985) 19–42.

apprehension about whether or not Israel performs properly the Sinaitic program. But the text reporting the journey after Sinai betrays Israel's repeated failures in between the wilderness of Sinai and the promised land. It is to mark this apprehension that the final redactor of the Pentateuch placed Moses' testament (Deuteronomy 1–34) at the end of the book. From the migration after Sinai on, what is critical is not the liberation that belongs to the past, but the ongoing implementation of the covenant existence that has been established at Sinai.

The recent and perhaps most provocative work in biblical studies today, especially in the developing world, is the theology that understands the central theological voice of the Bible to be that of liberation. Liberation theology reveals its own particular perspective of "solidarity with the oppressed" as the suitable theme by which to judge biblical texts. Its own research not only embraces certain aspects of socio-scientific ideologies operative in ancient Israel but also turns to embrace those texts that undergird a subversive and egalitarian society for the oppressed or the downtrodden.[33] One of the great contributions that liberation theology has brought to the discussion is the emphasis upon liberation and continuing reflection on its practical application. Theology that is separated from social matrices and actual practice appears to be irrelevant to human life.[34]

There is no doubt that in the above-discussed structure the theme of liberation also plays a significant role. Exodus 1–18 stands in its own right as a testimony about the escape from Egyptian servitude. Theologically conceived, however, it is not the story of liberation (Exodus 1–18) that is exalted in the structure of Exodus–Deuteronomy, but rather, the Sinai event (Exod. 19:1–Num. 10:10), which integrates the meaning of the liberation story.[35] The goal of the exodus is to serve Yahweh by making the covenant community constituted at Sinai (Exodus 19–40). The Sinai event complements the decisive concerns missing in the liberation story. That is, why did Yahweh liberate the people from the Egyptian bondage? Needless to say, the liberation story of Exodus 1–18 alludes to the question of why the liberation out of bondage would have to take place (e.g., Exod. 3:12; 5:1–3). However, it is not the language of exodus narrative but the language of the instructions or stipulations that explains in detail why the people called Israel was to be liberated. In view of this, we remain focused upon the control of the following textual meaning: the liberation or migration experience is

---

33. For recent discussion about liberation theology, see Perdue, *Collapse of History*, 69–110.

34. Gottwald, *The Tribes of Yahweh*, 701.

35. Knierim, *The Task of Old Testament Theology*, 356–59.

the instrument or means by which the theological program revealed in the Sinai narrative is enhanced. Despite all the important contributions that the exodus/liberation has made both to biblical and theological investigation, the liberation story is not fundamental in the conceptual layout of the extant Pentateuch. It is only at Sinai, not with the exodus, that the liberated community is organized around the sanctuary as a cultic-theocratic community.

This finding forces us to deal with another aspect that seems to be pertinent for our discussion. If the Sinai pericope is the fundamental part of the Pentateuch, how, then, do we relate the Sinai pericope to the rest of the Pentateuch? We have already discussed that in the interpretation of the relationship between the exodus and Sinai the purpose of Israel's liberation/salvation is to provide a formal constitution for entering into a covenant relationship between Yahweh and Israel. Basic to that discussion is that all the intrinsic parts of the Pentateuch are related under the aspect of the biography of Moses. Knierim describes this remark in his discussion:

> Specifically, the relationship between Genesis and Exodus–Deuteronomy means that in the work for Israel, especially in Moses' mediation of the revelation at Sinai as well as in his testament, the program is laid down by which Israel is called to be the paradigm for humanity in God's/Yahweh's creation. The decisive person for mediating this revelatory paradigm is Moses. Thus just as Moses is seen as the single decisive person for Israel's history and existence, so is he the decisive person for all of humanity's history and existence.[36]

In the narrative of Exodus–Deuteronomy, we realize the picture of Moses under which the whole narrative of the Pentateuch is governed. Returning to Knierim's thesis of the generic nature of the Pentateuch, we find a "biography of Moses" in that Moses is portrayed as the one who is not so much the spokesman of God to the people as the spokesman of God in behalf of the covenant that Yahweh establishes with his people. With this in mind, we can regard Moses as the "archetypal biblical prophet." In this respect, the liberated people emerges as the community of Yahweh to whom diverse groups of people are allied by the Mosaic covenant. George Mendenhall and others have realized for a long time the significance of ancient Near Eastern "vassal treaties" for the understanding of biblical covenant in its Mosaic form. In referring to Yahweh's covenant with Israel, the covenant appears to be the means by which the liberation remains a gift for the existence of Israel. Religio-historically speaking, the covenant tradition makes it clear that "a covenant to serve Yahweh alone would have been necessary only in

---

36. Knierim, "The Composition of the Pentateuch," 378.

society in which the existence of other gods was taken for granted."[37] This means that Israel is called to affirm the "suzerainty of Yahweh."[38] But this covenantal relation of Israel to Yahweh has finally to be adjudicated from the perspective that "the covenant relation means a way of righteousness and justice in the world, that the special covenantal role for Israel is to be the people who minister as a priesthood (Exod 19:3–6) in the world, standing before the world in behalf of God and before God in behalf of the world."[39] In this respect, the Mosaic covenant not only functions as the vehicle for the exclusive "monotheistic" faith of Israel, but also legitimates Yahweh's structure of creation for human existence.

The Sinai pericope has subdivisions. We have proposed that the Sinai pericope is cast in two larger literary blocks as higher structural levels — the revelation from the mountain (Exodus 19–40) and the revelation from the sanctuary (Lev. 1:1–Num. 10:10) — in that the first functions as preparatory for the second. It is legitimate to say that these two blocks were not organized on the basis of the juxtaposition of different literary strata or of traditions, however defined. The extant text of the Sinai pericope owes its basic structure to the Priestly writers who interwove their own concerns with the older JE traditions. Structurally and conceptually, these two parts are complementary and inseparable in order to make the liberated community the sacral community around the sanctuary.

Despite the second's importance, however, more significant is the topographical indicator that controls two types of migration at Sinai: Moses' up-and-down movement on the mountain, and the migration of Yahweh from the mountain to the sanctuary on earth. Both aspects are clearly visible in the composition of the Sinai story. Moses' ascending and descending of the mountain reflect the agenda under which Israel enters into a covenant with Yahweh by verbal commitment (Exod. 19:1–24:8). But the ongoing movement of covenant-making is not the end in itself. It prepares for the encounter with Yahweh by making and erecting the tabernacle sanctuary in the midst of Israel (Exod. 24:9–40:38). We have to keep in mind that the entire Mosaic ascending/descending narrative does not end in Exod. 24:8. Certainly, the perspective from

---

37. D. Sperling, "Israel's Religion in the Ancient Near East," in A. Green, ed., *Jewish Spirituality from the Bible through the Middle Ages* (New York: Crossroad, 1988) 23, 26; Levenson, *Sinai and Zion*, 23–42.

38. Levenson, *Sinai and Zion*, 43.

39. P. D. Miller, "Creation and Covenant," in S. J. Kraftchick, C. D. Myers Jr., and B. C. Ollenburger, eds., *Biblical Theology: Problems and Perspectives* (Nashville: Abingdon, 1995) 168. This perspective may be seen in many critical works: for example, J. D. Levenson, *Creation and the Persistence of Evil: The Jewish Drama of Divine Omnipotence* (San Francisco: Harper & Row, 1988) 135; R. Rendtorff, *Canon and Theology: Overtures to an Old Testament Theology* (trans. M. Kohl; OBT; Minneapolis: Fortress, 1993) 92–113, 125–34.

Exod. 24:9 on switches its concern to the ultimate goal of Yahweh's revelation, namely, the construction/erection of the tabernacle sanctuary in the midst of Israel. Yahweh moves down to earth from the top (?) of the mountain!

It is generally recognized that the aspects of Israel's responsibility to be Yahweh's vassal and to build the tabernacle sanctuary complement one another as the two central components of experiencing "Yahweh's commanding presence" in the exodus.[40] But the overall message conveyed by the above-mentioned conceptualization reflects that the covenant is not the ultimate goal. The covenant, important as it is as a condition, realizes its aim in building the sanctuary as the place of Yahweh's presence in the midst of Israel. In this light, the first "root experience" to be Israel (Exodus 1–18) serves as a provisional function for having the second root experience to be Israel, that is, entering into a covenant relationship with Yahweh alone (Exod. 19:1–24:8). But the second root experience of becoming the covenant community again paves the way for a third, establishing the sacral community around the sanctuary. All three are essential to identifying the nature of the Moses story. Yet, this process emphasizes the concept that the first (liberation) is preliminary, the second (covenant) is transitional, and finally, the third (sanctuary) is the ultimate. This is the most important theological program that we have found in the discussion of the Sinai story.[41]

After the sanctuary, which is on earth and not on the mountain, is erected, the tent of meeting/tabernacle represents the legitimate place to which Yahweh's revelation is transferred. The fact that Yahweh has spoken from the mountain through Moses to Israel would suggest a condition, the final condition, of his descending to the sanctuary in the Israelite camp. Once that condition is accomplished, the Sinai story says that Yahweh moves down to the camp on earth! This is undoubtedly Yahweh's first coming down to dwell among his community. For the first time the divine presence of Yahweh takes up its abode "among one

---

40. Mann, *The Book of the Torah*, 102; Knierim, "The Composition of the Pentateuch," 365. From the literary, traditio-historical point of view, we have to mention that the Yahwistic-Deuteronomic covenant story and the Priestly portions in Exodus 25–31 and 35–40 are split and inserted into the narrative governed by the Moses' ascent-descent cycle. As a result of this insertion, the covenant story functions as an introduction to the establishment of the sacral community around the sanctuary. We have to remember that connected with Sinai, the original Priestly narrative had only the story of the tabernacle. The Priestly story of the sanctuary had no Sinai covenant at all! In the sevenfold ascent-descent cycle of the progress of narration, as we have discussed above, the originally independent literary units have been woven together skillfully enough to be treated as a coherent story.

41. Knierim, "The Composition of the Pentateuch," 365; cf. Mann, *The Book of the Torah*, 105.

of the peoples of the earth."[42] Under this aspect, the organization of Israel is theocratic in nature. The instruction from the mountain stood in the past. The instruction from the tabernacle sanctuary stands in the present. Yahweh now provides the decisive instructions on how the Israelites remain fit for being in the tabernacling presence of Yahweh.

ON THE THEOLOGY OF THE PENTATEUCH

What has been discussed up to this point is that the Pentateuch in its final form is, as with any biblical text, conceptualized in that explicit expressions and inexplicit thoughts are structurally put together. We have been encouraged to look at this text as the representation of its own world, contrary to the virtually traditional discipline to look through the text, for example, as a window to the matrix for the textual meaning. In order to hear its literary truth, conceptuality, or textual affirmation about the reality presupposed in it, we have traced exegetical methods explaining its structure that affects the theology of the Pentateuch itself. In this way, the Pentateuch is seen to consist of various aspects that are beneath its surface: liberation from oppression, migrations to Sinai and to Moab, covenant-making, and sanctuary-building followed by revelation from the sanctuary. What is important here is that the sequence of these aspects appears to be conceptual. If we compare these aspects with one another, we find that the ultimate concern of the extant Pentateuch is put on its final aspect, that is, "the dwelling of Yahweh in tabernacle," or "the tabernacling presence of Yahweh." All other theological agenda, concerns, or perspectives presupposed in the structure are subservient to it. Therefore, we have to turn our attention to establishing the validity of the tabernacling presence of Yahweh in the place of the OT or biblical theology.

1. We would have to define, first of all, what the tabernacling presence of Yahweh is. The main word for the tabernacling presence of Yahweh is "tabernacle" (משכן). It refers in various contexts to a place of divine revelation, the place where sacrifice would be offered, or the place of dwelling, that is, God's presence in the tent. The verb "to dwell" (שכן), from which the noun is derived, refers to similar complexity of settlement. Its meaning is also embedded in "tent of meeting" (אהל מועד), which refers to the aspects other than space/locus particularly, but at the same time reveals the function of sanctuary implicit in "tabernacle" itself. It is an open question whether or not this lexical finding points to an inclusive worldview in which all other aspects are complementary. What we are going to undertake here is an

---

42. Mann, *The Book of the Torah,* 105.

interpretation of the tabernacling presence of Yahweh in the Pentateuch paying particular attention to the conceptual presuppositions on which all other perspectives are dependent. Indeed, these presuppositions represent, we believe, the bases for the truth claims of the extant Pentateuch.

There is no doubt that the concern for the tabernacling presence of Yahweh or the indwelling of God in the tent pervades the entire Bible. It is primarily found in the JE stratum and Priestly writings in the Pentateuch, as well as within historical, prophetic literature, and even in the NT writings.[43] This means that the concern for the tabernacle is by no means the property of the Priestly writers in ancient Israel. The Priestly writers did not invent it, nor were they the first or the last in the trajectory to speak of it.[44] Nevertheless, the evidence shows that the concern for the tabernacling presence of God in the Priestly writings is more fundamental than in any other part of the Bible. This concern is one, if not the central, factor by which the whole Pentateuch is organized.

Of course, there is diversity within this unity of concern, which deserves our special attention. For example, the Priestly portraits of the tabernacle sanctuary are by no means singular. It is described on one side as the "tent of meeting," which prescribes a portable sanctuary made of fabric and leather (Exod. 26:7–14). It is represented on the other side as the semi-permanent wooden structure with a designation "dwelling" or "tabernacle" (Leviticus 17–26). In addition, its shape with a bipartite design and its gold and bronze furnishings are regarded as a retrojection from a later institution, namely, the second temple, onto Solomon's temple (1 Kings 8:4).[45] But whatever the problem is with this evidence of diversity, the more elaborate concern for the tabernacle in the Priestly writings indicates that the final form of the Pentateuch has laid down a basic criterion against which everything it says must be evaluated. It is at this juncture that the problem of the OT theology of the tabernacling presence of Yahweh arises.

2. It is self-evident that along with what the text says or how the text says it, the quests for when, where, and by whom it is said also become criteria for discussing the validity of the text. The Pentateuch in

---

43. See C. R. Koester, *The Dwelling of God: The Tabernacle in the Old Testament, Intertestamental Jewish Literature, and the New Testament* (CBQMS 22; Washington, D.C.: Catholic Biblical Association of America, 1989).

44. Koester's study helps us at this point to discern the tabernacle imagery throughout the history of biblical literature. Although his focus lies on the role of the tabernacle in the earliest Christian sources, he contributes to our understanding that the OT portrait of the tabernacle is "a variegated one, comprised of texts and traditions that stem from different contexts and exhibit varying theological interests." See Koester, *The Dwelling of God*, 6–22.

45. Cf. Koester, *The Dwelling of God*, 10–11.

its final shape reflects a distinct setting, which is Priestly, and the concerns of a historical period, which is exilic-postexilic. On the basis of this literary-historical data, it has been said that the Priestly writers of the Pentateuch had adopted the older JE tradition of the tabernacle sanctuary (e.g., Exod. 33:7–11) — the tent of meeting that stood outside the camp — to expand upon their own tradition. This is what the priestly writers did in the Sinaitic portion of the Pentateuch after the Jerusalem temple had been destroyed.[46]

This understanding is crucial. During the exile, traditions and beliefs that had been developing in Israel over hundreds of years were brought to a reformulation. After the collapse of the national state and its temple, the exile became the matrix in which the traditional dimensions of Israelite faith were transformed.[47] We can hardly exaggerate the theological question by which the exile challenges Israel's faith: "What happened to Yahweh in the process of the exile?"[48] Or to put it somewhat differently, What does the Old Testament say about what happened to Yahweh during the exile? The theological crisis with which we struggle is the presence of Yahweh among his people that was put into deep jeopardy during the Babylonian captivity. The composition of the Pentateuch that we have considered is one representative of the theological reflections evoked by the exilic experiences. This observation leads us to think that the tabernacle sanctuary in the Priestly Pentateuch functions as a judgment or critique upon the Jerusalem temple, which was built, patronized, and abused by the Israelite monarchy. After the kingdom of Judah and its temple had been destroyed, the Priestly writers (Aaronites!) came to draw on the ancient tradition of the tent sanctuary with a message in mind for their own time: Israel had to be regenerated by Yahweh's tabernacling presence on earth.

For the Priestly writers, the tabernacle cult was seen to be fundamental to keeping Israel's life as God's people. They proclaimed, as a theological prescription, that "Yahweh had bound himself to a people, not to a place or a kingdom, and could meet his people in many differ-

---

46. For this perspective, I follow some critical works, such as M. Noth, *Exodus* (trans. J. Bowden; OTL; Philadelphia, Westminster, 1962) 17; F. M. Cross, *Canaanite Myth and Hebrew Epic: Essays in the History of the Religion of Israel* (Cambridge: Harvard University Press, 1973) 323–24; J. Blenkinsopp, "The Structure of P," *CBQ* 38 (1976) 275–92.

47. For example, see T. M. Raitt, *A Theology of Exile: Judgment/Deliverance in Jeremiah and Ezekiel* (Philadelphia: Fortress, 1977); D. L. Smith, *The Religion of the Landless: The Social Context of the Babylonian Exile* (Bloomington, Ind.: Meyer-Stone, 1989); see also essays in J. Barton and D. J. Reimer, eds., *After the Exile: Essays in Honour of Rex Mason* (Macon, Ga.: Mercer University Press, 1996) 5–26, 27–44, 45–58.

48. W. Brueggemann, "A Shattered Transcendence? Exile and Restoration," in Kraftchick, Myers, and Ollenburger, eds., *Biblical Theology: Problems and Perspectives*, 172.

ent locations"[49] if the tabernacle sanctuary took its place at the center of his people's encampment. This Priestly prescription for the tabernacle is not simply an attempt to legitimate an existing cultic institution by projecting it back into the wilderness period, but a theological blueprint to correct certain ideas or ideologies associated with Jerusalem and its temple.

3. One may argue that the dichotomy between the Sinaitic tabernacle and the Jerusalem temple is not to be sharply drawn.[50] This is to say that the concern for the dwelling of God in the Priestly tabernacle may not necessarily be a judgment on the Jerusalem temple. Indeed, the extant Pentateuch not only represents the Priestly tabernacle but reflects (although not names) the Deuteronomic central sanctuary. One may also have the impression that (as we read in, e.g., Ps. 26:8; 27:4–5; 74:7–8; Ezek. 40–48; 1 Chron. 6:32–48; 23:25–32; 2 Chron. 5:5; cf. 7:3) "tent" (מִשְׁכָּן) and "temple" (בֵּית יהוה) are put into synonymous parallel in biblical spirituality.[51] The tension between Sinai and Jerusalem or the tabernacle and the temple may be understood as a textual signal that yields "a spiritual dynamic that neither perspective alone could have produced."[52] Yet, this understanding and the biblical references given for it are only selected examples. The impression that the Bible stresses the continuity between the Mosaic tabernacle and the Jerusalem temple does not claim to be complete. The Bible does not present the description that the two complexes of tradition, the Sinaitic/Mosaic and the Zionistic/Davidic, are quite capable of coexistence without tension. The OT accounts of the tabernacle were shaped in various contexts and from multiple layers of traditions. They show varying theological interests. But the Priestly portrait of the tent sanctuary, especially described in Exod 25–31 and 35–40, reveals that the Priestly writer was probably an opponent of the Jerusalem temple: Yahweh had bound himself to a people and not to the building (e.g., Exod. 25:8; Lev. 26:11–12; cf. Josh. 22:19–29; 2 Sam. 7:5–7; Acts 7:44–46; 15:16; Rev. 21:3; John 1:14). What is particularly interesting here is that the distinctive theological emphases appear in the NT. In a setting where the differences between Christianity and Judaism were becoming increasingly clear, tabernacle imagery was theologically seen to establish the idea of the ever-onward call of

49. Koester, *The Dwelling of God*, 10. See R. E. Clements, *God and Temple* (Philadelphia: Fortress, 1965) 120–21; T. Fretheim, "The Priestly Document: Anti-Temple?" *VT* 18 (1968) 313–29; V. Fritz, *Tempel und Zelt: Studien zum Tempelbau in Israel und zu dem Zeltheiligtum der Priesterschrift* (WMANT 47; Neukirchen-Vluyn: Neukirchener, 1977) 149–53.

50. J. D. Levenson, "The Jerusalem Temple in Devotional and Visionary Experience," in Green, ed., *Jewish Spirituality*, 32–61; idem, *Sinai and Zion*, 15–218.

51. Levenson, "The Jerusalem Temple," 34–37, 50–51.

52. Levenson, "The Jerusalem Temple," 37; see also idem, *Sinai and Zion*, 187–217, esp. 206.

God to his people (Acts 7:44–46; 15:16; Rev. 21:3; John 1:14). In his study of the tabernacle imagery in the NT, Craig Koester remarked that the mobile sanctuary of the Sinai was attractive to early Christians because it corresponded with the identity of Christians as heirs of Israel's cultic heritage, while the static temple did not.[53]

The Priestly prescription for the tabernacle corrects, as a critique, certain ideas associated with the temple. This fact becomes clear when we read the Priestly accounts that the tabernacle was designed by Yahweh to be constructed by freewill offerings (Exod. 25:1–9; 35:4–29), unlike Solomon's temple, which utilized forced labor. Religio-historically, the sanctuary had been initiated by the deity, since it was in principle the gracious dwelling place of the deity on earth. In modern times, however, the decision to build a sanctuary is only made by a religious community for the sake of its gathering for worship. But according to the portrayal of the tabernacle in the Pentateuch, it is Yahweh himself rather than Israel who has the leading role in the construction of the sanctuary. The construction of the tabernacle represents a joyful "lifting up" (תרומאה) of the people's gifts to Yahweh (Exod. 35:5). The tent of meeting appears to be as a true meeting place where the divine will and human volition are reconciled with each other.

At this point, at a hermeneutical level, we see a convergence between the issues raised in the current discussion and those with which Wesleyan theologians have dealt. Randy Maddox, for example, pointed out that "Wesley construed God's power or sovereignty fundamentally in terms of *empowerment*, rather than control or *overpowerment*."[54] This is not to weaken God's power but to determine its character. As the one who governs, Yahweh enables Israel's obedience, but will not force it. Therefore, God's grace works powerfully in matters of human life and especially of Israel's ongoing life in the presence of Yahweh, thereby "empowering our responsibility, without overriding our responsibility."

4. How is Yahweh related to the world in the Pentateuch? The Priestly Pentateuch indicates that Yahweh freely met with Israel in the tent, but was not confined there. Put differently, the Pentateuch has portrayed Yahweh as a deity in search of his community. It points to Yahweh as the one who wants primarily to restore the order among creator, creature, and world. It is not accidental to see in the Priestly accounts of both creation and the tabernacle-building that the tabernacle ritual was anchored in the work of the Creator.[55]

---

53. Koester, *The Dwelling of God*, 84–85, 105, 185–86.

54. R. L. Maddox, *Responsible Grace: John Wesley's Practical Theology* (Nashville: Abingdon, 1994) 55.

55. Koester, *The Dwelling of God*, 10.

God's spirit, which was active when the world was created, played an active part as well in the construction of the tabernacle (Gen. 1:2; Exod. 31:3; 35:31). Such a perspective is also embedded in the theology of sabbath in which the experience of sabbath rest after creation is followed by the pattern of tabernacle-building.[56] This is the reason why the Moses story demonstrates that Yahweh rescued Israel. The goal of the exodus is not so much the promised land as it is to define Israel as a theocratic community, constituted and sustained by the tabernacling presence of Yahweh. Yahweh delivered Israel so that he might set up his tent (tabernacle) on earth.

How, then, could the holy Yahweh dwell in the midst of a sinful people? This question is solved by the prescriptions of Leviticus, which enable the presence of the cosmic God to indwell, to tabernacle, or to tent with his people. In effect, cult, as detailed in Exodus 19 through Num. 10:10, refers to the institutions of tabernacle and consecrated (Aaronite) priesthood, together with the associated rites of sacrifice and ordination by means of which Israel can sustain the presence of Yahweh in its midst.

The OT theology of the Pentateuch represents the availability of God in his portable shrine, which probably served as a source of consolation to Israel in exile. To those who were far from their temple, which lay in ruins, the most meaningful image of God was not that of a king enthroned in his stone palace (temple). It becomes clear that the tabernacling presence of Yahweh carries out the message of God's mobility and availability to all Israel. Here, again, the tent/shrine is indeed a judgment on the Jerusalem temple. The Pentateuch neither names Jerusalem nor refers to the kings who play a role in a political polemic. This theology would assure Israel that God is present and could be worshiped in many different locations, and it would also foster hope for the restoration of the sanctuary in the future. This theology is in part similar to and yet distinctly different from the theological blueprints that can be discerned in Ezekiel, Haggai, Zechariah, Deutero- and Trito-Isaiah, and the Deuteronomists.

---

56. See Blenkinsopp, "The Structure of P," esp. 281–83.

Selected Bibliography

Blum, E. *Studien zur Komposition des Pentateuch.* BZAW 189. Berlin: de Gryter, 1990.

Boorer, S. *The Promise of the Land as Oath.* BZAW 205. Berlin: de Gruyter, 1992.

Clements, R. E. *God and Temple.* Philadelphia: Fortress, 1965.

Clines, D. J. *The Theme of the Pentateuch.* JSOTSup 10. Sheffield: JSOT Press, 1978.

Crüsemann, F. *Die Tora: Theologie und Sozialgeschichte des alttestamentlichen Gesetzes.* Munich: Kaiser, 1992.

Eichrodt, W. *Theology of the Old Testament.* Trans. J. A. Baker. 2 vols. OTL. Philadelphia: Westminster, 1961–67.

Green, A., ed. *Jewish Spirituality from the Bible through the Middle Ages.* New York: Crossroad, 1988.

Knierim, Rolf. *The Task of Old Testament Theology: Substance, Method, and Cases.* Grand Rapids: Eerdmans, 1995.

Knight, D. A., and G. M. Tucker, eds. *The Hebrew Bible and Its Modern Interpreters.* Philadelphia: Fortress; Chico, Calif.: Scholars Press, 1985.

Koester, C. R. *The Dwelling of God: The Tabernacle in the Old Testament, Intertestamental Jewish Literature, and the New Testament.* CBQMS 22. Washington, D.C.: Catholic Biblical Association of America, 1989.

Kraftchick, S. J., C. D. Myers, Jr., and B. C. Ollenburger, eds. *Biblical Theology: Problems and Perspectives.* Nashville: Abingdon, 1995.

Levenson, J. D. *Sinai and Zion: An Entry into the Jewish Bible.* New York: HarperCollins, 1985.

Lohfink, N. *Theology of the Pentateuch: Themes of the Priestly Narrative and Deuteronomy.* ET. Edinburgh: T. & T. Clark, 1994.

Mann, T. W. *The Book of the Torah: The Narrative Integrity of the Pentateuch.* Atlanta: John Knox, 1988.

Mays, J. L., D. L. Petersen, and K. H. Richards, eds. *Old Testament Interpretation: Past, Present, and Future. Essays in Honor of Gene M. Tucker.* Nashville: Abingdon, 1995.

Noth, M. *Exodus.* Trans. J. S. Bowden. OTL. Philadelphia: Westminster, 1962.

Ollenburger, B. C., E. A. Martens, and G. F. Hasel, eds. *The Flowering of Old Testament Theology: A Reader in Twentieth-Century Old Testament Theology, 1930–1990.* SBTS 1, Winona Lake, Ind.: Eisenbrauns, 1992.

Perdue, L. G. *The Collapse of History: Reconstructing Old Testament Theology.* OBT. Minneapolis: Fortress, 1994.

Sun, H. T. C., K. L. Eades, J. M. Robinson, and G. I. Moller, eds. *Problems in Biblical Theology: Essays in Honor of Rolf Knierim.* Grand Rapids: Eerdmans, 1997.

Von Rad, G. *Old Testament Theology.* 2 vols. Trans. D. M. G. Stalker. New York: Harper and Row, 1962, 1965.

———. *The Problem of the Hexateuch and Other Essays.* Trans. E. W. Trueman Dicken. Edinburgh: Oliver and Boyd, 1966.

Whybray, R. N. *Introduction to the Pentateuch.* Grand Rapids: Eerdmans, 1995.

16

A Conflicted Book for a Marginal People: Thematic Oppositions in MT Jeremiah

Richard D. Weis

At the beginning of the twentieth century Bernhard Duhm expressed the judgment that in the case of the book of Jeremiah, "von einer methodischen Komposition, einer einheitlichen Disposition kann keine Rede sein." Later in the same paragraph he referred to the book as "die chaotische Masse."[1] While it has not been the unanimous conclusion of Jeremiah scholarship since 1901, this verdict has been repeated frequently by other researchers, down to the most recent studies.[2]

An aspect of the book of Jeremiah that has contributed to this widespread judgment of the book's synchronic incoherence is a series of stark thematic oppositions present in the final form of the book. Since some of these thematic oppositions involve theological statements, the book of Jeremiah at least arguably represents an instance of the coexistence of a plurality of theologies that Rolf Knierim identifies as the

Preliminary versions of this essay were presented for discussion in the March 1998 session of the Roundtable on Prophetic Literature in the Mid-Atlantic Region of the Society of Biblical Literature, and in a lecture at Westminster Theological Seminary, Philadelphia, Pennsylvania, in April 1998. I thank those in attendance on these two occasions, especially Stephen Cook, Michael O'Connor, Jean-Pierre Ruiz, Douglas Green, and Alan Groves, for their helpful reactions.

1. Bernhard Duhm, *Das Buch Jeremia* (HKAT 11; Tübingen: J. C. B. Mohr [Paul Siebeck], 1901) xx–xxi.

2. See, for example, Sigmund Mowinckel, *Zur Komposition des Buches Jeremia* (Kristiana: Jacob Dybwad, 1914) 5; James P. Hyatt, "The Book of Jeremiah: Introduction and Exegesis," *IB*, 5:787; John Bright, *Jeremiah* (AB 21; Garden City, N.Y.: Doubleday, 1965) lvi; John A. Thompson, *The Book of Jeremiah* (NICOT; Grand Rapids: Eerdmans, 1980) 30; Robert P. Carroll, *Jeremiah* (OTL; Philadelphia: Westminster, 1986) 38; William McKane, *A Critical and Exegetical Commentary on Jeremiah* (2 vols.; ICC; Edinburgh: T. & T. Clark, 1986–96) 1:xlix–l; Jack R. Lundbom, "Jeremiah, Book of," *ABD*, 3:711. More recently the case for acknowledging a greater degree of literary coherence in MT Jeremiah has been made by, among others, Mark E. Biddle, *Polyphony and Symphony in Prophetic Literature: Rereading Jeremiah 7–20* (SOTI 2; Macon, Ga.: Mercer University Press, 1996); A. R. Diamond, *The Confessions of Jeremiah in Context* (JSOTSup, 45; Sheffield: JSOT Press, 1987), esp. 177–88; Kathleen M. O'Connor, *The Confessions of Jeremiah: Their Interpretation and Role in Chapters 1–25* (SBLDS 94; Atlanta: Scholars Press, 1988), esp. 115–48; Mark S. Smith, *The Laments of Jeremiah and Their Contexts: A Literary and Redactional Study of Jeremiah 11–20* (SBLMS 42; Atlanta: Scholars Press, 1990).

problem facing Old Testament theology.[3] When seen in this way, it is small wonder that the book of Jeremiah has often been seen to be incoherent as a literary work, and explicable only as a pastiche of various materials and diverse redactional interventions.

Robert Carroll is one of the most strenuous recent advocates of this conclusion. In a 1995 essay titled "Synchronic Deconstructions of Jeremiah: Diachrony to the Rescue?" he argues that the book's extreme thematic oppositions render a coherent synchronic reading of the book of Jeremiah impossible, requiring a typically modernist diachronic (i.e., redaction-historical) explanation to restore a sense of coherence to the book. In particular, he points to oppositions in the portrayal of the effectiveness of prophets, and in the portrayal of the status and role of the king of Babylon.[4]

By contrast, I propose that these oppositions are actually an intentional and coherent response to varieties of complexity in the social location of the book's readers. To illustrate this I will focus on the opposing portrayals of the king of Babylon and the opposing instructions to Judean exiles in Babylon. My analysis will draw on a reader response approach, but will emphasize the social location of the reader and the way that frames interaction with the text. The results also have implications for the theological method proposed by Knierim.

THE OPPOSING PORTRAYALS AND INSTRUCTIONS

In his discussion of the opposing portrayals of Babylon and its king, Carroll calls attention to the strikingly different views of Babylon and its king presented in 25:1–14 and chs. 27–29 on the one hand, and chs. 50–51 on the other. In particular he points to the opposition between YHWH's reference to Nebuchadnezzar as עַבְדִּי, "my servant," in 25:9 and 27:6, and the representation of the same monarch in 51:34 as כַּתַּנִּין, "like the sea monster (or: dragon)."[5] However, the thematic opposition is significantly sharper and more extensive than Carroll suggests.

First, a third reference by YHWH to Nebuchadnezzar as עַבְדִּי is found in 43:10. In this context Nebuchadnezzar, as YHWH's servant, is opposed

---

3. Rolf P. Knierim, *The Task of Old Testament Theology: Substance, Method, and Cases* (Grand Rapids: Eerdmans, 1995) 1–2. The oppositions concerning Babylon and its kings, which will be treated in this essay, are specifically assessed in this way by Walter Brueggemann (*To Build, to Plant: A Commentary on Jeremiah 26–52* [ITC; Grand Rapids: Eerdmans, 1991] 257–59) and Ronald Clements (*Jeremiah* [IBC; Atlanta: John Knox, 1988] 261–65).

4. Robert P. Carroll, "Synchronic Deconstructions of Jeremiah: Diachrony to the Rescue?" in J. C. De Moor, ed., *"Synchronic or Diachronic?" A Debate on Method in Old Testament Exegesis* (OTS 34; Leiden: Brill, 1995) 39–51.

5. Carroll, "Synchronic Deconstructions of Jeremiah," 47.

to Egypt, not Judah. Nevertheless, the reporting of YHWH's designation of Nebuchadnezzar as עַבְדִּי is just as much a theological assertion as the references in 25:9 and 27:6, and functions similarly in its context. Thus, it is another component of the portrayal first encountered in 25:9 and 27:6.

Second, contrary to Carroll's suggestion that the application of the title of YHWH's servant to the king of Babylon is no particular cause for excitement, it is a highly unusual usage.[6] In the MT of Jeremiah there are two groups and two individuals on whom YHWH bestows the title עַבְדִּי or עֲבָדַי. The two groups are the prophets and "Jacob," that is, the people.[7] The two individuals are David, and Nebuchadnezzar, king of Babylon.[8] In the entire HB only the following figures are regularly described as YHWH's עֶבֶד: Moses, Joshua, David, the prophets, Jacob/Israel, Job, and Nebuchadnezzar. The three other figures given this title in the book of Jeremiah — the prophets, David, and Jacob/Israel — are also given the title in other literature of the exilic and postexilic eras. David and the prophets are so titled in the Dtr history, and Jacob/Israel receives the title in Second Isaiah.[9] Moreover, for the editor of MT Jeremiah, עַבְדִּי may have a specifically Davidic resonance. All three references to David under such a title are found in the MT version of the book only.[10]

Third, the references to Nebuchadnezzar as YHWH's servant are part of a larger pattern in which they are linked to one side of an opposition in the instructions to the Judean exiles in Babylon. The reference in 27:6 is part of a larger complex that embraces, in ch. 29, the letter of Jeremiah to the Judean exiles in Babylon following the deportation in 597.[11] That letter specifically instructs them (29:5–7):

בְּנוּ בָתִּים וְשֵׁבוּ וְנִטְעוּ גַנּוֹת וְאִכְלוּ אֶת־פִּרְיָן: קְחוּ נָשִׁים
וְהוֹלִידוּ בָּנִים וּבָנוֹת וּקְחוּ לִבְנֵיכֶם נָשִׁים וְאֶת־בְּנוֹתֵיכֶם תְּנוּ
לַאֲנָשִׁים וְתֵלַדְנָה בָּנִים וּבָנוֹת וּרְבוּ־שָׁם וְאַל־תִּמְעָטוּ: וְדִרְשׁוּ

---

6. Indeed, it clearly made some ancient readers uncomfortable. Jerome felt the need in his commentary (In Hieremiam libri VI, in S. Hieronymi Presbyteri Opera [CCSL 74, part 1.3, vol. 9; Turnout: Brepols, 1960] 239) to explain how Nebuchadnezzar was used by God, but could not properly be considered God's servant in the same sense as other figures.

7. The prophets: Jer. 7:25; 25:4; 26:5; 29:19; 35:15; 44:4. Jacob: Jer. 30:10; 46:27, 28.

8. David: Jer. 33:21, 22, 26. Nebuchadnezzar: Jer. 25:9; 27:6; 43:10.

9. David: 2 Sam. 3:18; 7:5; 1 Kings 11:13, 32, 34, 36, 38; 2 Kings 19:34; 20:6. Jacob/Israel: Isa. 41:8; 44:1, 2; 45:4.

10. All three occur in the well-known MT plus 33:14–26. On the other hand, as we will see below, one of the three references to Nebuchadnezzar as YHWH's servant probably occurs in both the LXX Vorlage and the MT. Most of the references to the prophets and Jacob as YHWH's servant(s) are found in both the LXX Vorlage and the MT.

11. Jeremiah 27–29 is often recognized as a coherent literary unit. See, for example, Carroll, Jeremiah, 523–24; Douglas R. Jones, Jeremiah (NCBC; Grand Rapids: Eerdmans, 1992) 337; Thompson, Book of Jeremiah, 528.

אֶת־שְׁלוֹם הָעִיר אֲשֶׁר הִגְלֵיתִי אֶתְכֶם שָׁמָּה וְהִתְפַּלְלוּ
בַעֲדָהּ אֶל־יְהוָה כִּי בִשְׁלוֹמָהּ יִהְיֶה לָכֶם שָׁלוֹם׃

Build houses, and settle down; plant gardens and eat their fruit; take
wives and beget sons and daughters, and take wives for your sons and
give your daughters to husbands, and let them give birth to sons and
daughters; become numerous there, and do not diminish; seek the welfare of the city where I have exiled you, and pray on its behalf to YHWH
because in its welfare you will have welfare.

The contents of chs. 50–51 stand in the sharpest possible contrast to
these portrayals of the king of Babylon as YHWH's servant, of Babylon
as the city whose welfare Judeans are to seek, and of Babylonian rule
as the context in which Judeans are to settle down, make a life for
themselves, and find their own welfare. As Carroll has pointed out, in
51:34 the king of Babylon is likened to the chaos monster or dragon
that elsewhere is understood as the opponent of YHWH, not YHWH's servant.[12] Jeremiah 50:17–18 declares that YHWH will "pay a visit to the
king of Babylon and his land, just as I paid a visit to the king of As-
syria" (הִנְנִי פֹקֵד אֶל־מֶלֶךְ בָּבֶל וְאֶל־אַרְצוֹ כַּאֲשֶׁר פָּקַדְתִּי אֶל־מֶלֶךְ אַשּׁוּר), because
"Nebuchadnezzar, king of Babylon, has gnawed [the] bones" of Is-
rael that had been devoured by Assyria (שֶׂה פְזוּרָה יִשְׂרָאֵל אֲרָיוֹת הִדִּיחוּ
הָרִאשׁוֹן אֲכָלוֹ מֶלֶךְ אַשּׁוּר וְזֶה הָאַחֲרוֹן עִצְּמוֹ נְבוּכַדְרֶאצַּר מֶלֶךְ בָּבֶל). Jeremiah 50:14
calls for an assault on Babylon "because it has sinned against YHWH"
(כִּי לַיהוָה חָטָאָה). Jeremiah 50:28 (cf. 51:11) characterizes the destruction
of Babylon as אֶת־נִקְמַת יְהוָה אֱלֹהֵינוּ נִקְמַת הֵיכָלוֹ "the vengeance of YHWH
our God, the vengeance for his temple," and in 51:24 YHWH declares,
וְשִׁלַּמְתִּי לְבָבֶל וּלְכֹל ׀ יוֹשְׁבֵי כַשְׂדִּים אֵת כָּל־רָעָתָם אֲשֶׁר־עָשׂוּ בְצִיּוֹן, "I will repay
Babylon and all the inhabitants of Chaldea for all their evil that they
have done in Zion." In 51:34–37 the inhabitants of Zion pray, not for
the welfare of Babylon, but for the avenging on Babylon of their torn
flesh and spilt blood, and in consequence of their prayer YHWH calls for
the utter destruction of Babylon. Throughout the two chapters are inter-
spersed exhortations to the audience of the speech, identified by YHWH
as עַמִּי, "my people" (51:45), not to settle down, but to flee Babylon.[13]

The contrasts could not be starker. The king of Babylon is the servant of YHWH on the one hand, and the chaos monster that opposes
YHWH and will be punished by YHWH on the other. Babylon is both the
home of YHWH's people for whose welfare they are to pray, and a place
from which they are to flee because YHWH responds to their prayers for
vengeance.

---

12. Carroll, "Synchronic Deconstructions of Jeremiah," 47.
13. Jer. 50:8; 51:6, 45, 50.

On the one hand, the mere existence of these oppositions in the text of MT Jeremiah calls for some explanation. On the other hand, the now well-established literary relationship between the Hebrew text behind the LXX and that which we know in the MT opens a door to deepening the description of the phenomena in front of us.[14] Specifically, we now have an avenue for assessing — by comparing the two text forms — whether these oppositions should be regarded as accidental or as intentional and redactional in nature.

When one compares the two versions of the book attested in the MT and the LXX, a striking thing emerges: the opposition appears to be a deliberate redactional creation. Adrian Schenker has examined the three cases where YHWH refers to Nebuchadnezzar as עַבְדִּי. In two cases (25:9 and 43:10) the term is present in the MT and absent in the LXX. Schenker's careful study demonstrates that these are not omissions or changes on the part of the LXX or its *Vorlage*, but alterations in the *Vorlage* of the LXX by the MT tradition.[15] In the third case (27:6) the LXX (reading δουλεύειν αὐτῷ, *pace* Schenker) at first glance seems to render a *Vorlage* לְעָבְדוֹ (also found at the end of the verse) instead of עַבְדִּי. Yohanan Goldman has persuasively argued that the most likely Hebrew text behind the LXX reading is עַבְדִּי.[16] Goldman also has demonstrated that 33:14–26, which contains all three references to David as עַבְדִּ, is likewise an addition to the LXX *Vorlage* by the MT tradition.[17] Among others, Tov, Bogaert, Schenker, and Goldman have established that the LXX *Vorlage* is the lineal ancestor of the MT in the redactional process.[18] Thus, the opposition between Nebuchadnezzar and David as עַבְדִּ, and

---

14. This is the view particularly associated with the work of Emanuel Tov ("L'incidence de la critique textuelle sur la critique littéraire dans le livre de Jérémie," *RB* 79 [1972] 189–99; "Some Aspects of the Textual and Literary History of the Book of Jeremiah," in Pierre-Maurice Bogaert, ed., *Le livre de Jérémie* [BETL 54; Leuven: Peeters and University Press, 1981] 145–67) and Pierre-Maurice Bogaert ("Les mécanismes rédactionnels en Jér 10,1–16 [LXX et TM] et la signification des suppléments," in Bogaert, ed., *Le livre de Jérémie*, 222–38). Among recent studies see in particular Yohanan Goldman, *Prophétie et royauté au retour de l'exil* (OBO 118; Freiburg: Universitätsverlag, 1992); idem, "Juda et son roi au milieu des nations: la dernière rédaction du livre de Jérémie," in Adrian H. W. Curtis and Thomas Römer, eds., *The Book of Jeremiah and Its Reception* (BETL 128; Leuven: Peeters and University Press, 1997) 151–82; Pierre-Maurice Bogaert, "Le livre de Jérémie en perspective: les deux rédactions antiques selon les travaux en cours" *RB* 101 (1994) 363–406; Hermann-Josef Stipp, *Das masoretische und alexandrinische Sondergut des Jeremiabuches: Textgeschichtlicher Rang, Eigenarten, Triebkräfte* (OBO 136; Freiburg: Universitätsverlag, 1994).

15. Adrian Schenker, "Nebukadnezzars Metamorphose vom Unterjocher zum Gottesknecht," *RB* 89 (1982) 498–527.

16. Goldman, *Prophétie et royauté*, 133–35.

17. Goldman, *Prophétie et royauté*, 9–37, 225–26.

18. Tov, "L'incidence"; Bogaert, "Les mécanismes rédactionnels"; Schenker, "Nebukadnezzars Metamorphose"; Goldman, *Prophétie et royauté*; idem, "Juda et son roi."

the expansion of the opposition between Nebuchadnezzar as YHWH's servant and as YHWH's opponent, are a direct result of intervention in the text by the tradents responsible for the MT.

The same tradents also have intervened in chs. 50–51 to heighten the broader pattern of oppositions built around the contrast between Nebuchadnezzar the servant and Nebuchadnezzar the enemy. In 50:14 the clause כִּי לַיהוָה חָטָאָה, "because it has sinned against YHWH," is present only in the MT, and seems more likely to have been added to the LXX *Vorlage* rather than subtracted from the MT. In 50:28 the MT plus נִקְמַת הֵיכָלוֹ, "the vengeance of his temple," may well be an assimilation to 51:11, but it nevertheless contributes to the sharpening of the opposition by linking YHWH's action specifically to the destruction of the temple, in which Nebuchadnezzar would also be regarded as having acted as YHWH's servant. Finally, 51:44b–49, a passage exhorting YHWH's people to come out of Babylon because its downfall is assured, is another likely MT addition. These additions to the LXX *Vorlage* do not create the portrayal of Babylon's role and fate, and the instruction to YHWH's people that oppose the corresponding portrayals and instructions in chs. 25, 27–29. That is already present in the LXX *Vorlage*, but they certainly serve to heighten the oppositional character of chs. 50–51.

That these interventions are in nature redactional, as opposed to text transmissional, seems self-evident from their mutually reinforcing character, and from the striking departure represented by YHWH's reference to Nebuchadnezzar as עַבְדִּי.[19]

PREVIOUS EXPLANATIONS OF THE OPPOSITIONS

Thompson apparently sees no issue requiring explanation here.[20] This perhaps is due to his interpretation that the bestowal of the title of YHWH's servant on Nebuchadnezzar merely describes him as YHWH's instrument.[21] This does not, however, take the use of the title apart from Nebuchadnezzar with sufficient seriousness. Indeed, Carroll is quite right in insisting that any attempt to interpret the book of Jeremiah as a whole must find an explanation for these oppositions.

The book of Jeremiah itself seems to offer a way of dissolving this opposition by suggesting a limited duration (seventy years or three generations) for the period when the king of Babylon rules as the servant of

---

19. The scope of the well-known rearrangement of the oracles against the nations between the LXX *Vorlage* and the MT also suggests redactional intervention, rather than incremental change during textual transmission.

20. Thompson, *Jeremiah*, 731.

21. Thompson, *Jeremiah*, 512. He is not alone in this, of course, since an analogous move was made as early as the fifth century C.E. by Jerome (see above, n. 6).

YHWH. Brueggemann and Clements, while their explanations have other more explicit aspects, both seem at some fundamental level to draw on this explanation in their language of historical periodization.[22] Wilhelm Rudolph and William Holladay make explicit appeal to such a solution.[23] This is not a satisfactory resolution of the contradiction, however. As the citations from chs. 50 and 51 make clear, the very things that Nebuchadnezzar does as YHWH's servant are those things for which he also is regarded as the enemy of YHWH. Thus, the oppositions remain tensed, unresolved.

Carroll regards a diachronic explanation of this thematic opposition as the only satisfactory explanation. He concludes that this and other oppositions render the text incoherent when it is read as a literary whole; the text can only be regarded as coherent if seen as a pastiche, an unintended accident of the superimposition of diachronically discrete layers of tradition.[24] Clements likewise resorts to an explicitly diachronic explanation, describing chs. 50–51 as "a relatively late appendage" to the book. However, he regards the change as intentional, with chs. 27–29 and 50–51 representing earlier and later stages in the theological reflections of the Jeremiah tradition.[25]

I suggest that the verdict that the text is incoherent without diachronic explanation is, as much as anything, due to particular assumptions about the nature of literary coherence. Specifically, it assumes that the coherence of a text or book is to be found at the conceptual level, that literary coherence is to be construed as conceptual uniformity or homogeneity, and that the only function of theological language and concepts is to describe God. Given such assumptions, it is difficult not to regard the oppositions discussed here as rendering the book of Jeremiah, when read as a literary whole, incoherent. However, as I will suggest below, conceptual uniformity is not the only way we might conceive of the coherence of literary works, and theological language might serve other functions.

Beyond the problems with a presupposition of coherence as conceptual uniformity, I would argue that a diachronic explanation of the

---

22. Brueggemann, *To Build, to Plant*, 258; Clements, *Jeremiah*, 264–65.

23. Wilhelm Rudolph, *Jeremia* (HAT 12; Tübingen: J. C. B. Mohr [Paul Siebeck], 1968) 297; William L. Holladay, *Jeremiah 2: A Commentary on the Book of the Prophet Jeremiah, Chapters 26–52* (Hermeneia; Minneapolis: Fortress, 1989) 431.

24. Carroll, "Synchronic Deconstructions of Jeremiah," 50–51.

25. Clements, *Jeremiah*, 263. Rudolph (*Jeremia*, 297–99) and Jones (*Jeremiah*, 523) adopt similar positions. William McKane (*Jeremiah*, 2:clxix–clxxi) seems to do so as well (see also his report of earlier literature in this line). Holladay (*Jeremiah 2*, 121) seems also to employ a diachronic explanation alongside his appeal to the seventy-year period as a way to resolve the opposition, but in reverse sequence from other scholars — the designation of Nebuchadnezzar as עַבְדִּי is later, not the views expressed in chs. 50–51.

oppositions discussed here is unsatisfactory on the basis of the evidence. The reasons for this are four. First, the opposition between instructions to settle down and seek the welfare of Babylon, and instructions to flee Babylon as the sought-after vengeance is brought on it is already present in the LXX *Vorlage*. Second, if one follows Goldman in reading δουλεύειν αὐτῷ in the LXX of 27:6 as a change from an original עַבְדִּי, then the opposing portrayals of the king of Babylon are also already in the LXX *Vorlage*. Third, while the MT additions perhaps only sharpen the opposing portrayals of Nebuchadnezzar, they *create* the Nebuchadnezzar-David opposition where none had existed. Fourth, the MT additions embrace not only two of the three references to the king of Babylon as YHWH's servant, but other matter that accentuates the oppositions associated with the opposing portrayals of the king of Babylon. These factors suggest two conclusions, both raising problems for any diachronic resolution of the oppositions. First, the thematic opposition existed before the redaction that produced the MT. Second, the sharpened and emphasized opposition found in the MT is the textual result aimed at by the redactional process, and as such should be presumed to have some kind of synchronic coherence that is worthy of investigation.

Brueggemann offers such a synchronic explanation when he suggests that the opposition of chs. 50–51 to chs. 27–29 (indeed, to the Jeremianic tradition as a whole) means that the "pro-Babylonian sympathy" of that tradition is "nullified and negated." As a result, YHWH's sovereignty is split apart from Babylonian imperial ambitions so that "only the sovereign power of [YHWH] matters."[26]

This explanation is unsatisfactory, however, for three reasons. First, it takes no account of, and does not adequately explain, the opposing sets of instructions to the *gôlāh* community in Babylon. Second, it is built fundamentally on the sequential explanation implied by the seventy-year period mentioned in the book, an explanation that is itself unsatisfactory, as we have seen above. Third, this explanation also assumes that coherence takes the form of conceptual unity and that the function of theological language is only to describe God.

A NEW EXPLANATION OF THE OPPOSITIONS

I propose that the apparent thematic incoherence on the part of the book of Jeremiah that we have discussed here is an intentional construction that is designed to assist its readers in maintaining a coherent identity in a situation of "marginality" as defined by Jung Young Lee in his

---

26. Brueggemann, *To Build, to Plant*, 258.

book of the same title.[27] Lee begins by reviewing conventional or "centralist" definitions of marginality as a situation of being "in-between" two cultures. This situation of "in-between" is defined as living "in two societies or two cultures and [being] a member of neither."[28] In general, this is regarded as a state of tension or divided identity, which the marginal person seeks to resolve through assimilation to the dominant culture. Lee goes on, however, to describe marginality from the point of view of more recent research coming out of marginal communities themselves. These understandings see the situation as fundamentally positive in nature, a condition that the persons in it seek to maintain because it gives them cultural dual citizenship, and locates them at a creative intersection of two cultures. He describes marginality from this perspective as being "in-both."[29]

I would suggest that the situation of the Babylonian *gôlāh*, and that of Persian-period Yehud and the Diaspora, are exactly situations of marginality as defined by Lee. The communities in question were small. A common estimate for the total number deported to Babylon is twenty thousand.[30] Carter estimates the population of early Persian-period Yehud at eleven thousand, and that of late Persian Yehud at seventeen thousand.[31] The size of Diaspora communities beyond these two is even more difficult to estimate, but in any case they were surely minority communities in their particular contexts. They tried to maintain an ethnically distinct identity in a larger and dominant Babylonian or Persian cultural context in which assimilation was a relatively easy and attractive option. In order to survive and thrive, the community that first read the final form of the book of Jeremiah had to affirm a distinct Judean identity, but it had to come to terms with being part of the larger Babylonian or Persian Empire. On the one hand, some degree of assimilation certainly occurred, as the names of the Davidides Sheshbazzar and Zerubbabel indicate. It represented a real threat of communal extinction. On the other hand, many of the traditions around which a distinct

27. Jung Young Lee, *Marginality: The Key to Multicultural Theology* (Minneapolis: Fortress, 1995).

28. Lee, *Marginality*, 43.

29. Lee, *Marginality*, 42–53.

30. Joseph Blenkinsopp, "Temple and Society in Achaemenid Judah," in Philip R. Davies, ed., *Second Temple Studies, 1: Persian Period* (JSOTSup 117; Sheffield: JSOT Press, 1991) 41; Brooks Schramm, *The Opponents of Third Isaiah: Reconstructing the Cultic History of the Restoration* (JSOTSup 193; Sheffield: Sheffield Academic Press, 1995) 54; Daniel L. Smith, *The Religion of the Landless: The Social Context of the Babylonian Exile* (Bloomington, Ind.: Meyer-Stone Books, 1989) 32.

31. Charles E. Carter, "The Province of Yehud in the Post-Exilic Period: Soundings in Site Distribution and Demography," in Tamara C. Eskenazi and Kent H. Richards, eds., *Second Temple Studies, 2: Temple Community in the Persian Period* (JSOTSup 175; Sheffield: JSOT Press, 1994) 134.

communal identity might be maintained presupposed national power and independence, which were not realistically attainable after 587/6. Indeed, to seek out such identities would lead to communal extinction of another sort. To survive and thrive in their marginal situation, the communities of Judean survivors had to deliberately construct and maintain an "in-both" identity that simultaneously accepted and resisted Babylonian or Persian dominance. Otherwise, their "in-between" situation would be resolved in favor of assimilation and the community would fade out of existence as a distinct identity, or it would be resolved in favor of violent resistance that would bring crushing reprisals.

The oppositions built around the characterizations of the king of Babylon and the instructions to the Judeans in Babylon precisely maintain the reader in the double identity necessary for an "in-both" existence. The king of Babylon is both friend and enemy of the community, thus YHWH's servant and foe. The Judeans under Babylonian domination must seek the welfare of Babylon and also flee it. That these dynamics might be addressed by portrayals of the king of Babylon and that city, and by instructions to the Judeans residing in it, is easy enough to see in the period when Babylon is the dominant power.

I contend that the dynamics would have been essentially the same under the Persians, and that the oppositions in the book of Jeremiah concerning Babylon and its king would speak as well to that situation.[32] To suggest that the dynamics described above characterized Yehud (and presumably other Diaspora communities as well) under Persian domination is not new. They are at work in the book of Esther, as demonstrated by Sidnie White Crawford.[33] Rainer Albertz also points to them in his discussion of the communal needs to which the formation of the Pentateuch responded.[34] They are certainly front and center in the books of Ezra and Nehemiah. That the Jeremiah texts about the king of Babylon could continue to address these dynamics was made possible by the use of the title "king of Babylon" by the Persian kings, beginning already with Cyrus.[35] Thus references to Babylon and its king in the Persian period would function as ciphers for Persia.

---

32. This is of particular relevance for MT Jeremiah, since this edition of the book is most commonly dated to the Persian period. See the review of literature on this point in Beat Huwyler, *Jeremia und die Völker: Untersuchungen zu den Völkersprüchen in Jeremia 46–49* (FAT 20; Tübingen: J. C. B. Mohr [Paul Siebeck], 1997) 63.

33. Sidnie A. White, "Esther: A Feminine Model for Jewish Diaspora," in Peggy L. Day, ed., *Gender and Difference in Ancient Israel* (Minneapolis: Fortress, 1989) 164–65, 173.

34. Rainer Albertz, *A History of Israelite Religion in the Old Testament Period* (trans. J. Bowden; 2 vols.; OTL; Louisville: Westminster John Knox, 1994) 2:472–73. Note his discussion of the "D composition" in particular.

35. See, for example, the text of the Cyrus Cylinder: "I am Cyrus, king of the world, great king, legitimate king, king of Babylon, king of Sumer and Akkad" (*ANET*, 316).

Thus, when seen from the point of view of the social situation of the reader, these oppositions in the book of Jeremiah are eminently coherent. Their coherence is not that of conceptual uniformity, however, but the coherence of opposites maintained in tension, the very balancing act needed to maintain a coherent social identity for the reader. The opposition is intentional, and the reader is not expected to resolve it. Instead, the opposition is aimed at maintaining the two sides of the "in-between," "in-both" identity necessary to keeping the readers' community alive as a distinct cultural entity under Babylonian, or — in the case of the MT version of the book — Persian dominance. We may also conclude that the function of the theological statements within this set of oppositions is not primarily to describe God, but to maintain communal identity. To attempt to reconcile them into a conceptually coherent picture of the Deity is to misunderstand their intention.

IMPLICATIONS FOR METHOD IN OLD TESTAMENT THEOLOGY

Although we have been engaged in the exegetical enterprise that in Knierim's methodology precedes the theological task,[36] the results of our study have implications for that task and methodology. A brief review of those implications may be useful.

Knierim proposes a twofold task for the discipline of OT theology. The first element is the examination of the fundamental way(s) in which the relationship between YHWH and the world is named in the HB/OT, so as to establish criteria for determining the relationships and degrees of validity among the diversity of theologies and texts in the HB/OT. Knierim specifically names these criteria as the theology of YHWH's creation of, and dominion over, the world, and the "theology of justice and righteousness." The second element is the assessment of the individual theological expressions in the light of those criteria.[37]

Insofar as statements about YHWH's relation to the king of Babylon and vice versa, which we have examined above, are theological statements in Knierim's meaning of that term,[38] we have been confronted already in our exegetical work with the problem and task of OT theology as Knierim defines them. Interestingly, the two fundamental theological criteria identified by Knierim do not seem especially helpful in making sense of the opposing portrayals and instructions relating to Babylon in the book of Jeremiah. Both portrayals of the king of Babylon, and both sets of instructions to the exile community in Babylon, are

---

36. Knierim, *Task of Old Testament Theology*, 60–69.
37. Knierim, *Task of Old Testament Theology*, 16.
38. That is, statements about the relation of YHWH and reality (Knierim, *Task of Old Testament Theology*, 10–11).

grounded in a theology of YHWH as creator and ruler of the universe (27:5 and 51:15–19).[39] Nor is a theology of justice and righteousness particularly helpful in adjudicating between the two sides of the opposition, since it may be argued that the destruction of Jerusalem and success of Babylon, and the destruction of Babylon and restoration of Jerusalem, are both presented in the book as YHWH's just acts.

I suggest that the problem is not to be attributed to Knierim's choice of fundamental criteria, but to two methodological issues. First, Knierim's theological method appears to share an assumption with the various unsatisfactory attempts to resolve or explain the oppositions reviewed above, namely, that overtly theological language in the HB always primarily functions to describe God. By contrast, we have seen that the best explanation of this thematic opposition in the book of Jeremiah understands its primary purpose to be not theological, but sociological — the maintenance of communal identity — rather than the description of God. This suggests a need to take more seriously the contextuality of theological expressions, not only at the level of exegesis, but in the discipline of OT theology itself. The second issue is the question of what constitutes the theological elements whose relationships and validity must be assessed in the second stage of the theological task as Knierim defines it. All the previous attempts at assessing the relationship between the opposing portrayals of Babylon and its king have treated the two sides of the opposition as two discrete elements, whose relationship must be conceived somehow. Our conclusion about that relationship, while proceeding from that starting point, suggests that there is only a single complex element here. To put it differently, the opposition itself, rather than being an obstacle to be overcome, is the central theological element here, not its two component sides.

---

39. Note also Schenker's valuable discussion of the allusions to theological understandings of creation in Jeremiah 27 ("Nebukadnezzars Metamorphose," 500–508).

Selected Bibliography

Albertz, Rainer. *A History of Israelite Religion in the Old Testament Period*. Vol. 2: *Exile to the Maccabees*. OTL. Louisville: Westminster John Knox, 1994.

Blenkinsopp, Joseph. "Temple and Society in Achaemenid Judah." In *Second Temple Studies, 1: Persian Period*, ed. Philip R. Davies. JSOTSup 117. Sheffield: JSOT Press, 1991.

Brueggemann, Walter. *To Build, to Plant: A Commentary on Jeremiah 26–52*. ITC. Grand Rapids: Eerdmans, 1991.

Carroll, Robert P. "Synchronic Deconstructions of Jeremiah: Diachrony to the Rescue?" In *Synchronic or Diachronic?" A Debate on Method in Old Testament Exegesis*, ed. J. C. De Moor. OTS 34. Leiden: E. J. Brill, 1995.

Carter, Charles E. "The Province of Yehud in the Post-Exilic Period: Soundings in Site Distribution and Demography." In *Second Temple Studies, 2: Temple Community in the Persian Period*, ed. Tamara C. Eskenazi and Kent H. Richards. JSOTSup, 175. Sheffield: JSOT Press, 1994.

Clements, Ronald. *Jeremiah*. IBC. Atlanta: John Knox, 1988.

Duhm, Bernhard. *Das Buch Jeremia*. HKAT 11. Tübingen and Leipzig: J. C. B. Mohr (Paul Siebeck), 1901.

Goldman, Yohanan. *Prophétie et royauté au retour de l'exil*. OBO 118. Freiburg: Universitätsverlag, and Göttingen: Vandenhoeck & Ruprecht, 1992.

Holladay, William L. *Jeremiah 2*. Hermeneia. Minneapolis: Fortress, 1989.

Knierim, Rolf P. *The Task of Old Testament Theology: Substance, Method, and Cases*. Grand Rapids: Eerdmans, 1995.

Lee, Jung Young. *Marginality: The Key to Multicultural Theology*. Minneapolis: Fortress, 1995.

Rudolph, Wilhelm. *Jeremia*. HAT 12. Tübingen: J. C. B. Mohr (Paul Siebeck), 1968.

Schenker, Adrian, O.P. "Nebukadnezzars Metamorphose vom Unterjocher zum Gottesknecht." *RB* 89 (1982) 498–527.

Smith, Daniel L. *The Religion of the Landless: The Social Context of the Babylonian Exile*. Bloomington, Ind.: Meyer-Stone Books, 1989.

Thompson, John A. *The Book of Jeremiah*. NICOT. Grand Rapids: Eerdmans, 1980.

Tov, Emanuel. "L'incidence de la critique textuelle sur la critique littéraire dans le livre de Jérémie." *RB* 79 (1972) 189–99.

17

Text Criticism, Text Composition, and Text Concept in 2 Samuel 23 and 24

William Yarchin

It is not uncommon for compositions in the HB — ranging in size from entire scroll complexes like the Torah to smaller passages like a psalm or even a verse — to juxtapose disparate materials in peculiar combinations. The last four chapters of 2 Samuel provide a parade example. Here we find six clearly demarcated, self-standing text units (21:1–14; 21:15–22; 22:1–51; 23:1–7; 23:8–39; 24:1–25) that do not exhibit an immediately apparent rationale in their arrangement relative to each other. In the following pages I will identify the compositional relationship between only the last two text units, addressing this question: Why is 2 Sam. 23:8–39 (a list of David's soldiers) followed by the story of David's census and the resulting plague upon Israel in 2 Samuel 24?

In general, I adopt here the methodological approach of Rolf P. Knierim, who has advanced the study of the HB by exploring how intra-textual concepts provide compositional coherence within and among text units.[1] In the case of the Samuel books, where the MT does not consistently preserve the best reading, investigation of compositional questions inevitably entails text critical questions.[2] As we will see, this

---

1. See especially his "The Composition of the Pentateuch," in *The Task of Old Testament Theology: Substance, Method, and Cases* (Grand Rapids: Eerdmans, 1995) 351–79; *Text and Concept in Leviticus 1:1–9. A Case in Exegetical Method* (FAT 2; Tübingen: J. C. B. Mohr [Paul Siebeck], 1992); "The Book of Numbers," in E. Blum, C. Macholz, and W. Stegemann, eds., *Die Hebräische Bibel und ihre zweifache Nachgeschichte* (FS R. Rendtorff; Neukirchen: Neukirchener, 1991) 155–69.

2. In the light of readings preserved in MT Chronicles, 4QSam[a], LXX[L], and/or other textual witnesses, the MT reading in Samuel is in many cases not to be followed. The value of the Greek text in the textual criticism of Samuel has been well documented by J. Shenkel (*Chronology and Recensional Development in the Greek Text of Kings* [Cambridge: Harvard University Press, 1968] 5–21) and E. Tov ("The State of the Question: Problems and Proposed Solutions," in R. Kraft, ed., *1972 Proceedings of the International Organization for Septuagint and Cognate Studies and the Society of Biblical Literature Pseudepigrapha Seminar* [Missoula: Scholars Press, 1972]). D. Barthélemy has established that in the latter half of 2 Reigns, Codex Vaticanus (LXX[B]) features the *kaige* rescension, which appears to revise the OG toward a proto-Masoretic text (*Les Devanciers d'Aquila* [VTSup 10; Leiden: Brill, 1963] 91–143). O. Thenius (*Die Bücher Samuels* [KHAT 4; 2d ed.; Leipzig: S. Hirzel, 1864]), J. Wellhausen (*Der Text der Bücher Samuelis* [Göttingen: Vandenhoeck & Ruprecht, 1871]), S. R. Driver (*Notes on the Hebrew Text and the Topography of the Books of Samuel* [2d ed.;

is particularly true in the list of David's soldiers, where a key text-critical factor — the textual attestation to the Hebrew root שׁלשׁ — has a decisive effect on discerning the composition of the whole list. The present essay, then, includes an English translation of David's list that reflects the most defensible textual readings. I follow with an analysis of the structure and composition of the list and, based on that analysis, I examine the position of the list vis-à-vis ch. 24. I argue that the compositional connection between the list of soldiers and the census plague story is compelling, sequentially linked by the concept of development in David's military organization — a development that exceeded its proper constrictions, resulting in disaster for Israel.

TEXT-CRITICAL FOCUS:
THE "THREE," THE "THIRTY," AND THE "OFFICERS"

The Hebrew text of 2 Sam. 23:8–39 includes one feature in particular that impinges directly on the question of the composition of the pericope. I refer to the appearance of the root שׁלשׁ in its various permutations in vv. 8, 13, 18, 19, 22, 23, and 24 as attested in the Hebrew, Greek, Syriac, and Aramaic witnesses and in the Masoretic notes, both here and in the parallel passage of 1 Chron. 11:10–47. What follows is a summary of the readings preferred by the majority of modern critics and reflected in most modern translations.

1. In v. 8 MT הַשָּׁלִשִׁי is emended to רֹאשׁ הַשָּׁלִשָׁה, "chief of the three," based on LXX[L] (while 1 Chron. 11:11 Ketib and most Greek witnesses read הַשָּׁלוֹשִׁים, and 1 Chron. 11:11 Qere reads הַשְּׁלִישִׁים).

2. In v. 13 MT Ketib שְׁלשִׁים מֵהַשְּׁלשִׁים is emended to שְׁלשָׁה מֵהַשְּׁלשִׁים, "three from the thirty," based on the Qere and 1 Chron. 11:15.

3. In v. 18a MT Ketib רֹאשׁ הַשְּׁלִשָׁי is emended to רֹאשׁ הַשְּׁלשִׁים, "chief of the thirty," based on the Peshitta (while the Qere הַשְּׁלשָׁה, 1 Chron. 11:20, and the other versions indicate "three").

Oxford: Clarendon, 1913]), and subsequent scholars have ingeniously utilized what has come to be called the Lucianic (LXX[L] = Gk MSS boc₂e₂) witnesses to the OG in assessing readings within Samuel. For the history of the status held by the Lucianic or Antiochan MSS in the minds of text critics, see the survey by E. Ulrich, *The Qumran Text of Samuel and Josephus* (HSM 19; Missoula, Mont.: Scholars Press, 1978) 15–28.

While the ancient Hebrew witnesses in the readings provided by 4QSam[a] characteristically stand with the Lucianic readings against MT (F. M. Cross, "The History of the Biblical Text in the Light of Discoveries in the Judean Desert," *HTR* 57 [1964] 292–93), E. Tov has argued that this observation should not be considered an established fact in every case ("The Textual Affiliations of 4QSam[a]," *JSOT* 14 [1979] 37–53). S. Pisano has further demonstrated that readings from this Qumran ms are not to be employed in a cavalier manner (*Additions or Omissions in the Books of Samuel* [OBO 57; Fribourg, Switzerland: Universitätsverlag, 1984]). Overall, great care must be exercised regarding the various ancient witnesses to the Hebrew text of the Samuel book.

4. In v. 18b MT ולו שם בשלשה is emended to ולא שם בשלשה, "but he was not among/did not attain to the three" (based on 1 Chron. 11:20 Ketib and a small number of Masoretic MSS), or to ולו שם בשלשים, "and he had a name among the thirty" (based on context, since the next verse plainly states that Abishai did not have a name among the three).

5. In v. 19 MT מן השלשה is emended to מן השלשים, "more than the thirty," based on the Peshitta and v. 23a.

6. In v. 22 MT ולו שם בשלשה הגברים is emended to ולא שם בשלשה הגברים, "but he did not have a name among the three heroes" (based on a small number of Masoretic MSS and the same emendation at v. 18b), or to ולו שם בשלשים, "and he had a name among the thirty" (based on the Peshitta and the same emendation at v. 18b).

In sum, this is how most scholars untangle the issue of the three and the thirty:

1. Jeshbaal[3] is Chief of the "Three" (v. 8);

2. Three men from the "Thirty" joined David at Adullam (v. 13);

3. Abishai was Chief of the "Thirty" (v. 18a), yet he did not attain to the "Three," or alternatively he had a name among the "Thirty" (v. 18b), and he was honored more than the "Thirty" (v. 19a);

4. Benaiah also had no name among the "Three," or possibly had a name among the "Thirty" (v. 22b);

5. Finally, the name Asahel begins a list of the names of the "Thirty" (v. 24a).

According to these readings the pericope features two groups of warriors: a group called the "Three," with Jeshbaal at its head, and another group known as the "Thirty," led by Abishai, and listed beginning with Asahel. Most of the emendations that support this understanding, however, are based on uncritical use of the evidence from the Masoretic tradition, the Chronicles text, and the versions, as D. Barthélemy has shown in a penetrating analysis of the textual problems of this pericope.[4] For a full understanding of the complexities of the textual evidence his argument should be consulted firsthand; reviewed here are the most pertinent results of his research:

---

3. The name ישב בשבת, though attested in the Vulgate, Targum, and Peshitta, is probably a corruption from ישבשת by assimilation to בשבת in the preceding line. ישבעם, attested in LXX[B], is itself best explained as a de-baalized form of ישבעל, a form attested in LXX[L]. I read this latter form (see P. K. McCarter, *II Samuel: A New Translation with Introduction, Notes, and Commentary* [AB 9; Garden City, N.Y.: Doubleday, 1984]: 489; cf. D. Barthélemy, ed., *Critique textuelle de l'Ancien Testament* [OBO 50/1; Fribourg, Switzerland: Éditions Universitaires; Göttingen: Vandenhoeck & Ruprecht, 1982] 1:311).

4. Barthélemy, *Critique textuelle*, 1:312–21.

1. In 2 Sam. 23:8b the MT Ketib tradition has preserved an archaic expression (רֹאשׁ הַשָּׁלִשִׁי) "Elite of the Guard," or "Elite Guard" or "Shalishite Guard"; the *yod* of the second word denotes a military group, as it does for the כרתי and the פלתי regiments of David's military,[5] and the first word would not mean "chief," since שׂר is explicitly this text's term for troop leadership. The Chronicles text reflects a degree of ignorance regarding this ancient phrase, and so we find a wavering between the Ketib and Qere traditions as to how to render it, whether שָׁלִשִׁים or שָׁלוֹשִׁים. In any event, reliance on MT of Chronicles at these points is unsound. Second Samuel 23:8b and 18a should be read רֹאשׁ הַשָּׁלִשִׁי, "of the Shalishite Guard."

2. At v. 13a MT מֵהַשְּׁלֹשִׁים shows signs of assimilation to the Chronicles text (which itself is the result of assimilation from the archaic sense of the שׁלשׁ root), and the Peshitta and Targum readings indicate the same archaic meaning for רֹאשׁ noted for vv. 8 and 18. Accordingly, v. 13a should be read שְׁלֹשָׁה מֵהַשְּׁלֹשִׁים רֹאשׁ, "three from the officers—a band."

3. The MT מִן הַשְּׁלֹשָׁה at v. 19a is the result of a secondary assimilation to the parallel in 1 Chron. 11:21 already corrupted by assimilation to the "three" that precedes (in v. 18b) and follows (in v. 19b), while the Peshitta and Targum divide between שָׁלִשִׁים and שָׁלִשִׁים. In short, the testimony from the various witnesses is exceedingly complex at this point.

My acceptance of Barthélemy's text-critical judgments on the issue of the root שׁלשׁ in this pericope is evident in the following translation. So also is my rendering of רֹאשׁ in vv. 8 and 18 in the sense attested often in the HB as a technical term designating a troop of combatants,[6] שָׁלִשִׁי as a proper title for a certain רֹאשׁ, and שָׁלִשִׁים as "officers"[7] or "adjutants."[8] My interpretation of this pericope, therefore, will be based on the following specific points:

1. Jeshbaal is of the Shalishite company.

2. Three from the Officers' group joined David in vv. 13ff.

3. Abishai is of the Shalishite group, is recognized by the Three, and is honored more than the Officers.

4. Benaiah is recognized by the Three, and is honored more than the Officers.

5. Asahel is registered among the Officers.

---

5. Cf. 2 Sam. 8:18; 15:18; 20:7, 23; 1 Kings 1:38, 44.

6. As in Judg. 7:16, 20; 9:34, 37, 43, 44; 1 Sam. 11:11; 13:17, 18; Job 1:17; cf. E. P. Dhorme, *A Commentary on the Book of Job* (Nashville: Nelson, 1967) 11; idem, *L'emploi métaphorique des noms de parties du corps en hébreu et en akkadien* (Paris: Librairie orientaliste Paul Geunther, 1963) 31.

7. See B. A. Mastin, "Was the *šalîš* the Third Man in the Chariot?" in J. A. Emerton, ed., *Studies in the Historical Books of the Old Testament* (VTSup 30; Leiden: Brill, 1979) 138, 153; N. Naaman, "The List of David's Officers (*šalîšîm*)," *VT* 38 (1988) 71–79.

8. See Thenius, *Die Bücher Samuels*, 275, 279.

TRANSLATION

[8]These are the names of the warriors who belonged to David.

Jeshbaal the Hachmonite,[9] of the Shalishite company: He wielded his sword[10] against eight hundred, [all] slain at one time. [9]After him, Eleazar son of Dodo the Ahohite, of the Three Heroes with David: When they mocked the Philistines they [the Philistines] mustered right there for battle, and Israel withdrew.[11] [10]But he stood his ground[12] and smote the Philistines to the point that his hand grew weary and cleaved to the sword, and Yahweh wrought a great victory that day. Then the people rallied behind him, but only to plunder.

[11]After him, Shamma son of Agee the Hararite: The Philistines gathered themselves at Lehi,[13] where there was a field-plot of lentils. Now, the

---

9. In Jeshbaal's patronym, MT תחכמני is likely a corrupted form. Barthélemy suggests that MT is the result of assimilation by the influence of the final letter of the preceding word, such that the original initial *he* corrupted to *taw* (*Critique textuelle*, 311). McCarter maintains that the error is orthographic, and, referring to the spelling in 2 Chron. 11:11, he notes that "graphic confusion of *bn* and *t* was possible in the scripts of the fourth and third centuries B.C." (*II Samuel*, 489). In any event, we should read החכמני.

10. Neither the Ketib nor the Qere of MT makes any sense, and the widely disparate translations of the various versions indicate that the intelligibility of the primitive text eluded textual tradents at an early stage. The modern attempts at emendation are well covered by S. R. Driver (*Notes*, 364), and do not inspire confidence. The most widely accepted solution is to read according to MT of 1 Chron. 11:11 הוא עורר את חניתו, "he wielded his spear." But Barthélemy has shown that the Chronicler's phrase is itself an assimilation to 2 Sam. 23:18 (*Critique textuelle*, 312–13), and McCarter, while he reads with the Chronicler, acknowledges that MT of the Samuel text is probably closer to the primitive reading. In sum, while the Qere reads a puzzling patronym (cf. AV), the context and parallel with v. 18 and 1 Chron. 11:20 call for a verbal clause, yet there is no textual support for changing MT. I acknowledge the point made by Barthélemy: "Etant donné qu'il ne faut pas céder à une assimilation aux parallèles et que la critique textuelle ne nous donne aucun autre moyen d'échapper à la forme ruinée du *M, il faut respecter celle-ci (à titre de ruine précieuse)" (p. 313). Even so, for the sake of translation, I follow 1 Chron. 11:11.

11. The difficulty with MT is threefold: (1) standard Hebrew prose would require a particle such as אשר before the verb נאספו; (2) the root חרף in the *pi'el* is nowhere else attested in construct with ב (F. Böttcher, *Neue exegetische-kritische Ährenlese zum Alten Testament* [Leipzig: Barth, 1863]); (3) a much smoother הוא היה עם דויד בפס דמים והפלשתים נאספו שם למלחמה is attested in 1 Chron. 11:13, which, it is argued, preserves more faithfully the original בחרפם הפלשתים בפס דמים והפלשתים from which MT Chronicles and MT Samuel had lost some through haplography (McCarter, *II Samuel*, 490). Many scholars prefer to read with the Chronicler (e.g., J. Wellhausen, *Der Text der Bücher Samuelis*, 217; Driver, *Notes*, 365; H. P. Smith, *A Critical and Exegetical Commentary on the Books of Samuel* [ICC; Edinburgh: T. & T. Clark, 1899] 383). But as Barthélemy has pointed out, the MT tradition as represented in the Aleppo Codex and the Cairo Codex reads a *qameṣ ḥatuf* at בחרפם, indicating a *qal* infinitive ("poke, jab, mock"), such that this verbal construct refers to the actions of David and Eleazar vis-à-vis the Philistines instead of the reverse (*Critique textuelle*, 31–4). Read with MT according to Aleppo and Cairo.

12. Cf. J. Mauchline, *1 and 2 Samuel* (NCB; Greenwood, S.C.: Attic Press, 1971) 316; and see NEB.

13. The MT makes no sense (AV: "unto a troop"), particularly in the light of the words immediately following. The scholarly consensus since S. Bochart (*Hierozoicon. Sive bipertitum opus de Animalibus* [London: T. Roycroft, 1663] 200–201) has been to repoint to לְחָיָה,

people had fled from before the Philistines, [12]but he stationed himself in the midst of the plot and defended it, and struck down the Philistines; Yahweh wrought a great victory.

[13]There went down three of the Officers — a band — and they came on account of the harvest[14] to David at the cave of Adullam. Now, there was a contingent of Philistines camping in the Valley of Rephaim, [14]and while David was in the stronghold, a Philistine outpost was at Bethlehem. [15]David felt a longing, and said, "O that someone would give me to drink water from the well of Bethlehem that is at the gate!" [16]So the Three Heroes broke through the Philistine camp and drew water from the well of Bethlehem that was at the gate, carried it, and brought it to David. But David refused to drink it, and as he poured it out before Yahweh [17]he said, "Far be it from me, O Yahweh, that I should do this — the very blood of the men who went at the risk of their own lives?" And he simply refused to drink it.

Such were the exploits of the Three Heroes.

[18]Abishai brother of Joab, son of Ṣeruiah, of the Shalishite company: He wielded his sword against three hundred slain; so he gained a reputation among the Three. [19]Honored more than the Officers,[15] he became their Captain. But he was not included among the Three.

[20]Benaiah son of Jehoiada, son of a formidable warrior, of many exploits at Kabṣeel: He struck down two distinguished warriors[16] of Moab; he also, on a snowy day, went down and struck down the lion in the pit. [21]In addition, he struck down an Egyptian of noteworthy appearance:[17]

---

the locative form of the toponym Lehi (e.g., Thenius, *Die Bücher Samuels,* 278–79; K. Budde, *Die Bücher Samuel* [KHAT 8; Tübingen and Leipzig: J. C. B. Mohr [Paul Siebeck] 1902) 320; McCarter, *II Samuel,* 490). Read with this emendation, attested by LXX[L].

14. Because the parallel Chronicles text reads אל הצור, and because MT would apparently refer to a point in time (an expression for which אל is never used [so Driver, *Notes,* 366; but not so McCarter, *II Samuel,* 490–91]), many scholars read with LXX[L] and the Chronicler: "to the mountain top" (e.g., H. P. Smith, *Books of Samuel,* 385) or suggest emendations such as קציר ראש (e.g., Budde, *Die Bücher Samuel,* 321; cf. NEB, JB). But LXX[L] is clearly an assimilation to the Chronicler's text, which itself preserves a distinct textual tradition. The fact is that MT need not refer to a point in time or in space, but rather to *purpose* or *reason* ("on account of"), as we see in 2 Sam. 21:1: אל שאול, "on account of Saul." Note the following observation: "There is a tendency in Hebrew, especially manifest in Samuel, Kings, Jeremiah, and Ezekiel, to use אֶל in the sense of עַל, being used exceptionally in a phrase or construction which regularly, and in accordance with analogy, has עַל" (BDB 41a).

15. Reading שְׁלשִׁים with the Targum.

16. Most scholars supply בני after שֵׁני, as does LXX (e.g., Driver, *Notes,* 368). I retain MT, following A. A. Anderson, who notes the suggestion in HAL 80 of "warrior" (2 *Samuel* [WBC 11; Waco, Tex.: Word, 1989] 276). The choice of the particular word to denote a military opponent was probably intentional for its resemblance to the word in the next line for "lion" (AV: "two lion-like men of Moab").

17. Scholars have tended to read the Qere איש for the Ketib אשר and מדה with 1 Chron. 11:23 for מראה, yielding "a man of stature," similar to an emended reading at 2 Sam. 21:20. But as Barthélemy has pointed out, the Chronicler's reading is itself an embellished reading in the light of precisely 2 Sam. 21:20, as is also the Qere here in 2 Sam. 23:21 (*Critique textuelle,* 318). Read with the MT Ketib.

in the Egyptian's hand was a spear; he [Benaiah] went down against him with a staff and took the spear from the hand of the Egyptian by force and slew him with his own spear. [22]Such were the exploits of Benaiah son of Jehoiada, and he gained a reputation among the Three Heroes. [23]He was honored more than the Officers,[18] but he was not included among the Three. David appointed him over his bodyguard.

[24]Asahel brother of Joab, among the Officers;[19]

Elhanan son of Dodo of Bethlehem; [25]Shammah the Harodite; Elikah the Harodite; [26]Helas the Paltite; Irah son of Iqesh the Tekoaite; [27]Abiezer the Anathotite; Sibbechai[20] the Hushite; [28]Salmon the Ahohite; Maherai the Netophatite; [29]Helev son of Baanah the Netophatite; Ittai son of Rivai from Gibeah of the Benjaminites; [30]Benaiahu the Piratonite; Hiddai of the wadis of Gaash; [31]Avialbon the Arbatite; Azmavet the Barhumite; [32]Elyahba the Shaalbonite; Jashen the Gunite;[21] Jonathan son of [33]Shammah the Hararite; Ahiam son of Sharar the Hararite; [34]Eliphelet son of Ahasbai the Maakatite; Eliam son of Ahitophel the Gilonite; [35]Hesrai the Carmelite; Paarai the Arbite; [36]Yigal son of Nathan from Sobah; Bani the Gadite; [37]Seleq the Ammonite; Nahrai the Beerotite, Armor-bearer to Joab son of Seruiah; [38]Ira the Jitrite; Gareb the Jitrite; [39] Uriah the Hittite.

A sum of thirty-seven.

COMPOSITION ANALYSIS

Second Samuel 23:8–39 appears to be composed of three macrosections, preliminarily presented as follows:

1. Superscription: names of David's warriors   8a
2. Concerning the warriors   8b–39a
3. Subscription: sum of the warriors   39b

---

18. Reading שְׁלִשִׁים with the Targum.

19. Reading שְׁלִשִׁים with the Targum.

20. First Chronicles 11:29 and LXX[M,N] read סבכי. LXX[A,B] (ἐκ τῶν υἱῶν) apparently had in their respective *Vorlagen* the consonants of MT. Although it is possible that MT Chronicles and LXX[M,N] reflect assimilation to 2 Sam. 21:18, it is also possible that MT and LXX[L] (Σαβενει) are the result of graphic confusion: כ with נ in addition to ס with מ (McCarter, *II Samuel*, 492). Read סבכי, "Sibbechai."

21. It appears that בני before Jashen is a dittography from the preceding word, and that the gentilic that would further identify Jashen is missing from MT (Barthélemy, *Critique textuelle*, 321). First Chronicles 11:34 supplies the gentilic הגזוני, while LXX[L] reads הגוני. McCarter opts for the Chronicler's reading, arguing that הגוני would have arisen through confusion of *zayin* and *waw* and not the other way around (*II Samuel*, 492–93). D. Barthélemy favors הגוני, since it is a form attested elsewhere in Num. 26:48 (*Critique textuelle*, 322). Both critics agree that LXX at 2 Sam. 23:32 and Chronicles correctly read בן following Jonathan, making him the son of Shammah. I read ישן הגוני יהונתן בן שמה, "Jashen the Gunite; Jonathan son of Shammah."

Macrosection 2 (vv. 8b–39a) consists of two large subsections, vv. 8b–23 and vv. 24–39a. These two subsections distinguish themselves from each other syntactically and substantively. Of particular interest is the fact that the first section (vv. 8b–23) features a certain preoccupation with the same category of individuals, namely, the Three Heroes group. The text's implication is that Jeshbaal, Eleazar, and Shamma comprise the Three (this point will be further substantiated below), and the text's concern over the relationship of Abishai and Benaiah to the Three distinguishes vv. 8b–23 from vv. 24–39a, where no implicit or explicit reference to the Three appears.

2 Samuel 23:8b–23

This section begins with the name "Jeshbaal the Hachmonite," who occupies the text's spotlight as an individual no farther than v. 8b. The text identifies this warrior (first by his gentilic, followed by his association with the Shalishite company) and then refers to a remarkable exploit he had performed. In v. 9 the Eleazar text segment begins with the word אחריו, indicating that this segment is distinct from, yet connected to, that of Jeshbaal. Eleazar's segment exhibits a structure essentially identical to that of Jeshbaal: gentilic identification followed by a brief account of a distinguishing exploit. Finally, the description of Shamma's exploit is structured similarly to that of Eleazar, in a narrative style.

With v. 13 the text shifts its focus from the identification and exploits of individual warriors to a somewhat lengthier anecdote. Dropping the connective אחריו ("after him"), the text here at the beginning of v. 13 employs for the first time in the whole of vv. 8–39 a *waw*-consecutive + imperfect at the beginning of a segment. The effect is to distinguish vv. 13ff. from vv. 8b–12, while at the same time establishing a temporally sequential connection with vv. 8b–12. This distinction sets apart the Jeshbaal, Eleazar, and Shamma segments together as a single section relative to vv. 13ff.

The narrative of vv. 13–17a is structured similarly to the exploit descriptions of Eleazar and Shamma, with an introduction that sets the scene (vv. 13–14), an account of a remarkable exploit (vv. 15–16a), and a reference to the outcome of the exploit (vv. 16b–17a). Unlike the preceding segments of Jeshbaal, Eleazar, and Shamma, however, the figure of David is very much present — even crucial — in every subsection: in vv. 13–14 the key factor is the location and situation of David relative to the Philistine posts and to the three officers who come to Adullam to join him in protecting the harvest; it is David who sparks the daring exploit of the three (in fact, their excursion to Bethlehem and back is described in language that almost exactly mirrors David's expression of his desire for water from the distant well); in vv. 16b–17a it is David who delivers the punch of the anecdote by unexpectedly refusing to drink the water that the three had delivered to him in accordance with his wish.

This latter action of David in vv. 16b–17a highlights a particular distinction of the water-fetching anecdote relative to the exploit descriptions in vv. 8b–12. As he pours forth the water before Yahweh, David binds himself to an oath regarding the lives (= the blood) of these particular men. The oath words pronounced over the outpoured water presuppose the *unity* of the three, as the water is pronounced to be their blood altogether — three lives embodied in the one stream of water. Through his ritual action David recognizes the trio to be a uniquely distinguished group; they have demonstrated their devotion to him to such a degree that he ritually binds himself to their being alive. In his refusal to drink their "blood," David honors not the death of the three individuals but their life *as a group*. The Three are spoken of here as a highly unusual group: honored with the honor bestowed upon those who have sacrificed their lives (whose "blood" has flowed), yet they live. Thus was formed from the three unnamed ones a unique group bedecked with David's highest honor.

So vv. 13–17a have to do with a group of Three, and vv. 8b–12 have to do with three individuals. Verse 17b offers a summative reference to the exploits of "the Three Heroes" (שְׁלֹשֶׁת הגברים). To which "three" does this clause refer? The answer to this question is important for understanding the composition of vv. 8b–23, for if reference in v. 17b is restricted to the Three of vv. 13–17a, then v. 17b does not tie vv. 8b–17a together as a unit.

What stands out in all of the three exploits in vv. 8b–12 is that in each case the individual warrior acted *alone,* so that the feat is truly the exploit of a single hero. Honor for the exploit goes in each case to that specific person and derivatively to his traditional group (the Ḥachmonites, the Aḥoḥites, etc.).

In contrast to the individuality of the exploits related in vv. 8b–12 stands the nature of the exploit narrated in vv. 13–17a, where we are told nothing of any individual feats of derring-do — not even patronymics, much less any individual names — but instead, we are told of a concerted action by "three from the officers" functioning *as a unit,* as a ראשׁ. A further contrast appears in the fact that this group's exploit did not serve to benefit Israel directly, as no enemies were slain, no "great victory" wrought. Rather, the group's exploit was motivated by their devotion to David personally, whom they honored by their action. The three individuals became a group and operated together as a unit for David's sake. They "went down" to join *him* at Adullam; they risked their lives by traveling to Bethlehem and back to serve *him*. In other words, the three individual heroes became the Three Heroes group by virtue of their distinguished united service to David.

The two sections, however, are not set adrift from each other. We have already noted the *waw*-consecutive + imperfect formulation in v. 13a that begins the anecdote of the Three. The temporal connection made by וירדו ("they went down") brings vv. 8b–12 and vv. 13–17a into a sequentiality such that the first section, though itself not composed as a narrative, is nonetheless introductory to the latter section. Verses 8b–17a then have all to do with exploits by warriors. Verses 13–17a tell of the one exploit, in a passage full of exploits, that stood out from the rest: relatively noncombative,[22] a group of three functioning as one, solely for the sake of David. The compositional sequence of the three individual exploits followed by the one group exploit points to the formation of the Three Heroes group of vv. 13–17a from the three warriors of vv. 8b–12. Hence v. 17b refers to the whole of vv. 8b–17a,[23] making the whole a section devoted to the שלשת הגברים — the Three Heroes group: vv. 8b–12 concentrate on the group's *composition*, that is, on the identities and individual exploits of Jeshbaal, Eleazar, and Shamma respectively, while vv. 13–17a focus on the group's *formation*, that is, on the single extraordinary group exploit and on David's response by virtue of which the record can speak of such a group designated by the term שלשת הגברים. As a section, then, vv. 8b–17 concern the composition and formation of the Three Heroes group: first are noted the individuals that compose the group (vv. 8b–12), then the David-centered exploit that catalyzed the three as a group (vv. 13–17a), followed by a summary notice concerning all the above reviewed exploits of the Three (v. 17b).[24]

---

22. The anecdote is not devoid of combat references, to be sure, but the aspect of combat per se is not as prominent in the anecdote of the Three as in the descriptions of the exploits in vv. 8b–12. The little story of the Three entails more danger than actual combat.

23. Otherwise, the plural particle אלה in v. 17b is difficult to explain; it most naturally refers to all the exploits recounted in vv. 8b–17a. Cf. Mauchline, *1 and 2 Samuel*, 317; H. W. Hertzberg, *I & II Samuel* (OTL; Philadelphia: Westminster, 1964) 405.

24. The majority of twentieth century interpreters have followed Wellhausen, who suggested that the appearance of the anecdote of the three unnamed warriors in vv. 13–17 is due to an editor's insertion of these verses between vv. 8b–12 and vv. 18–23 (*Der Text der Bücher Samuelis*, 214); so, for example, Anderson (*2 Samuel*, 274), Mauchline (*1 and 2 Samuel*, 317), and Driver (*Notes*, 365–66). This suggestion rests on reading v. 13a as "from among the Thirty"; according to vv. 19 and 23 the Three do not seem to have been counted among the Thirty, and so vv. 13–17 make it appear as though the Three were identified with Yeshbaal, Eleazar, and Shamma. But we have seen that a "thirty" reading of v. 13a is questionable at best, and, with the syntactical and structural signals of vv. 8b–17, the impression is more likely that the text as it stands — regardless of its editorial development — connects the three warriors of vv. 8b–12 with the three of vv. 13–17a.

2 Samuel 23:18–23

As a segment, vv. 18–19 are composed similarly to the individual warrior-segments of vv. 8b–12. First the text identifies Abishai by his family bonds and by the name of his military outfit (v. 18aα). Then we read of Abishai's distinguishing exploit (v. 18aβ). Following the report of the exploit, the text turns to the outcome of Abishai's exploit, in the form of the status he achieved. The text is very precise about these honors. First of all, we are told that Abishai "gained a reputation among the Three" (v. 18b). Then, we learn that he was elevated above the Officers in that he received more honor than they and that he became their captain (v. 19a). Finally, the text notes that despite his ascendancy, Abishai was not among the group of Three (v. 19b). The Benaiah segment is structured almost identically.

The Abishai and Benaiah segments are both composed very much like the segments of the individual warriors of vv. 8b–12 but stand apart on one point in particular. Unlike the individual exploits of Jeshbaal, Eleazar, and Shamma, the exploits of Abishai and Benaiah are given recognition in the fact that these two men receive appointments to official leadership positions: Abishai became the Captain of the Officers and Benaiah was appointed Chief over David's bodyguard.[25]

In addition, each of these two heroes is said to have been honored "more than the Officers" as a result of his exploit(s) and each is said to have been highly esteemed in the eyes of the Three Heroes (this is the meaning of the ולו שם בשלשה phrase in vv. 18b and 22b) while not being reckoned among that group. The text presents the same sequence for both heroes: exploit(s), followed by recognition by the Three, followed by honor greater than the Officers, followed by appointment to a specific leadership office. The impression made by this rigidly followed sequence is that the sequence is significant, tracing a causative trail. Recognition of the heroic achievement in the estimation of the Three *resulted in* being honored more than the Officers *as manifested in* appointment to office. The text speaks of the achievements reached by Abishai and Benaiah respectively in terms of their status relative to the Three. In composing the Abishai and Benaiah segments in just this way the text presupposes (1) the existence of a group known as the Three (Heroes); (2) the significance of recognition by the Three in evaluating heroic exploits; and (3) the influence of recognition by the Three for rank relative to the Officers and for appointment to leadership positions.

---

25. On the syntax of v. 23b, cf. 2 Sam. 20:23, which refers to Joab's position over the army.

As a section immediately following vv. 8b–17 and linked to that section, vv. 18–23 is a section concerned with the influence of the Three Heroes group as that influence is manifest in the appointments of Abishai and Benaiah to key leadership positions within David's military organization. This connection between vv. 8b–17 and vv. 18–23 points to vv. 8b–23 as a single text-unit governed in its composition by the concept of the Three Heroes group: the individual members who comprised the group, the formation of the group, and the legacy of the group in the delegation of authority among David's other officers. In the whole of 2 Sam. 23:8–29, then, we have a major subsection in vv. 8b–23, the structure of which is presented in its essentials as follows (cf. the outline of 23:8–39 below):

A. Pertaining to the Three Heroes group	8b–23
1. Composition and formation of the group	8b–17
a. Component members of the group	8b–12
b. Formation of the group (exploit anecdote)	13–17a
c. Summative notice of the exploits of the Three	17b
2. Hierarchical legacy of the group in David's military organization	18–23
a. In Abishai: Captain of the Officers	18–19
b. In Benaiah: Head of the Bodyguard	20–23

2 Samuel 23:24–39a

In contrast to vv. 8b–23, vv. 24–39a make no explicit reference to the Three Heroes group whatever. The latter section, however, has often been taken to refer to members of another group known as "the Thirty" (despite the fact that the individuals listed in vv. 24–39a total thirty-seven according to v. 39b). The evidence for the existence of a group so designated in Israel during the monarchic period has received a good deal of attention. K. Elliger argued that the existence of a formally designated "thirty" group may reflect an Egyptian tradition of a band of thirty officials in the service of the Pharaoh.[26] But research by B. Mazar has undermined Elliger's thesis, and P. K. McCarter and N. Naaman have each registered serious doubt as to whether

---

26. K. Elliger, "Die dreissig Helden Davids," in H. Gese and O. Kaiser, eds., *Kleine Schriften zum Alten Testament* (TB 32; Munich: Kaiser, 1966) 109–10. What motivates Elliger's specific proposal is the need to reconcile the presence of the term "the Thirty" in MT of 2 Sam. 23:8b–39b with the sum of thirty-seven reported in v. 39b. Elliger's position is that, as an Israelite institution, the "Thirty" would, over time, contain more or fewer members than an actual count of thirty, since its name derived from an ancient tradition of a royal company.

there ever was a recognized regiment of thirty within the Israelite royal army.[27]

But ultimately the text-critical factors render the question moot. As noted in our review of the text-critical issues, D. Barthélemy has demonstrated the likelihood that the earliest attested text tradition did not feature שָׁלִשִׁים in vv. 19, 23, and 24, but rather שְׁלֹשִׁים. The text-critical landscape on this specific question is anything but smooth, but I am persuaded that prior to interpretation of שְׁלֹשִׁים in 2 Samuel 23 (as early as MT Chronicles) as "thirty," probably due the influence of שְׁלֹשִׁים in v. 39b, *the text tradition in 2 Samuel 23 did not at all refer to a group known as "the Thirty."* Even though this text-critical conclusion remains in debate, the cumulative weight of evidence reviewed above points away from such a group of thirty.

This means that, while vv. 24–39a is a section distinct from vv. 8b–23, it is not composed as a representation of a group of "the Thirty" in distinction from "the Three Heroes" of vv. 8b–23.[28] To the extent that vv. 24–39a do represent a group of any particular title, it would be of "Officers" (שָׁלִשִׁים), as the section begins with the words עשה אל אחי יואב בְשָׁלִשִׁים. This would be the corps over which Abishai had been appointed Captain according to vv. 18–19.

The principle according to which the names in vv. 23–39a are organized remains to be identified. It has been recognized at least since Budde that these names are mostly of individuals who hail from the Israelite territories west of the Jordan between Ephraim and the Negev, and more specifically at the beginning of the list the majority of names belong to the Bethlehem region.[29] Beginning with Benaiah in v. 30,

---

27. Mazar points out that the Egyptian inscriptional evidence cited by Elliger actually refers to three groups of ten judges and hence to groups of *ten* in the service of Pharaoh instead of thirty. Mazar favors a possible Aegean origin for the "thirty" tradition that was configured in this early list in Samuel according to the ties of the first thirty names to the geography of the Cisjordan ("The Military Elite of King David," in S. Ahituv and B. A. Levine, eds., *The Early Biblical Period: Historical Studies* [Jerusalem: Israel Exploration Society, 1986] 84–100). McCarter has noted that none of the groups of "thirty" mentioned in the Hebrew Bible (Judg. 10:4; 12:9; 14:11; 1 Sam. 9:22) is a military entity save 1 Chron. 11:42 (which is itself dependent on the Chronicler's perception of a "thirty" motif in 2 Sam. 23:8a–39, as evident in the שְׁלֹשִׁים readings in 1 Chronicles 11; cf. our text-critical discussion above): "Thus the evidence for a pre-Davidic history of the institution of the Thirty is meager" (*II Samuel*, 497). Naaman notes that the "thirty" is otherwise unattested as a standing military body during the Israelite monarchic period, and thus, if it ever existed, the "thirty" would have to have dropped from the scene shortly after its formation ("The List of David's Officers," 73).

28. Contra most scholars: for example, Budde (*Die Bücher Samuel*, 318); F. Stolz (*Das erste und zweite Buch Samuel* [ZBK 9; Zurich: Theologischer, 1981] 296); R. P. Gordon (*1 & 2 Samuel: A Commentary* [Exeter: Paternoster, 1986] 311); Anderson (*2 Samuel*, 274); W. Brueggemann (*First and Second Samuel* [IBC; Louisville: John Knox, 1990] 347).

29. Budde, *Die Bücher Samuel*, 324. The exceptions are Abiezer from Anathoth (v. 27a)

the names are connected with clans and regions beyond the Judah/ Bethlehem area, such as the hills of Ephraim and the Jordan depression.[30] The text's geographic focus returns to the Jerusalem and Judah area at v. 33 and remains so through v. 36a, and concludes with non-Israelite warriors in vv. 38a–39a.[31] Unless we assume that David came onto the scene with a full-blown regiment of officers from the various geographic quarters represented in this section of text, it is likely that the composition of this text reflects the *development of David's military organization*. Though one cannot be overly insistent on this point, such a compositional concept is — however implicitly — signaled by the clustering of names from the Bethlehem and Judah region near the beginning of the list and by the appearance of Transjordanian and non-Israelite clan locations at the end. The mention of Asahel indicates that these men had come into David's service before David had taken Jerusalem (cf. 2 Sam. 2:18–23).[32] It is likely then that these individuals were eventually recognized as שָׁלִשִׁים in David's army, if not by their individual exploits (as in vv. 8b–23) then by their early association with David in a military context. Hence, vv. 24–39a would reflect the development of David's army as it grew from its Bethlehemite and Judahite beginnings to include warriors from more distant parts of Israel.[33] Verses 24–39a, then, constitute a section whose composition is governed by the

---

and Salmon of the Ahohites from Benjamin (v. 28a). There is some uncertainty as to the location of the Ahoah mentioned in v. 28a. McCarter locates Ahoah in Benjamin on the basis of 1 Chron. 8:4 (*II Samuel*, 494), while Elliger connects it to *wadi el-hoah* in the southern area of Judah ("Helden Davids," 87ff.).

30. On the location of Piraton (v. 30a), see Y. Aharoni, *The Land of the Bible: A Historical Geography* (2d ed.; Philadelphia: Westminster, 1979) 440; McCarter (*II Samuel*, 498); cf. Judg. 12:13ff. On the identification of Shaalbon with modern Selbît in the Aijalon, see Elliger ("Helden Davids," 93ff.) and Aharoni (*Land of the Bible*, 311). The reading in v. 32b is a difficult text-critical problem; see the discussion above. Elliger suggests Gimzo on the Benjaminite border with Philistia ("Helden Davids," 96–97), while Mazar ("Military Elite," 95 n. 49) and McCarter (*II Samuel*, 498) favor Gizon near Aijalon.

31. The Sobah of v. 36a has been identified by Elliger as the Aramaean Sobah ("Helden Davids," 102–3), but Mazar claims that the location has been identified "with absolute certainty" as modern Subah near Bethlehem ("Military Elite," 96 n. 59); cf. Aharoni, *Land of the Bible*, 443. The reference intended in the הגרי identification of Bani in v. 36b remains elusive; suggestions include a "Hagrite" gentilic (so McCarter, *II Samuel*, 499) and a "Gadite" gentilic (so Elliger, "Helden Davids," 103). Either way, the Transjordan is probably the geography to which the text points. Mazar has shown that the Beerothites, like the Yitrites of Kiriath-Jearim, are of Hivite stock and hail from the Benjaminite territory ("Military Elite," 96).

32. Elliger, "Helden Davids," 118.

33. See Elliger, "Helden Davids," 113–15; also Hertzberg, *1 & 2 Samuel*, 407–8. J. Mauchline writes, "That the earliest group should have been recruited from Judah, the second substantially from the territory near to, or north of, Jerusalem, and the third partly from areas which became incorporated into David's empire would support the idea of a gradual development of this order of chivalry" (*1 and 2 Samuel*, 321).

concept of development within David's military organization: it begins
with the officers from Israelite and Judahite clan locations and proceeds
to those officers from Transjordan and non-Israelite clan locations. The
structure of this section looks like this:

Concerning the Officers	24–39a
1. Those from Judahite and Israelite clan locations	24–36a
2. Those from Transjordan and non-Israelite clan locations	36b–39a

2 Samuel 23:8–39

We have seen that vv. 8b–23 comprise a section of text built around
the group of the Three Heroes in a way that shows the membership of
that group to be exclusive, based on a special bond with David himself,
and noteworthy in the delegation of authority over officers who are in
David's service. To the extent that the status of Abishai and Benaiah
ben Yehoiada respectively is shown in vv. 18–23 to have been based on
the presupposed status of the Three as shown in vv. 8b–17, the whole
of vv. 8b–23 is concerned with the development of the elite in David's
military corps. Essentially the same concept of military organizational
development continues in vv. 24–39a, the composition of which reflects
the development of David's corps from the earliest days to his Hebron
days, at which point David's troops included warriors from Transjordan
and from Hivite and Hittite origin. P. K. McCarter has observed that
the organizing principle of 23:8–39 is rank. This is correct insofar as
the individuals listed in vv. 8b–23 rank over the individuals listed in
vv. 24–39a. But the text, through just this composition of vv. 8b–23 and
vv. 24–39a respectively and together as a whole, is organized to reflect
the way(s) in which such ranking was *developed*.

In vv. 24–39a the ranking is by the emergence of David the warrior
chief from his Bethlehemite beginnings to his influence over Judah, as
supported by the warriors whose names are listed loosely according to
the point in that emergence at which each one became a part of his
corps. In vv. 8b–23 the ranking is by the unique group effort of the
Three and the subsequent hierarchizing of command is by their influence. In the whole of vv. 8b–39a, the ranking is by the emergence of
the Three (with their special tie to David), who are connected to the
appointment of Abishai and Benaiah ben Yehoiada to positions of leadership over the remainder of the warriors. Hence, this entire section of
2 Sam. 23:8–39 is organized according to a pattern of a ranking that is
the product of a hierarchical development among David's warriors. The
superscription (v. 8a) and subscription (v. 39b) show that this development in ranking is a matter of official record. The structure of the entire
pericope in its essentials is presented as follows:

Unlike lists of figures within the monarchic government such as 2 Sam. 8:15–18, 20:23–26, and 1 Kings 4:1–8, this text does not concern itself with authority levels within the judicial and cultic sides of monarchic leadership. Rather, the list of 2 Sam. 23:8–39 is restricted to the military sphere exclusively. Reflecting the development of hierarchical authority among the warriors that followed David, this list shows such development to have emanated from the centrality of David himself. The strength of David's military is seen to grow with the hierarchical development of levels of authority (centered in David, who himself is "centered" in Bethlehem), and with the numerical development of his officer corps ("centered" in Bethlehem/Judah). As a list-text, the whole of 23:8–39 reflects the development of David's warrior organization.

2 SAMUEL 23:8–39 AND 2 SAMUEL 24

In the light of this analysis of David's warrior list, let us turn to the question of compositional coherence between the list and the story of David's census of Israel. I will argue that the concept of military strength development connects the two texts in a sequence that makes sense.

In 2 Sam. 24:1 Yahweh becomes angry at Israel and puts it in David's mind to conduct a census of Israel and Judah. The sudden mention of Yahweh's renewed anger against Israel has long puzzled interpreters, and the usual approach is to make rational sense of it. But it is likely that here we have an example of irrational (i.e., unaccountable) divine anger, in contrast to the 1 Chronicles 21 version of this story, where Satan is the one who instigates David to take a census.[34] At any rate, the

---

34. P. Considine has discerned three types of irrational divine anger in ancient East Mediterranean literature: (1) divine anger whose cause is unknown and unknowable; (2) divine anger whose cause is unknown but capable of being discovered; and (3) divine anger whose cause is stated in the text but is out of character or attitude of the offended deity on other occasions ("The Theme of Divine Wrath in Ancient East Mediterranean Literature," in *Studi Micenei ed Egeo-Anatolici,* fasc. 8 [Incunabula Graeca 28; Rome: Edi-

clear result of this divine anger will be a census conducted by royal decree.

In every other narrated instance of census-taking in the HB the purpose is military preparedness, usually just prior to an actual battle or campaign.[35] But in our story, an enduring peace had evidently been established already; otherwise, David could not have sent his chief war officer on a nine-month mission to the remotest parts of the kingdom. Indeed, scholars suggest that Joab's apprehension (24:3) was due to certain dangers involved in numbering the people for war during peacetime. F. Keil pointed to an uneasiness among the people if they were to be numbered for battle;[36] similarly, W. McKane suggests that such a census would arouse fears and suspicions among the relatively independent tribes of the early monarchy;[37] G. von Rad maintained that the census as a preface to conscription would constitute a disturbing intervention into the old sacral institution of holy war;[38] McCarter holds that the danger would lie in the inevitable violation, during a general enrollment for war, of the military rules for purity that obtained in the ancient world — the sort of violation that the fee collection would insure against (cf. Exod. 30:11–16).[39] In any event, the result remains the same: David would be commissioning a census for which there was no evident justifiable reason, whether that justification lie in a divine commissioning or an impending military threat.

The narration in 2 Samuel 24 points in this same direction. The dialogue between "the king" (not "David"!) and Joab in vv. 2–4a serves not just to report the royal commissioning of the census but also to reflect the fact that the census is *unjustified*. Verse 4a implies that Joab and his lead soldiers are being compelled by nothing more than sheer royal authority (דבר המלך) to proceed with a census whose justification requires more than royal authority.

Thanks to the narration of v. 1, the reader is very much aware that the reason David could not (or at least did not) provide his officers

---

zioni dell'Atenao, 1969] 114). He reckons 2 Sam. 24:1 as an example of the first type. A counterpoint to Yahweh's irrational anger appears later in this story (24:16) when Yahweh displays irrational divine mercy in sparing Jerusalem from destruction.

35. See Num. 1:2–3; Josh. 8:10; Judg. 20:14ff.; 1 Sam. 11:8; 5:4; 2 Sam. 18:1; cf. also Judg. 7:3; 1 Kings 20:15, 27; 2 Kings 3:60.

36. C. F. Keil, *Die Bücher Samuels*, vol. 2 of *Biblischer Commentar über die prophetischen Geschichtsbücher des Alten Testaments* (2d ed.; Leipzig: Dörffling & Franke, 1875) 391.

37. W. McKane, *I & II Samuel* (TBC; London: SCM, 1963) 302.

38. G. von Rad, *Der heilige Krieg im alten Israel* (Göttingen: Vandenhoeck & Ruprecht, 1969) 37–38. Cf. also H. P. Smith, *Books of Samuel*, 389; J. G. Baldwin, *1 and 2 Samuel: An Introduction and Commentary* (Leicester: InterVarsity, 1988) 295; Brueggemann, *First and Second Samuel*, 352.

39. McCarter, *II Samuel*, 514.

with a satisfactory reason for the census is that from David's perspective there *was* no reason for it.[40] We are told there that Yahweh *instigated* (סות) David to conduct the census. This is not the same as Yahweh having *commissioned* (צוה) David. In the latter case, David would have been authorized, not by virtue of his royal office, but by virtue of divine command. The effect of vv. 2–4a following closely on the heels of v. 1 is to indicate to the reader that the census about to commence is divinely instigated but not divinely authorized. Presupposed here is that the census is justified by virtue of the authority under which it is commissioned.[41] Whether by omitting the instructions for the census fee from the commission, or by some other omission, David had failed to do what this text presupposes a king must do to safely conduct a census, namely, to secure sufficient (i.e., divine) authority. This may explain why, although later in the narrative the resultant plague will take its toll on the *people*, the plague is a punishment of *David*, for it is he who erred (as David himself will emphasize in v. 17).

This focus on the royal office as the authority for the census is underscored not only by the exclusive use of the term המלך in vv. 2–4a with reference to David, but also by the narration of the census-taking itself (vv. 4b–9). As Joab and his officers go forth to the task, the text mentions that their departure was לפני המלך (v. 4b). The use of this term in context is very likely to signify the military aspect of the procession out of Jerusalem, which in turn points to the ultimately military purpose of the census.[42] The undertaking is thus accountable to and on behalf of the king as warrior. Similarly, the narration of the census-taking concludes (v. 9a) with the tally of the census being delivered אל המלך. In this way the report of the census process that the king had commissioned reflects a movement going out from the king, traversing the land (v. 8a), and returning back to its source in the king. At

---

40. Cf. Stolz, *Samuel*, 302.

41. For a fuller treatment for the need for proper authorization to conduct a census and of the acquisition of such authorization through a census fee, note the following from A. Schenker: "Wer einen Preis zum voraus bezahlt, um etwas zu tun, was ohne solche Vorauszahlung mit Strafe belegt würde, wozu er zuerst keine Vollmacht hatte. Der Preis, den er voraus erlegt, hat den Zweck, ihm ein Recht einzubringen, an dem ihm der Inhaber dieses Rechtes gleichsam einen Anteil verkauft. Die Bezahlung der Gebühr durch den Käufer ist die Anerkennung seiner eigenen Nicht-Zuständigkeit und die Bitte um Übertragung dieser ihm an sich nicht zustehenden Vollmacht, während die Annahme dieses Preises durch den Inhaber der Vollmacht bedeutet, dass er sie dem Zahlenden überträgt und ihm an diesem Recht Anteil gibt" (*Der Mächtige im Schmelzofen des Mitleids: Eine Interpretation von 2 Sam 24* [OBO 42; Freiburg, Switzerland: Universitätsverlag; Göttingen: Vandenhoeck & Ruprecht, 1982] 17–18).

42. So C. J. Goslinga, *Het tweede boek Samuël* (COut; Kampen: J. H. Kok, 1962) 460; Hertzberg, *I & II Samuel*, 412; cf. also Mauchline, *1 and 2 Samuel*, 322. See 2 Sam. 15:18 and 18:4.

the end of the census narrative (v. 9), we have the king in Jerusalem, now the holder of the product of a census he had authorized without himself having been authorized. The warrior-king now knows the number of warriors that he can mobilize, and there the matter stands. Irrespective of what a king would do with the information that David possesses, in the telling of this particular narrative David does nothing with it. It is almost as if to hearken back to Joab's question: the king now "knows the number of the people" (v. 2b), but what justifies or authorizes this knowing? According to v. 4a, only sheer royal authority justifies it, and the implication is that the authority of the king alone is insufficient justification for a census. David has conducted an unauthorized census, that is, a census undertaken apart from the sort of authorization that would circumvent the consequences of an otherwise authority-violating venture. Those consequences occupy the focus of the rest of the narrative in ch. 24: judgment by plague; intercession; and a divine relenting.

CONCLUSION

From what has been reviewed here we can discern the compositional flow from the list of David's warriors into the story of David's census. Both texts have in common the development of David's military organization. The conceptual link between 23:8–39 and 24:1–25 is that of warrior leadership under David with specific reference to the development and organization of military resources. Moreover, this conceptual link is dynamic and not static: David the king-as-warrior acts to excess, since in ch. 24 he acts without the necessary authority to conduct a census, and in doing so brings calamity upon Israel.

Additional evidence illuminating this conceptual link can be found in other biblical texts and in texts from the ancient Levant. In a recent article, K. C. Hanson offers a cultural analysis of ancient Hittite, Greek, and Israelite narratives that depict royal figures violating certain culturally assumed norms, and the disastrous consequences that follow. He concludes that these narratives, including 2 Samuel 24, "implicitly or explicitly function as 'cautionary tales' against royal arrogance."[43] In the present essay we have seen how, in the light of certain text-critical judgments on the MT of 2 Sam. 23:8–39, it is possible to recognize a compositional flow into 2 Samuel 24 implying the royal deviance from the norm that Hanson has pointed out. The present juxtaposition of these two pericopes moves the reader from the honorable development

---

43. K. C. Hanson, "When the King Crosses the Line: Royal Deviance and Restitution in Levantine Ideologies," *BTB* 26 (1996) 21.

of David's military force that yields salvation for Israel to the excessive development of his forces that proves catastrophic for Israel.

BIBLIOGRAPHY

Aharoni, Y. *The Land of the Bible: A Historical Geography.* Trans. A. F. Rainey. 2d ed. Philadelphia: Westminster, 1979.

Anderson, A. A. *2 Samuel.* WBC 11. Waco, Tex.: Word, 1989.

Baldwin, J. G. *1 and 2 Samuel: An Introduction and Commentary.* Leicester: Inter-Varsity, 1988.

Barthélemy, D. *Les Devanciers d'Aquila.* VTSup 10. Leiden: Brill, 1963.

———, ed. *Critique textuelle de l'Ancien Testament.* OBO 50/1. Fribourg, Switzerland: Éditions Universitaires; Göttingen: Vandenhoeck & Ruprecht, 1982.

Bochart, S. *Hierozoicon. Sive bipertitum opus de Animalibus.* London: T. Roycroft, 1663.

Böttcher, F. *Neue exegetische-kritische Ährenlese zum Alten Testament.* Leipzig: Barth, 1863.

Brueggemann, W. *Power, Providence, and Personality: Biblical Insights into Life and Ministry.* Louisville: John Knox, 1990.

———. *First and Second Samuel.* IBC. Louisville: John Knox, 1990.

Budde, K. *Die Bücher Samuel.* KHAT 8. Tübingen and Leipzig: J. C. B. Mohr (Paul Siebeck), 1902.

Considine, P. "The Theme of Divine Wrath in Ancient East Mediterranean Literature." In *Studi Micenei ed Egeo-Anatolici.* Fasc. 8. Incunabula Graeca 28, pp. 85–159. Rome: Edizioni dell'Atenao, 1969.

Cross, F. M. "The History of the Biblical Text in the Light of Discoveries in the Judean Desert." *HTR* 57 (1964) 281–99.

Dhorme, E. P. *L'emploi métaphorique des noms de parties du corps en hébreu et en akkadien.* Paris: Librairie orientaliste Paul Geunther, 1963.

———. *A Commentary on the Book of Job.* Trans. H. Knight. Nashville: Nelson, 1967.

Driver, S. R. *Notes on the Hebrew Text and the Topography of the Books of Samuel.* 2d ed. Oxford: Clarendon, 1913.

Elliger, K. "Die dreissig Helden Davids." In *Kleine Schriften zum Alten Testament,* ed. H. Gese and O. Kaiser, pp. 72–118. TB 32. Munich: Kaiser, 1966.

Gordon, R. P. *1 & 2 Samuel: A Commentary.* Exeter: Paternoster, 1986.

Goslinga, C. J. *Het tweede boek Samuël.* COut. Kampen: J. H. Kok, 1962.

Hanson, K. C. "When the King Crosses the Line: Royal Deviance and Restitution in Levantine Ideologies." *BTB* 26 (1996) 11–25.

Hertzberg, H. W. *I & II Samuel.* Trans. J. S. Bowden. OTL. Philadelphia: Westminster, 1964.

Keil, C. F. *Die Bücher Samuels.* Vol. 2 of *Biblischer Commentar über die prophetischen Geschichtsbücher des Alten Testaments.* 2d ed. Leipzig: Dörffling & Franke, 1875.

Mastin, B. A. "Was the *šalîš* the Third Man in the Chariot?" In *Studies in the Historical Books of the Old Testament,* ed. J. A. Emerton. VTSup 30, pp. 123–54. Leiden: Brill, 1979

Mauchline, J. *1 and 2 Samuel*. NCB. Greenwood, S.C.: Attic Press, 1971.

Mazar, B. "The Military Elite of King David." In *The Early Biblical Period: Historical Studies*, ed. S. Ahituv and B. A. Levine, pp. 83–103. Jerusalem: Israel Exploration Society, 1986. (Originally published in *VT* 13 [1963] 310–20.)

McCarter, P. K. *II Samuel: A New Translation with Introduction, Notes, and Commentary*. AB 9. Garden City, N.Y.: Doubleday, 1984.

McKane, W. *I & II Samuel*. TBC. London: SCM, 1963.

Naaman, N. "The List of David's Officers (*šalîšîm*)." *VT* 38 (1988) 71–79.

Pisano, S. *Additions or Omissions in the Books of Samuel*. OBO 57. Fribourg, Switzerland: Universitätsverlag, 1984.

Rad, G. von. *Der heilige Krieg im alten Israel*. Göttingen: Vandenhoeck & Ruprecht, 1969.

Schenker, A. *Der Mächtige im Schmelzofen des Mitleids: Eine Interpretation von 2 Sam 24*. OBO 42. Freiburg, Switzerland: Universitätsverlag; Göttingen: Vandenhoeck & Ruprecht, 1982.

Shenkel, J. D. *Chronology and Recensional Development in the Greek Text of Kings*. HSM. Cambridge: Harvard University Press, 1968.

Smith, H. P. *A Critical and Exegetical Commentary on the Books of Samuel*. ICC. Edinburgh: T. & T. Clark, 1899.

Stolz, F. *Das erste und zweite Buch Samuel*. ZBK 9. Zurich: Theologischer, 1981.

Talmon, S. "The Presentation of Synchroneity and Simultaneity in Biblical Narrative." In *Studies in Hebrew Narrative Art throughout the Ages*, ed. J. Heinemann and S. Werses, pp. 9–26. ScrHier 27. Jerusalem: Magnes, 1978.

Thenius, O. *Die Bücher Samuels*. 2d ed. KHAT 4. Leipzig: S. Hirzel, 1864.

Tov, E. "The State of the Question: Problems and Proposed Solutions." In *1972 Proceedings of the International Organization for Septuagint and Cognate Studies and the Society of Biblical Literature Pseudepigrapha Seminar*, ed. R. Kraft, pp. 3–15. Missoula, Mont.: Scholars Press, 1972.

———. "The Textual Affiliations of 4QSamᵃ." *JSOT* 14 (1979) 37–53.

Ulrich, Eugene Charles, Jr. *The Qumran Text of Samuel and Josephus*. HSM 19. Missoula, Mont.: Scholars Press, 1978.

Waltke, B., and M. O'Connor. *An Introduction to Biblical Hebrew Syntax*. Winona Lake, Ind.: Eisenbrauns, 1990.

Wellhausen, J. *Der Text der Bücher Samuelis*. Göttingen: Vandenhoeck & Ruprecht, 1871.

Contributors

Antony F. Campbell, S.J., is Professor of Old Testament at Jesuit Theological College within the United Faculty of Theology, Parkville, Victoria, Australia.

Sok-chung Chang is Assistant Professor of Hebrew Bible at Kwandong University, Kangnung, Korea.

Keith L. Eades is Assistant Professor of Christian Studies at California Baptist University, Riverside, California.

Deborah Ellens is an independent scholar in Claremont, California.

Randy G. Haney is Adjunct Professor of Philosophy and Religion at Mt. San Antonio College, Walnut, California.

John E. Hartley is Professor of Old Testament at Haggard Graduate School of Theology, Azusa Pacific University, Azusa, California.

Rodney R. Hutton is Professor of Old Testament at Trinity Lutheran Seminary, Columbus, Ohio.

Rolf P. Knierim is Professor Emeritus of Old Testament at Claremont School of Theology and Avery Professor Emeritus of Religion at Claremont Graduate University, Claremont, California.

Won W. Lee is Assistant Professor of Religion and Theology at Calvin College, Grand Rapids, Michigan.

David B. Palmer is an independent scholar in San Dimas, California.

Tércio M. Siqueira is Professor of Old Testament at Faculdade de Teologia da Igreja Metodista, Rudje Lamos (São Paulo), Brazil.

Yoshihide Suzuki is Professor of the Faculty of Humanities at Niigata University, Niigata, Japan.

Marvin A. Sweeney is Professor of Hebrew Bible at Claremont School of Theology and Professor of Religion at Claremont Graduate University, Claremont, California.

Tai-il Wang is Professor of Old Testament at Methodist Theological Seminary, Seoul, Korea.

Richard D. Weis is Dean of the Seminary and Professor of Old Testament Theology at the United Theological Seminary of the Twin Cities, New Brighton, Minnesota.

William Yarchin is Associate Professor and Chair of the Department of Religion and Philosophy at Azusa Pacific University.

Scripture Index

Author Index